HELLENISTIC CULTURE AND SOCIETY

General Editors: Anthony W. Bulloch, Erich S. Gruen,
A. A. Long, and Andrew F. Stewart

Religion in Hellenistic Athens

Religion
in Hellenistic
Athens

Jon D. Mikalson

UNIVERSITY OF CALIFORNIA PRESS

Berkeley / Los Angeles / London

University of California Press
Berkeley and Los Angeles, California

University of California Press, Ltd.
London, England

© 1998 by
The Regents of the University of California

Library of Congress Cataloging-in-Publication Data
Mikalson, Jon D., 1943-
    Religion in Hellenistic Athens / Jon D. Mikalson.
        p.   cm. — (Hellenistic culture and society ; 29)
    Includes bibliographical references and index.
    ISBN 0–520-21023-9 (alk. paper)
        1. Athens (Greece) — Religion.   2. Hellenism.   I. Title.
    II. Series.
BL793. A76M55   1998
292'.00938'5 — dc21   97-35407
                                                             CIP

Printed in the United States of America

9   8   7   6   5   4   3   2   1

The paper used in this publication meets the minimum requirements
of American National Standards for Information Sciences —
Permanence of Paper for Printed Library Materials, ANSI
Z39.48–1984.♾

καὶ νῦν γὰρ ἐκτὸς ἐλπίδος γνώμης τ' ἐμῆς
σωθείς, ὀφείλω τοῖς θεοῖς πολλὴν χάριν.

Sophocles *Antigone* 330–31

Contents

Abbreviations

FGrHist	F. Jacoby, *Die Fragmente der griechischen Historiker* (Berlin/ Leiden, 1923–58)
GR	*Greece & Rome*
GRBS	*Greek, Roman, and Byzantine Studies*
Hesp.	*Hesperia*
HSCP	*Harvard Studies in Classical Philology*
HTR	*Harvard Theological Review*
ID	*Inscriptions de Délos*
IE	H. Engelmann and R. Merkelbach, *Die Inschriften von Erythrai und Klazomenai* (Bonn, 1972–73)
IG	*Inscriptiones Graecae*
JHS	*Journal of Hellenic Studies*
KA	R. Kassel and C. Austin, *Poetae comici Graeci* (Berlin, 1983–)
PA	J. Kirchner, *Prosopographia Attica* (Berlin, 1901–03)
PAAH	Πρακτικὰ τῆς Ἀκαδημίας Ἀθηνῶν
RE	A. Pauly, G. Wissowa, and W. Kroll, *Real-Encyklopädie der classischen Altertumswissenschaft* (Stuttgart, 1893–)
REG	*Revue des études grecques*
Reinmuth	O. W. Reinmuth, *The Ephebic Inscriptions of the Fourth Century B.C.* (Leiden, 1971)
RhM	*Rheinisches Museum*
Schwenk	C. J. Schwenk, *Athens in the Age of Alexander: The Dated Laws and Decrees of the "Lycourgan Era," 338–322 B.C.* (Chicago, 1985)
SEG	*Supplementum Epigraphicum Graecum*
SIG³	W. Dittenberger, *Sylloge Inscriptionum Graecarum*, 3rd ed. (Leipzig, 1915–24)
TAPA	*Transactions of the American Philological Association*
YCS	*Yale Classical Studies*
ZPE	*Zeitschrift für Papyrologie und Epigraphik*

Introduction

Religion in Hellenistic Athens, like Greek religion in the classical period and Christianity at later times, was a complex system of deities, rituals, and beliefs that responded to human needs. As the needs and circumstances of the Athenians changed, so changed their religion, but very gradually. I emphasize the word "change," a neutral term, because the understanding of Hellenistic religion and of Athenian religion in particular has been significantly impeded by value judgments either condemning them as degenerating from the classical ideal or praising them for making progress toward Christian conceptions. In the most general terms, the devaluation of Hellenistic religion has led to cynicism about the motives and institutions of the worshippers of the period and to a failure to recognize sufficiently the continuity with classical religion. The search for proto-Christian elements similarly neglects the body of evidence showing continuity with classical religion and inclines scholars to overvalue or misinterpret what may appear as new or different in Hellenistic religion. These judgments can be combined in such a way that centuries of Hellenistic religion are treated as a mere transition period between two dynamic and fulfilling religious systems, that of classical Greek religion and that of early Christianity. According to this view, in the Hellenistic period classical Greek religion, which was closely tied to the political unit of the city-state, progressively meant less and less to the citizens as the city-states lost their independence and power; the citizens turned progressively more to private cults and beliefs; these private cults, in turn, were often imported from the East and offered more personal, direct relationships between individuals and the deities; and, finally, the collapse of state religion and the new, personal orientation of Hellenistic cults prepared the ground for Christianity.[1]

Even more misleading than value judgments are two fundamental methodological errors in the study of Hellenistic religion that have distorted our conception of it: the failure to distinguish religious phenomena and evidence by date and by place. If for these purposes we date the "Hellenistic period" from the death of Alexander the Great in 323 B.C. to Octavian's victory at Actium in 31 B.C., we find that much of the evidence commonly used to describe religion in this period is drawn from the Roman imperial period, from the first, second, and even third centuries A.D. The Greek world under the Roman emperors became very different—socially, economically, politically, and, I would claim, religiously—from what it had been in the Hellenistic period, and it is simply wrong to impose, for example, the description of the Isis cult taken from Apuleius' *Metamorphoses* (second century A.D.) on the Isis cult on Delos in the second century B.C., or the musings of the hypochondriac Aelius Aristides (second century A.D.) on the Asclepios cult of third century B.C. Athens. In volume 2 of his monumental *Geschichte der griechische Religion* (1974), Martin Nilsson made a strong distinction, in theory and in the organization of his book, between religion in Hellenistic and in Roman times, and our understanding of Hellenistic religion has been set back by his successors' failure to maintain this distinction.[2]

Nilsson also argued that we should recognize differences in religion

1. The general outlines and details of this view of Hellenistic religion may be found in Gehrke 1990, 185–92 (with extensive bibliography, 249–53); Koester 1982, 164–204; F. Walbank 1981, 209–21; Peters 1970, 446–79; Grant 1953, xi–xxxviii; Tarn and Griffith 1952, 336–60. Nilsson's work (1967–74, vol. 2) remains the best general study and survey of religion in the period. For recent and succinct statements of the problem, see Graf 1995; Price 1984, 14–15.

W. S. Ferguson's monumental *Hellenistic Athens* (1911) has remained the fundamental source for religion in Hellenistic Athens and is widely cited in the most recent studies of Hellenistic Athens. Ferguson saw in the development of religion in Athens many of the elements described above, and it is because of his critical importance to this area of study and because of others' dependence upon him that in what follows I occasionally address his arguments directly and explicitly. My focus on Ferguson should be taken as an acknowledgment of his accomplishment and importance. He laid out the factual foundation for the study of religion in Hellenistic Athens, a major contribution, and my disagreements with him concern not those facts but some of his interpretations of them.

2. Nilsson's same distinctions of time and place, with the same good results, are to be found in Z. Stewart 1977 and in the writings of Nock 1972.

among the old mainland Greek cities, the old Greek colonies in Asia Minor, and the cities founded much later by Macedonian generals and kings in Asia Minor. That is, in our study of Hellenistic religion we must maintain distinctions of place as well as of time. Even for Nilsson this distinction, because he was describing religion topically, was unwieldy and nearly impossible to maintain, but it needs to be reasserted and maintained. Otherwise we are inclined to impose, for example, a religious belief or cult known from second century B.C. Alexandria on contemporary Athens or, even worse, to imagine it part of a religious system, a religious *koinē* that all or most Greeks of the Hellenistic period shared. Again, individual cities in the Mediterranean area even within the Hellenistic period differed significantly in their societies, economics, traditions, politics, and religion. To neglect these fundamental distinctions of place and time is to create a Hellenistic "religion" that was never practiced at one time or one place by anyone.

My purpose is to examine Athenian practiced religion of the Hellenistic period—that is, the religion of one people in one period—and to note changes within that period. I also intend to examine it on its own merits, to see how it reflected the constant and changing needs of both the state and the individual. My study of these two hundred and fifty years of religion in Athens, from the death of Alexander in 323 to the sack of Athens by the Roman general Sulla in 86 B.C., indicates that changes did occur, but that they were not nearly so dramatic or linear, or even necessarily of the same nature, as the common conceptions of Hellenistic religion would suggest. We require, I think, far greater precision than we have had about what changes occurred, when they occurred, where they occurred, and, especially, why they occurred and whom they affected. In the conclusion, when we have completed our survey of Athenian religion, we will attempt to relate religion in Hellenistic Athens to current and more general views of Hellenistic religion.

To determine change we need a base, a status against which activities and events of later periods can be measured. For this base I have chosen the ten years following the battle of Chaeroneia (338 B.C.) when, under the leadership of Lycourgos, the Athenians reaffirmed and, one might say, consolidated their religious (as well as other) beliefs and institutions on the classical model. In chapter 1 I describe from the relatively rich documentation of that period fundamental personal religious beliefs and state cultic institutions and activities. In subsequent chapters, I set out, in chronological order, reasonably distinct historical periods, to show both elements of continuity and change and the context in which they occurred. This diachronic orientation will, I trust, contribute to understanding the sequence and nature of change in Athenian Hellenistic religion. I attempt to note with some precision the first datable example of each new phenomenon. In this I take particular caution against retrojecting data from later to earlier times. For example, we know that a corps of Athenian young men aged eighteen to twenty (ephebes) served together for two years of training already in the Lycourgan period, and we know that in the second century B.C. these ephebes had one year of service with a full and large program of religious activities. It is very inviting, but ultimately unhelpful, to retroject the activities known for ephebes of the second century upon those of the fourth century. My procedure is rather to give what evidence we have for the fourth-century ephebes and then later to introduce that for the second-century ephebes and to note the changes. New evidence may well change the picture one day, but regularly to use late evidence to describe or understand earlier periods is quite likely to cause us to miss real changes and to fail to make connections with political and social situations that contributed to those changes. For this study it seemed better to let the evidence speak for itself in chronological sequence, however lacunose it might be. I conclude the study with a review of the major religious developments in Athens and an attempt to relate these developments to trends in religion found elsewhere in the Greek world in the Hellenistic period.

Continuity in religion is the norm, but some particularly Greek concepts promoted this continuity at Athens and elsewhere in the ancient Greek world. First is the fundamental Greek belief that, in religious matters, one should act κατὰ τὰ πάτρια ("in the ancestral way"). This belief, found in the earliest to the latest Greek prose and poetry, naturally led to religious conservatism of a high degree. A second Greek belief also came into play, that it was "impious" to "dishonor" a god. One might actively worship—that is, "honor"—a god, and presumably that cult thrived. But to disestablish a cult, to close a sanctuary, tear down the *temenos* wall, dismantle the altar, and to, for example, farm the property or to use it for other secular or religious purposes would be actively to "dishonor" the god, and that was always thought to be dangerous. Cults might be allowed to repose in benign neglect, but we have no record of a decision to eliminate a cult not devoted to the worship of a king or other such political figure. Even major state cults might suffer, at certain periods, benign neglect. In such cases priests or priestesses would continue to serve, annual festivals would continue to be celebrated, but revenues, attendance at festivals, the number of dedications, new construction, and, in general, the status of the cult might be diminished as the citizens found the needs once provided for by this deity better served by another. But the cult itself, because of the ever-present danger of "dishonoring" the god, would not be eliminated. The result was, in Athens and elsewhere, that as the years went by the number of cults increased but very few cults disappeared entirely.[3] Cults, once founded, tended, like departments and programs in a modern government bureaucracy, to live on and on, some no longer having a significant role in state religion, some virtually forgotten. Also as in a government bureaucracy, new cults could be added to the existing structure with no attempt or thought to eliminate redundant cults.

Some cults become lost for us, and that means that they disappear from the epigraphical, archaeological, and literary record. Presumably, in some cases the cult did in fact come to an end, and there were no longer priests or priestesses, a sanctuary, sacrifices, dedications, or worshippers. For some, cult activity and prosperity may have slipped below the level of public notice, with members unable to afford inscriptions or attract the attention of orators or historians. Some cults disappear for us for centuries, only to reappear in the late Hellenistic or Roman periods. For them the question will be whether the reappearance is in fact a new foundation, the revival of a largely dormant institution, or simply another attestation of a cult or festival not likely, by its nature, to have left a continuous record.

In Athens exclusively foreign cults disappeared when their foreign devotees left the city; citizen cults would die completely only when, as in 200 B.C., sanctuaries were pillaged and destroyed by foreign invaders and not rebuilt. Apart from these rare occurrences, change in Hellenistic religion has two forms: the introduction of new cults and a changing degree of importance among existing cults. The former is relatively easy to document, but care must be taken to determine who participated in the new cults and whom they affected. Changes in the relative status of existing cults is much more difficult to determine and can only be traced, often quite hypothetically, in cases where new or existing cults seem to be assuming functions once commonly centered in another cult. Although the sources and evidence are never adequate to understand fully these changes, we need to point to what evidence there is if we wish to understand how Hellenistic Athenian religion came to differ from its classical predecessor.

3. Cf. Bruneau (1970, 660) on Delian cults after 166.

The nature of the evidence also makes the study of change in Hellenistic Athenian religion difficult. Most of the evidence, particularly from the later periods, is from inscriptions, and, although they are fairly abundant in comparison with those of other cities and can often be exactly dated, they still provide a very lacunose record in terms of time and subject. Attestations of a festival might be, for example, a hundred years apart, and then only the briefest mention of the real or planned occurrence of the festival. And for religious matters these inscriptions provide only the external details, the names of priests and priestesses, the occurrence of sacrifices and expenses therefrom, inventories of dedications, changes in cult procedures, and such matters. Much or most of my description and argument will depend on this very partial record, and I, like all who work with epigraphical material, recognize the risks and dangers inherent in this. A newly discovered epigraphical text, a new fact, will always have the potential to explode an argument or conclusion. But such is the way of progress in the historical study of ancient religion.

After the age of Lycourgos we have little to reveal the personal beliefs and devotion of Athenian worshippers, and I present that little I found. There is little evidence for continuity in this regard, but there is also little evidence for change, and we must beware of unsupported claims that, somehow, the religious "mentality" of the Athenians underwent significant changes in these years. Here we must be particularly cautious with statements of philosophers and other "intellectuals" who practiced at Athens. Most were not Athenians and did not participate in Athenian religion, and we need to consider their role in Athenian society and what influence they appear to have had on that society. Let me state here that my purpose is a history of religion in Hellenistic Athens as it was practiced in cult by the Athenians. The theories about religion and the gods and the comments on religious matters by philosophers, themselves extremely interesting and important areas of inquiry, are investigated only to the extent that they appear to have affected the religion practiced by the Athenians. In philosophy and theology change is the norm, but not so in cult and religious belief. There the norm is a continuity that we will see unmistakably in religious institutions and ritual. And we should assume similar continuity in religious beliefs and attitudes unless there is clear evidence to the contrary.

I see in the history of Athenian religion from 338 to 86 B.C. a more or less regular pattern: after 338 B.C. the Athenians, under the leadership of Lycourgos, as part of a general national revival, reasserted their traditional beliefs, rehabilitated their major sanctuaries, and placed their cults on a firmer financial basis. In the course of the next 250 years Athenian religion was affected by various external and internal pressures for change, but as each pressure was removed, the Athenians, explicitly or implicitly, returned to the Lycourgan model. The return, however, was never and could never be complete. Precedents had been set and attitudes on some subjects had been changed, and the effects of this become apparent in the reaction to the next set of pressures. But always, when the Athenians were free to act as they chose, there was at least a putative restoration of τὰ πάτρια ("the ancestral ways") as they were defined in the Lycourgan era. This repeated pattern of τὰ πάτρια, dislocation, and partial restoration of τὰ πάτρια parallels political developments in the period where the pattern is democracy, dislocation caused usually by foreign influence, and partial restoration of the traditional democracy. It will not be surprising that the religious and political patterns tend to be waves on the same frequency, because dislocations in both were caused largely by foreign influences and restorations in both tended to occur when the Athenians, however briefly, could manage their government and lives as they pleased.

The major influences for change in Athenian religion of the Hellenistic period I see to be political events and dislocation of populations. The political events were essentially Athenian domestic reactions to foreign pressures, as when, for example, they chose of their own accord to award divine honors to Antigonos Monophthalmos and his son Demetrios in 307 B.C. Such events, though relatively few and more or less explicable from current religious beliefs and practices, served as precedents for the future and, despite periodic reactions against them, eventually determined the shape of Athenian state religion. More important than these relatively infrequent events were, however, dislocations of populations. For old Greek city-states like Athens, religion was almost indissolubly tied up with *their* local deities, shrines, and cult practices and was almost without exception limited to *their* citizens and members of their households. A Milesian, for example, could move to Athens and live as a metic, but he would be unable to continue his Milesian religious customs and would be able to participate in Athenian religion only in the most limited, superficial ways. Some Egyptian and other oriental cults, unlike most Greek cults, appear to have been relatively easily transplanted, and this may be one explanation for their growing popularity in the period. The movement of peoples from their homelands, accelerating in the course of the Hellenistic period, was, I submit, the major force for change in personal, practiced religion, both in Athens and elsewhere. The initial stages seem of minimal importance in Athens, with, for example, a small group of Egyptians worshipping their Isis or a similar group of Citians from Cyprus worshipping their Aphrodite Ourania. The full force of population dislocation will become clear, however, when we examine Athenian relationships with Delos after 166. With the Delians expelled from their island, with Athenians administering religious affairs on Delos and returning to Athens after their years of service there, we shall see in both cities signs of religious change, of the explosion of foreign cults and Athenian participation in them, of syncretism, and of some (but not all) other elements commonly associated with Hellenistic religion. Spiritual changes and changed personal beliefs resulted from exposure to and participation in these foreign cults, and for Athenians this exposure and participation began with their stays on Delos and with the resulting permanent or temporary separation from their own, inherited cults and religious traditions. A very unusual set of circumstances involving religious and social affairs on Delos when the Athenians occupied it, their administration of Delian cults, and their return to Athens all contributed to bringing "Hellenistic religion" to Athens. The effects, however, were much greater on Athenians during their stays on Delos, for in Athens, even as Athenians who administered and participated in the cults of Delos returned home, traditional Athenian religious cults and structures still predominated. I argue, however, that Athens was finally opened to Hellenistic religious influences from the East by the experience on Delos.

On technical matters: the spelling of Greek names here, as everywhere, is inconsistent, but I aim to be consistently inconsistent. Greek personal names I generally transliterate, but with "c" for kappa and "ch" for chi: hence "Lycourgos," not "Lykourgos." I am reluctant, however, to make strangers of very old friends: hence "Aeschylus" and not "Aiskhulos" or "Aischylos." The epithets of deities I generally transliterate more strictly because their etymological significance thus emerges more clearly. For the names of the Attic demes I follow Traill 1975. For the abbreviations of authors' names and the titles of their writings, I follow *The Oxford Classical Dictionary* (2nd ed.). The translations throughout are my own, and I indicate by square brackets [ ] passages of restored Greek, by curved brackets ( ) supplements I have made to clarify the meaning. To make further inquiry easier and to distinguish between homonymous individuals I give most Athenians their *PA* (Kirchner,

Prosopographia Attica) or their *APF* (Davies, *Athenian Propertied Families*) numbers. These numbers will also help in the consultation of the invaluable new *Lexicon of Greek Personal Names*, vol. 2, by Michael Osborne and Sean Byrne (1994).

Most of the hundreds of inscriptions cited in the text and notes have been edited, reedited, emended, and commented upon by a number of scholars in a wide variety of publications. Many have long bibliographic trails, and I have attempted to reduce where possible references to the inscriptions themselves and to discussions of them to the citations in *Supplementum Epigraphicum Graecum* (*SEG*), the annual survey of epigraphical scholarly work. The cross-referencing system of the appendix will lead from the *SEG* reference to the original publication. On occasion a single *SEG* entry gives accounts of several publications, and for these one should turn directly to *SEG*.

The year dates given to events and documents in this study are based ultimately upon the lists of eponymous archons for whom the Athenians "named" their years. The sequential list of archons for the Hellenistic period, after many years of painstaking work by scholars, is now mostly secure. Some uncertainties remain, however, and in particular John Morgan's recent work indicates that several archons of the late third century may be dated one year too early. When his work is published, revisions to the dates I have given may have to be made, but they will in no way, I think, affect the conclusions to be drawn about religious matters. And, finally, I regret that Christian Habicht's *Athen: Die Geschichte der Stadt in hellenistischer Zeit* (Munich, 1995) and Robert Parker's *Athenian Religion: A History* (Oxford, 1996) have appeared too late to be incorporated into this study.

On this foray into the Hellenistic period I have had the pleasant sense of treading in the footsteps of three of my teachers, Paul L. MacKendrick at the University of Wisconsin and Sterling Dow and Zeph Stewart of Harvard University, and of their teachers, Arthur Darby Nock and William Scott Ferguson. In recent years I have been helped immeasurably by Christian Habicht and Stephen Tracy, both of whom have read the manuscript at various stages, have saved me from errors great and small, and have pointed me in important new directions. Glenn Bugh and Diskin Clay read parts of the manuscript in its early phases and contributed much. In 1995–96, as a Sesquicentennial Associate of the University of Virginia and Whitehead Visiting Professor at the American School of Classical Studies in Athens, I had not only the opportunity,

environment, and library necessary to complete this work but also colleagues such as Judith Binder, Alan Boegehold, John Camp, and Carol
Lawton who daily enriched my knowledge of religion in both classical
and Hellenistic Athens and had many immediate, practical suggestions
to offer. To them, to the director of the American School, William D. E.
Coulson, and to the staff of the School I owe much.

1

The Age of Lycourgos

In 330 B.C. Lycourgos, son of Lycophron, of the deme Boutadai, prosecuted a certain Leocrates for treason.[1] For six years, since 336/5, Lycourgos had dominated Athenian politics, largely through control of the city's finances, and he would continue to do so until 324. Leocrates had fled Athens, with money and mistress in hand, immediately after the victory of Philip II, king of Macedon, over the combined Athenian and Theban forces at Chaeroneia in 338, at the very moment when Athenians were expecting Philip to turn his wrath upon their city. Philip spared Athens, but Leocrates chose to live abroad, in Megara, for eight years. When Leocrates took up his life in Athens again, Lycourgos brought him to court on several charges: treason, because by abandoning the city, he subjected it to the enemy; dissolution (of the power) of the people, because he had not withstood the danger on freedom's behalf; impiety, because for his part, he would have been responsible for the sanctuaries being torn to pieces and the temples being razed; maltreatment of parents, because he was letting disappear their tombs and depriving them of the traditional rites of the dead; and desertion and refusal to serve in the armed forces, because he, by flight, avoided military assignment (*Leoc.* 147).

Lycourgos' speech against Leocrates is critically important, though usually overlooked, as a source for the religion of Athenians of its time,

---

1. For Lycourgos' times, family, and for many other aspects of his political and religious activity, see Tracy 1995; Faraguna 1992; Merker 1986; Humphreys 1985; Schwenk 1985; Mitchel 1970; MacKendrick 1969, 22–24; Durrbach 1931.

330 B.C., and for understanding the development of Athenian religion in the fourth century as a whole.[2] For us it will serve as the centerpiece of a report on the status of Athenian religion in the 330s and 320s: that is, of the status of Athenian religion at the very beginning of the Hellenistic period, the status against which we must measure changes in Athenian practiced religion in the last quarter of the fourth century, in the third and second centuries, and in the first century up to the sack of Athens by the Roman general Sulla in 86 B.C.

We first cull from the speech what Lycourgos says on religion and religious matters and then attempt to place Lycourgos' statements into the context of his life and career, and, finally, into the context of what we know, from other sources, of the religion practiced in fourth-century Athens. The first question is what Lycourgos said; the second question is whether what he said is idiosyncratic or reflective of the views and practices of his contemporaries.

Lycourgos "believes" ($\dot{\eta}\gamma o\hat{\upsilon}\mu\alpha\iota$), literally as a creed, that "the concern of the gods watches over all human activities, but especially over piety toward parents, toward the dead, and toward the gods themselves" (*Leoc.* 94). From parents we have received the beginning of life and the most benefits, and "it is the greatest impiety not only to sin against them but also not to spend one's life benefiting them" (94). He relates a story, a bit mythical but fit for the younger men to hear, telling of an eruption of Mount Etna on Sicily, when burning lava flowed through a village. It caught and killed those who, in fleeing for safety, had abandoned their parents, but it spared the one young man who had stayed behind to rescue his aged, infirm father. He and his father alone were saved, and the site of the event is still called "the Place of the Pious." From this one ought to see, Lycourgos concludes, "that the divine ($\tau\dot{o}\ \theta\epsilon\hat{\iota}o\nu$) is well intentioned ($\epsilon\dot{\upsilon}\mu\epsilon\nu\hat{\omega}\varsigma\ \ddot{\epsilon}\chi\epsilon\iota$) to good men" (95–96). Athenians in general excel other men in acting in a holy way toward parents (15), but Leocrates had left behind his parents to the enemy (97). Leocrates' father, now dead, would be, if the dead have any perception of the affairs of the living, Leocrates' harshest judge (136).

By his cowardly and lengthy flight, Leocrates abandoned the tombs of his ancestors to the enemy and neglected the cult owed them (8, 59, 97, 147). The old men among the jurors will vote Leocrates guilty because, for his part, he surrendered them to the enemy so that they would

2. On the political aspects of the speech, see Tracy 1995, 14–16.

be not cared for in old age or buried in the free soil of their fatherland (144). The Greeks fighting the Persians at Plataea in 479 had sworn to bury all the allied troops who died in battle (81), but Leocrates did not stay even to help collect and bury his fellow Athenians who had died on the battlefield at Chaeroneia. Now he passes by their tomb shamelessly, although, so far as it depended on him, they would have been unburied (45, 144).

In regard to the gods themselves, Leocrates betrayed their temples, their statues, their sanctuaries, their honors outlined in the laws, and their sacrifices that have been handed down by the ancestors (1). So far as Leocrates was concerned, the gods' sanctuaries would have been destroyed and their temples razed (147). Because of this, Lycourgos' indictment is, if correct, "just," "pious," and "on behalf of the gods" (1; cf. 2, 27, 35, 38, 97, 146). The Athenians surpass other men in their piety toward the gods (15), but Leocrates brought no help to their sanctuaries (8), and in his flight felt not the slightest fear in abandoning the Acropolis and the sanctuary of Zeus Soter and Athena Soteira (17). "The help from the gods does not aid traitors, and with good reason. For their first act of injustice is impiety concerning the gods, by depriving them of their traditional, ancestral rites" (129). Now "Leocrates will call upon the gods to save him from these dangers, but which gods? Surely not those whose temples, statues, and sanctuaries he betrayed" (143). The ancestors of the Athenians, having taken Athena as their patroness, named their city after her so that those who honor the goddess would never abandon the city. Leocrates took no thought of the traditions, of his fatherland, or of its sanctuaries, and, so far as he could, caused divine aid to be lost (26).

And not only did Leocrates betray the gods of the state. When living in Megara Leocrates had his house in Athens sold and had removed from there to Megara the domestic cults of his family, those cults which his ancestors had founded and, in the traditional and ancient ways of the Athenians, had handed down to him. Ignoring these traditions, Leocrates reestablished these cults as strangers in a land foreign and alien to them, amid Megarian not Athenian traditions. He felt no fear at their very name, "cults of the fathers" (25).

Why did Leocrates return to Athens after years of exile? "Some god led him to his punishment, so that, having fled the glorious danger (in battle), he might find an inglorious death and be subject to those whom he betrayed. For so the gods mislead the minds of wicked men" (91–92). Thus "As you vote, jurors, think that the temples and the sanctuaries are asking you to help them," and remember that "though you vote in secret, the gods will know your way of thinking, and if you favor the traitor you subject yourselves to punishment from the gods" (146–50).

Such are the ways that Lycourgos in this speech details and applies his belief that "the concern of the gods watches over all human activities, but especially over piety toward parents, toward the dead, and toward the gods themselves." Lycourgos expresses his thoughts on other religious topics also, in particular on oracles, on the religious services called liturgies, and on oaths.

In *Against Leocrates* Lycourgos cites, each time without a hint of skepticism, four Delphic oracles: one historical, one possibly historical, and two literary. Each oracle promotes, successfully, a political or moral purpose. In ca. 361 Callistratos of Aphidna (*APF* 8157), a prominent statesman and orator, was condemned to death by the Athenian people. He fled the city and eventually went to Delphi to inquire about his return. Delphic Apollo told him that if he returned to Athens he would find justice (literally, "he would find the laws"), and so he returned and took refuge at the altar of the Twelve Gods in the Agora. Nonetheless he was put to death by the Athenians. The point is, Lycourgos claims, that justice for criminals is punishment, and the god rightly returned the criminal to his victims. "It would be terrible (δεινόν)," he says, "if the same messages should be given to the pious and to criminals" (93).

In the seventh century B.C. the Lacedaimonians, fighting the Messenians, sent to Delphi and were told that they should take an Athenian leader and they would then win the war. They therefore fetched the general Tyrtaeus from Athens and with his help defeated the Messenians. The Lacedaimonians also learned from the poetry of Tyrtaeus the moral system upon which they based their education of the young (105–9). In even more remote, legendary times the Peloponnesians were besieging Athens and learned from Delphi that they would capture the city if they did *not* kill its king Codros. Codros learned of the oracle and, by a ruse, induced the invaders to kill him. The Peloponnesians, when they realized what they had done, withdrew, and Codros by his sacrifice saved the city (83–89). Similarly, in the reign of Erechtheus Athens was about to face an invasion by Eumolpos, his Eleusinians, and the Thracians. Erechtheus learned from Delphi that the Athenians would be victorious if, before the invasion, he sacrificed his daughter. Lycourgos read out fifty-five lines from Euripides' *Erechtheus*, in which Praxithea, Erechtheus' wife, for intensely patriotic reasons, expresses her approval of the sacrifice. Erechtheus' daughter was sacrificed, or sacrificed herself, and Athens was again saved, because of Delphic Apollo and the patriotism of her leaders and citizens (98–101).

In fourth-century Athens the wealthiest citizens were subject to appointment, by an archon, to a liturgy, a service that might involve paying the expenses for a chorus at the City Dionysia or other state festival (*chorēgia*) or for a team of athletes in competition at the Great Panathenaia (*gymnasiarchia*).[3] Defendants in criminal trials often listed the liturgies they had performed, hoping thereby to win favor with the jury. Lycourgos, no doubt anticipating one line of Leocrates' defense, expressed his annoyance at such persons, because they undertook these liturgies on behalf of their own families but then expected public rewards. The liturgist himself, Lycourgos claimed, was awarded a crown for his service but was in no way benefiting others. Public gratitude should go to those who supported a trireme or helped build the city walls or provided in other ways for public safety from their private funds. Here one could see the virtue (ἀρετήν) of the givers, but in liturgies one sees only the prosperity of those who have spent the money (139–40).

Finally, the oath is, according to Lycourgos, what holds the democracy together. The government consists of three things—the archon, the juryman, and the private citizen; each of these gives a pledge under oath, and for good reason. Many men, after deceiving others, escape detection and receive no punishment, either then or perhaps for their whole life. But the gods know who has committed perjury and they will punish him. If, perchance, the individual should escape, his family falls into great misfortunes (79). Those who remain true to their oaths have the goodwill (εὔνοιαν) of the gods with them as a help (βοηθόν) (82).

We have some record of each of the three oaths Lycourgos cites, that of the archon, the juryman, and the private citizen, and each, fortunately, comes from a roughly contemporary source. From the *Constitution of the Athenians* (55.5) we learn that archons-select went to the Agora, made sacrifices on a specially designated stone near the Stoa Basileios, and then mounted this stone and swore that they "would govern justly and according to the laws; that they would not take gifts because of their office; and that if they should take anything, they would set up a golden statue."[4] The archons-select then had to repeat this oath on the Acropolis.

3. On these liturgies, see Davies 1967 and *APF*, xvii–xxxi. See also below, chapter 2, pp. 54–56.

4. On the "sacred stone" and the Stoa Basileios in front of which it sat, see Camp 1992, 53–57, 100–105.

Lycourgos is concerned that the jurors bring a vote in accordance with their oath (εὔορκον ψῆφον, 128) and that they not, in violation of their oath, allow speakers to get off the topic (13). The oath to which he refers is recorded by Demosthenes:[5]

I will vote in accordance with the laws and decrees of the Demos of the Athenians and of the Boule of five hundred. And I will not vote to have a tyrant or an oligarchy. If someone attempts to destroy (the power) of the Demos of the Athenians or if he speaks or brings a vote contrary to this, I will not be persuaded. Nor will I vote for the cancellation of private debts or for the redistribution of the land or houses of Athenians. I will not bring back those who have been exiled or condemned to death. I will not myself banish, nor will I allow anyone else to banish, the residents here contrary to the established laws and decrees of the Demos of the Athenians and of the Boule. And I will not confirm in office a person in such a way that he holds one office when he is subject to audit for another, and these offices include the nine archons, the *hieromnēmōn*,[6] those who are chosen by lot with the nine archons on this day, a herald, an embassy, and delegates to the council of allies. Nor will I allow the same man to hold the same office twice or the same man to hold two offices in the same year. And I will not accept bribes because of my jury service, not I myself nor another for me nor in any other way with me knowing of it, not by a trick or by any contrivance. And I am not less than thirty years old. And I will listen to both the prosecutor and the defendant equally, and I will bring my vote on the basis of the issues being prosecuted. (Dem. 24.149–51)

The juror swore this oath by Zeus, Poseidon, and Demeter, and he cursed himself and his family to utter destruction if he transgressed any of these provisions. But he prayed that if he kept this oath, he might have "many good things." It is this oath that Lycourgos asks the jurors to abide by.

Of the oath of private citizens Lycourgos says, "You have an oath which all the citizens swear when they are enrolled onto the register of demes and become ephebes, that you will not shame your holy weapons or leave your position in battle, that you will defend your fatherland and hand it down better than it is" (76). The full text of this oath, preserved on a fourth-century inscription from the deme Acharnai, is as follows:[7]

I will not bring shame upon these sacred weapons nor will I abandon my comrade-in-arms wherever I stand in the ranks. I will defend both the holy and profane things. I will not hand on the fatherland smaller than I

5. On the jurors' oath, see A. Harrison 1968–71, 2:48.
6. The *hieromnēmōn* was Athens' delegate to the Amphictionic Council that administered Delphi in this period.
7. For text and commentary, see Tod 1948, #204. See also Siewert 1977.

received it, but larger and better, so far as it lies in my power with the assistance of all the other citizens. I will obey the officials who govern wisely and the laws, both those which are already established and those which are wisely established in the future. If anyone attempts to destroy them, I will not allow it, so far as it lies in my power with the assistance of all the other citizens. I will hold in honor the ancestral sanctuaries. The following gods are witnesses: Aglauros, Hestia, Enyo, Enyalios, Ares and Athena Areia, Zeus, Thallo, Auxo, Hegemone, Heracles, the territory of the fatherland, the wheat, barley, vines, olive trees, and fig trees.

These are the three oaths—of the archon, the juryman, and the private citizen—that, in Lycourgos' view, "hold the democracy together" (79). The jurymen are to uphold theirs as they vote on Leocrates' guilt. Lycourgos has read to them the ephebic oath and then details how Leocrates broke each of its provisions (76–78). As a traitor Leocrates' crime is against his fellow citizens. As a perjurer it is against the gods.

It is also the Athenian ephebic oath upon which, according to Lycourgos, the Greek allies formed the oath that they swore before they joined battle with Xerxes' Persians at Plataea in 479 B.C. Lycourgos had also this oath read to the jurors, the text of which survives on the very stone that preserves the ephebic oath:[8]

I will not make life more important than freedom, nor will I abandon my leaders whether they be alive or dead. I will bury all of our allies who die in the battle. And when we have defeated the barbarians, I will destroy no one of the cities that fought on Greece's side, but I will exact a tenth from all those who chose the barbarians' side. I will most certainly not rebuild any of the sanctuaries burned or razed by the barbarians, but I will leave them for our descendants as a memorial of the impiety of the barbarians.

Because the Greeks, including the ancestors of the jury, remained faithful to the terms of this oath, they had the goodwill of the gods as their helper (80–82).

And, finally, the ancestors of the jurymen had sworn, by the decree of Demophantos of 410 B.C., to kill any man betraying the fatherland by word, by deed, by hand, or by vote. This oath survives in Andocides' speech on the Mysteries (1.96–98):[9]

Let the oath be this: "I will kill, [by word and deed and vote] and by my own hand, if I am able, whoever destroys the democracy at Athens and if anyone holds an office in the future after the democracy has been destroyed

8. Tod 1948, #204, for text and commentary.
9. On this decree and oath, see MacDowell 1962, 134–36.

and if anyone attempts to set up or help set up a tyrant. And if someone else kills him, I shall consider him holy in the view of the gods and *daimones* since he has killed an enemy of the Athenians, and after selling the property of the dead man I will give half of it to the killer and will deprive him of nothing. And if someone dies killing or attempting to kill anyone of such men, I will treat well him and his children as I do Harmodios and Aristogeiton and their descendants. Whatever oaths have been sworn at Athens or in the army or elsewhere against the Demos of the Athenians, I do away with and dismiss." Let all Athenians swear these things on the sacred victims before the Dionysia. And let them pray that for the one keeping his oath there be many and good things, but that if he violates this oath, he and his family may perish utterly.

In Lycourgos' view the jurors have inherited this oath from their fathers, who gave it, like a hostage of the happiness of the commonwealth, to the gods. And, in the case of Leocrates, they must prove themselves no worse than their fathers (127).

Such are the main religious sentiments expressed by Lycourgos in his prosecution of Leocrates. They permeate the speech, giving it much of its content and structure. They provide, so far as they go, a consistent and unified view of the role of the gods in Athenian political life, of humans' responsibilities to the gods, and of sin and piety. In sum, the gods are concerned with all human activities, in particular those concerning parents, the dead, and the gods themselves. The pious person will care for his parents while living; will see to the proper burial, tomb, and tomb cult of the dead; and will protect and maintain the sanctuaries, temples, statues, honors, sacrifices, and traditional rituals of state and domestic gods. Through impiety in these areas divine aid can be lost to the individual and the city. The gods seek out and see to the punishment of individual sinners and know even their secret thoughts and votes.

Lycourgos takes for granted the accuracy of the oracles from Delphic Apollo, treating identically those of historical times and those found in poetry. He views them as promoting justice, morality, and patriotism, and as beneficial to and favoring the Athenian state. Oaths are, as he puts it, critical to "holding together the democracy," and the provisions in the oaths of the archons, jurors, and ephebes put under religious sanctions much of the political behavior of Athenian citizens. The gods will punish perjurers or their descendants, but offer goodwill and help to those who keep their oaths. Lycourgos is skeptical of the public benefit of the religious liturgies of the wealthy, seeing them as only ostentatious demonstrations of private wealth, especially in comparison to services that the wealthy might provide in rebuilding the city's walls or supporting the navy. And, finally, Lycourgos claims Athenians surpass other Greeks in their piety toward parents and the gods, and that Leocrates' impious behavior is the exception.

The *Leocrates*, a forensic speech, was delivered in court before a jury numbering, probably, five hundred Athenian citizens and was later published for all Athenians to read. As a general rule one can assume that prosecutors and defendants speaking in such trials attempted to avoid controversy on points not essential to their case, that they attempted to show themselves in tune with the moral and religious norms of their peers. For this reason courtroom orations are a particularly valuable source for the social, moral, and religious standards of their time.[10] This general rule, unfortunately, does not apply to the *Leocrates*, because its tone and purpose are patently didactic. Lycourgos was giving moral, patriotic, and religious instruction, and in large sections the effect is more that of Pericles' "Funeral Oration" from Thucydides than that of a forensic oration of Isaeus or Demosthenes: hence Lycourgos' review of events in Athens' legendary or historical past, his anecdotes, and, in particular, his reading of oaths and of passages from Euripides and Aeschylus. We cannot therefore assume that because the *Leocrates* is a forensic speech, Lycourgos assumed his auditors all shared these beliefs. Nor, however, should we deduce from the speech's didactic character that the audience did *not* share these beliefs.[11] Lycourgos may have thought that in those times and in that case, Athenians needed to be reminded of their fundamental beliefs. And here it should be noted that Lycourgos presents these beliefs as commonly known, not as beliefs currently being ignored, challenged, or rejected, except by the impious Leocrates. He does not defend the beliefs themselves against attack; he simply presents them and applies them to Leocrates. Lycourgos' frequent appeal to the traditions and laws of the fathers and ancestors also should not incline us to assume that he was trying to revive old, long-dead beliefs. Such appeals are soundly based in the Greek oratorical

---

10. Mikalson 1983, 7–8.

11. That Leocrates' jury was exactly divided on its vote and that Leocrates was thus acquitted (Aeschines 3.252) need not make us question the audience's acceptance of Lycourgos' religious arguments. There may have been points of law or fact which Lycourgos avoided or concealed but which influenced the jury.

tradition as far back as Homer and can be found throughout the orations of the classical period. That Lycourgos describes beliefs and practices as traditional and ancestral by no means indicates that they are not current. It rather proves that they have a good pedigree and are deserving of continued respect. I would thus argue that there is nothing in the speech itself to allow us to judge the commonality or sincerity of the religious statements that Lycourgos makes. For that we must turn to other, contemporary sources.

I begin by examining these religious beliefs in the context of Lycourgos' career and other activities in the domain of religion. For those of us skeptical of politicians' and lawyers' words—and Lycourgos was functioning as both in the *Leocrates*—we need to see how words correlate with deeds, how what Lycourgos says in the *Leocrates* accords with his public career. Then I turn to other sources from the period to assess how Lycourgos' sentiments and actions appear to fit into the tenor of his times. As I discuss both topics, I shall add, as they appear, other religious elements from the period to complement those found in the *Leocrates*.

In 307/6 B.C., about seventeen years after his death, the Athenians voted for Lycourgos the highest honors the state then offered its citizens: a statue in the Agora and dining privileges in the Prytaneion for descendants. The formal decree, proposed by Stratocles, survives and serves to indicate how Lycourgos' near contemporaries viewed his contributions to the state.

> In the archonship of Anaxicrates (307/6), in the sixth prytany, that of the tribe Antiochis, Stratocles, son of Euthydemos, of the deme Diomeia, proposed: whereas
>
> > Lycourgos, son of Lycophron, of the deme Boutadai, inherited from his ancestors long-standing goodwill toward the Demos [. . .], and his ancestors, Lycomedes and Lycourgos, were honored by the Demos when they lived and received burial at public expense in the Cerameicos when they died because of their goodness and manliness; and
> > Lycourgos himself, when engaged in state affairs, made many good laws for the fatherland, and having been treasurer of the general revenues for the city for twelve years and having spent from the general revenues 18,600 talents, and having collected, on credit, 650 talents from private citizens, and having spent all these for the needs of the city and the Demos, and having appeared to have administered all these things justly, he was crowned by the city many times; and

having been selected by the Demos again, he collected much money into the Acropolis and he prepared adornment for the goddess, viz. golden Nikai, gold and silver processional vessels, and gold adornment for 100 *kanēphoroi;* and

elected for the oversight of military preparations he brought many weapons and 5,000 missiles into the Acropolis and prepared 400 seaworthy triremes, having repaired some and constructed others anew; and

in addition to these things, he received the ship sheds, the armory, and the theater of Dionysos half built and completed them, and he completed the Panathenaic Stadium, and he built the gymnasion at the Lyceum, and he adorned the city with many other buildings; and

after King Alexander subjugated all of Asia and thought it his right to give orders to all Greeks, and after Alexander demanded Lycourgos from us as his enemy, the Demos did not, despite fear of Alexander, give Lycourgos up; and

although many times submitting public audits of what he administered, when the city was free and under a democracy, he was throughout all that time not convicted of any crime and not susceptible to bribes;

So that all may know that (the Demos of the Athenians) consider most valuable, when they are alive, those who choose to handle public affairs justly for the benefit of democracy and freedom, and when they die, express their always-to-be-remembered gratitude,

It has been decided, with good fortune, by the Demos to praise Lycourgos, son of Lycophron, of the deme Boutadai, for his virtue and justice, and for the Demos to erect a bronze statue of him in the Agora, unless somehow the law forbids it, and to give the privilege of dining in the Pyrtaneion for all time to the eldest of his descendants. And all the state decrees Lycourgos proposed are to be in force, and the secretary of the Demos is to erect (copies of) them on stone plaques and to stand them on the Acropolis near the dedications. And for the engraving of the plaques the treasurer of the Demos is to give fifty drachmas from the Demos' fund for decrees. ([Plut.] *X Orat.* 852A–E)[12]

This decree records Lycourgos' accomplishments in the areas of law, finance, politics, military preparedness, public works, and religion as they were viewed, retrospectively, by the next generation. I present the text *in toto* because this, better than any summation, puts Lycourgos' religious activities into the context of his whole career. It gives, for us, a much-needed perspective. As we concentrate our attention henceforth

12. Pausanias (1.29.16) in his description of Lycourgos' activities virtually summarizes this decree. A fragmentary copy of the decree survives on stone (*IG* II² 457). For *IG* II² 513 as a fragment of another copy of the decree, see M. Osborne 1981, 172–74. On the variations among these texts, see Oikonomides 1986; Cuvigny 1981, 87–89 (and notes).

on the religious activities of Lycourgos, which were major, we must keep in mind that they were only one part, and probably not the most significant part, of his public career.

Stratocles' decree takes up issues of Lycourgos' family, financial management, "adornment" (*kosmos*) of the goddess and the city, the building program, and, finally, personal character. We now take up the religious aspects of these in the same order.

Lycourgos was of the *genos* of the Eteobutadai, the aristocratic kinship group that traced its ancestry to Erechtheus, the earth-born king of Athens and foster child of Athena, the same Erechtheus whose story Lycourgos tells in *Leocrates* 98–101.[13] To a member of the Eteobutadai was allotted the priesthood of Poseidon-Erechtheus, whose cult was centered in the Erechtheum, the heart of Athenian state religion. One of Lycourgos' sons, Habron, was allotted this priesthood and he ceded it to his brother Lycophron.[14] Habron dedicated in the Erechtheum a plaque depicting himself handing over the trident to his brother. Lycourgos and his sons were also represented by wooden statues in the Erechtheum, and all this suggests that Lycourgos too held the priesthood during his lifetime.[15] And thus not only was Lycourgos born into a pro-democratic and patriotic family as Stratocles' decree declares, but he was also, by birth, aristocratic and closely tied, as closely as an Athenian male could be, to the major state cult of Athena Polias and Poseidon in the Erechtheum.

Lycourgos, like his father and grandfather, was given a burial at public expense, and he and his descendants were buried very near the Academy, just opposite the sanctuary of Athena Paionia.[16] Lycourgos had, reportedly, been a student of Plato, the founder of the Academy, and had studied also with the rhetorician Isocrates ([Plut.] *X Orat.* 841B). He once hired sophists to teach his sons and, when challenged on this, replied that if someone promised to make his sons better, he would give him not just 1,000 drachmas but half his fortune (842C–D). Lycourgos also roughed up and had thrown into prison a tax collector who was harassing Xenocrates, then head of the Academy (842B–C; Plut. *Flam.* 12.7). Lycourgos had ties also with the Lyceum, for there he built a gymnasion and had it planted with trees ([Plut.] *X Orat.* 841C–D);

---

13. On the Eteobutadai, see Bourriot 1976, 1304–47.

14. On the sons of Lycourgos and especially on Habron, see Merker 1986. On the priesthood of Poseidon-Erechtheus, see Aleshire 1994, 327–35.

15. [Plut.] *X Orat.* 841A–B, 842F–843A, 843E–F.

16. [Plut.] *X Orat.* 842E; Paus. 1.29.15. For the discovery and epitaphs of the tombs of Lycourgos' family, see *SEG* 37.160–62.

and, after his death, Democles, a student of Theophrastos, spoke in defense of Lycourgos' sons (842D–E).[17] We note these close associations Lycourgos had with philosophers of his time because the relationship of philosophy, statesmen, and popular religion will be important to understanding religion in the late fourth century and throughout the Hellenistic period.

Lycourgos, the decree of Stratocles states, "made many good laws for the fatherland," and several of these concerned religious matters:

1. To reestablish a lapsed contest of comic actors in the theater at the Chytroi festival, and to enroll the victor in the City Dionysia ([Plut.] *X Orat.* 841F).[18]

2. To have a contest of dithyrambic choruses for Poseidon in Piraeus, with 1,000 drachmas to the winners, 800 drachmas to second place, and 600 to third (842A).[19]

3. To forbid women from riding on wagons in the procession to Eleusis for the Mysteries. The purpose, according to the *Vita*, was that ordinary women not be made inferior to the rich.[20] The fine was 6,000 drachmas. Lycourgos' own wife then apparently violated the law, and Lycourgos paid the 6,000 drachmas to buy off sycophants ready to prosecute him (842A–B).[21]

4. To establish new provisions for handling sacred funds and dedications to the gods. The fragmentary text of Schwenk #21 of 335/4 records two laws: the one certainly proposed by Lycourgos gives detailed instructions for the making, storage, inventorying, and repair of objects dedicated to several deities. For some actions the approval of Apollo at Delphi was required.[22]

---

17. On Democles and this incident, see Merker 1986, 46.

18. For the nature of these contests, see Hamilton 1992, 38–42; Pickard-Cambridge 1988, 15–16. Hamilton (42) describes Lycourgos' reforms: "A plausible reconstruction is that when Lykourgos rebuilt the Theater of Dionysos he revived the Chytrine contests, shifted their venue from the Limnaian precinct to his new theater, and made them much more elaborate."

19. For the nature of this contest, see Pickard-Cambridge 1962, 4, 57. Oddly, Poseidon's cult is poorly attested for Piraeus. There is only one mention, of a "plaque of Poseidon" (*SEG* 26.72.42, 46–47 of 375/4). See Stroud 1974, 183.

20. For an example of such behavior, see Dem. 21.158.

21. Cf. Plut. *Mor.* 541F, *Comp. Nic. Crass.* 1.3; Aelian *VH* 13.24.

22. On Schwenk #21, see Faraguna 1992, 368–69, 371–79.

5. To set up bronze statues of Aeschylus, Sophocles, and Euripides, to copy and protect in a public building the texts of
their plays, and to specify that the secretary of the city read
these to the actors. The actors then were to follow them exactly
(841F).[23] This law might not necessarily be termed "religious,"
but it does affect the performances at various state and deme
drama festivals. It also suits well the man who in court quoted
a long passage of Euripides and spoke with approval of the
poetry of Tyrtaeus. Two other of his laws also concerned
"literary" matters, the comedy competitions of the Chytroi
and the dithyrambic competition in Piraeus.

All five laws have in common that they created *kosmos* in both its
meanings, "order" and "adornment," in religious affairs. The dithyrambic competition and the renewed comedy competition were new or-
naments, as all such public festivals were *kosmoi* of the city. The law
on preservation of the tragedies regularized their texts, as the wagon
law would the procession to Eleusis. And, finally, Schwenk #21.CEF
10–32 persistently refers to the dedications to be made and remade as
kosmos. The provisions established there would bring *kosmos* (as both
"beauty" and "order") to these dedications. We shall find such *kosmos*
to be a persistent theme in Lycourgos' personal involvement in religious affairs.

In the implementation of law, apparently most often on the side of
the prosecution, Lycourgos spoke "many times about sacred matters"
([Plut.] *X Orat.* 843D). We know from titles and surviving fragments
that he spoke[24]

1. *About the Priestess of Athena.* The priesthood of Athena Polias
was also hereditary to one branch of the *genos* of the Eteobutadai, and in this speech Lycourgos detailed many of her
activities as well as those of the priestesses of Athena Nike,
Hygieia, and Skiras (frags. 6.1–22).

2. *About Priestly Perquisites.*

23. Pausanias (1.21.1–2) discusses statues of the three tragedians in the theater of
Dionysos. For the argument that these were the Lycourgan statues and for later copies,
see Richter 1962, 24–29.
24. For a discussion of these speeches, see Durrbach 1932, xxxvi–l. Citations of the
fragments are from Conomis 1970.

3. *About Oracles.*

4. *Against Menesaichmos,* an individual who had violated a rule of sacrifice on a *theoria* (religious embassy) to Delos. Here Lycourgos described Athenian, Delian, and Delphic rites and myths related to Apollo (frags. 14.1–11).

5. *Against Euxenippos* of Lamptrai (*APF* 5866), who, it was alleged, had falsely reported a dream he had received in the sanctuary of Amphiaraos concerning the division of territory in Oropos.[25] Hyperides' speech (4) in Euxenippos' defense survives.

The scanty surviving fragments of these speeches suggest that Lycourgos discussed in some detail matters of ritual and regularly offered the jury lessons in Athenian cult and myth history. Two fragments from other speeches recall also the hortatory nature of the *Leocrates*: "It is not holy to leave unpunished one who transgresses the written laws by which the democracy is preserved" (10.2) and "One ought to help one's friends and family, short of committing perjury" (15.2). We note finally Lycourgos' speech *Against Autolykos,* an Athenian who fought at Chaeroneia but had removed his family from Athens immediately before the battle and, as a result of Lycourgos' prosecution, was put to death for it.[26] In this speech, as in the *Leocrates,* Lycourgos mentioned family tombs (3.3). Clearly the tone and substance of Lycourgos' attack on Leocrates were consistent with this and his other legal activities concerning religion and the state.

Lycourgos' base of political power was as treasurer of the general revenues, and he is praised for multiplying more than twentyfold the revenues of the state ([Plut.] *X Orat.* 842F). From Stratocles' decree we know that, in his twelve years, he spent 18,600 talents: that is, 1,550 talents per year. He also raised 650 talents as loans from individuals.[27] Much of this money must have been used for defense, for the rebuilding of the walls and the navy. But religious sanctuaries clearly also benefited from Lycourgos' financial wizardry, particularly with new buildings, new equipment, and some new festivals. And Lycourgos' involvement was not just at the policy level; in 329/8 he personally ordered a payment to an architect at Eleusis (*IG* II² 1672.11) and in 333/2 a teamster

---

25. On Oropos and its importance to Athens in this period, see below, p. 33.

26. Cf. *Leoc.* 53 and Harp. s.v. "Αὐτόλυκος."

27. The *Vita* claims 250 talents ([Plut.] *X Orat.* 841D); Stratocles' decree, 650 talents (852B). If both refer to the same fund, Stratocles' decree is probably correct.

was paid for his work at Eleusis on the basis of a decree that Lycourgos had personally proposed (*IG* II² 1673.64–65).[28]

Some measures taken by Lycourgos appear intended to bring order (*kosmos*) to what may well have been confused, lax, and perhaps failing financial programs of the dozens of largely independent sanctuaries and cult organizations, many of which owned land and possessed precious dedications of gold and silver. Careful records and inventories of dedications made to the major state deities and stored in sanctuaries had begun already in the 430s, then probably because Pericles viewed these dedications as part of the city's reserve capital, reserves that in an emergency could be and later were "loaned" at interest to the state. D. M. Lewis sees these early inventories as the result of "putting Athens' financial machinery in order to face the coming Peloponnesian War" (1985b, 72).[29] The disaster at Chaeroneia may have generated a similar concern, and such inventories were kept throughout the Lycourgan period.[30] But these precious dedications were also part of the adornment (*kosmos*) of the state,[31] and the second law partially preserved in Schwenk #21, proposed by Lycourgos, has this as its focus. It provides for, conditional on the approval of the oracle of Apollo, the making of new dedications and the repair of old gold and silver ones — all as *kosmos* for such important deities as Zeus Soter, Zeus Olympios, Dionysos, Athena Itonia, Agathe Tyche, Amphiaraos, Asclepios, Artemis Brauronia, and Demeter and Kore. Clearly this was to be done under a (perhaps new) degree of state supervision.[32]

By 335/4 Lycourgos had also established the "dermatikon" fund, which accrued from the sale of the skins (δέρματα) of animals sacrificed

---

28. For the date of *IG* II² 1673, see Clinton 1972, 83–113. For more on *IG* II² 1672 and 1673 and their possible relationship to a Lycourgan reestablishment of the ἀπαρχαί, see Faraguna 1992, 357–58.

29. More generally, see Lewis 1985b, 71–81. See also Linders 1987.

30. Dated inventories for these years survive from the Acropolis, *IG* II² 1462 of 329/8 (on which see Nagy 1984) and 1497 of 329/8–327/6 and 1472 of 326/5–321/0; from Eleusis, *IG* II² 1544 of 333/2; and from the Asclepieion on the south slope of the Acropolis, Aleshire, Inv. III, ending in 329/8. A series of inventories of silver *phialai* dates ca. 330 (*IG* II² 1553–78; on these and similar new texts, see Lewis 1959a, 1968). Many of the surviving fragments of similar inventories probably date also to these years. On Lycourgan inventories of the treasurers of Athena, see Lewis 1988, 297–98.

31. On such dedications being part of the glory of the city, see Linders 1987.

32. *IG* II² 1498–501a appear to be an Lycourgan age inventory of a large number of bronze statues and plaques from the Acropolis, many damaged and all perhaps in a "scrap heap," which were to be melted down, presumably to be remade into new dedications. See Harris 1992.

at several major state festivals and sacrifices.[33] These skins were valuable, and now the state, which presumably had paid for the animals, could recoup some of its expenses. This revenue, nearly 6,000 drachmas for the second half of 334/3 (*IG* II² 1496.68–92), previously may well have been an undeserved bonus to the various cult establishments and their officials. At about the same time, perhaps in the same year, the state also revised certain elements of the annual Panathenaia, using new revenues from the leasing of "Nea" either to finance existing sacrifices and banquets or to introduce new ones.[34]

Lycourgos himself was wealthy, and the 650 talents he raised as loans from individuals to the state, perhaps beginning immediately after Chaeroneia, indicate that he was not averse to soliciting financial favors from the wealthy on behalf of the state. In the *Leocrates* we saw that Lycourgos in 330 preferred individuals contribute for rebuilding the walls and manning the triremes rather than for drama competitions and other such festival activities. We do find, however, private wealth coming to the support of some of Lycourgos' building projects, and him encouraging or being grateful for it. Deinias of Erchia (*APF* 3163), at Lycourgos' request, donated land so that the remodeling of the Panathenaic Stadium could be completed ([Plut.] *X Orat.* 841D). Eudemos of Plataea, a foreigner, was honored, on Lycourgos' proposal, by the state in 330/29 for supplying teams of oxen to help with this same project (Schwenk #48).[35] And, finally, Lycourgos himself proposed a crown for Neoptolemos of Melite (*APF* 10652) because he promised he would gild an altar of Apollo in the Agora in accordance with Apollo's oracle (*X. Orat.* 843F). Liturgies for ephemeral religious activities may have been falling into disfavor and would soon be eliminated, but clearly private contributions for construction of sacred buildings and their *kosmos* were welcomed by Lycourgos. We see here the beginnings of a planned and systematic new manner of the use of the resources of the rich for the benefit of the community in religious affairs.[36]

33. Harp. s.v. "δερματικόν." The fund was being used by 335/4 and was considered "the money of the gods" (Schwenk #21.CEF 23). *IG* II² 1496 records revenues from the fund from 334/3–331/0, on which see below, pp. 36–39.

34. Schwenk, #17A and B, on which see now Rosivach 1991. On the identity of the land called Nea, see below, note 51.

35. On the nature of Eudemos' contribution, probably valued at 4,000 drachmas, see Clinton 1972, 105.

36. On the development of this new manner of providing funds for state religious activities in the Lycourgan period, see Faraguna 1992, 381–96.

From Stratocles' decree we learn that Lycourgos had "adornment" (*kosmos*) made for "the goddess," surely Athena Polias. This *kosmos* included golden statues of Nike, gold and silver processional vessels, and gold jewelry (*kosmos*) for one hundred basket carriers (*kanēphoroi*).[37] The context of the discussion of this in the *Vita* (841D) suggests that Lycourgos financed it, at least in part, with the 650 talents he obtained on loan from private individuals. The amount seems enormous, but is understandable if, like Pericles, Lycourgos viewed such hardware as capital reserves of the state, available as an emergency fund. Lycourgos would then be restoring, in similar form, the reserves depleted by the Peloponnesian War and never replenished.[38] It would also be an act of piety, repaying a long outstanding debt to the patroness of the city. The choice of statues of Nikai seems to confirm this. By the late fifth century at least eight such statues had been dedicated, probably to commemorate military victories. But then all the Nike statues except one were melted down for coinage in 407/6, in the worst financial times of the Peloponnesian War. That left a debt of at least seven, and the "supports" for seven Nikai are recorded in inventories of 371/0 and 369/8.[39] Thus, quite likely, Lycourgos had remade seven of the fifth-century Nikai, the gold of each weighing about two talents (ca. 120 lbs.). *IG* II² 1493–95 indicate that by 334/3, the gold for the Nikai and the processional vessels was being collected and officials to oversee the project had been appointed.[40] The whole project was probably among the now lost provisions of the law of 335/4 concerning dedications (Schwenk #21).

Apart from serving as financial reserves, the processional vessels and the jewelry of the *kanēphoroi* also contributed to the *kosmos* of the Panathenaia, as did the remodeling of the Panathenaic Stadium and the sacrifices provided for in Schwenk #17A and B. Here Lycourgos' familial connection to the cult of Athena Polias and the decision to provide *kosmos* for the city no doubt coincided. The "*kanēphoric kosmos*" is explicitly mentioned in Schwenk #21.CEF 10, and, if the accepted dating of these various documents is correct, Lycourgos must have turned to these religious matters very early in his administration.

The Athenians wished to honor Lycourgos also for his building pro-

---

37. Cf. Paus. 1.29.16.

38. Schwenk 1985, 125–26; Mitchel 1962, 215 n. 8, 226.

39. *IG* II² 1424A.378, 1425.382. On these statues of Nike, see Faraguna 1992, 377–79; Linders 1987, 119–20; Mitchel 1962; D. B. Thompson 1944. On Thompson's suggestion that Alexander offered to restore these Nikai, see Mitchel 1970, 6.

40. On *IG* II² 1493–95, see Mitchel 1962, 213–19.

gram: he completed the ship sheds and armory in Piraeus, the theater of Dionysos, and the Panathenaic Stadium. He built also a gymnasion at the Lyceum and "adorned" (ἐκόσμησε) the city with many other buildings. The sources indicate that he simply completed the sacred buildings, the theater of Dionysos and the Panathenaic Stadium.[41] We do not know to what extent Lycourgos was responsible, except for holding the purse strings, for other construction in sanctuaries also occurring during his administration. This included the temple of Apollo Patroös, the monument of the eponymous heroes of the ten tribes, the small temple to the north of that of Apollo Patroös, all in the Agora; the portico of Philon at Eleusis; the sanctuary of Plouton and repairs to the City Eleusinion in Athens; and repairs to the Amphiaraion and the building of a spring house of Ammon.[42]

Athens was obviously buzzing with construction, both sacred and secular, in the time of Lycourgos' administration, rivaling perhaps that under Pericles. As F. W. Mitchel puts its, "Only if we stop to consider that Athens had completed no significant building since the Erechtheion and the temple of Athena Nike, can we duly appreciate the Lycourgan building program" (1970, 48). Here we note that in Stratocles' decree the sacred buildings are lumped together with military (ship sheds and armory) and educational (gymnasion) structures.[43] All are, again, part of Lycourgos' "adornment" (kosmos) of the city.

After Alexander had defeated and destroyed Thebes in 335, he demanded from Athens those who had encouraged and aided the rebel-

41. Theater of Dionysos: [Plut.] X Orat. 841D, 852C; IG II² 457; Paus. 1.29.16. Panathenaic Stadium: [Plut.] X Orat. 841D; IG II² 457. On the theater, see Pickard-Cambridge 1946, 134–74. For the throne of Dionysos in the theater being Lycourgan, see Maass 1972, 76.

42. Temple of Apollo Patroös: Camp 1992, 159–61; Lambert 1993, 209–12, 357; Hedrick 1988; H. Thompson and Wycherley 1972, 136–39. Monument of eponymous heroes: Camp 1992, 97–100; Rotroff 1978, 208–9; H. Thompson and Wycherley 1972, 38–41; Shear 1970. Temple just north of that of Apollo Patroös, sometimes assigned to Zeus Phratrios and Athena Phratria: Lambert 1993, 209, 357; H. Thompson and Wycherley 1972, 139–40. Portico of Philon: Mylonas 1961, 133–35. Cf. IG II² 1673 of 333/2. Plutonion and Eleusinion in Agora: IG II² 1672.162–68, 182–83, 193 ff. (of 329/8); Clinton 1992, 18–21. Repairs at Amphiaraion and building of spring house of Ammon: Schwenk #28 of 333/2. Cf. Schwenk #41.16–17 of 332/1 and below, pp. 33 and 37. On secular as well as sacred elements of the Lycourgan building program, see Faraguna 1992, 257–69.

43. The intermingling of military and religious resources is suggested also in an anecdote related by Plutarch (Mor. 818E–F): Demades, probably as treasurer of the military fund, in 331 dissuaded the Athenians from aiding those revolting from Alexander by saying he would use for this expedition the fund from which he had intended to distribute fifty drachmas to each citizen at the Choes festival. On this incident see Faraguna 1992, 256.

lious Thebans, including Demosthenes and Lycourgos. An Athenian embassy, headed by Phocion, dissuaded Alexander and saved all but the general Charidemos.[44] It is this incident that Stratocles' decree makes into a tribute to Lycourgos. Neither Demosthenes nor Lycourgos was won over by Alexander's clemency. When, eleven years later, Athenians debated granting divine honors to Alexander, Demosthenes quipped, "If he wishes, let him be the son of Zeus, or the son of Poseidon" (Hyperides 5.31).[45] For his bitterly witty response Lycourgos characteristically turned to religious ritual ([Plut.] *X Orat.* 842D): "What kind of god would he be, when (worshippers) will have to purify themselves on leaving his sanctuary?" Deities avoided pollution, and Athenians normally purified themselves *before* approaching them. The "god" Alexander would, uniquely, pollute his worshippers.

Lycourgos was not, however, averse to all innovation in religion in Athens. However much he was devoted to completing, building, and repairing the sanctuaries of the traditional deities and to reestablishing for them the *kosmos* of Periclean times, he was open to new ideas. In 329/8 he was one of the ten *epimelētai* ("overseers") who administered the new quadrennial festival for Amphiaraos, the healing deity whose cult center in Oropos Athens received from Alexander in 335 (Schwenk #50).[46] Lycourgos also established a new festival contest, but on very traditional lines, for Poseidon in Piraeus ([Plut.] *X Orat.* 842A). Piraeus was clearly a focus of his attention as he rebuilt the navy and completed the ship sheds and armory. There too, on Lycourgos' proposal, the Citians of Cyprus were granted permission, in 333/2, to purchase land for a sanctuary of their native deity, Aphrodite Ourania, as the Egyptians had been before for their Isis (Schwenk #27). Both these cults should be imagined, at this time, as very small, practiced only in Piraeus and only by Citian and Egyptian nationals.[47] Neither cult survived long,

---

44. On this embassy, see Tritle 1988, 117–18.

45. On this debate in the Ekklesia and on Alexander's very short-lived cult in Athens, see chap. 2, pp. 46–49. On Demosthenes' quip, see Worthington 1992, 264; Nock 1972, 135.

46. On this new quadrennial festival, see Tracy 1995, 92; Knoepfler 1993. Tracy (7) disagrees with Knoepfler and accepts the traditional view that Philip in 338, not Alexander in 335, returned Oropos to Athens.

47. On the Piraeic cults of Isis and Aphrodite Ourania at this time, see Simms 1989; Schwenk 1985, 141–46; Vidman 1970, 11–12. The Piraeic Aphrodite Ourania is distinct from the Aphrodite Ourania who had long had a sanctuary and altar in the Agora, west of the Stoa Poikile. On the latter, see Shear 1984, 24–40; Edwards 1984; Foster 1984. On this and on all cults of Aphrodite in Athens, see Pirenne-Delforge 1994, 15–79, esp. 16–25.

and in chapter 5 we shall see what became of them. They were probably introduced at this time to accommodate the needs of foreign traders
living in Piraeus, as had been the cult of Bendis for Thracians almost a
century earlier.[48]

Stratocles' decree concludes with praises of Lycourgos' character. He
was never convicted of a crime and did not take bribes; that is, he was
honest (cf. *X Orat.* 842F, 843F). He demonstrated his goodwill ($\epsilon\ddot{v}voia$)
toward democracy and freedom. He possessed virtue ($\dot{a}\rho\epsilon\tau\dot{\eta}$) and justice ($\delta\iota\kappa\alpha\iota\sigma\sigma\dot{v}\nu\eta$) (cf. 841F, 842F). In addition the *Vita* credits him with
being of good repute (841F), a hard worker (841C–D, 842C), and out-
spoken (842D).

Such a man Leocrates encountered in 330, eight years after he had
slunk out of Athens in fear of Philip, had taken with him his money,
mistress, and household gods, and had sold his very house in Athens
for a new life in Megara. The substance and tone of Lycourgos' attacks
on Leocrates are in perfect accord with what else we know of Lycourgos' character and career. Lycourgos was engaged in a fundamental renewal of the state of Athens: financially, militarily, educationally, and
religiously. As we shall soon see, he did not do and could not have done
this alone, nor did he initiate all the individual measures. He was working within a tradition, but the defeat at Chaeroneia in 338 must have
provided significant impetus for the movement.

Stratocles' decree, read as a whole, suggests that the religious aspects
of this national revival, our concern, were no more and no less important than financial policy and national defense in the eyes of Athenians
nearly twenty years after Lycourgos' death. We should take it as a sign
of the health and vigor of popular religion in the time that it was
thought necessary for it to have such a prominent role in the national
revival. On the public side of religion Lycourgos brought fiscal order
and *kosmos* to state cults. Both, apparently, went together, and fiscal responsibility was not a cover for parsimony. Inventorying and melting
down of old dedications made possible new, more beautiful ones. Re-
couping some expenses meant more money for both old and new festivals. Careful financial management and fund-raising meant the building, remodeling, and repair of sacred buildings. Coins were made into
statues of the gods. And all of this contributed to the *kosmos* of the city.

The *Leocrates* affords us a precious look at some elements of the private side of the religious attitude we see expressed in contemporary pub-

48. On the foundation of Bendis' cult in Athens, see Simms, 1988.

lic documents. The oaths by ephebes, jurors, and archons, the sanctity of which Lycourgos emphasizes, give support to the moral and patriotic duties of young and old alike. For the gods the Athenians were remodeling, repairing, and adorning the temples, sanctuaries, statues, and dedications that Leocrates had betrayed. On the Acropolis, which Leocrates abandoned, was the cult of Athena Polias, who now had back her Nikai and had for her festival a new stadium, new processional vessels, and gold jewelry for one hundred *kanēphoroi*. Given such correspondences between the *Leocrates* and the public religious activities in Athens, we may assume, without evidence to the contrary, a similar correspondence between it and the private religious attitudes and beliefs of the Athenians in 330 B.C. We may take what Lycourgos says about the gods, about oracles and oaths, and about piety and impiety as what was still acceptable to say in a public forum about religion: hence the value of the *Leocrates* for understanding religion in late-fourth-century Athens.[49]

In assessing the religious tenor of the times it is important to recognize that Lycourgos was not alone in promoting these various religious projects. As we have seen, Deinias of Erchia (*APF* 3163), who in 367/6 had been a member of the board of *pōlētai* (administrators of state con-

---

49. Many of Lycourgos' statements about religion, both in general and in particular, can be paralleled from orators who lived in his period, from his purported teachers Isocrates and Plato, and from [Dem.] 59, a speech from the late fourth century. Examples include the following: That the goodwill of the gods is the reward of piety (*Leoc.* 82, 127; Dem. 3.26, 19.239–40, [11.2, 16]; Isoc. 6.59, 7.29–30, 8.33–34, 15.281–82). That the gods become hostile as the result of impiety (*Leoc.* 93, 129; [Dem.] 59.74–77; Isoc. 8.120; Pl. *Leg.* 9.871A–B). That the gods may be allies in war (*Leoc.* 82; Dem. 18.153, [11.2]) and may help Athens through divination (*Leoc.* 93; Dem. 19.297–299; Aeschines 3.130; Din. 1.98). That piety involves observing traditional sacrifices (*Leoc.* 97; [Dem.] 59.74–77; Pl. *Leg.* 5.738B–C) and respect for the dead (*Leoc.* 94, 97; [Dem.] 43.65; Aeschines 1.13–14). That gods punish perjurers (*Leoc.* 79; Dem. 19.239–240, [59.126]) but feel goodwill toward those who keep their oaths (*Leoc.* 127; Dem. 3.26). That perjury may adversely affect one's children (*Leoc.* 79; Dem. 54.40–41, 19.292, 23.67, 29.26, 33, 54 [59.10]; Aeschines 3.111), and, for the state, general prosperity (*Leoc.* 127; Dem. 3.26), divine help in war (*Leoc.* 82; [Dem.] 11.2), and hopes for the future (*Leoc.* 79; Dem. 19.239–40; Aeschines 2.87; Isoc. 18.3). That the ephebic oath is important (*Leoc.* 76–79; Dem. 19.303) and that treason is a violation of it and hence impiety (*Leoc.* 76–79; Dem. 8.8, 18.240, 323, 19.156). That the gods help in prosecution of such impieties (*Leoc.* 1–2, 91–92; Din. 1.98, 3.14) and direct their attention (*Leoc.* 146; Dem. 19.239–40; [59.109, 126]) and assign guilt (*Leoc.* 146; [Dem.] 59.109; Aeschines 3.120–21) to jurors who do not convict the impious.

These parallels indicate that Lycourgos' claims were common and familiar to Athenian audiences. For general discussion of these and similar beliefs, see Mikalson 1983.

tracts) and over the years had performed numerous liturgies (Dem. 20.151), contributed land for the completion of the Panathenaic Stadium ([Plut.] *X Orat.* 841D). Eudemos of Plataea was, at Lycourgos' proposal, honored for contributing teams of oxen for work on the stadium (Schwenk #48). As in previous decades, the boards of overseers of Eleusis and the treasurers of Athena, along with other such committees, continued to exercise their traditional functions. In the membership of ad hoc committees made up to deal with two new religious projects, the reorganization of the sanctuary of Amphiaraos and the sending of the sacred delegation (Pythaïs) to Delphi, we can identify individuals involved in religious innovations and activities in which Lycourgos personally participated.[50]

In 335 Athens had received from Alexander the neighboring territory of Oropos and the sanctuary of Amphiaraos there.[51] In 333/2 Pytheas of Alopeke (*PA* 12346), *epimelētēs* of the waterworks, was honored for repairing and remodeling Amphiaraos' sacred spring house (Schwenk #28).[52] In 331/0 the antiquarian and Atthidographer Phanodemos of Thymaitadai (*PA* 14033) was honored for the legislation that he drafted concerning sacrifices and a new quadrennial festival of Amphiaraos,[53] as well as for providing funds for the festival and repair of the Amphiaraion (Schwenk #41). In 329/8 the state crowned the same Phanodemos along with Lycourgos, Demades of Paiania (*APF* 3263), Niceratos of Kydathenaion (*APF* 10742), Sophilos of Phyle (*PA* 13422), Thrasyleon of Acharnai (*PA* 7329), Epiteles of Pergase (*PA* 4963), Epichares of Paiania (*PA* 4999), Thymochares of Sphettos (*APF* 13964), and Cephisophon of Cholargos (*PA* 8419) for overseeing, as elected *epimelētai*, the first Athenian celebration of the quadrennial Amphiaraia (Schwenk #50). Similarly honored, in 328/7, were Euthycrates of Aphidna (*PA* 5601), Philostratos of Acharnai (*APF* 14726), and Chairestratos of Rhamnous (*PA* 15172) for overseeing, for the Boule, a dedication in the Amphiaraion. Twenty-four members of the Boule as well as

---

50. These two groups of individuals have been admirably analyzed by Lewis 1955, 27–36. See also Faraguna 1992, 215–43; Humphreys 1985, 210–12; Schwenk 1985, 244–48.

51. For the date, see Knoepfler 1993. For the division of the land of Oropos among the Athenian tribes and for the troubled question of whether the land called Nea, the rental of which provided funds for victims for the annual Panathenaia, was in Oropos, see Rosivach 1991, 436–39; Langdon 1987. On all aspects of the cult of Amphiaraos at Oropos, see Petrakos 1968.

52. On Pytheas and his office, see Habicht 1989 = 1994, 328–32.

53. For the possibility that the very fragmentary *SEG* 32.86 may be part of this legislation, see M. Walbank, 1982. But Humphreys (1985, 227–28 n. 33) prefers the Epitaphia.

ten others, including Phanodemos, Demades, and Cephisophon, contributed money for this dedication (Schwenk #56).

In 326/5 the Athenians sent a sacred delegation (Pythaïs) to Delphi
to deliver the first-fruits to Apollo Pythios,[54] the first such delegation
since 355 (Isaeus 7.27), and the ten men elected as *hieropoioi* ("sacrificers")
to make the sacrifices and supervise the *theōria* were the now familiar
Phanodemos, Demades, Niceratos, and Lycourgos, and with them Hip-
pocrates (son of Aristocrates), Boethos (son of Nausinikos), Glaucetes
of Oion (*APF* 2921), Clearchos (son of Nausicles), Neoptolemos of
Melite (*APF* 10652), and Cleochares of Kephisia (*APF* 8647) (*SIG*³ 296).

The men who were participating with Lycourgos in these religious
projects were, as D. M. Lewis (1955, 27–36) has shown, generally older,
experienced, and wealthy. At least five—Cephisophon, Deinias, Demades, Glaucetes, and Niceratos—were sixty or more years of age in
330/29. Eight (Cleochares, Deinias, Demades, Glaucetes, Neoptolemos,
Niceratos, Philostratos, and Thymochares) because of their wealth are
numbered in J. K. Davies' *Athenian Propertied Families* (1971) among the
206 attested members of the upper financial class in the period 333/2–
301/0.[55] Demades and Niceratos both served terms as treasurer of the
military fund, Sophilos as "general over the land." Thymochares was
later to serve as a general under Demetrios of Phaleron. In the *Leocrates*
Lycourgos recommends, over festival liturgies, support for ships of the
navy, and Cleochares, Deinias, Demades, and Niceratos had each provided this service, some several times. Demades and Glaucetes followed
up the Pythaïs with continued service to Delphi as *proxenoi* ("representatives in Athens of foreign [here Delphic] interests").[56] Epiteles served
Delphi as both *nāopoios* ("temple builder")[57] and *proxenos*, and in 323/2
he proposed a decree on Athenian participation in the Nemean games
(Schwenk #79).

Neoptolemos of Melite (*APF* 10652) and Xenocles of Sphettos (*APF*
11234) may be representative of the prosperous Athenians who provided
financial and personal support to the Lycourgan religious revival. Neop-

54. Such *theōriai* to Delphi were sent irregularly and infrequently in the fifth and fourth
centuries, on a signal of lightening sent by Zeus to Athens. For the Pythaïdes in the fifth
and fourth centuries, see Daux 1936, 528–31.

55. For references and further details on the careers of these and other individuals discussed here, see *APF* and Lewis 1955, 27–36.

56. On Demades' role in the restoration of the Nikai in and after 334/3, see Mitchel
1962, 213–22.

57. *Nāopoioi* were representatives from various states who oversaw capital improve-
ment projects at Delphi. See Roux 1979, 96 ff.

tolemos' participation in the Pythaïs was but a small part of his civic activities.[58] A very rich man (Dem. 21.215), he was honored by the state "for the many projects to which he, as *epistatēs* ('supervisor'), contributed his own funds" (Dem. 18.114). He made a dedication on the Acropolis (*IG* II² 4901) and, when honored by the state with a crown, gave it to Athena (*IG* II² 1496.43–46). In his home deme of Melite he was responsible for work in the sanctuary of Artemis Aristoboule ("Of the Best Council"), which his fellow demesman Themistocles had privately built to commemorate his victory at Salamis but which at this time was being administered by the deme (*SEG* 22.116).[59] When Apollo requested it, Neoptolemos paid for the gilding of the new altar of Apollo and received for this a crown and statue from the state, on Lycourgos' motion ([Plut.] *X Orat.* 843F–844A). And, finally, this same Neoptolemos dedicated a beautiful and quite well preserved relief sculpture representing Dionysos being delivered to the Nymphs, and among the figures are Artemis and Apollo, for both of whom Neoptolemos had provided other services.[60]

Xenocles of Sphettos, who was one of the richest men of his time, active in public life for forty years, a staunch democrat, and a close friend of Lycourgos, served as Lycourgos' stand-in as financial administrator for one four-year term.[61] Xenocles' religious interests were directed neither to the Amphiaraion nor to Delphi, but to Eleusis. As *epimelētēs* of the Mysteries, in 321/0 or 318/7, he dedicated statues of Demeter and Kore; that same year he built a stone bridge over the Cephisos on the processional route to Eleusis, at his own expense.[62] The bridge, constructed in part for the convenience of the initiates, recalls Lycourgos' legislation concerning the procession. Xenocles, unlike Neoptolemos, is known for festival liturgies, having served as *chorēgos* and having won as gymnasiarch of his tribe in the Panathenaia of 346/5 (*IG* II² 749, 3019). Years later, in 307/6, after the abolition of such liturgies, he is the first known *agōnothetēs* ("contest producer"), responsible for all the year's dramatic and choral competitions in the city's festivals (*IG* II² 3073, 3077).[63]

Despite his services, Xenocles was not beloved by each and every

---

58. On Neoptolemos, see Faraguna 1992, 220–21.

59. On the origins, history, and (now excavated) sanctuary of Artemis Aristoboule, see Garland 1992, 73–78.

60. Edwards 1985, #15, 419–38; Shear 1973, 168–70.

61. On Xenocles' career, see Faraguna 1992, 228–29; Habicht 1988a = 1994, 323–27.

62. *IG* II² 1191, 2840, 2841, and *Anth. Pal.* 9.147; on which see Habicht 1988a, 325 = 1994, 325.

63. On the replacement of the several *chorēgoi* by one elected *agōnothetēs*, see chapter 2.

Athenian. He is one of several of the prominent Athenians we have encountered thus far to be the object of a curse tablet. On one such lead tablet some individual intended "to bind, to bury, and to make disappear from men" Xenocles, Demeas the son of Demades, and one hundred other men and women. On similar curse tablets of the period are targeted Lycourgos (twice), Demosthenes (twice), Hyperides, Phocion, and the Callistratos condemned by Lycourgos (*Leoc.* 93). These specific tablets seem all to have been motivated by political and legal disputes.[64]

We thus see a number of prosperous, prominent, and often elderly Athenians supporting religious activities, but not necessarily in a uniform, orchestrated way.[65] Some, like Xenocles, contributed to festivals; others, like Neoptolemos, may have shared Lycourgos' reservations about such liturgies. Xenocles favored Eleusis; Demades and Glaucetes, Delphi; Phanodemos and several others, Amphiaraos; and Neoptolemos assisted a local sanctuary. This variety suggests that personal motives weighed equally with civic ones in the support these men brought to religion, as was probably also true for Lycourgos in his devotion to the cult of Athena Polias.

As a final step in establishing the status of Athenian religion at the very beginning of the Hellenistic period we turn to the festivals and sacrifices of the state cult in the age of Lycourgos. Precious for this purpose is *IG* II² 1496, the four-year record (334/3–331/0) of revenues the state received from the sale of the skins (*dermata*) of victims at state-supported festivals and sacrifices. The document distinguishes between the nine festivals, which are listed by name, and the six sacrifices (θύσιαι), which are listed by recipient. The distinction is meaningful,[66] because the festivals are all of long standing while most of the sacrifices seem innovations of the fourth century. The festivals are the Asclepieia, Bendideia, City Dionysia, Dionysia in Piraeus, Eleusinia, Lenaia, Olympieia, Panathenaia, and Theseia. The drama festivals of the City Dionysia, Lenaia, and Dionysia in Piraeus, as well as the Eleusinia, Olympieia, and Panathenaia, are very old, each going back at least to the sixth century B.C. The Theseia, held on Pyanopsion 8, was probably founded in 476/5 with the recovery of Theseus' bones from Scyros.

64. On curse tablets, see Habicht 1993 = 1994, 14–18; Gager 1992. The specific tablets cited are Ziebarth 1934, 1023 #1, 1027 #2; *Kerameikos* 14 (1990): 148–49; Gager 1992, #42, 58.

65. Cf. Humphreys 1985, 212.

66. Mikalson 1982.

The Athenians received Theseus "as if he were coming home," with processions and sacrifices, and he was henceforth honored annually with sacrifices (Plut. *Thes.* 36).[67] The Asclepieia was probably introduced with the arrival of Asclepios in 420/19.[68] The Bendideia of Bendis, on Thargelion 19, was also introduced late in the fifth century.[69]

The sacrifices of *IG* II² 1496 are to Agathe Tyche, Ammon, Demokratia, Eirene, Hermes Hegemonios, and Zeus Soter. All the sacrifices, except that to Ammon, occur in more than one year and hence are already an established part of the state program. By 335/4 Agathe Tyche ("Good Fortune") already had a temple[70] and treasury and was to receive additional *kosmos* from the provisions initiated by Lycourgos (Schwenk #21.CEF 19–20).[71] *SEG* 26.121.44, from the first century B.C., indicates a sanctuary in Piraeus. Four private dedications to her are assigned to the fourth century: *IG* II² 4610, 4644 (found in the City Asclepieion), and 4564 (to Twelve Gods and Agathe Tyche). In the fourth, *IG* II² 4627, she is presented as the wife of Zeus Epiteleios Philios, and the deities and sculpture suggest that the Agathe Tyche of this dedication contributed to the success of marriage and family. Two slightly later texts, however, seem to associate her with military victories,[72] and that may be why she is so little in evidence after Athens' defeat in the Lamian War in 323/2.

Ammon, the oracular god of Egypt, was known to Athenians in the fifth century and was consulted in Egypt by both Cimon (Plut. *Cim.* 18.6–7) and Alcibiades (Plut. *Nic.* 13.1). A *phialē* dedicated to Ammon is recorded in the Athenian inventories as early as 375, and *SEG* 21.241 of 363/2 lists a number of dedications made to him and other deities by the Athenian state.[73] Pytheas of Alopeke, again in his role as *epimelētēs* of the waterworks, built a new spring house near the sanctuary of Ammon in 333/2 (Schwenk #28.13–15), and the sanctuary itself may date as

67. Cf. Plut. *Cim.* 8.5–6 and Paus. 3.3.7. On the recovery of Theseus' bones and the foundation of his cult, see Garland 1992, 82–98.

68. On which see Clinton 1994; Aleshire 1989, 7–15; Garland 1992, 116–35.

69. For the introduction of Bendis, see Simms 1988.

70. Lycourgos, frag. 5.6 Conomis. On a possible sacrifice to Agathe Tyche in 304/3 and on her cult in Athens, see Woodhead 1981, 361–62. See now also Tracy 1994. For fourth-century sculptured representations of the goddess, see Palagia 1982, 109; 1994

71. For the increasing importance of Tyche in religious thought in the fourth century, see Mikalson 1983, 59–62.

72. *Hesp.* 63 (1994): 233–39; *SEG* 30.69.

73. Cf. *SEG* 21.562. On these inventories and in general on Ammon in Athens in this period, see Woodward 1962.

early as 363/2.[74] Around 330 Pausiades of Phaleron is honored for services as priest of Ammon along with the priests of Dionysos, Poseidon Pelagios, and Zeus Soter (*IG* II² 410). His deme and the associated cults suggest the Ammoneion was in Piraeus. That the sacrifice for Ammon in *IG* II² 1496.96–97 was made in only one of the four years (333/2) may indicate that it was for a special occasion, perhaps the dedication of Pytheas' spring house.[75]

The sacrifices to Demokratia in 332/1 and 331/0 (*IG* II² 1496.131–32, 140–41) should probably be associated with the dedication of a statue to her by the Boule in 333/2 (*SEG* 32.238).[76] The cult may have been founded in 403 after the restoration of the democracy,[77] but these quite large sacrifices and the dedication may reveal a renewed interest. The cult of Eirene had been established in 375/4 to celebrate Timotheus' victories over the Lacedaimonians, which led to peace (Isoc. 15.109–10).[78] The cult of Hermes Hegemonios ("Leader"), according to the scholiast to Aristophanes *Ploutos* 1159, was founded on the basis of an oracle, and this Hermes was apparently known by the time of the *Ploutos* (388 B.C.). In the first century B.C. a Hermes Hegemonios in Piraeus received a dedication from three generals (*IG* II² 2873).

The *dermatikon* revenues from the sacrifices to Zeus Soter ("Savior") are the largest preserved of those from all the festivals and sacrifices. The cult is first certainly attested in Aristophanes' *Ploutos* (1173–90).[79] There the god is associated with "saving" merchant sailors and defen-

---

74. Woodward 1962, 6–7.

75. Woodward 1962, 7.

76. For arguments for the identification of this statue with a late-fourth-century torso (S 2370) found in the excavations of the Agora, see Palagia 1982. Later (1994) Palagia followed Shear in assigning the torso to Agathe Tyche.

77. On the cult of Demokratia in Athens, see Raubitschek 1962.

78. Deubner 1932, 37–38; Jacoby, *FGrHist* 3B, suppl. 1:523–26. For a possible festival of Eirene, see Robert 1977.

79. On cult of Zeus Soter see Rosivach 1987; Garland 1987, 137–38. Garland (137, 239) associates the provisions of *IG* I³ 130a (of ca. 432) with Zeus Soter, but there is nothing in the text to warrant this. Since there are two Zeuses given the epithet Soter in Athens, one Zeus Eleutherios of the Stoa of Zeus in the Agora and the other in Piraeus, care must be taken in assigning references to Zeus Soter. It is not sufficient to assume all references "in political contexts" are to Zeus Eleutherios/Soter, as Rosivach (263) does. The Piraeic Soter may well have picked up political associations (see chapter 4). Of the references of importance in this chapter, Lycourgos *Leoc.* 17, 136–37; *IG* II² 1669; Plut. *Mor.* 846D, *Dem.* 27.6–8 certainly belong to the Soter of Piraeus. Most likely Schwenk #21.CEF 13 and *IG* II² 410 do also. Given the late and Piraeic nature of most of the other sacrifices in *IG* II² 1496, I take the reference to Zeus Soter there to be to the Zeus of Piraeus (against Rosivach, 280 n. 49).

dants in law cases.[80] Pausanias' description of the statuary and dedications in the sanctuary in Piraeus suggests also a tie with military victories (1.1.3). In the second half of the fourth century, major construction was underway in Soter's Piraeic sanctuary (*IG* II² 1669). One *epistatēs* of this construction was Leochares of Pallene (*APF* 9175), son of Leocrates, perhaps the father of the very Leocrates who Lycourgos claimed disregarded this deity in his flight from Piraeus in 338 (*Leoc.* 17).[81] In 323, as part of his restoration after the Harpalos affair, Demosthenes was contracted "to adorn the altar of Zeus Soter."[82] The sacrifices to Zeus Soter in *IG* II² 1496 were no doubt part of a festival later to become known as the Diisoteria.[83]

Given the large number of festivals, sacrifices, and rituals performed in Athens each year,[84] the list in *IG* II² 1496 is comparatively short; but, I think, it quite likely records all the state-supported sacrifices and festivals that required a substantial number of victims. Other rites and rituals such as the Plynteria, Thargelia, Thesmophoria, and so forth did not utilize this type of victim. Nor did the Eleusinian Mysteries. The first celebration of the quadrennial Amphiaraia in 329/8 would postdate *IG* II² 1496.[85] It is to these festivals and sacrifices listed in *IG* II² 1496 and later additions of the same type that I shall direct attention as we

80. Lycourgos too imagines that Leocrates in his defense will appeal to Zeus Soter and Athena Soteira (*Leoc.* 17).

81. Cf. Humphreys 1985, 229 n. 40. A statue of Leocrates' father, dead by 330, had been dedicated in the sanctuary of Zeus Soter (*Leoc.* 136–37). If the Leochares of *IG* II² 1669 is in fact our Leocrates' father, the construction described in *IG* II² 1669 must antedate 338.

82. Plut. *Mor.* 846D; *Dem.* 27.6–8. It is commonly but mistakenly thought that Demosthenes spent either thirty (*Mor.* 846D) or fifty (*Dem.* 27.8) talents on this "adornment." This large sum was, in fact, part of the contrivance (ἐσοφίσαντο) the Athenians used to make it possible for Demosthenes to pay his outstanding fine (χρηματικῆς ζημίας) for involvement in the Harpalos affair. The Athenians every year paid a contractor to prepare and adorn the altar of Zeus Soter for his annual sacrifice, and this year they awarded the contract, at the highly inflated sum of, probably, fifty talents to Demosthenes. Demosthenes certainly need not and did not spent the fifty talents on the altar. They would go to pay his fine. Demosthenes would be responsible only for having the altar duly prepared, and the cost for that was probably modest, no doubt less than 100 drachmas. The altar of Zeus Soter was probably chosen both for its symbolic value and for the sacrifice's proximity of place and perhaps time to Demosthenes' return. Cf. Androtion *FGrHist* 324 F 8; Jacoby ad loc.; and Goldstein 1968, 42–44.

83. The name "Diisoteria" is not attested until 140/39 (*IG* II² 971.41–45).

84. Mikalson 1975a.

85. The quadrennial Hephaistia reported in [Arist.] *Ath. Pol.* 54.7 to have been introduced in 329/8 is chimerical, a mistake for the quadrennial Amphiaraia discussed above. See Knoepfler 1993; Rhodes 1993, 610.

proceed through the Hellenistic period. We shall be seeing the continuation, development, and changes each experienced. Apart from these, three cults were also prosperous in the age of Lycourgos: that of Asclepios in Piraeus and on the south slope of the Acropolis, that of Demeter and Kore and associated deities in Eleusis and its branches in Athens, and that of Artemis of Brauron. Extensive and precisely dated Lycourgan accounts and inventories survive for each, as do dedications and other epigraphical records.[86] We know, for example, that in 335, after Alexander destroyed Thebes, the Athenians "in grief" canceled the celebration of the Eleusinian Mysteries (Plut. *Alex.* 13.1). After that the Mysteries were surely held each year and are attested for 333/2 (*IG* II² 1673.44, 62) and 331/0 (1672.244–45). Excellent modern studies are available for the cults of Asclepios, the Eleusinian deities, and Artemis of Brauron,[87] and in this study we shall note only significant changes reflective of the period. And, finally, we shall attempt to establish the continuity of numerous ancient rites and rituals which were, no doubt, celebrated annually but which, by chance, have left only rare attestations. For example, we know that the Choes was still celebrated ca. 331 (Plut. *Mor.* 818E–F) and in 329/8 (*IG* II² 1672.204). The Haloa is attested for 329/8 (*IG* II² 1672.124, 144), and in 325/4 the Thargelia was being expected (*IG* II² 1629.196–99). Here the attestations are infrequent, but each will demonstrate survival and provide a *terminus ante quem* for the ritual or festival.

The evidence, though even more sparse, indicates that the Athenians of the Lycourgan period were regularly participating, as a state, in international religious affairs, particularly by sending religious embassies (*theōriai*) to international games or cult centers. The Pythia, the agonistic festival at Delphi, was being held quadrennially, and an Athenian *archetheōros* for it is attested for 331/0 (*Hesp.* 37 [1968]: 375–76, line 26). Around 330 the Athenians sent a *theōria* to Dodona "to adorn," as ordered by the oracle there, the statue of Dione (Hyperides 4.24–26).

---

86. E.g., for Asclepios: dedications and inventories of dedications, Aleshire, Inv. III and *SEG* 30.163; others, Schwenk #54, *SEG* 35.74, and *IG* II² 4392. For Eleusis: financial accounts, *IG* II² 1670–73; dedications and inventory of dedications, *IG* II² 1544, 2839–41; other, *IG* II² 1933–34; for the Lycourgan building program at Eleusis, see Mitchel 1970, 45. For Artemis of Brauron, dedications and inventories of dedications, *IG* II² 1522–24, 4594.

87. For Asclepios, Aleshire 1989, 1991; Edelstein and Edelstein 1945. For Eleusis, Clinton 1992, 1988, 1974; Mylonas 1962. For Artemis of Brauron, see summary and bibliography in Rhodes 1993, 607–8.

Lycourgos himself, as we have seen, was one of the ten *hieropoioi* of the Pythaïs to Delphi in 326/5. Demosthenes headed the Athenian *theōria* to the Olympic Games of 324 (Din. 1.81–82), and in 323/2 the Athenians were making provisions for their *theōria* to the Nemean Games (Schwenk #79). And, finally, we have seen that Lycourgos prosecuted Menesaichmos for ritual error on a *theōria* to Delos (frag. 14.1–11 Conomis). From these scattered references we may conclude that the Athenians were at this time regularly sharing in the traditional international religious life of the Greeks, in marked contrast, as we shall see, to the later periods when they were under Macedonian domination.

Among the attempts to bring *kosmos* to Athenian life after 338 was also the restructuring, probably ca. 336/5, of the *ephēbeia*, a two-year period of formal training and acculturation of about five hundred Athenian young men aged eighteen to twenty (ephebes), all administered by an annually elected official termed the *kosmētēs*.[88] We have already encountered the oath of the ephebes in Lycourgos' *Leocrates* (76), and the *Constitution of the Athenians* of ca. 325/4 gives the fullest description of the institution (42.2–5):

After (the citizenship of) the ephebes has been examined (and approved), their fathers, gathering together by tribes, after swearing an oath, choose from their fellow tribesmen three men over forty years of age, men whom they consider best and most suitable to oversee the ephebes. From these the Demos elects one of each tribe to be *sōphronistēs*. And they elect from the other Athenians one to be *kosmētēs* over them all. These gather together the ephebes, first make a tour of the sanctuaries, and then travel to Piraeus. (The ephebes) serve as a garrison force, some for Mounichia and the others for Akte. (The Demos) elects also for them two *paidotribai* ("trainers"), and also instructors who teach the ephebes to fight in armor, archery, javelin throwing, and to work the catapult. The Demos gives for support one drachma (per day) for each *sōphronistēs* and four obols for each ephebe. A *sōphronistēs* receives the payments of his fellow tribesmen and buys the supplies in common for all, because they dine together by tribes, and he takes care of all other things. This is the way they spend the first year.

In the second year, when an Ekklesia is held in the theater, the ephebes make a display of military maneuvers for the Demos and, after receiving a shield and spear from the city, patrol the land and spend time in the forts. They serve on garrison duty for two years, wearing cloaks, and they are free from all taxes. They do not initiate or respond to lawsuits so that they may have no excuse for being absent, except for trials involving inheritances and

---

88. On the *ephēbeia* and on changes to it in this period, see Rhodes 1993, 494–95, 502–10; Faraguna 1992, 274–80; Siewert 1977; Reinmuth 1971; Pélékidis 1962.

guardianships or if a priesthood comes to one by family connection. And, after the two years have passed, the ephebes join the other Athenians.

This institution was, in this period, primarily and fundamentally military, not religious, and this is not the place to treat the complex questions of its origin and various activities. But even at this stage in its development the *ephēbeia* made young Athenian males familiar with the sanctuaries and religious traditions of their homeland. We shall see later that the ephebes come to play a very large role in state religion, but even now, just after 336/5, they are clearly participating. They received a formal tour of the sanctuaries of Attica and may have participated in the new quadrennial Amphiaraia (Reinmuth #15).[89] Other records of their religious activity for this period are not numerous, consisting solely of three separate dedications in different places by ephebes of different tribes, all from 333/2. The ephebes of Aiantis made a dedication to the hero Mounichos for a victory in a torch race, a competition by tribes that was surely part of a religious festival (Reinmuth #6).[90] Similarly the ephebes of Erechtheis made a dedication for a torch race victory at Rhamnous (*IG* II² 3105 + *SEG* 31.162).[91] And, finally, the *sōphronistēs* and forty-four ephebes of the tribe Leontis made a dedication to their tribal hero Leos after they had received crowns from the Demos and their tribe "because of their virtue (ἀρετῆς) and their self-control (σωφροσύνης)" (Reinmuth #9). These are the earliest indications of what will become a very large program of ephebic religious activity in the Hellenistic period.[92]

I conclude this chapter with a brief discussion of *IG* II² 410, a decree of ca. 330 which honored with gold crowns Meixigenes of Cholleidai, the priest of Dionysos(*APF* 9754); Himeraios of Phaleron, the priest of Poseidon Pelagios (*APF* 7578);[93] Nicocles of Hagnous, the priest of Zeus

---

89. See Rhodes 1993, 505; Lewis 1973, 255. On the date of Reinmuth #15, see Tracy 1995, 25–26.

90. On the possible festivals and on the hero Mounichos as the eponymous hero of this year's class of ephebes, see Habicht 1961, 145–46 = 1994, 42–44.

91. On this text, see Palagia and Lewis, 1989.

92. See Humphreys 1985, 206–8 for speculation from admittedly "rather tenuous" indications on what other religious rituals Lycourgan ephebes may have performed.

93. The epithet "Pelagios" serves to distinguish this Poseidon from Poseidon Erechtheus, Hippios, Soter of Sunium, and the various other Poseidons of Attica. He may well be the Poseidon for whom Lycourgos established the cyclical choruses in Piraeus (see above, p. 23).

Soter (*PA* 10897); and Pausiades of Phaleron, the priest of Ammon (*PA* 11727).[94] They along with ten *hieropoioi* were selected by the Boule to sacrifice to Dionysos and the other gods (surely those represented by the individual priests). They have reported "good things" about these sacrifices — no doubt that the omens were good.[95] Their sacrifices, at the Boule's request, were "for the health and safety of the Boule and Demos of the Athenians and of their children, wives, and other possessions."

We have thus far examined, through Lycourgos' *Leocrates*, continuity in religious belief and both continuity and innovation in deities and cults from the fifth century through the Lycourgan era. Thus far continuity heavily outweighs innovation. In the sacrifices of *IG* II² 410, commissioned by the Boule[96] for the "health and safety of the Boule and the Demos and their wives, children, and property" and made to Dionysos, Poseidon Pelagios, Zeus Soter, and Ammon, all from Piraeus, we see, I think, signs of the beginning of a new orientation, in both thought and place, of Athenian practiced religion. The place has shifted from the Acropolis cults of Athena Polias and Poseidon-Erechtheus to Piraeus, and two relative newcomers, Zeus Soter and Ammon, are among the deities honored. The Piraeus setting is not surprising, given the importance placed on the development, religious and secular, of the harbor in the Lycourgan era. We shall later investigate how political circumstances influenced the religious development of Piraeus and dictated, or rather interrupted, its religious relationship with the city of Athens. In the phrase "for the health and safety" I see a sign of a changed religious outlook, one whose concern is now becoming defensive, perhaps even pessimistic in contrast to the higher expectations and optimism of the fifth century. Athens no longer is militarily and economically preeminent, threatening others. Under the power of Macedon she is now the one threatened and will remain threatened throughout the Hellenistic period. Athens' needs are now different from what they were in the fifth century, and we should not be surprised to see state cult accommodating itself to these new needs. "Health and safety" had always been gifts of the gods,[97] but so had many others. But in the turbulent

94. The *terminus ante quem* for *IG* II² 410 is the death of Himeraios at the hands of Antipater's agents in 322/1. On this see below, chapter 2, pp. 49–50.

95. On boards of *hieropoioi* established for making such mantic sacrifices, see [Arist.] *Ath. Pol.* 54.6; Rhodes 1972, 129.

96. For other, later examples of such sacrifices commissioned by the Boule, see Rhodes 1972, 43 n. 6.

97. Mikalson 1983, 16–24, 42, 45–48, 53, 55–56, 67–68, 71, 89.

times of the last half of the fourth century and in the following centuries, the obtaining of health and safety plays an increasingly large role in state cult. "For health and safety" soon becomes formulaic in state decrees treating sacrifices and other religious matters, and various types of gods promising these come to the fore.

Asclepios' cult was very strong in the fourth century and remained so throughout the Hellenistic and Roman periods. In 332/1 the newly enfranchised Amphiaraos himself, the proprietor of a healing sanctuary and obvious favorite of the Lycourgan age, is given a gold crown worth 1,000 drachmas, because "he takes good care of the Athenians and the others who come to his sanctuary for the health and safety of all those in the land" (Schwenk #40). That the healing gods provide health and safety is understandable, but their greater prominence, vis-à-vis the fifth century, is also revealing.[98] What *IG* II² 410 indicates is the extension of such concerns among the official documents of state cult to deities not fundamentally concerned with healing.[99] Later we shall see how other "saving gods" of various pedigrees come forth to promise safety in the political arena, amid these changes *IG* II² 410 of ca. 330 B.C. serving both as a marker and a harbinger of developments in religious thought in Hellenistic Athens.

In the fourteen years between the battle of Chaeroneia and the death of Alexander, the Athenians, under the leadership of Lycourgos, as part of a general civic, military, educational, and economic revival, devoted considerable attention and money to the *kosmos* of long-established cults, including building and remodeling sanctuaries, erecting and refurbishing dedications, and reorganizing the finances of many festivals and cult centers. It is noteworthy that the rebuilding of the religious infrastructure was considered no less important than rebuilding the walls, the ships, and the national economy. State religion was still vital to Athenian society.

This effort on the religious side should not be put down to mere nostalgia any more than were the efforts on the military and economic side. The cults enhanced had been practiced throughout the fourth century, but may, like much else in Athens, have become somewhat shabby from the economic and military tribulations of the century. I am speaking

---

98. See, e.g., Garland 1992, 132–35.

99. The only prior attestation of the phrase "for health and safety" in state documents is *IG* II² 223 B.5 of 343/2, a decree which Phanodemos proposed. On this text see below, chapter 4, p. 132.

not of the restoration of lapsed practices and cults but of the refurbishing of existing ones. If I am correct in my assessment of Lycourgos' *Leocrates*, religious beliefs and attitudes remained very much what they had been in the late fifth century and throughout the fourth century. Participation in this religious effort was, as we have seen, widely based. Lycourgos' contributions were certainly great, but in his religious projects he was aided by many prominent Athenian citizens and was supported by the majority votes of the body politic. In addition, Lycourgos was often continuing or completing projects, such as the theater of Dionysus and the Panathenaic Stadium, that had been begun in the generation before Chaeroneia.

The religious environment of the 320s would have been familiar, natural, and comfortable to an Athenian of the 420s. There were innovations, but they were limited and in accord with the classical traditions. The Athenians of the fourth century introduced the cult of Ammon for their own use, but the new cults of Isis and Aphrodite Ourania were for foreign nationals dwelling in Piraeus, just as in the fifth century Bendis had been for Thracians. Piraeus had been, was, and would continue to be the natural home for new cults of foreign residents. With new emphasis on economic growth and the navy, Piraeus was also the natural site for developments of all types, including the religious ones of the festival of Poseidon and the sanctuary of Zeus Soter.

The one significant hint of change I see in religious attitudes is a rising concern for "the health and safety of the Demos of the Athenians, their children, wives, and other property": hence the prominence of Asclepios and Amphiaraos. Developments in this regard in the political arena will soon be coming, but we can note already the large sacrifices to Eirene and Zeus Soter.[100] Hand in hand with this concern is, I believe, the inauguration and quick growth of the cult of Agathe Tyche. If events in political and personal life were thought to depend on Tyche, the state and its citizens may have been more inclined to think of their gods as "saviors" than as "givers." But such changes are, in the age of Lycourgos, in their very beginnings: what at the beginning of the Hellenistic period is most striking is the continuity of Athenian religion with its classical past.

---

100. In the comical situation of Ar. *Plut.* 1171–90, the cult of Zeus Soter becomes unnecessary when Ploutos ("Wealth") recovers his powers. One might infer that the greater the dangers to the state, whether they be economic or military, the greater the need for Zeus Soter. Ehrenberg (1962, 271 n. 2) suggests, correctly I think, that Zeus Soter appears only in the later plays of Aristophanes "because of the general deterioration of the political and economic conditions."

2

The Decade of Demetrios of Phaleron

On the death of Alexander in 323, Athens led a revolt against Macedonian domination of Greece, the so-called Lamian War. The revolt failed, and Antipater, Alexander's governor of Macedonia and "general of Europe," imposed the following conditions on Athens in the peace settlement: that Athens establish 2,000 drachmas as a minimum property qualification for citizenship rights; that a Macedonian garrison be installed at Mounichia, overlooking the Piraeus harbors; and that Demosthenes, Hyperides, and other leading anti-Macedonians be surrendered to Antipater. Antipater died in 319, and two years later his son Cassander reestablished Macedonian control of Athens. He made as his overseer of Athens an Athenian, Demetrios of Phaleron, who retained control until 307/6. These political developments and in particular the reign of Demetrios of Phaleron had significant consequences for the religion of this and later periods, and those we examine here.

But first we step back to the summer of 324/3, the year before Alexander's death, when it became known in Athens and other Greek cities that Alexander, now in Ecbatana, wished "divine honors."[1] In Athens the thought of divine honors for a Macedonian monarch had been

1. For a survey of the evidence and abundant scholarship on the divine cults of Alexander, see Badian 1981; Habicht 1956, 28–36, and 1970, 245–55. In particular for religious aspects of Alexander's cult in Athens and the debate in the Ekklesia about it, see Badian 1981, 54–55, 64–65; Habicht 1956, 28–36, with corrections of 1970, 246–50; Balsdon 1950, 383–88; Nock 1928, 21–22 = 1972, 1:134–35. Atkinson 1973 is fatally flawed by misunderstandings of, among other things, the import of the law concerning "introducing new

floated some years before. In 338, shortly after the battle at Chaeroneia, Isocrates in a published letter to Philip II had indicated that should he, as Isocrates advised, demolish the power of the Persian empire, "there was nothing left but for him to become a god" (*Epis.* 3.5).[2] Philip's son Alexander had succeeded in this Herculean task, and now the Athenians along with other Greek states had to tackle the question of such "divine honors."

In 324/3 the Athenians in the Ekklesia formally debated offering such divine honors to Alexander. The same Demades who under Lycourgos had been a *epimelētēs* of the Amphiaraia and a *hieropoios* of the Pythaïs to Delphi and had continued his service to Delphi made the proposal to recognize Alexander as a son of Zeus.[3] We have previously noted Lycourgos' and Demosthenes' caustic comments on the idea (chapter 1, pp. 29–30), but in this meeting of the Ekklesia Demosthenes evidently warned against quarreling with Alexander on the point (Din. 1.94).[4] In the face of opposition Demades made a similar point: the Athenians in begrudging Alexander heaven might, because of him, lose their land (Val. Max. 7.2, ext. 13). With religious arguments raised against it but political ones for it, Demades' proposal passed, and for a brief time Alexander was a god in Athens.

Alexander's death and the revolt against Macedon in 323/2 no doubt

---

gods" and the role a divine Alexander would have played in Athens. In all discussions of the cult of Alexander at Athens, the warnings of Bickerman (1963) on the insufficiency of the evidence should be kept in mind.

2. Isocrates is, perhaps, not to be taken literally here but as pushing to an extreme a metaphor known since Homer (e.g., *Il.* 24.258–59). On this see F. Walbank 1987, 371–72; Balsdon 1950, 363–68. In 346 Isocrates, in proposing the same expedition to Philip, was much less extravagant in the promised rewards. Philip's model there was to be Heracles and his task was divinely commissioned (5.113–14, 151–52). Clement (*Protr.* 4.54.5) claims that after Chaeroneia the Athenians enacted a law to "worship" (προσκυνεῖν) Philip as a god, and Fredericksmeyer (1979) accepts Clement's claim. Badian (1981, 67–71) strongly opposes it. It may be, as Badian suggests, that Philip's statue was set up in Heracles' sanctuary in Cynosarges as a σύνναος θεός. If in fact Philip was honored as a god in Athens before his death, it would be most surprising that this fact does not appear in our sources for the Lycourgan period or for the debate about divine honors for Alexander in 324/3. In any case, Philip and Alexander in their lifetimes were clearly experimenting with identifying themselves with various gods and heroes (Fredericksmeyer 1979, 1981; Edmunds 1971).

3. On Demades' role, see Worthington 1992, 271–72; Williams 1989; Mitchel 1970, 14–18.

4. On Demosthenes' changing positions on this issue, see Worthington 1992, 60–62, 262–64.

brought a quick end to this nascent cult. Hyperides, in a funeral oration for the Athenian dead of the Lamian War, spoke, perhaps hyperbolically, of the cult in the present tense; he described "seeing sacrifices made for men" and "statues, altars, and temples being carefully completed for men."[5] These are the things the Athenians "even still now" (καὶ νῦν ἔτι) are being forced to do (6.21). This passage of Hyperides is the only indication that Alexander's cult survived, even by days, the Lamian War. There is no trace of it in the following months or years.

In Hyperides' view the Athenians were "forced" (ἀναγκαζόμεθα) to institute this cult, and it was the result of the insolence (ὑπερηφανίαν) and boldness (τόλμαν) of the Macedonians. "What was holy concerning the gods was being destroyed" (6.21–22). The sources suggest that Athenian religious sentiments were unanimously opposed to the cult but yielded to political pressures. When the political pressure was removed, the religious principles came to the fore. Soon after Alexander's death Demades was fined ten talents for introducing the king's cult (Ath. 6.251B; cf. Ael. *VH* 5.12). He was charged, most probably, not with a political or constitutional crime but with impiety "for introducing new gods."[6] He could not pay the fine and temporarily lost his citizen rights.

Demades' prosecution inaugurated two further trials for impiety, directed against members of the pro-Macedonian faction in Athens.[7] The philosopher Aristotle himself had served as tutor to Alexander for eight years, and he and his successors at the Lyceum, including Theophrastos, were staunchly pro-Macedonian. In 322 the Eleusinian *hierophantēs* sought to charge Aristotle with impiety for composing a paean on Hermeias, tyrant of Atarneus. Hermeias was devoted to Alexander and was a potential philosopher-king of the Platonic model.[8] He had hosted Aristotle for three years at Assos and given him in marriage Pythias, his niece and adopted daughter. After Hermeias' death in 341 Aristotle erected a cenotaph for him at Delphi and composed a choral song, in the guise

---

5. According to Hyperides, "statues, altars, and temples are being completed carefully (ἐπιμελῶς συντελούμενα) for human beings but negligently (ἀμελῶς) for the gods" (6.21). The latter may include projects initiated under Lycourgos, some of which were apparently never completed.

6. So Habicht (1970, 219–20), vs. Atkinson (1973, 320), Williams (1989, 24), and Worthington (1992, 271–72), who think it was a γραφὴ παρανόμων. The evidence is not conclusive for one or the other.

7. On these trials see Winiarczyk 1989, 166, 182–83; Derenne 1930, 185–201.

8. On this whole affair and on the song, accusation, and the development of the literary tradition about them, see Düring 1957, 272–83; Boyancé 1937, 298–310; Wormell 1935. On the charge and the role of the hierophant, see Clinton 1974, 21.

of a hymn to Arete ("Virtue"), praising Hermeias' virtue; likening him, indirectly, to Achilles, Ajax, Heracles, and the Dioscouroi; and promising him immortality in song. The song was probably intended for a memorial service but was then, it was charged in 322, sung regularly at common meals at Aristotle's school. These honors, the song, and the recitations of it certainly go beyond the usual respect paid even to the most illustrious dead mortals in Athens at the time, and they and a perverted interpretation of the song would make plausible the charge that Aristotle was honoring Hermeias as a god.[9] The formal charge in 322 was, no doubt, the same as that against Demades, of introducing a cult not officially authorized by the state. Aristotle fled the city and died before the trial could take place. The purposes of the accusation were in large part political, directed against a leading pro-Macedonian, but the trial also reflects newly aroused Athenian sentiments against more-than-human honors given to foreign political leaders. In 319 the anti-Macedonian Hagnonides of Pergase (*PA* 176) charged Theophrastos with impiety, but obtained barely one-fifth of the jurors' votes.[10] Here we know nothing of the specific charges. In both cases we see the nexus of religion and politics, for the defendants were eminent pro-Macedonians. Religion was clearly an effective and superficially apolitical tool to be used against political opponents, as it had been also in the sixth and fifth centuries.[11] The equally important nexus of religion and philosophy in these impiety cases we shall consider later. For now we may, however, see these impiety trials as the aftermath of the "forced" introduction and later failure of the cult of Alexander. The strong religious sentiments found in the age of Lycourgos retained their power and could be effectively employed in the realm of politics.

That traditional religious sentiments still ran deep in individuals is also exemplified in the fates of those prominent Athenians who incited the Athenians to revolt from Macedon and whom Antipater demanded be sent to him for punishment. In 322 Demosthenes, Hyperides, Aris-

9. The decisive question may have been whether Aristotle's song was a paean, appropriate only for a god, or a *skolion*, a drinking song for banqueters (Ath. 15.696A–697B). In the *Deipnosophistae* it is reported, although the attribution is questioned, that Aristotle said in his own defense, "If I chose to sacrifice to Hermeias as a god, I would not be building for him a memorial as if he were mortal, nor would I have adorned his body with funeral honors if I had wished to immortalize (ἀθανατίζειν) his nature (φύσιν)." Düring (1957, 281) and Wormell (1935, 85) reject this as an obvious forgery.

10. D.L. 5.37. See Ferguson 1911, 35–36.

11. As Plato has Euthyphron say to Socrates, "such things are easily slanderable to the common people" (εὐδιάβολα τὰ τοιαῦτα πρὸς τοὺς πολλούς, *Euthphr.* 3B).

tonicos of Marathon (*PA* 2028), and Himeraios of Phaleron (*APF* 7578)[12] were condemned by the now pro-Macedonian Ekklesia, on Demades' motion, and all fled the country. They were chased down by an agent of Antipater, and all, following the earliest traditions of Greek religion, took refuge in sanctuaries: Demosthenes at the sanctuary of Poseidon on nearby Calauria, the others in the shrine of the hero Aeacos on Aegina. According to Plutarch's vivid account in *Demosthenes* 28.1–30.5, Antipater's agent Archias, a Thurian commanding Thracians, had Hyperides, Aristonicos, and Himeraios dragged (ἀποσπάσας) from Aeacos' sanctuary and sent to Antipater at Cleonae for execution.[13] Demosthenes with poison committed suicide. If we are to trust Plutarch, Demosthenes sarcastically bid Archias, an actor, to play the role of Cleon in the *Antigone* and deny his body burial. As he felt the poison working, Demosthenes attempted to leave the sanctuary: "O dear Poseidon, while still alive I leave your sanctuary. So far as Antipater and the Macedonians are concerned, not even your temple is left pure" (29.6). Demosthenes wanted to preserve the purity of the sanctuary by leaving it before his death and by anticipating the Macedonians' impious violation of asylum. In his last act, the Demosthenes of Plutarch attempted to maintain traditional piety, but, collapsing and dying beside the altar, he failed. This whole nexus of asylum, sanctuary, and the pollution of death is classical,[14] and to the extent that Plutarch's account of these events is accurate, it maintains its full vigor at the end of the fourth century.[15]

The Macedonian garrison arrived on the Mounichion Hill shortly before Demosthenes' death, on Boedromion 20, 322, the first occupying power since the Spartans in 403 B.C. The timing of their arrival, Plutarch claims, added "not a little to the suffering" the Athenians felt, for it was the day on which the initiates traditionally held the procession from Athens to Eleusis for the Mysteries:

12. This Himeraios, who had served as a priest of Poseidon Pelagios ca. 330 (chapter 1, pp. 42–43), was the brother of Demetrios of Phaleron.

13. Cf. Plut. *Phoc.* 29.1 and [Plut.] *X Orat.* 846E–F. For other sanctuaries from which Hyperides was reportedly taken, see *X Orat.* 849A–C and Suda *Y* 294.

14. See Mikalson 1991, 69–77.

15. Demochares (*APF* 3716), Demosthenes' nephew, later expressed the opinion that Demosthenes died not by the poison, but that by the honor (τιμῇ) and foresight (προνοίᾳ) of the gods he was rescued from the savagery of the Macedonians and given a quick and painless death (Plut. *Dem.* 30.4 = *FGrHist* 75 F 3). There is here a possible allusion to the death of Sophocles' Oedipus in *Oedipus at Colonus*.

Because the ritual was thrown into confusion, many reflected on (the difference between) the older actions of the divine forces and those today. Long ago, at the height of (Athenian) good fortunes, mystic visions and voices occurred to terrify and astound the enemy, but now at the same rites the gods (merely) watched the most grievous sufferings of Greece.[16] The time that (before) was most holy and pleasant was being treated with *hybris* and (henceforth would be) known for these very great evils. A few years previously the Athenians received an oracle from Dodona, "to guard the summits of Artemis," lest others seize them. But then, in the days (of preparation for the festival), the fillets they used to wrap the mystic chests were dyed and took on not (their usual) purple color but a sallow, corpselike one. And, what was more, all the private garments when dyed kept their natural color. And, as an initiate bathed his piglet in the Cantharos Harbor (on Boedromion 16), a shark attacked it and swallowed the lower parts of the body, up to the belly. The god was showing clearly to them that, deprived of the lower parts of their country and those bordering on the sea, they would retain the upper city. (Plut. *Phoc.* 28.1–3)

Plutarch reflects the interests of his time in collecting the oracles and unfavorable omens surrounding the event, but he may be recording fourth-century attitudes in describing Athenian concern that the gods, unlike a century and a half previously, had failed to protect even their own rites. If the gods no longer protect such rites, could they be *sōtēres* ("saviors") of the Athenians in larger terms? We find other such expressions of religious despair in Athens only during the plague of 431 and the defeat at Syracuse in 413.[17]

The omens and oracle accompanying the Macedonian occupation proved true. The Macedonians were to hold this fortress on Mounichia, with a few interruptions, until 229 B.C. and were to disrupt the normal relations, religious and other, between Piraeus and the city. Two years to the month after the Macedonians occupied the fortress, in Boedromion 320, the now familiar Demades proposed an administrative reshuffling to ensure that the Piraeic roads on which the procession for Zeus Soter and Dionysos was held were smoothed and otherwise made ready (*IG* II² 380). It seems that the main streets of Piraeus, a center of Lycourgan renovation, had fallen into disrepair. Zeus Soter and Dio-

---

16. In the Persian invasion of 480, at the battle of Salamis, "a great light flashed from Eleusis, and a sound and voices covered the Thriasian Plain, as if of many men together leading in procession the mystic Iacchos. And from the multitude of shouting men a cloud seemed to rise up little by little, and then to sink down and to fall upon the triremes" (Plut. *Them.* 15.1).

17. See, e.g., Mikalson 1984.

nysos appear, from this inscription, the major deities of Piraeus, with Dionysos now sharing in Zeus' procession, not having one of his own. Demades, formerly pro-Macedonian but now in vocal opposition to the Macedonian garrison, seems to be attempting to restore some luster to Piraeus and to the procession. He may be repairing the results of neglect caused, perhaps, by bad economic times in Piraeus and by those sentiments Plutarch records on the occupation of Mounichia.

But in religious terms, the occupation of the Mounichion Hill by the Macedonian garrison meant far more than bumpy and dirty roads for processions. Before this date Piraeus functioned in religious matters, vis-à-vis the state, simply as a deme.[18] It was larger, more prosperous, and more cosmopolitan than most, but it was still a deme. Unlike other demes, however, it had the harbors and was the center of international commerce; thus it became, as we have seen, the residence of many foreigners and the site of their cults. The results of the isolation of Piraeus from the city were, in religious terms, twofold.[19] First, some of its cults that, like most deme cults, served primarily local interests became increasingly "national" in character, looking to the interests of the people of Piraeus almost as an independent state. They thus become parallel to the city's Acropolis cults, which were now less accessible to Athenians of Piraeus. The cult of Zeus Soter, which had already begun to move in this direction, now does so increasingly. Second, the foreign cults in Piraeus, of Isis and others, might have been expected to penetrate the city and be taken up by Athenians there, sometimes even as state cults. The sometimes partial, sometimes complete isolation of Piraeus from 322 to 229 probably delayed this natural development significantly. These are all matters we shall trace through the later periods of Athenian religious history.

One victim of the Macedonian garrison may have been Artemis. As Artemis Mounichia she had her sanctuary just below the very hill that served as a fortress for the garrison,[20] and during the occupation Athenians very likely would not have had access to it. They certainly would have been reluctant to send their wives and daughters there to celebrate Artemis' rites. Artemis' very ancient cult was prominent in the fifth and

18. On Piraeus in general, see Garland 1987.

19. For analogous effects on the similarly isolated Salamis, see Taylor 1993, 226–44.

20. On Artemis Mounichia, see Palaiokrassa 1991, 1989; Garland 1987, 113–14; Parke 1977, 137–39. On the hero Mounichos, see Palaiokrassa 1991, 26–27, 36–37; Kearns 1989, 186–87; Habicht 1961, 145–46 = 1994, 42–43

fourth centuries,[21] but in the fourth century the last mention of her is a passing remark by Demosthenes in 330 (18.107). From then until the last quarter of the second century B.C. there is no epigraphic evidence that her cult was being celebrated.[22] Likewise the hero Mounichos, the eponymous hero of the hill and founder of Artemis' cult there, received a dedication in the mid–fourth century (*IG* II² 4590) and one from the ephebes in 333/2 (Reinmuth #6). After that he disappears from the record.

Keeping in mind the disgruntlement the Athenians felt in 322 when the gods did not protect their rites, we may suspect they felt even more strongly about the Artemis who failed to protect even her sanctuary and hill. This sentiment may also have contributed to the apparent decline of Artemis' cult at Brauron,[23] which was very popular in the fifth and the first three-quarters of the fourth century. The cult was still being practiced in the 320s ([Arist.] *Ath. Pol.* 54.7; Din. 2.12; [Dem.] 25.hypothesis), but it is last attested by the dedication of two crowns by the *hieropoioi* of the quadrennial Brauronia, probably in 313/2 (*IG* II² 1480.12–16).[24] Since Artemis Brauronia was closely related to Artemis Mounichia by myth and ritual, she may have felt Athenian disfavor as well.[25] Here too the Athenians may not have wished to entrust their wives and daughters to a countryside not entirely under their control. When we see new state cults of Artemis emerging in later centuries, they and even that of Artemis Mounichia are of a quite different character.

We now turn to the last of the conditions imposed on Athens by the Macedonians, Cassander's installation of Demetrios of Phaleron as vir-

---

21. The tenth Athenian month, Mounichion, was named after her festival. The demesmen of nearby Thorikos sacrificed to her regularly in the first quarter of the fourth century (*SEG* 33.147.40).

22. For the last quarter of the second century B.C., see *IG* II² 1006.29–30 of 122/1; 1011.16 of 106/5; and 1028.21 of 101/0. Palaiokrassa's survey (1991, 1989) of the archaeological evidence shows no break in the cult, but the amount of evidence for the Hellenistic period appears too limited to establish an unbroken continuity. She associates some rebuilding in late fourth century with the destruction of Mounichia by Demetrios Poliorcetes in 307/6 (Diod. 20.46.1), but the rebuilding, especially if it involved a temple, might well have been Lycourgan, preceding the destruction by Demetrios.

23. On Artemis of Brauron, see Rhodes 1993, 607–8; R. Osborne 1985, 154–74.

24. For the date see Rhodes 1993, 607–8.

25. On the relation between the two Artemis cults, see Palaiokrassa 1991, 1989; Garland 1987, 113–14; R. Osborne 1985, 162–63. An incompletely published inscription (*REG* 76 [1963]: 134–35) records an inventory and planned repairs to the major buildings of the site "in the third century B.C." Apart from indicating prior neglect the inscription may, depending on its date, point to plans for renewal after the departure of the Macedonian garrison from Mounichion.

tual tyrant of Athens in 317. Demetrios held power until removed in 307/6 by Cassander's rival, Demetrios Poliorcetes.[26] Demetrios of Phaleron was an accomplished orator, a student and writer of Peripatetic philosophy, a lawgiver, and a bon vivant.[27] His authority in Athens during the period was supreme, and we may assume that significant changes in religious institutions were due to or approved by him. They include (1) the elimination of festival *chorēgiai;* (2) legislation limiting expenditure on funerals and funerary monuments; and (3) the institution of officials (*gynaikonomoi*) who, among other duties, oversaw some restrictions on the number of participants at private ritual activities. These reforms all alike seem intended to limit major expenditures for religious purposes by the rich, but for what reason and with what results we must examine.

Since their beginnings the choruses that were essential to the tragedies, comedies, and dithyrambs at various Athenian religious festivals had been paid for by wealthy individuals in Athens. The individual sponsoring the chorus was the *chorēgos*, his service was a *chorēgia*, and he might erect a "choregic" monument to celebrate a victory.[28] The *chorēgoi* for the tragedies and comedies of the City Dionysia were appointed by the archon eponymous, those for the Lenaia by the archon basileus. Dithyrambs were presented as competitions among choruses of each of the ten tribes, and the tribes appointed the *chorēgoi*. At some time in the fourth century, before ca. 325, the tribes began to appoint also the *chorēgoi* for the comedies. The expenses were considerable. From Lysias 21.1–5 we hear that one *chorēgos* spent 3,000 drachmas for his tragic chorus in the City Dionysia and 2,000 for a men's chorus at the Thargelia in 410; 5,000 for a dithyrambic chorus and victory monument in 409; more than 1,500 for a boy's chorus, probably in 404; and 1,600 for a comic chorus in 402.

In the mid–fourth century there were at least forty-five such *chorēgoi*: twenty-eight for the City Dionysia (twenty for the dithyrambic competitions of men and boys, three for tragedy, and five for comedy), seven for the Lenaia (five for comedy, two for tragedy), and ten for the dithyram-

---

26. The political connections probably motivated and are nicely reflected in a lead curse tablet, found in the Cerameicos, which has as its victims Cassander, his brother Pleistarchos, his general Eupolemos, and Demetrios of Phaleron (Gager 1992, #57).

27. On the career of Demetrios of Phaleron, see Tracy 1995, 36–50; Green, 1990, 44–49; MacKendrick 1969, 31–34; Wehrli 1949; Bayer 1942.

28. On all elements of the *chorēgia*, see Pickard-Cambridge 1988, 86–93. On φιλοτιμία, the "virtue" behind such public services, see Whitehead 1983.

bic competitions (men and boys) at the Thargelia.[29] At some time in the course of Demetrios' tenure all these and other *chorēgiai* by appointed individuals were eliminated. All the *chorēgoi* were replaced by a single, elected *agōnothetēs* ("contest producer"). The last of the long series of choregic inscriptions date to 320/19.[30] Xenocles of Sphettos (*APF* 11234), in 307/6, is the first recorded *agōnothetēs* (*IG* II² 3073), and there it is said that "the Demos were the *chorēgos*" (ὁ δῆμος ἐχορήγει)for this celebration of the Lenaia.

Why the change? It would relieve a relatively small group of rich families from a considerable outlay of money, and some see this to be Demetrios' purpose.[31] Aristotle, Demetrios' teacher, had suggested (*Pol.* 1309a14–20) that democracies, for the sake of their own stability, spare the rich costly and useless *chorēgiai* and *lampadarchiai* ("sponsorships of torch races"). Demetrios himself reportedly questioned the value of the choregic monuments for analogous reasons: "For the victors the tripod is not a dedication of victory, but a 'last libation' over the exhausted resources and a 'cenotaph' of failed families" (*FGrHist* 228 F 25).

But henceforth "the Demos" were to be the *chorēgos*, and the innovation might be seen as a democratization of the festivals. This would be in accord with Demetrios' extension of citizen rights by reducing the property qualification to 1,000 drachmas from the 2,000 instituted by Antipater. Now the people, by election of the chief official and by financial support, were to take control of their own festivals. In political terms Demetrios may have intended not to save his wealthy rivals money but to limit their opportunities for display and publicity.[32]

Whether Demetrios was intending to help or restrict the rich is a question for political historians to settle. Why he turned to the *chorēgiai* is an issue for religious history and can be viewed in the context of the preceding two decades. Lycourgos had brought economies and order to the finances of state cults and to their handling of dedications. The result had been not "economizing" at the expense of religion but a new *kosmos* for the sanctuaries in terms of buildings and dedications, as well as for the splendor of some of the major festivals. Demetrios may have wished to bring similar economy, order, and *kosmos* to the very expen-

---

29. Davies 1967, 33–35.
30. *IG* II² 3055, 3056. On the chronology, see Raubitschek 1943, 54–55.
31. Pickard-Cambridge 1988, 92; Ferguson 1911, 55–58.
32. Gehrke 1978, 173.

sive and popular festivals that featured dramatic and choral competitions. If it helped his friends or harmed his enemies, so much the better. The introduction of the *agōnothesia* would certainly bring order to the somewhat chaotic and arbitrary system by which these choruses had been financed for generations.

There had also been criticisms, public and private, of the institution of the *chorēgia* in the past twenty years. Lycourgos, as we have seen, preferred that individuals contribute to the building of walls and the support of the navy. To him *chorēgiai* were only for the glory of the family of the *chorēgos*, a conspicuous display of wealth (*Leoc.* 139–40). Aristotle goes so far as to call such services "not useful" (*Pol.* 1309a18).[33] And Demetrios' own criticism, given above, has meaning only if some *chorēgoi* had endured genuine financial hardships. The *chorēgia* was thus an institution in need of reform, and reformed it was. The results of a reform may differ, however, from its purposes, and we now look at these results.

The first attested *agōnothetēs* was Xenocles of Sphettos, whom we met earlier as a supporter of Lycourgos' religious program (chapter 1, pp. 34–36). After Demetrios' overthrow, in the restored democracy, Xenocles took up his old interests. Forty years before he had twice served as a liturgist for the Panathenaia. Now, as elected *agōnothetēs*, he was to manage all the choruses of the festivals. Clearly not all liturgists had wanted to be relieved of such duties.[34] Some former *chorēgoi* emerge now as *agōnothetai*.[35] Eleven or fourteen years earlier, as *epimelētēs* of the Mysteries, Xenocles had used his own money to build a bridge over the Cephisos. Did he, as *agōnothetēs*, contribute to the costs of the festivals? Was the *agōnothetēs* expected to help finance the festivals he superintended? If so, this would be a major development in the nature and in the public perception of the festivals. No longer would the success of the competitions and the glory therefrom be owed to several individuals; attention instead would focus on one man, the *agōnothetēs*.

---

33. Cf. Antiphon 1.3.8; Lysias 26.4; Dem. 21.169, 225; [Xen.] *Ath. Pol.* 1.13; Theophr. *Char.* 26.6; Antiphanes frag. 202 KA.

34. Aristotle (*Pol.* 1309a16–20) says the rich, "even if they wish them," should be prevented from performing such liturgies.

35. Xenocles himself had also probably served as a *chorēgos* (Habicht 1988a = 1994, 323–27 on *IG* II² 749). We see the transition from *chorēgos* to *agōnothetēs* also in *IG* II² 649. Philippides of Paiania (*APR* 14361) in 293/2 is honored for, among other things, having performed his duties both as *chorēgos* and *agōnothetēs* "piously and well" in his lifetime (21–23, 30–32). His father Philomelos had been a *chorēgos* (7–14). For Philippides' numerous other liturgies, see *APF* 14670.

And also, since the office was elected, the candidates were presumably volunteers actively seeking the position. The state probably would provide the base expenses, and hence the festival would be more democratic, but the *agōnothetēs* might, at his own expense, provide the extras that would make it truly memorable.

There is no evidence that Xenocles contributed his own money, but he certainly had the necessary fortune and, years earlier, the inclination to do so. We know that the *agōnothetēs* of 284/3 did contribute and was honored for it. When Philippides of Kephale (*APF* 14356), the rich Athenian poet of New Comedy, was elected *agōnothetēs* in the year of the archonship of Isaios, "he heeded the Demos, a volunteer, at his own expense, he sacrificed the ancestral sacrifices for the Demos . . . , and he gave to the Athenians all their contests" (*IG* II² 657.38–50). The authority remained with the people, but the financial contributions of the *agōnothetēs* were acknowledged, welcomed, and honored. And these contributions could be enormous. The prominent statesman Eurycleides of Kephisia (*PA* 5966) as *agōnothetēs* in the last third of the third century B.C. spent 63,000 drachmas (*IG* II² 834).[36] From the status of the office in 284/3, when the contributions are not treated as an innovation, we might expect that the *agōnothesia* from its inception involved an outlay of personal funds.

In 309/8 Demetrios served as archon eponymous. Duris of Samos, a contemporary historian, after describing the profligacy, debauchery, and personal vanity of Demetrios, continues: "in the procession of the Dionysia which Demetrios as archon held, the chorus sang for him poems of Seiron of Soli, poems in which Demetrios was addressed as 'sun-formed.'" The relevant line is then quoted: "The exceptionally noble, sun-formed *(ἡλιόμορφος)* archon honors you (viz., Dionysos) with divine honors" (*FGrHist* 76 F 10). If Demetrios limited himself to the traditional duties of the archon eponymous as detailed in the *Constitution of the Athenians* (56.4) of about fifteen years earlier, the procession was that of the City Dionysia.[37]

But it is the song that deserves attention. If we are to take seriously the malicious Duris here,[38] we must place the song at the end of the

---

36. On Eurycleides and *IG* II² 834, see Habicht 1982b, 118–27.

37. From Demochares (*FGrHist* 75 F 4) it would appear that Demetrios provided for his procession a large mechanical snail and had donkeys parade through the theater. On the text and on these bizarre elements, see F. Walbank 1957–67, 2:358–59.

38. On Duris see Billows 1990, 333–36.

procession, just prior to the sacrifices to Dionysos. It was composed by a foreigner, not an Athenian. "Noble" (εὐγενέτας) is a reasonable adjective for the now-distinguished Demetrios, but "sun-formed" is not. A rare word, it could as easily be taken as "rotund" as suggesting any solar theology. And Demetrios was, according to the same passage of Duris, a notorious glutton.[39] Given the quality of the source and the uncertainty of the meaning of the line, we should not, I think, take it as evidence of a movement toward the divinization of Demetrios. And there is no other evidence, apart from a large number of honorific statues,[40] pointing in this direction.

Duris' description also does not make Demetrios' archonship a *terminus post quem* for the establishment of the *agōnothesia*. The *agōnothetēs* may have been initially responsible only for the *agōnes* ("contests") of the festivals, with the archons retaining their traditional responsibility for the processions.[41] Then Demetrios need not, as archon, have been the first, prototypical *agōnothetēs*. As eponymous archon he had a constitutional role to play in the City Dionysia, but it need not have been that of *agōnothetēs*. It seems likely that the establishment of the *agōnothesia*, like similar reforms of Lycourgos, would have occurred relatively early in Demetrios' reign.

One further significant innovation in the financing of festivals occurred just prior to Demetrios' reign. Cassander had placed his general Nicanor in Menyllos' place as commander of the Macedonian garrison in Mounichia in 319.[42] In the turmoil after Antipater's death Nicanor took control of the whole Piraeus and harbors. At this time the Athenian general and statesman Phocion persuaded Nicanor to try to win Athenian favor by becoming an *agōnothetēs* (Plut. *Phoc.* 31.2). Plutarch's use of the term here is probably anachronistic, but we have, for the first time, a complete foreigner contributing to the expenses of Athenian festivals,[43] for

---

39. Cf. the report of Carystios in Ath. 12.542E–F.

40. D.L. 5.75; Pliny *NH* 34.27; Nepos *Milt.* 6.4; Strabo 9.398; Plut. *Mor.* 820E–F. On the statues of Demetrios of Phaleron, see Tracy 1995, 49 n. 75.

41. The *Ath. Pol.* distinguishes carefully between the *agōnes* and the *pompai* of the festivals in its descriptions of the responsibilities of the archons (56–57). At the time of the writing of *Ath. Pol.*, ca. 325, the archon eponymous was responsible for the City Dionysia's contests and, with the *epimelētai*, for its procession (56.4–5).

42. On this Nicanor, perhaps not as commonly thought Aristotle's son-in-law of Stagira, see Tracy 1995, 42 n. 38; Bosworth 1994.

43. It should be emphasized here that Nicanor was being asked to contribute to existing festivals, not to create new ones. Ferguson (1911, 30) and Gehrke (1978, 173) leave somewhat the opposite impression.

the purpose, ultimately unsuccessful, of winning the goodwill of the populace. Hitherto on occasion resident foreigners had served as *chorēgoi*,[44] but it is a considerable step from that to having a foreign general contributing to the festivals. The former, often wealthy, might be naturally contributing to the *kosmos* of the city in which they resided, often permanently. The latter can have had only political motives. This event serves as a harbinger of the later politicization of the festivals by foreigners.

In a general description of Athenian attempts to restrict extravagance at funerals, Cicero summarizes Demetrios' own account of his efforts in this regard (*Leg.* 2.63–66 = *FGrHist* 228 F 9): "Demetrios says that the magnificence of funerals and tombs grew to be almost what it is now at Rome. This practice he himself reduced by legislation. . . . He reduced expenditure not only by a punishment but also by time. He ordered that the procession to the tomb be before dawn. He also put a limit on new tombs, for he did not want anything to be set up over the mound of earth except a column not higher than three cubits or a table or a basin,[45] and he placed a certain magistracy in charge of this."

The requirement that the processions be held before dawn indicates that more than economy was intended. Like the sixth-century B.C. funerary legislation of Solon, the purpose must have been to prevent ostentation, whether in practice or in monuments, and this is commonly viewed as a limitation on the aristocratic and wealthy.[46] In this regard Demetrios' law would be analogous to Lycourgos' law that women not ride on wagons in the procession to Eleusis for the Mysteries, lest "ordinary women be made to feel inferior to the rich" (chapter 1, p. 23).

The behavior of women at funerals was always a concern of Greek funerary legislation, and it may be that the magistrates Demetrios had

44. The metics Lysias and his brother Polemarchos had served as *chorēgoi* near the end of the fifth century, which Lysias presents as laudable but not exceptional (12.20). A Theban was *chorēgos* for the Rural Dionysia of the deme Eleusis in mid–fourth century (*IG* II² 1186). The scholiast to Ar. *Plut.* 953 implies that metics were allowed to be *chorēgoi* for the Lenaia but not for the City Dionysia. There was also a law forbidding foreigners as chorus members in the Dionysia, a law that Demades blatantly violated (Plut. *Phoc.* 30.3). On metics and *chorēgiai*, see Whitehead 1977, 80–82.

45. On the difficulty of finding evidence of this change in the excavations of the Cerameicos, see Stichel 1990. For a somewhat forced reinterpretation of Cic. *Leg.* 2.66 to give the meaning that one could not erect as tomb monuments either *stēlai* more than three cubits high, or reliefs, or stone vases, see Stichel 1992. For the development and nature of elaborate family grave precincts in Athens just before the time of Demetrios, see Garland 1982.

46. Garland 1989; Gehrke 1978, 167.

superintend this legislation were the *gynaikonomoi* ("regulators of women") whom he had also introduced.[47] Their authority evidently extended beyond women, at least to the point of regulating religious activities at which women might be present. The *gynaikonomoi* also enforced Demetrios' legislation limiting the number of guests at weddings and private sacrifices to thirty (*FGrHist* 328 F 65; Ath. 6.245A–C). Funerals, weddings, and sacrifices were the major occasions for the gatherings of extended families, and it must have been the size, ostentation, and expense of these which Demetrios sought to limit by law.

All of the innovations and legislation described thus far would have saved the wealthy money, but it may well have been money they would have preferred to spend to sustain or raise their families' reputations in the social and political arenas. The financial burdens of the *chorēgiai* now fall upon far fewer, but these fewer probably paid far more, and they seem to have done so willingly. It is unlikely that the wealthy welcomed limitations on their weddings, funerals, and private sacrifices, and state officials were needed to enforce these new provisions. At least one result, if not purpose, of Demetrios' religious legislation was to reduce the great disparity between the religious obligations and ceremonies of the very wealthy and the rest of the citizens. The private religious activities of the rich became less grand, less ostentatious. The dramatic festivals were now more directly under the control of the state, but, paradoxically, they also would be more associated each year with the generosity of one individual.

Political historians will have to decide whether in all of this Demetrios' prime motivation was to harm the wealthy or benefit the middle and lower classes.[48] But Demetrios was also a philosopher, a philosopher who in his lifetime produced a corpus of Peripatetic writings second only to that of the prodigious Theophrastos.[49] Theophrastos had been his teacher,[50] and during his reign Demetrios helped the Eresian acquire a private garden (D.L. 5.39). Also during his reign he rescued the atheist Theodoros of Cyrene from charges of impiety (D.L. 2.101). In earlier years, in 322, he had served on an embassy with Xenocrates of Chalcedon, who headed the Academy from 339 to 314 B.C.[51] He was, of all

---

47. On Demetrios' *gynaikonomoi*, see Gehrke 1978, 162–63.
48. For a recent treatment of this, see Gehrke 1978.
49. For Demetrios' writings, see D.L. 5.80–81; for Theophrastos', D.L. 5.42–50.
50. D.L. 5.75; Strabo 9.398A; Cic. *Leg* 3.14, *Off*. 1.3, *Fin*. 5.54; Suda Δ 429.
51. Demetr. *Eloc*. 289.

previous and later men in authority in Athens, the most philosophical (cf. Cic. *Leg*. 3.14), and it is during his ten-year reign that we can expect to have the best chance to see the influence of philosophy on contemporary religion. We pause here, therefore, to introduce a topic fundamental to understanding Hellenistic practiced religion: the influence of philosophy, philosophers, and philosophical statesmen on state and private religion.

Aristotle, as we have noted, had written in the *Politics* (1309a16–20) that democracies, for the sake of their own stability, should spare the rich costly and useless *chorēgiai*. And under Demetrios these were eliminated. Plato in the *Laws* had recommended various limitations on expenses for funerals and funerary monuments (*Leg*. 12.958D–960B), and Demetrios had some such enacted. Aristotle speaks of the institution of *gynaikonomoi*, and Plato and Theophrastos both urge restrictions on the activities of women and the extravagance of the citizens.[52] H.-J. Gehrke, by a careful comparison of the philosophers' statements on these subjects and Demetrios' innovations (1978), has shown that there are significant and decisive differences. Sometimes officials with the same names have very different functions; sometimes the purposes seem quite different. To this extent Gehrke's work is very valuable. But he goes too far, I suspect, in then rejecting *all* philosophical influence on Demetrios' lawgiving and in accepting *only* political purposes, arising from current circumstances, for the innovations.[53] The need and means of such reforms were obviously a common topic of discussion in the philosophical schools, and it is inconceivable that the statesman/philosopher Demetrios would have been unaffected by them. From them he may well, as a philosopher, have recognized the need and some of the means for reform without, as a statesman, having accepted the often utopian purposes and systems of the philosophical models. Demetrios was quite obviously not attempting a wholesale transformation of Athenian religion or society on Platonic or Aristotelian principles. He did not, for example, as Plato would have him do, eliminate dramatic festivals.[54] On the contrary, as archon in 309/8 he staged the procession of the City Dionysia. But some of the needs and problems that affected contem-

52. Arist. *Pol*. 1300a4–5, 1322b39. See, e.g., Plato *Leg*. 6.775A–776B and Theophr. frags. 157, 158 W.

53. Williams (1987), though not treating Gehrke's arguments in detail, stresses Demetrios' close affiliation both earlier and later with the Peripatetic School and reaffirms the common view that Demetrios was influenced by his philosophical background in his political and social reforms.

54. E.g., *Rep*. 3.394B–398B, 10.595A–608B.

porary religion were clearly among current philosophical topics, and Demetrios may well have selected and remodeled certain elements of those discussions to suit the circumstances of his time and people. The results on practiced religion are not to be denied, but they are certainly limited and, in the total scheme of things, concern primarily administrative details.

In one regard we find the philosopher Demetrios articulating some religious concerns of his time. A fragment of his essay (*FGrHist* 228 F 39) on the power and nature of *tychē* ("fortune") seems to capture his generation's feelings about her. *Tychē* is "unintelligible" (ἀσύνετος) to us and accomplishes her work "contrary to our calculations" (παρὰ λογισμὸν τὸν ἡμέτερον). She "demonstrates her power in what is contrary to our expectations" (ἐν τοῖς παραδόξοις). For Demetrios the events of the past fifty years—the virtual disappearance of the once powerful Persian empire and the rise and prosperity of the once humble Macedonians—reveal her power. *Tychē* has now given the "good things" to the Macedonians, "until she plans something else for them."

There are various sides to *tychē*—the good and the bad, the divine and the profane.[55] In both literature and life throughout the fifth and fourth centuries, *tychē* had often been given responsibility, as an impersonal, profane force, for the evils of life, especially for death.[56] This continues in the late fourth century: in New Comedy characters, especially slaves, fault her for a host of misfortunes.[57] But throughout the fourth century there is in the orators an increasing tendency to attribute to *tychē* responsibility for some beneficial activities once more commonly assigned to the gods.[58] We may see the culmination of this trend in the establishment, by 335/4, of the state cult of Agathe Tyche ("Good Fortune"). In New Comedy too, characters, again usually slaves, regularly invoke *tychē* as a cause of the often welcome turns of events that characterize this genre, but usually with a caveat about the fickleness of fortune.[59] In Menander's *Aspis* (97–148) *tychē* even appears on stage as a goddess directing affairs, and there she claims that "if something unpleasant were happening to these characters, it would not be fitting for me, a goddess, to be attending them" (97–98). She is here, unmistak-

---

55. For a general account of *tychē*, see Nilsson 1967–74, 2:200–210.
56. Mikalson 1983, 19, 50, 59–62; 1991, 22–28.
57. E.g., Men. *Aspis* 213–15, *Dysc.* 339–40, 800–804, *Pk.* 802; Philemon frag. 166 KA.
58. Mikalson 1983, 61–62.
59. E.g., Men. *Aspis* 248–49, *Dysc.* 800–804, *Epitr.* 351, 1107–8.

ably, Agathe Tyche. In popular religion the Olympian gods were generally given responsibility for what was good in life, and when *tychē* is conceived of as beneficial Agathe Tyche, she too can become a deity.

The fragments of the New Comedy poet Philemon suggest that he, no less than Menander, had characters muse on the nature of *tychē*. A man's *tychē* is "born with him" (9 KA); "One must work to assist *tychē*" (56); "*Tychē* is not a god. What happens to each man is called *tychē*" (125); "What people themselves do for themselves does not involve *tychē*" (137). In these and similar comments (116, 161, 166, 178) Philemon's characters, like Demetrios, treat *tychē* as an impersonal, ineluctable force that must be recognized and accommodated in human life. In the last third of the fourth century the Athenians, through their cult of Agathe Tyche, must have thought it possible to influence her, but it is possible that this effort was short-lived. There is no evidence for her cult in the third century, and we do not hear of her again until the last quarter of the first century when her sanctuary in Piraeus, along with many others, was to be repaired (*SEG* 26.121). After the fourth century the Athenians may have, in general, reverted to the fifth-century view of *tychē* as essentially a negative, profane, unapproachable force, more like Philemon's or Demetrios' *tychē* than the *tychē* of the state cult or of Menander's *Aspis*. Hence Demetrios' essay on *tychē* may be, if not influential on, at least reflective of late-fourth-century views of *tychē*.[60]

Such are, in various areas, the religious activities of the philosopher/statesman Demetrios,[61] but the real influence of philosophers on Athenian religion of the late fourth century lies, I think, elsewhere. In Athens at this time virtually all the prominent philosophers—among them Aristotle, Theophrastos, Xenocrates, and Theodoros—were foreigners, neither heirs to Athenian religious traditions nor full participants in state cults. They were also, as foreigners living abroad, isolated from the religious practices of their native cities. Inheriting from Plato more elevated, abstract conceptions of deity and cult, unable to maintain the cults of their homelands if they had chosen to do so, and not full participants in Athenian cult nor, perhaps, familiar with or sympathetic to

60. Peter Green, as do many others, assigns major importance to Tyche as a divine figure and profane concept in the Greek world throughout the Hellenistic period (1990, 53–54, 396, 400–401, 453, 586). In Athens, I would claim, there is no evidence, outside of philosophical circles, for her influence after the end of the fourth century.

61. For Demetrios' contributions to the Hellenization of the Egyptian cult of Sarapis, see below, chapter 7.

Athenian religious traditions, they formed within Athenian society separate, close-knit groups that were, perhaps, by ancient standards, largely areligious. As a result of all this, and in their great respect for their philosophical mentors, these foreign philosophers and their adherents seem to have begun to use traditional religious terminology and ritual both to express respect for their esteemed predecessors and to shape some activities of their groups.

In 387 Plato began teaching at the Academy gymnasion, the long-established public gymnasion named after the hero Academos and located less than a mile outside of the Dipylon.[62] Academos, Athena, Zeus, Prometheus, Hephaistos, Hermes, and Heracles all had cults in or near the gymnasion,[63] but none of them was to serve as the patron of Plato's new school. Plato himself established a cult of the Muses there to serve that function (D.L. 4.1; cf. *FGrHist* 328 F 224). In the 380s Plato had acquired property adjoining the gymnasion and built there a home and a building for his school. Presumably he placed his new Mouseion on his own property.[64] To introduce a new cult to state property would have required state approval and, perhaps, state oversight. Plato presumably could and did, as a citizen, introduce and establish on his own property a private cult.

The Muses were thus, probably from its very beginnings as a formal school, the patron deities of the Academy.[65] That Plato chose them is significant. They had had a small role in Athenian state cult. In the fifth century the state administered some funds belonging to them (*IG* I[3] 369.66, 86), and they had an altar near the Ilissos (Paus. 1.19.5).[66] In the private realm Sophocles, according to a late biography (*Vita* 6), as-

---

62. On the Academy, its history, location, and physical remains, see Wycherley 1978, 219–25.

63. Judeich 1931, 413. On the hero Academos (or Hecademos), see Kearns 1989, 157.

64. The late biographical tradition understandably places the Mouseion in the Academy (e.g., Olympiodoros in Westermann 1845, 387; D.L. 3.25, 4.1). Here one must keep in mind the loose application of the term "Academy," which was used variously for the sanctuary of Academos, the gymnasion, Plato's school, and the whole district (Wycherley 1978, 209).

65. Since first proposed by Wilamowitz (1881, 279–88), Plato's school has often been called a *thiasos*—a private religious association, devoted to the Muses—but Lynch (1972, 106–34) has shown that there is no evidence that it was such or was ever called such in antiquity.

66. The garden of the Muses (*IG* II[2] 2613, 2614) may well have been that of the Lyceum, though not in the private garden of Theophrastos. See Ritchie 1989; cf. Wycherley 1962, 11–12. The Mouseion Hill, facing the Acropolis, was named not for the Muses but for the legendary poet Musaios who was reportedly buried there (Paus. 1.25.8).

sembled a *thiasos*, a private religious association, for the Muses "from the educated" (ἐκ τῶν πεπαιδευμένων). And in the mid–fourth century private teachers had cults of them at their schools just as there were cults of Hermes at gymnasia (Aeschines 1.10).[67] These Muses are in no sense uniquely or particularly Athenian, but rather derive from the Panhellenic literary tradition beginning with Homer and Hesiod. They thus could be adopted and "worshipped" by Greek literati of virtually all cities, and the usual limitations of the participation by foreigners in established Athenian cults would not apply. This would suit Plato's purposes, for he clearly intended his school to be Panhellenic. Of the nineteen "students" of Plato listed by Diogenes Laertios only three are Athenian (3.46). Because the Muses were primarily private deities, Plato was free to create Muses who would suit the purposes of his school. He was free, essentially, to create a religious cult compatible with his beliefs and pedagogy.[68] Thus while the Academy, like many other Athenian institutions, had its divine patronage and cult, the similarities may have been only superficial.

Plato shared with Apollo a birthday, Thargelion 7. To what extent Plato thought this significant we do not know. But soon after his death in 347, perhaps at his very funeral, a story was circulated suggesting that Apollo, not Ariston, was Plato's "biological" father (D.L. 3.2). This story, apparently put forth by Speusippos, Plato's nephew and immediate successor as head of the Academy, is the first indication of the divinization or heroization of the Academy's founder. As an epitaph, perhaps late, puts it: "Phoebus begot Asclepios to save the body and Plato to save the soul" (D.L. 3.45). Plato would, if the story be believed, rank with Heracles and Asclepios, sons of deities and benefactors of mankind who were both worshipped widely in Athens. According to later tradition Aristotle founded an altar (βωμός) at the tomb of Plato, and this may be confirmed by Aristotle's own elegiac poem on Plato.[69] This altar at Plato's tomb, if in fact it was his, would indisputably indicate a hero

---

67. On the role of the Muses in schools of "elementary" education, see Lynch 1972, 115–16.

68. For possible reasons why the Muses would have appealed to Plato philosophically, see Boyancé 1937, 261–67; Wilamowitz 1881, 279–88. Lynch (1972, 115) sees little religious significance in the Mouseia of the philosophical schools.

69. For sources on the altar, see Plezia 1977, *Carmina* T 4a–d; for Aristotle's poem, see Plezia, 1977, *Carmina* F 3 = West 1972, Aristotle #673. The poem is not complete, and the interpretation of the critical lines 2–3 is uncertain. The altar may be either of Plato himself or of "Revered Friendship" (σεμνῆς φιλίας). The later tradition obviously took it to be an altar of Plato (Plezia 1977, *Carmina* T 4a–d).

cult established for him by 322 B.C.[70] Plato would then be the first Athenian since Harmodios and Aristogeiton in the sixth century to be given a hero cult.[71]

It seems clear that immediately after his death Plato was treated as more than human, perhaps as a founding hero (like a founder of colony) whose grave in the Academy received special veneration.[72] The last, at least, would be in accord with Plato's own recommendation (*Rep.* 5.468E–469B) that outstandingly good men should be venerated as good *daimones* after their deaths.[73] A particular occasion of this veneration would have been his birthday, shared with Apollo. Here, again, as in the cult of the Muses, religious forms are being adapted to new kinds of deities and new purposes.

Aristotle seems not to have received such veneration after his death, in part, perhaps, because he won no such devotion when alive from a large group of students and citizens.[74] Also, his final departure from Athens, in 322, as we have seen, was to avoid a trial on charges of impiety. But that charge, seemingly concocted, was that he was rendering greater than human veneration to Hermeias, the deceased tyrant of Atarneus. There must have been some public suspicion that such things were going on in the philosophical circles. Aristotle, in fact, may have been surprisingly conventional in some areas of religion. In his will he provided for a dedication of a statue of his mother to Demeter at Nemea (or "wherever seems best") and for the fulfillment of a vow by the dedication of life-size statues to Zeus Soter and Athena Soteira in his home city Stagira (D.L. 5.16). He provided nothing, however, for Athenian deities, and in this he was probably not unlike the other foreign philosophers who resided, short term or long term, in Athens.

The Peripatetics, probably in imitation of the Academy, also had a Mouseion as their central sanctuary. Theophrastos, the student and successor of Aristotle, in his will (D.L. 5.51–57) provided for the remodeling and repair of the buildings of this sanctuary, that the statue of Aristotle and other dedications be reinstalled, that the altar be repaired, and that other necessary work be done. The original status (public or pri-

---

70. Mikalson 1991, 29–45.

71. Sophocles may also have been given heroic honors, as or in association with Dexion; for evidence see Clinton 1994. On the cult of Dexion, see below, chapter 5.

72. Novotny (1977, 222–23) sees a Pythagorean influence in the divinization of the master by his devotees.

73. Novotny 1977, 223.

74. Düring 1966, 17.

vate) of this Mouseion is uncertain. It was probably not, as long assumed, in the private garden of Theophrastos.[75] Ritchie (1989) would identify it with the altar of the Muses by the Ilissos (Paus. 1.19.5), and this would suggest that it was a public sanctuary appropriated by the Peripatetics. This seems to me inherently unlikely, but in any case by the time of his death in 287/6 Theophrastos felt fully confident to arrange the financing of the Mouseion, the disposition of its statuary and offerings, and its building plans, all without the hint of state oversight or approval. Whether this Mouseion began as public or private, by the third century it was under the control of the Peripatetics, and the Peripatetic school, like the Academy, had what might superficially appear to be a conventional private cult.

It is against this "religious" background of the two major philosophical schools that we might view some of the events of the last quarter of the fourth century. Both schools were strongly pro-Macedonian, and many in them had personal ties with the royalty of Macedon. The largely foreign Academics quite probably, and the equally foreign Peripatetics possibly, gave more than human veneration to certain human individuals. The patron deities and cults of both schools were divorced from those of most contemporary Athenians. Hence, after the abortive attempt to establish a cult of Alexander, the Athenian populace turned on these philosophers with religious charges: against Aristotle in 322, unfairly it seems, for treating Hermeias like a god, and a few years later against Theophrastos. The charges of impiety would be all the more credible because these men were Athenian in neither citizenship nor religion.

I would propose that philosophers were being attacked not for their doctrines but for pro-Macedonian politics *and* non-Athenian religious practices. But it is precisely these practices—the divinization or heroization of prominent political and philosophical figures, couched in eulogistic language—that would soon prevail when the Athenians, in 307/6, officially and willingly deified Antigonos Monophthalmos and his son Demetrios Poliorcetes. Such divinization was familiar in Asia Minor, but the model for it in Athens comes from the philosophical schools and their many foreign students and leaders.

The instruments by which this model was expanded from the schools to the state were surely those prominent politicians who had close ties to the schools. Lycourgos, as we have seen, was personally acquainted

75. Ritchie 1989; Lynch 1972, 99–102.

with several philosophers; had defended Xenocrates, then head of the Academy; and was buried in the garden of the Academic Melanthios. After Lycourgos' death his sons were defended by Democles, a student of Theophrastos (see chapter 1, pp. 22–23). Demetrios of Phaleron himself was a student of Theophrastos and a philosopher in his own right. These politicians and no doubt many others had intimate knowledge of the Academics and Peripatetics and must have known of their cults of the Muses and their veneration of founders and leaders. When the time came, the politicians so inclined could transfer these concepts to the politically beneficial divinization of Macedonian royalty. And thus, in conclusion, this major innovation in Athenian religious practice, the divinization of foreign kings, which failed with Alexander but was soon to "succeed" with Antigonos and Demetrios Poliorcetes, mostly likely had its origins not in the theories and doctrines but in the practices of the contemporary schools of philosophy.

The single most authoritative study of Athenian religion in the Hellenistic period is W. S. Ferguson's monumental *Hellenistic Athens*, published in 1911. Ferguson's views have been widely accepted and are the standard version promoted by the handbooks and other common sources for Athenian religion. I conclude this chapter on Demetrios of Phaleron with a summary and critique of Ferguson's views, because he himself at precisely this point in *Hellenistic Athens*, at the end of the reign of Demetrios of Phaleron, gives his first summary of the status of Athenian religion.

For Ferguson traditional Athenian religion, the beliefs of Athenian citizens as we know them from the classical period, was in serious, irremediable decline by the last quarter of the fourth century B.C.— certainly by the time of the ouster of Demetrios of Phaleron by Demetrios Poliorcetes in 307 B.C. Ferguson claimed that the comic poet Philemon reflected "the popular sentiments," a poet for whom

life has no lasting satisfactions: evil predominates. It has no clear meaning or purpose: it is sustained by no religious hope of any kind. The gods are there, and by them oaths are taken and sacrifices are offered, but they are there simply as old finery which we do not like to destroy, but for which we have no further use. They no longer enter into the thoughts of men, and whether one wills to believe in them, or wills to disbelieve in them, makes little difference in the life of individuals. (1911, 86)

The claims that for the Athenian people in the last quarter of the fourth century, life was "sustained by no religious hope of any kind," that the gods were like clothes for which there was no use, that the gods "no longer entered the thoughts of men" are, on their face, astonishing. Not twenty years before, Lycourgos, as we have seen, had finished devoting twelve years to the restoration, financial and physical, of both major and minor sanctuaries and festivals in Athens. To judge from the inscriptions, traditional Athenian religion in 326 was stronger in finances and in state support than it had been since the end of the Peloponnesian War. What had happened in twenty years to reduce Athenian popular religion from prosperity to oblivion?

Ferguson attributed this collapse to a fundamentally changed intellectual climate, occasioned largely by the philosophical schools. We have examined above the relationship of these philosophical schools to various reforms of Demetrios and also to the proposed but hitherto unsuccessful ruler cult. But what is the evidence that philosophical theories, even when shared by the head of state, went beyond this and suddenly overthrew religious beliefs which the citizens of Athens had held for centuries?

For this Ferguson turned to New Comedy, not to that of Menander but to that of Philemon from Syracuse, who, the most popular poet of his time, became a naturalized citizen of Athens. It was on the basis of fragments of Philemon that Ferguson judged that "the gods are simply there as old finery," that "they no longer enter into the thoughts of men," and that whether one believes in them or not makes no difference. But two errors, one methodological and one interpretative, invalidate Ferguson's sweeping conclusions. First, one cannot deduce from fragments of tragedy or comedy, without a fuller context, the views of the dramatist. The fragments prove only that some characters in some situations in comedy could say such things.[76] Second, even if we ignore the methodological problem, the fragments of Philemon simply do not support Ferguson's conclusions. Ferguson used Kock's edition (1880–88) of the fragments, and in more recent scholarship several of the fragments Ferguson used are now no longer attributed to Philemon.[77] But even if we follow Ferguson in using Kock's edition, the fragments argue not for the unimportance of the gods but the unknowability of them (118ab, 166 K). And even these unknowable gods are to be respected

76. Mikalson 1991, 5–8.

77. Of Kock's fragments used in this discussion, 118ab, 166, 178, 246, and 247 are not from Philemon (KA VII:317). Of the genuinely Philemonian fragments in Kock, 57 = 60 KA, 67 = 70 KA, 181 = 197 KA, and 199 = 168 KA.

and worshipped (118ab K). Elsewhere in these fragments we find ideas conventional in fifth-century drama: that the gods are aware of just men (57 K); that one might ask from the gods a long life (178 K); that one should hold one's parents in honor (199 K); and that, in Aeschylean terms, the gods punish the unjust even after death (246 K).[78] In one genuine fragment of Philemon (67 K), a character brings ritually correct offerings to Artemis. In 181 K, possibly genuine, Ferguson's fundamental argument is contradicted: "Those who reverence god have good hopes for safety."

Ferguson dismissed the native Menander in favor of the foreigner Philemon. For Ferguson Menander survived, like Philemon, only in fragments, but since the discovery of the *Dyscolos* and its publication in 1959 we have the advantage of seeing how Menander, in 317/6, presented religion in a complete play. The god Pan speaks the prologue, and a focal point of the action is the sanctuary he shares with the Nymphs in the rural deme Phyle. The *Dyscolos* offers a unique and precious, albeit literary and comic, recreation of the activities around such a rural sanctuary. The site, deity, characters, and action are far less dignified than those of tragedy and less fantastic than those of Old Comedy, but the fundamentals of religion remain the same.

A woman receives a seemingly unfavorable dream from a deity, here Pan, and she comes to the sanctuary to make offerings to the deity to avert its potential dangers (407–18). The offerings and ritual are traditional but are, through the cook and the slave, given an unusually detailed and lively, occasionally comic, description. A young woman, by diligently "fawning upon" and "honoring" the Nymphs, has persuaded them to help her (36–39).[79] The gods individually and as a group regularly come to characters' lips in the various forms of casual imprecations and exclamations familiar from Old Comedy.[80] Individuals regularly and often casually pray to the gods for help, and the gods do help.[81] Sostratos' mother travels about the deme every day, sacrificing to one god

78. For parallels see Mikalson 1991: justice and the gods, 178–79 and *passim;* parents, 171–73 and *passim;* punishment after death, 212–13.

79. Cf. Men. *Dysc.* 197, 347. "Honor" is the *vox propria* for the appropriate human response to divinity throughout the classical period (Mikalson 1991, 183–202) and recurs in this play at lines 202, 381, and 479.

80. Men. *Dysc.* 74, 85, 94, 112, 138–39, 142, 148, 151, 160, 162, 182, 191–92, 201, 221, 234, 293, 311–13, 320, 341, 357, 415, 434–35, 459, 467–68, 503–4, 516, 531, 544, 592, 600–601, 612, 621–22, 633, 639, 659, 666–67, 675, 681, 690, 718, 750–51, 774, 777, 788, 826, 835, 874, 876, 889, 908.

81. Men. *Dysc.* 197, 203, 571–73, 660–61.

or another (260–63). The gods are invoked as witnesses of a betrothal (761–62) and are credited with giving a young man "good sense" (736). In short, the gods do everything, given the subject of the play, that fifth-century tragedians and comic writers had them do.

There is in the *Dyscolos* little if anything critical of contemporary religion. Cnemon finds fault with blood sacrifices, in that humans give to the gods only the inedible portions and then feast on the rest (447–53). But he is the misanthrope who views the neighboring sanctuary as only a nuisance and who refuses to lend implements to people sacrificing there. In the view of one character, the Nymphs take their vengeance on him for this by having him fall into the well, and this proves that the gods exist (εἰσὶν θεοί, 639–44; cf. 876–78). And, at the play's end, after at least a partial change of heart, Cnemon joins the post-sacrificial feast and festivities.

This is not the place to undertake a full study of religion in Menander or New Comedy, but only to make the point that the one complete play and the numerous fragments of New Comedy do not justify Ferguson's conclusion that popular religious beliefs were, in any sense, in decline at the end of the fourth century.[82]

A second argument, developed by Ferguson and widely accepted by others before and after him, is that classical religion was closely associated with the political and social institutions of the polis—which is true—and that when Athens lost all semblance of freedom in international politics (in 322, after the Lamian War) and in internal politics (after the installation of Demetrios of Phaleron by the Macedonians in 317), religious belief and trust in state cult must have fallen too. But why? The religion of the Athenian polis was always internal; during the empire of the fifth century it certainly received welcome financing from abroad, but its principles, beliefs, gods, cults, and sanctuaries were, in good part, unique to Athens and depended little on anything or anyone from abroad. The political and social institutions with which traditional religion was affiliated—the Ekklesia, Boule, tribe, deme, phratry, family, and so forth—all continued to operate in the fourth century and would do so, in one form or another, for centuries under a wide variety of democracies, oligarchies, and monarchies.[83] And there is abundant evidence from the inscriptions alone that, certainly in the late fourth

82. For a brief general survey of religion and the gods in New Comedy, see Nilsson 1967–74, 2:194–98.

83. See now Tracy 1995, 18.

and third centuries, the religious side of Athenian life in politics and in social and family life remained vital.

If, as Ferguson claimed, the gods and religious belief were virtually dead by the end of the fourth century, how are we to explain the abundant religious activity we find attested then, immediately thereafter, and for centuries to come? Here is how Ferguson attempted it:

> The religious attitude of Philemon is not peculiarly his. The deities of the Athenians were associated in thinking and in cult with a decaying social and political order, so that its fate was bound to affect theirs. Every instinct of the people, however, prompted the conservation of institutions which bore the impress of all that was most glorious in the past of Athens. The majority did not despair of the city-state, even though it was hard to understand the ways of its gods. Hence there could be no abandoning the ancient festivals and usages. On the contrary, things must be the more scrupulously adhered to because of the strong undercurrent of doubt and wonder. It was, accordingly, not an accident that the popular party, on recovering the government in 307 B.C., acknowledged the spiritual kinship to Lycourgos of Boutadae; for his *pietism* and *fanaticism* [italics mine] for archaizing harmonized with a general tendency. It was his spirit which manifested itself in the persecution of Theophrastus for impiety, the expulsion of Theodorus the atheist, and the attempted regulation of the schools of philosophy. (1911, 87)

By this argument, it was precisely the underlying unbelief and godlessness of the Athenian people that led them to restore their traditional religious beliefs, to attack philosophers who preached atheism. By this argument, the more sacred buildings the Athenians built, the more sacrifices they made, and the more prayers they offered, the more they revealed their disbelief and doubt. Hence all the dedications and other evidence of religious activity become a testament to pervasive doubt, disbelief, and atheism.

There is something fundamentally wrong here. Does evidence of religious activity—making sacrifices, restoring sanctuaries, and renewing festivals—reasonably indicate disbelief? We know that such activities took place. They are facts. But what do we know of the purported general disbelief among the people? Ferguson's source for that was fragments from the comic theater, and we have seen that methodologically the fragments cannot be used for that, and, even if they are so used, they do not support claims of pervasive disbelief among the people. We are left, rather, with all the expected signs of a religious revival: the building and remodeling of sanctuaries, the refurbishing and organization of dedications, the widespread participation in religious activities, and in general a new attention to the *kosmos* of the religious side of Athenian life. Ferguson was, I think, fundamentally mistaken in his assessment of Athenian religion at the end of the fourth century. He relied overmuch on and misinterpreted small fragments of a foreign writer of comedy, and he gave undue importance to the influence of the philosophical schools. And then he offered a perverse interpretation of the widely attested religious activity in Athens to prop up his hypothesis. These points are critical to understanding not only the religious atmosphere at the end of the fourth century but also the development of religion in the whole Hellenistic period in Athens. If like Ferguson we think that the Athenians had given up on their gods and cults at the end of the fourth century, then we are inclined to treat all evidence for public religious activity in the following centuries as somehow debased, insincere, a lifeless shadow of what these same practices must have meant in the classical period. We become disinclined to view this evidence as indications of genuine, living religious belief.

Religion in Athens at the end of the reign of Demetrios of Phaleron was, fundamentally, what it had been at the end of the age of Lycourgos and what it had been throughout the fourth century. There were some administrative changes, as in the elimination of the *chorēgiai*, and these had some significant effects. We also see, but in the limited ways I have described, some influence of the foreign philosophers, though its most serious results lay in the future, with the eulogizing and divinization of Macedonian monarchs and princes in later years. Apart from these, Athenians, I believe, continued to make sacrifices, offerings, dedications, and prayers in the very same manner and to the very same deities, and for the very same purposes and with the very same spirit they had displayed in the previous century.

Ferguson, in the passage cited above, wrote of Lycourgos' "pietism" and "fanaticism for archaizing" in religious affairs. In chapter 1 I attempted to show Lycourgos as the leader in a general revitalization of Athenian institutions, among which was religion. This movement had wide support, and Lycourgos was not demonstrably "pietistic" or "fanatic" in offering renewed support to religious cults and sanctuaries. Here we note that in 307/6, after the restoration of the democracy, the Athenians voted the decree of Stratocles that, as described in chapter 1, expressed the citizens' gratitude to Lycourgos for his many contributions, including those involving the religious cults. We may see this decree not only as a reaffirmation of traditional democratic principles but also as a restatement of the value and importance of the religious reforms of Lycourgos. And thus, at the end of the decade of Demetrios of Phaleron, we find Athenians aligning themselves, in religious terms, with the age of Lycourgos. The age of Lycourgos, in turn, was continuous with the late fifth and fourth centuries, and we have thus established a continuity of religion from the end of the fifth century to the end of the fourth. There were some innovations, especially the introduction of foreign cults established in Piraeus for foreigners. There were new influences, especially from foreign potentates and their representatives and from resident, but foreign philosophers. Both may become important in later centuries; but by 307/6 B.C, they are only seminal, and Athenian popular religion remained much what it had been at the end of the fifth century.

3

Twenty Years of the Divine Demetrios Poliorcetes

In 314 B.C. Antigonos I Monophthalmos ("One-Eyed"), a Macedonian general with a large army and plans to lay claim to Alexander's empire, declared in the so-called Proclamation of Tyre that all Greek city-states should be free, ungarrisoned, and autonomous. At last in 307/6 he sent his son Demetrios, soon to earn the epithet Poliorcetes ("Besieger"), to liberate Athens. Demetrios defeated Cassander's garrison at Mounichia and two months later, as liberator, entered Athens. He freed Athenians from Cassander, gave them back their border forts, drove the "tyrant" Demetrios of Phaleron in flight to Cassander, and restored the democracy. And, within months, his father Antigonos sent a large shipment of grain and ship timbers to Athens.

Thus began a stormy twenty-year relationship between Athens and Demetrios Poliorcetes, a relationship that brought turmoil to Athenian politics and Athenian religion.[1] The pro-democratic and pro-independence factions in Athens must have viewed the events of 307/6 with great enthusiasm. They were freed from Cassander and his hated garrison. They again would have control of their own land and harbor. The tyrant had been deposed, and Antigonos' proclamation and Demetrios' actions made the restoration of traditional Athenian democracy viable. Antigonos' gift of grain helped alleviate a chronic problem, and the ship

1. For the chronology, sources, and details of the Athenian cults of Antigonos and Demetrios, I am much indebted to Habicht 1956; for the political events and chronology of the period, to Billows 1990 and Shear 1978.

timbers made possible a rebuilding of the navy. The prospect in 307/6 must have been for a restoration of Athens, both internally and in foreign affairs, to the conditions of the age of Lycourgos. And, should they be needed, the powerful Antigonos and Demetrios would serve as guarantors of this welcome new status. Antigonos and Demetrios were both "saviors" (sōtēres, σωτῆρες) and "benefactors" (εὐεργέται) of Athens, far beyond that which any foreign power, Macedonian or other, had been since the ouster of the Peisistratids in the sixth century B.C.

In 306 Demetrios left Athens to tend to his father's campaigns in Asia and the Aegean. The Antigonids continued to provide financial support, but militarily Athens was on her own. She was soon attacked by Cassander's forces, and in 304 Demetrios had to return to Athens to rescue her from Cassander's siege. Again Athens was "saved" by Demetrios and again was deeply grateful. Her physical safety and her democracy were preserved.

In 301 the Antigonids suffered a crushing defeat by a coalition of the forces of Seleucos, Lysimachos, and Cassander at the battle of Ipsos in Asia. Antigonos, aged eighty-one, was killed, and Demetrios was severely weakened. Athens, alert to the new political situation, declared neutrality and for five years maintained amicable relations with all the Macedonian principals: Demetrios, Cassander, Lysimachos, Seleucos, and Ptolemy. In 296 Demetrios attempted militarily to reassert his control over Athens, but he succeeded in taking only Rhamnous and Eleusis. In 295/4, after a long and devastating siege of the city itself, he captured it and garrisoned Piraeus and the Mouseion Hill adjacent to the Acropolis. In 288/7 Athens revolted from him and drove his garrison from the Mouseion Hill, but not from Mounichia, Piraeus, Rhamnous, and Eleusis. Demetrios made a final attempt, again unsuccessful, to take Athens by force. Then, as part of a peace treaty with Ptolemy, he withdrew from Athens to Asia but maintained control of Eleusis, Rhamnous, Phyle, Salamis, Sounion, and Piraeus through garrisons. This was the last the Athenians were to see of Demetrios Poliorcetes himself.

On four occasions Demetrios lived in Athens for a time, in 307/6 and 304/3 as liberator, in 295/4 and 291/0 as conqueror. These "visits" serve to punctuate major religious developments during the period and provide the structure for this chapter.

As we have seen in chapters 1 and 2, in 307/6, after the liberation of Athens and the restoration of the democracy, in Stratocles' decree the Athenians expressed their respect for Lycourgos and perhaps their aspirations for a return to the conditions of his age. There Lycourgos, nearly twenty years after his death, is honored for his and his ancestors' pro-democratic spirit, for his economic, building, and religious activities, for his military preparations, for his opposition to Alexander, and for his honesty (for the text of the decree, see chapter 1, pp. 20–21). In all of these areas the comparison to the recently deposed "tyrant" Demetrios of Phaleron would have been obvious.

The Stratocles, son of Eudemos, of the deme Diomeia (*APF* 12938) who proposed this reassertion of Lycourgan values is a pivotal figure in the intertangled political and religious history of his time. He emerged immediately as a strong—probably the strongest—supporter of Demetrios Poliorcetes and set the agenda for the many honors, political and religious, that the Athenians showered upon the Macedonian general and his father. In the years 307–301 Stratocles proposed no fewer than twenty decrees that were passed by the Ekklesia and survive on stone.[2] For fifteen, the content of the decree is known, and of these at least ten award civil honors and/or citizenship to ambassadors, friends, or agents of Demetrios.[3] Their dates reveal that Stratocles' political career was in hiatus during the reign of Demetrios of Phaleron, even though it had begun at least by 324/3 when he was one of the prosecutors of Demosthenes in the Harpalos affair.[4] Stratocles was thus both initially pro-democratic and, after 307, a supporter of Demetrios Poliorcetes. His family, which can be traced back two generations, was wealthy and had performed the usual liturgies expected of the rich (*APF* 12938). His reputation in the later biographical tradition is uniformly bad; he had come to represent the supposed degeneracy of the Athenians who fawned upon Demetrios. Plutarch takes out on Stratocles his dislike of Demetrios Poliorcetes and the divine honors he was given at Athens. Stratocles was, according to Plutarch, "audacious" (παράτολμος), lived "licentiously" (ἀσελγῶς), and seemed to imitate the "coarseness" (βωμολοχίαν) and "loathsomeness" (βδελυρίαν) of the fifth-century demagogue Cleon in his behavior toward the Demos (*Dem.* 11–12; cf. 24.5).

In terms of the religious history of the time we need to distinguish between foreign influences on Athens and the reception of these influ-

2. *IG* II² 456, 457, 460, 469, 471, 486, 492, 495, 496 + 507 (add.), 503, 559 + 568 (add.), 560, 561, 566 + *SEG* 3.86, 640, 971; *Hesp.* 1 (1932): 44–46, #4; *Hesp.* 11 (1942): 241, #46; *Hesp.* 7 (1938): 297; and *SEG* 16.58, 36.164.

3. *IG* II² 469, 471, 486, 492, 496 + 507 (add.), 559 + 568 (add.), 560, 561; *SEG* 16.58, 36.164.

4. Dinsmoor 1931, 13–14.

ences by the Athenians. Demetrios Poliorcetes, in a sense, represents the former, Stratocles the latter. But we must remember that the divine honors for Demetrios which we shall detail were only proposed by Stratocles. They were approved by the majority vote of the Ekklesia. And those divine honors given to Demetrios in 307/6 were proposed and no doubt enacted by the pro-democratic faction in Athens.

Demetrios Poliorcetes came to Athens in June 307/6 as her liberator from the rule of Cassander and Demetrios of Phaleron, as restorer of the democracy, and as guarantor of Athenian autonomy. Here Plutarch describes the reception the Athenians gave him:

> Demetrios found the mouth of the (Piraeus) harbor unbarred and sailed in. He was now in full view of all. From his ship he gave a signal for calm and silence, and when this was accomplished, through a herald he proclaimed that his father had sent him, with good fortune, to free the Athenians and to throw out the garrison and to restore to the Athenians their laws and ancestral constitution. After this proclamation was made, the majority (of the Athenians) immediately put their shields down before their feet and applauded. And, shouting, they were bidding Demetrios to disembark, calling him "benefactor" ($\epsilon\vec{v}\epsilon\rho\gamma\acute{\epsilon}\tau\eta\nu$) and "savior" ($\sigma\omega\tau\hat{\eta}\rho\alpha$). (Plut. *Dem.* 8.4–9.1)

Two months later, when Demetrios entered the city itself, the Athenians voted their benefactor and savior honors. The most detailed account of these honors is from Diodoros 20.46.1–4:

> After Demetrios had razed the whole of Mounichia, he restored freedom to the Demos (of the Athenians) and established friendship and alliance with them. On the proposal of Stratocles, the Athenians voted to erect gold statues of Antigonos and Demetrios on a chariot near Harmodios and Aristogeiton; to award them both crowns worth 200 talents; to erect an altar and call it "of the Saviors" ($\Sigma\omega\tau\acute{\eta}\rho\omega\nu$); to add to the (existing) ten tribes two, Demetrias and Antigonis; to perform for Demetrios and Antigonos each year contests, a procession, and a sacrifice; and to weave (Antigonos and Demetrios) into the robe ($\pi\acute{\epsilon}\pi\lambda o\nu$) of Athena. The Demos (of Athens), having been destroyed in the Lamian War by Antipater, after fifteen years unexpectedly recovered their ancestral constitution. . . . And Antigonos, after ambassadors arrived from Athens and delivered the decree about the honors and described (the need for) grain and wood for shipbuilding, gave them 150,000 *medimnoi* of grain and sufficient wood for 100 ships. He also drove out the garrison from (the island of) Imbros and returned that city to the Athenians.

The honors voted for Antigonos and Demetrios were certainly grand and exceeded, each of them, honors hitherto paid to living men, but all are explicable as extensions of Athenian religious traditions.[5] Let us look at them individually.

1. GOLD (PROBABLY GILDED) STATUES NEAR HARMODIOS AND ARISTOGEITON.

Honorary statues had, in the late fourth century, become fashionable. There were, reputedly, 360 of Demetrios of Phaleron, all but one of which were destroyed in 307.[6] Stratocles' decree of 307/6 provided a bronze statue for Lycourgos, and Demosthenes was similarly honored forty years after his death. The gold of the Antigonos-Demetrios group is, however, special and brings to mind the chryselephantine statue of Athena Parthenos by Phidias.[7] The Antigonid group was to be erected "near Harmodios and Aristogeiton," a siting usually prohibited by law,[8] but appropriate. Antigonos and Demetrios were, like Harmodios and Aristogeiton, "tyrant-removers" if not tyrannicides, and, because of them, democracy was restored. Conon had been honored with a statue in the Agora, the first such honor after that of Harmodios and Aristogeiton, for overthrowing the "tyranny" of the Spartans in 394. In 371/0 Iphicrates, a hero of the Corinthian War, was given a bronze statue and the full range of honors accorded Harmodios and Aristogeiton. And, finally, centuries later, the statues of the assassins of Julius Caesar were erected alongside the tyrannicides.[9]

2. CROWNS FOR DEMETRIOS AND ANTIGONOS, WORTH 200 TALENTS.

Crowns in the form of wreaths, even gold ones, were regularly awarded to citizens and noncitizens alike for meritorious service

---

5. For modern discussions of the various divine honors given to Antigonos and Demetrios Poliorcetes in Athens, see Weber 1995, 298–305; Green 1990, 48–50, 403; Billows 1990, 149–50, 234–36; Rosivach 1987, 269–74, 281–82; F. Walbank 1987; Fredericksmeyer 1979, 45–47; Kertész 1978; Habicht 1956, 44–58, 240–41, and 1970, 255–56.

6. See chapter 2, note 40.

7. Houser (1982, 234, 236) claims that previously gold "had been reserved by Greeks for images of the gods."

8. *IG* II² 450 of 314/3 and 646.37–39 of 295/4; [Plut.] *X Orat.* 852E. See Habicht 1956, 46–47.

9. For the statues of Conon, Demosthenes, Iphicrates, and Brutus and Cassius, see Wycherley 1957, *Testimonia* 16, 29, 117, 119, 158, 261–62, 697–99, 702, 712; Shear 1978, 55–56. On the awarding of statues in this period, see Dow 1963, 83–86.

in the fourth century. The honoree would then often dedicate his crown to Athena, and it would be stored in the Parthenon as part of her sacred property. Demosthenes had received such a crown worth 1,000 drachmas for his services to the state. But the cost of the gold wreaths for Antigonos and Demetrios (1,200,000 drachmas) is staggering, even in those inflationary times. The presumption may have been that Demetrios would dedicate these crowns to Athena, and thus the gold would not have left Athens but would have been transferred from the secular to the sacred treasury.[10] Even so, one may suspect that in the original decree the 200 talents were intended to cover the costs not only of the crowns but also of the gold statues and all other honors to be paid to Antigonos and Demetrios.[11]

3. A (SINGLE) ALTAR, TO BE CALLED "OF THE *SŌTĒRES*."

Here we move from honors on the human level, however elevated, to those appropriate only for a deity. By building an altar the Athenians established a cult of Antigonos and Demetrios as the "Saviors." The altar presumes sacrifices, and sacrifices presume a priest. According to Plutarch, the priest of the Soteres was elected annually (*Dem.* 10.3),[12] and that serves, if needed, as one further indication of the political nature of this cult. The Soteres were, indisputably, viewed as "gods" (θεοί), even though in the inscriptions of the time and possibly in the original decree the term θεοί was not used, perhaps intentionally.[13]

The contests, procession, and sacrifice described by Diodoros were presumably for the annual festival of the Soteres. The elaborateness of this proposed new festival would put Antigonos and Demetrios, as a pair, on a par with the major deities of Athens—with Athena Polias and

---

10. See, e.g., *IG* II² 1477B.15–21 as reedited in *Hesp.* 40 (1971): 454 and Lewis 1988, 304–5.

11. Billows (1990, 258) views this sum, however inflated, as money paid to Antigonos by the Athenians. Given the situation, this seems improbable, especially since Antigonos soon had to send 140 talents to Athens (*IG* II² 1492.97–103).

12. Plutarch (*Dem.* 10.3, 46.1) also claims that the new priest of the Soteres replaced the eponymous archon and, until 288, gave his name to the year for which he served. The inscriptions of the period, however, show that this did not happen, regardless of what the decree ordered. See Habicht 1956, 45 n. 3.

13. For lack of θεοί in inscriptions, see Habicht 1956, 44 n. 2. For contemporary texts see *SEG* 25.141.22 of ca. 303; *IG* II² 646.40 of 295/4; *IG* II² 3424. Plutarch (*Dem.* 10.3), probably erroneously but understandably, writes of the σωτῆρας θεούς.

her Panathenaia and with Dionysos Eleuthereus and his City Dionysia. We shall soon see the form that this new festival was finally to take.

4. TO ADD TO THE (EXISTING) TEN TRIBES TWO, DEMETRIAS AND ANTIGONIS.

This change[14] required an enlargement of the Boule from five to six hundred and a major reorganization of the demes, a structure that had been unchanged since Cleisthenes in 508 B.C. There were religious effects also. Each of the ten tribes had a cult and priest of its eponymous hero, and now the new Antigonidai must have worshipped Antigonos as their eponym, the Demetriadai Demetrios. The original ten eponyms were all heroes: that is, legendary, dead mortals like Ajax and Erechtheus receiving cult.[15] Presumably the new eponyms were thought gods, not heroes. As eponyms of tribes, Antigonos and Demetrios would each have had a priest and have received annual worship from the members of his tribe. These tribal cults were distinct from Antigonos' and Demetrios' combined cult as *sōtēres*.

5. FIGURES TO BE WOVEN INTO *PEPLOS* OF ATHENA.

A new embroidered *peplos* was presented to the Athena Polias of the Erechtheum at each quadrennial celebration of the Great Panathenaia. The embroidery typically represented the victory of the Olympian gods over the Giants. The decree probably intended that among the Olympians Antigonos and Demetrios be represented for the presentation to be made in 302/1 B.C. (see below, p. 99). Here the Soteres would be imagined, like the Olympians, as overcoming the forces of evil and chaos in the world.[16]

All of the above were classified as "honors" ($\tau\iota\mu\alpha\iota$), and it is as "honors" that they are intelligible within the Greek tradition at both the human and divine levels. According to Plutarch (*Dem.* 8.1), Antigonos and

14. Cf. Pollux 8.110; Steph. Byz. s.v. "Αντιγονίς."
15. On the eponymous heroes, see Kearns 1989, 80–92; Kron 1976.
16. Compare the charges brought against Phidias in the fifth century for allegedly representing himself and Pericles on the shield of Athena Parthenos (Plut. *Per.* 31.4).

Demetrios wanted to give freedom to all Greeks "for the sake of their own glory and honor" (ὑπὲρ τῆς εὐδοξίας καὶ τιμῆς). What was this "glory and honor" to be? "Honor" may, of course, be given to men; more important, in Greek popular religion "honor" is what, fundamentally, pious men were expected to render to the gods. Each god had one or several functions (τιμαί), and for the performance of these and for his power in these areas received "honor" (τιμή) from mortals. The god then might choose to "honor" the person or city who "honored" him. Elsewhere I have argued that this relationship of man to god was very similar to that of subjects to their king.[17] Kings had functions to perform and the power to perform these. The subjects honored the king for these and showed their honor in the form of gifts. Essentially, in the Greek tradition the same emotion and thought are involved in the honor shown both to men and to gods, but the functions of the human and divine honoree are qualitatively different. One can honor a man for a multitude of civic, social, military, and athletic activities. One renders honor to the gods for what, basically, lies wholly or partially beyond human control: safety in war, at sea, and in other dangers; health; and economic prosperity.[18] And one exhibits this "honor" through the gifts of sacrifice, prayer, hymns, dedications, and festivals.

It must have seemed to the pro-democratic faction in Athens that Antigonos and Demetrios were, unlike any humans before them, providing just such "divine" benefits to them: safety from the assaults of Cassander and his like; food to ensure physical health;[19] and, with the restoration of the democracy and Piraeus, the prospect of economic good times. In addition to these traditional gifts the Antigonids were also providing "autonomy" and "freedom" of the state.[20] Antigonos promised these to all Greeks in 314, reasserted their importance in his settlement of 311 with Cassander, Ptolemy, and Lysimachos, and had his son Demetrios deliver them to Athens in 307/6.[21] In the fifth century Athenians had taken largely into their own hands the preservation of their freedom and autonomy, but since Chaeroneia in 338 Athenian international political status was

17. Mikalson 1991, 196–201.
18. Mikalson 1991, 183–202.
19. On the Athenians' chronic need and concern for food, which had often been in short supply since 335 B.C., see Tracy 1995, 30–35.
20. On the relationship of these terms, which were virtually synonymous in this period, see Billows 1990, 194–97.
21. On Antigonos' policy concerning the freedom and autonomy of the Greeks, see Billows 1990, 197–205.

beyond their control, determined by the actions of Macedonian generals such as Antipater, Cassander, and Antigonos. For foreign affairs the Athenians were as dependent on them as they were on the gods for health, safety, and prosperity, and the Macedonian generals alone could—as Antigonos alone did—give Athenians their precious autonomy. But we should be careful not to limit Athenian gratitude and divine honors to Antigonos and Demetrios solely to these political services. They are important in understanding the Athenian response, but also important are the safety in war, food, and prosperity traditionally attributed, in part, to the gods. It is for all of these elements—some more traditional, some relatively new in this period—that Athenians rewarded Antigonos and Demetrios with the same "honors" that they had previously given the gods: altars, sacrifices, and festivals. In retrospect this was a momentous step in Athenian religious history, but one understandable in the political circumstances and religious traditions of the time.

As Hellenists raised on Homer, Greek tragedy, and Greek philosophy, we are inclined to see the fundamental distinction between gods and men lying in the immortality of the former and all that follows from it. That is essentially a theological distinction, to be found in the literature of the archaic and classical periods. Always more central to popular religion were the functions of the various deities, whether the deities be ouranic or chthonic, divine or heroic. And it is because of similarity of function, not of *physis*, that Antigonos and Demetrios could be ranked among the gods. The Athenians were receiving from Demetrios and Antigonos what formerly they could expect only from their gods.

Antigonos and Demetrios were to be the Soteres of the Athenians, and the epithet *Sōtēres* describes, as divine epithets often did, precisely what the new "gods" provided—that is, "safety" in the physical, economic, and political realms. If, as I have claimed, the model for human piety toward the gods was the relationship of a subject to his king, it may be not coincidental that the Athenians, first of the Greeks and simultaneously with these divine honors, proclaimed Demetrios "king" (Plut. *Dem*. 10.3).[22] Certainly not consciously, but in accord with their religious (though not political) traditions, the Athenians were fitting Demetrios into a model that would allow them to give him divine honors.

---

22. Demetrios as "king" is first attested in Athenian inscriptions in Mounichion 305 (*IG* II² 471.15–16) and this remains his title until the revolt of 288/7. The title is not found again until 249/8 (*IG* II² 777.9), a decree passed by a pro-Macedonian government. See Shear 1978, 16–17.

Despite Plutarch's disapproval of the divine honors given to Antigonos and Demetrios, his account of them and of the times suggests that they were bestowed willingly, sincerely, and relatively spontaneously. In other, contemporary documents we see that such honors came to Antigonos and Demetrios also from varying segments of Athenian society. *IG* II² 3424 records a list of eleven Athenian citizens who, at their own expense, dedicated statues of the Soteres; there were originally even more contributors. The surviving remnants of the closing poem (lines 12–19) may suggest that these Athenians intended their dedication to be an example for others to follow. In *SEG* 30.69 of 304/3 the state undertakes to pay the prytanists of the tribe Akamantis for the costs (300 drachmas) of cattle sacrificed to the Soteres, Athena Nike, and, probably, Agathe Tyche on behalf of Athenians who were on campaign with Demetrios.[23] Here there is discussion of the former "slavery" of the Greeks and of their current freedom and autonomy (lines 7–9). The Akamantid sacrifice to the Soteres is to be repeated each Elaphebolion hereafter as a memorial of successes reported at this time (19–23). The best preserved of these texts, *SEG* 25.149 of the same period, describes honors to be rendered to Demetrios by Athenian volunteers serving with him on campaign:

The select volunteers voted: [whereas,

> Demetrios] the Great [previously] came into [Attica with a naval and infantry] force and [threw out] the opponents of [democracy and set free] the land of the Athenians and [most other Greeks, and now] has stood by [the Athenians] to help with an [even greater] force,
>
> and, having overcome [his enemies, has already aligned] many cities under the kingship [of his father Antigonos, himself enduring every] danger and labor,
>
> and he honors [those with him] and is very concerned [with their safety,]
>
> and he leads those in need of [freedom and helpfully takes part with us] in the affairs in the Peloponnesos, and he [immediately went there with select volunteers] and threw out the [enemy] from the land,

[with good fortune] it was voted by the select volunteers [to praise because of his virtue and goodwill] Demetrios, son of Antigonos, a king, [son of a king, and to erect] an equestrian [statue of him] in the Agora next to Demokratia,[24] and [to encourage Athenians and] the other Greeks to set

---

23. On the text, date, and background of *SEG* 30.69 (= *SEG* 25.141 + *Hesp.* 16 [1947]: 153, #46) see Habicht 1990b = 1994, 19–22; Woodhead 1981.

24. On surviving fragments of this statue, see Houser 1982.

up [for Demetrios altars and sanctuaries], and for those participating in the sacrifices [performed on behalf of Antigonos and Demetrios] to sacrifice also to Demetrios Soter, [presenting] the most sacred and beautiful [victims for sacrifice,] and to [proclaim the honors] given to the king by the select volunteers [so that, just as they themselves] have honored their benefactors [at their own expense, so also others] may follow and honor [them with the most illustrious] honors.

These three texts from different groups in the years just after 307/6 confirm the associations the Athenians as a group had made between their safety and freedom, Greek freedom, democracy, and the divine honors they were giving to Demetrios. The feeling of gratitude is almost palpable even on these formal, stone records. If we can trust the restorations, *IG* II² 3424 and *SEG* 25.149 even reveal a proselytizing spirit completely uncharacteristic of classical religion. *SEG* 25.149 differs from the others in that new honors are awarded only to Demetrios, not to his father; that agrees with the contemporary development of the cult of the *Sōtēres*. Demetrios was the *Sōtēr* present in the land and minds of the Athenians, and he quickly dominated and soon monopolized the cult he initially shared with his father.[25]

Demetrios also received rewards like those of the gods, it seems, in the symposia of high society. Alexis (116 KA) in a comedy represented symposiasts toasting Demetrios just as they did Aphrodite and Eros.[26] The playful spirit of this society, in which Demetrios and Stratocles themselves no doubt participated,[27] is apparent. For the divine Demetrios Alexis was willing even to break the conventions of his genre in order to provide such topical, graceful compliments. And thus from the Ekklesia to the sanctuary of the tribal hero Akamas, from the theater to the symposium, praises and divine honors were being showered upon Demetrios.

After Demetrios' departure in 307 Athens entered into the Four Years' War with Cassander. Athens enjoyed some initial successes, but by 304 Cassander had established control over Boeotia and the Athenian forts at Panacton and Phyle by land and over Salamis by sea. Preparing to

25. Habicht 1956, 48.
26. Antiphanes 81 KA has a similar toast for "the revered goddess and the sweetest king." Since Antiphanes I died in 334, the fragment, if it is his, cannot refer to Demetrios. If the fragment belongs to Antiphanes II, as seems probable, the "sweetest king" would be Demetrios. See KA ad loc. On the references to Demetrios in New Comedy, see Weber 1995, 301–3.
27. E.g., Ath. 13.577C–F, 579A, 580D–E, 596F; Plut. *Dem.* 11.

face a siege, Athens summoned Demetrios. Demetrios landed at Aulis and recovered Boeotia, Phyle, Panacton, and Salamis. He had again "saved" Athens and spent the winter of 304/3 there. During this time he also restored to power the party of Stratocles.

The political outlook of Stratocles and his followers appears, however, to have changed significantly between Demetrios' first arrival in 307/6 and his second visit in 304/3. Previously staunchly democratic, they appear to have become, in the course of the exercise of and loss of their power, more oligarchic and, after their previous successes with Demetrios, strongly pro-Macedonian and pro-Demetrian. In 303/2 there was apparently an unsuccessful democratic uprising against them, an uprising resulting in the exile of Demochares (303/2) and Philippides (302/1). The extension and elaboration of the divine honors given to Demetrios in 304/3 and in subsequent years were all probably due to this oligarchic party of Demetrios' supporters. The honors of 307/6 had, as we have seen, widely based support, but that is not necessarily true of the honors we now examine.

In 304/3 a cult of Demetrios Kataibates ("Descender") was established at the very spot in Attica where Demetrios had dismounted from his chariot.[28] *Kataibatēs* was the epithet usually reserved for Zeus, to designate the Zeus cults founded at spots hit by Zeus the god of lightening. In such a way Zeus "descended" to earth.[29] To apply the epithet to Demetrios, for his descent from his chariot, might be viewed as a wordplay, a pun—one of several such puns we shall see applied to the cults of Demetrios. Some Athenians were, surely, deeply grateful to Demetrios, but even in their expression of gratitude they, or the ones responsible for these honors, could not, perhaps, restrain their wit.

Demetrios therefore had, on his arrival in 304, three distinct cults in Athens: as *Sōtēr* with his father Antigonos, as a tribal eponym, and as *Kataibatēs*. He was thus ranked with the major deities and heroes of Athens, with Athena Polias, Zeus Olympios, and the likes of Ajax and Erechtheus. In 304, however, unlike in 307, Demetrios appears to have taken these honors literally. He began to act, in Athens, as though he were a god. And among the divine models he might have chosen, he picked Dionysos. According to Plutarch (*Dem.* 2.3), Demetrios emulated Dionysos because Dionysos was the god most terrifying (δεινό-

28. On cult of Demetrios Kataibates, see Plut. *Dem.* 10.4, *Mor.* 338A; Clem. Al. *Protr.* 4.54.6. See also Habicht 1956, 48–50.

29. See Nilsson 1967–74, 1:71–73.

τατον) in warfare but in peacetime most suited for delights and graces (τρέψαι πρὸς τὴν εὐφροσύνην καὶ χάριν ἐμμελέστατον). One thinks of the two sides of the Dionysos of Euripides' *Bacchae*, the god who also happened, by force at times, to win the whole Greek and much of the Asian world to his service.[30]

On his way to Athens in 304, Demetrios had, probably for a brief time, taken up quarters *in* the temple of Apollo Delios,[31] an unparalleled act in Greek religious history to this point. In Athens he chose the residence of his older sister (as he liked her to be called; Plut. *Dem.* 24.1), Athena Polias, and was quartered in the opisthodomos of the Parthenon.[32] This was again an unparalleled act which could only be taken by detractors of Demetrios as gross impiety, but which followed logically from the honors the Athenians themselves had awarded the Macedonian king. Athena was, it was said, entertaining him as a *xenos* ("foreign guest"), but, as Plutarch describes it (*Dem.* 23.3), Demetrios was not a "very orderly *xenos*" nor one behaving "gently as befits a virgin (παρθένῳ)" hostess. This new, young, handsome Dionysos reputedly devoted himself wholeheartedly to debauchery and affairs with freeborn wives and sons of the Athenians and with a bevy of beautiful courtesans.

Demetrios' residency in the opisthodomos (not in the cella, at least) of the Parthenon and his behavior there must have shocked many Athenians, as it did Plutarch four hundred years later. That the divine honors the Athenians had awarded to Demetrios had led to this should be viewed largely as the fault of Demetrios. In his dress,[33] in his choice of lodging, and in his behavior he chose to indulge fully in his newfound divinity. The Athenians of 307/6 could have imagined no such abominations resulting from the honors they were awarding their benefactor and savior.

Demetrios' Athenian agents in all of this were quite likely Stratocles and his party, in part because they were grateful for the restoration of their influence when Demetrios' returned, in part perhaps because some of them shared the symposia and courtesans that Demetrios provided. Stratocles carried the seemingly boundless honors one step further by

30. On Demetrios and Dionysos, see Ehrenberg 1946, 190–93.

31. Habicht 1956, 197.

32. Philippides frag. 25 KA; Plut. *Dem.* 23.3, 26.3, and *Comp. Dem. et Ant.* 4.2; Clem. Al. *Protr.* 4.54.6.

33. Plut. *Dem.* 41.4–5; Duris, *FGrHist* 76 F 14.

proposing that Demetrios be treated as an oracular god: that "every-thing which King Demetrios bids be considered holy in respect to the gods and just in respect to men" (Plut. *Dem.* 24.4–5). Henceforth am-bassadors to Demetrios were to be considered *theōroi* (as were ambas-sadors to Delphi), and Demetrios' responses were to be viewed as or-acles (Plut. *Dem.* 11.1, 13.1–2; *Mor.* 338A). On this very point we hear of the first Athenian opposition to the divine Demetrios. Demochares, son of Laches, of Leukonoion (*APF* 3716), staunchly pro-democratic, spoke against the proposal (Plut. *Dem.* 24.5). For this and no doubt other anti-Demetrian sentiments he was exiled.[34] Demetrios and his Athenian sup-porters around Stratocles were in absolute control, and those who op-posed them on political or religious grounds were clearly well advised to bide their time. The wait, it turned out, was for only three years.

In the interval, probably in 302/1, the Ekklesia voted heroic honors for three important generals and agents of Demetrios: Adeimantos of Lampsacos, Oxythemis of Larissa, and Bourichos. Each had provided valuable services for Athens in the past, and Adeimantos, a close friend of Theophrastos (D.L. 5.57), had already received a crown from the Athe-nians in 302 (*SEG* 14.58). Oxythemis had been given Athenian citizen-ship in 304/3 (*IG* II² 558).[35] According to Demochares (*FGrHist* 75 F 1), these men were then given altars, *heroa* (hero sanctuaries), libations, and paeans. Since King Demetrios was a god (θεός), his lieutenants must be given the lesser, heroic honors.[36] These hero cults, if ever in fact estab-lished, probably did not outlive Demetrios' defeat at Ipsos in 301, for, apart from Demochares' complaint, they have left no record.[37] Upon hear-ing the news of these honors for his subordinates, Demetrios reportedly was surprised and commented that in his time, no Athenian "was great or strong in spirit" (Demochares, *FGrHist* 75 F 1). Such, perhaps accu-rately, was the attitude of the new deity toward his devotees in 302/1. The disaffection was shared by the devotees. When Antigonos was killed and Demetrios suffered a serious defeat at Ipsos in 301, the Athenians re-volted from their divine patron and established a moderate government.

---

34. On Demochares' exile, see Billows 1990, 337–39; Marasco 1984; Shear 1978, 47–51.

35. On *SEG* 14.58, see Badian and Martin 1985. On *IG* II² 558, see M. Walbank 1990, 445–46: M. Osborne 1981–82, 1:118–19, 2:124–26.

36. See Price 1984, 33–34.

37. Nor is there record of the "sanctuaries" (ἱερά) of Demetrios' courtesans Leaina and Lamia also mentioned by Demochares (*FGrHist* 75 F 1). On *FGrHist* 75 F 1, see Marasco 1984, 191–98. In all this Demochares' hostility to Stratocles and Demetrios must be taken into account.

As he was returning to Athens from an expedition to the Peloponnesos, probably that expedition extolled in *SEG* 25.149 of ca. 303/2 (above, pp. 84–85), Demetrios turned his attention to the Eleusinian Mysteries:

> And then, departing for Athens, Demetrios wrote that he wished, as soon as he arrived, to be initiated and to receive the whole initiation, from the Small Mysteries through the Epopteia.[38] This was something not permitted and had not happened before, but the Small Mysteries were performed during (the month) Anthesterion, the Great Mysteries during Boedromion. And (initiates) celebrated the Epopteia after leaving an interval of, at the least, one year from the Great Mysteries.
>
> After (Demetrios') letter was read, only Pythodoros, the *dādouchos* ("torchbearer"), dared to speak in opposition, and he accomplished nothing. But after Stratocles proposed that they, by vote, call Mounichion Anthesterion, (the Athenians) performed the Small Mysteries at Agrai for Demetrios. And, after this, Mounichion, having just become Anthesterion, was made Boedromion, and Demetrios received the remaining rites and, at the same time, he received also the Epopteia. And for this reason Philippides (the comic poet), attacking Stratocles, wrote:
>
>> The man who compressed the year into one month.
>
> and, about (Demetrios') lodging in the Parthenon,
>
>> The man who took the Acropolis to be a hotel
>> and introduced courtesans to the virgin (τῇ παρθένῳ).
>> (Plut. *Dem.* 26)[39]

That Demetrios, as a man, wished to be initiated into the Eleusinian Mysteries is not surprising, but his request that the Mysteries be accommodated to his schedule, and not vice versa, was unprecedented. But Demetrios now, seemingly, viewed himself as one of the Athenian gods. It might seem odd that a god should want initiation into another deity's mysteries, but as the "new" Dionysos Demetrios had the model of the "old" Dionysos. The "old" Dionysos alone of the Olympians had, according to Eleusinian lore, been initiated into these mysteries.[40] Demetrios could also feel affinity with Demeter through his name and, perhaps more important, by similarity of function. He, like Demeter, provided the Athenians grain. In 307/6 his father had sent to Athens

---

38. On the Eleusinian Mysteries and their stages, see Mylonas 1961.
39. Cf. Diod. 20.110.1.
40. Mylonas 1961, 212–13.

150,000 *medimnoi* of grain; Demetrios himself was to send another 100,000 *medimnoi* in 295/4 (Plut. *Dem*. 34.4); and, no doubt, throughout his association with Athens he facilitated or controlled the shipment of the desperately needed grain from abroad. We shall soon see how the Athenians, perhaps in gratitude for the grain shipment of 295/4, tied Demetrios even more closely to the cult of Demeter.

From Plutarch's account of this episode a bit more of the opposition to Demetrios emerges. Pythodoros, the Eleusinian *dādouchos*, expressed, probably in the deliberations of the Ekklesia, his opposition to the manipulation of the program of the Mysteries at which he officiated. This criticism comes, naturally, from the priestly quarter. Philippides, however, the long-standing opponent of Demetrios, on the comic stage ventured an attack not on Demetrios but on his Athenian agent Stratocles (Plut. *Dem*. 26 above = Philippides frag. 25 KA).[41] The witticism on the manipulation of the calendar is perhaps harmless, but there lies just below the surface of the barb about the courtesans and the virgin Athena the desecration that Stratocles' accommodations of Demetrios had occasioned. In 302/1 the result of such criticisms for Philippides, as for Demochares, was exile.

Within a few years, however, the Parthenon was to suffer even more. In the period of Athenian independence and neutrality after the battle of Ipsos in 301, Lachares (*PA* 9005), an Athenian of unknown family and deme, gained political power in a civil war and became a virtual tyrant.[42] It was to drive him out and to restore his own control that Demetrios returned to Athens in 295/4: "Again Demetrios attacked Attica, and, having gotten control of Eleusis and Rhamnous, he was pillaging the land. He captured a ship holding grain and bringing it to the Athenians and hung its merchant and captain, and, as a result, others turned away in fear. A serious famine occurred in the city and, in addition to the famine, a lack of other supplies" (Plut. *Dem*. 33.3). Pausanias gives a fuller account of the career and fall of Lachares:

Cassander—for he had a terrible hatred toward the Athenians—made into a close friend Lachares who, up to that time, was a leader of the Demos. Cassander persuaded Lachares to plan for a tyranny, and of the tyrants we know Lachares was the harshest in matters that concern men and the most unsparing

41. Cf. Plut. *Dem*. 12.4–5.
42. On Lachares' career, see, in addition to passages translated here, Polyaenus 3.7.1–3, 4.7.5, 6.7.2; Plut. *Mor*. 379D, 1090E; Ath. 9.405F; Ferguson 1929, 1–20; Shear 1978, 52–53; Habicht 1979, 1–21; M. Osborne 1981–82, 2:144–52.

toward the divine. Demetrios the son of Antigonos already had a quarrel with the Demos of the Athenians, but even so he did away with the tyranny of Lachares. And, as the city wall was being captured, Lachares ran off to the Boeotians. It was suspected that Lachares was well supplied with money, for he had taken down the gold shields from the Acropolis and had stripped off the removable jewelry and decoration from the very statue of Athena. For the sake of this (money) the men of Coronea killed him.[43] (Paus. 1.25.7)

The siege of Athens by Demetrios in 295/4 forms another important episode in the religious history of Athens, as the result of both Lachares' actions and the further honors given to Demetrios. According to Pausanias, Lachares removed the golden shields dedicated on the Acropolis and the "removable" adornment (τὸν περιαιρετὸν κόσμον) of the statue of Athena. He may have done this, as modern tyrants do, to provide a treasure for his life in exile, but he apparently used the gold and silver also to pay his mercenaries (*POxy.* 17.2082 = *FGrHist* 257a). A few pages later Pausanias, after describing Lycourgos' contributions to Athens, says, "Lachares, having become a tyrant, stole all these things which were made of silver and gold. But the buildings were still there even in my time" (1.29.16). The comic poet Demetrios II in his *Areopagites* (1 KA) had a character claim that "Lachares made Athena naked."

What had Lachares done? Quite probably, if we combine the two passages of Pausanias, he had removed and melted down *all* the gold and silver stored on the Acropolis. This would have included the golden shields, the jewelry and perhaps even the gold of the chryselephantine statue of Athena Parthenos by Phidias, and the many dedications recorded on the inventories of the fourth century.[44] Centuries of precious dedications were lost, and, tellingly, the last surviving inventory of Acropolis dedications dates to 303/2.[45] The blow to the cults of Athena Polias and other Acropolis deities must have been enormous, not so much in economic terms—for dedications such as these generated no income—but in prestige, respect, and τιμή. Athena and her colleagues were unable to protect even their own property.[46] We shall see

43. Lachares was, in fact, probably not killed by the Coroneians of Boeotia. See Kirchner on *PA* 9005.

44. On the question whether Lachares took the gold of the statue itself, see Linders 1987, 117.

45. Miller and Koumanoudes 1971, 456 n. 13; Lewis 1988.

46. On Lachares' violation of the asylum of his Athenian opponents in Athena's temple during the preceding civil war, see *FGrHist* 257a. This too could be construed as Athena's failure to protect "her property." See Mikalson 1991, 69–77.

later that after Athens' successful revolt from Demetrios in 288/7, there was a period of disorder for the cult of Athena Polias, and it was slow to regain its former prominence. Eventually the Panathenaia was reinstated and would continue to be celebrated throughout antiquity, but damage had been done. The Athena Polias cult represented and promoted by Lycourgos was now in decline and, apart from the Panathenaia, would remain so for some time.

In 295/4, after his expulsion of Lachares, Demetrios installed a pro-Macedonian oligarchy in Athens, and from them he received new honors.[47] Plutarch (*Dem.* 12) claims that the proposer of the decree surpassed even Stratocles in his servility. Demetrios was, as often as he visited Athens, to be received with the hospitality usually shown Demeter and Dionysos. Money for a dedication was to be given to the citizen who excelled in the splendor and cost of this reception. The month Mounichion was to be named Demetrion, and the last day of the month was to be called Demetrias. Thus, henceforth, Mounichion 30 would be known as the Demetrias of Demetrion. The City Dionysia was to be, according to Plutarch, renamed the Demetrieia.[48] According to Duris (*FGrHist* 76 F 14), in the theater of Dionysos, where the Demetrieia was to be celebrated, Demetrios was represented (ἐγράφετο) on the proscenium "riding on the world."

In 304/3 Demetrios had been the *xenos* (guest) of Athena Polias, but henceforth, as often as he visited, he was to receive gifts of *xenia* from the whole state, and these gifts were to be those usually reserved for Demeter and Dionysos—prayers, hymns, and sacrifices. Demetrios' self-identification with Dionysos was discussed previously, but here his identification with his namesake Demeter becomes obvious. He had been initiated into her mysteries, however irregularly, during his last visit, and, like her, he provided essential grain to the Athenians, especially after the devastation of the crops and near starvation caused, this very year, by Lachares and Demetrios himself. Demetrios now, like Demeter, controlled Athens' grain supply, and like her he should be honored whenever he came to town.

In 307/6 Demetrios had arrived in Piraeus on Thargelion 26 (Plut.

47. On the oligarchy see M. Osborne 1981–82, 2:144–53; Habicht 1979, 22–33; and Shear 1978, 53–55. For the date and character of the new honors, see Habicht 1956, 50–55: Jacoby on *FGrHist* 328 F 166.
48. For further sources see Philochoros, *FGrHist* 328 F 116; Harp. s.v. "ἔνη καὶ νέα." The contemporary name of the festival was "Demetrieia" (Dinsmoor 1931, 15), not "Demetria" as in Plut. *Dem.* 12.1.

Dem. 8.3–5), and hence neither the month (Mounichion) nor the day of the month (the thirtieth) was named after him because of the events of his first visit.[49] Mounichion was, however, the month the Athenians manipulated so that Demetrios could celebrate all three stages of the Mysteries in 303/2, and naming the month after him may have had a touch of humor.[50] The new Demetrion was, according to Philochoros (*FGrHist* 328 F 116), to be a "holy month," celebrated as one long festival. Demetrias, as each thirtieth day was to be named, was no doubt to be Demetrios' monthly festival day, like those of Apollo (the seventh) and Artemis (the sixth). Unlike the sacred days of the Olympians it fell in the last half of the month, in fact at the "moonless" time usually reserved for evil spirits and regarded by the Athenians with some trepidation.[51] Could this too have been an in-joke? There is, however, no evidence that the renaming or sanctification of the month and day was ever effected. Contemporary inscriptions retain the traditional names for both, and business continued to be transacted in Mounichion and on the thirtieth days.[52]

The City Dionysia was, apparently, not renamed the Demetrieia, as Plutarch claims, but the name "Demetrieia" was added to the name "City Dionysia."[53] A day or more of celebration for Demetrios may have been added to the traditional City Dionysia, as Habicht suggests (1956, 53), or—more likely in view of Demetrios' identification with Dionysos—existing elements of the festival may have been remodeled to accommodate the new Demetrios/Dionysos. This amalgamation of the Demetrieia and City Dionysia was, however, short-lived, and after Athens' revolt from Demetrios in 288/7 the City Dionysia appears again alone (without the Demetrieia) on inscriptional records (*IG* II² 653, 654, 657). The Demetrieia of Demetrios, as Habicht has argued (1956, 53–54), is distinct from the cult of the Soteres because it is here Demetrios/Dionysos, not Demetrios Soter, who is receiving worship. After 288/7 the Athenians continued to need *sōtēria* ("safety"), and a cult of the Soteres, as we shall see, survived—but with different Soteres. Clearly

49. Plutarch (*Thes.* 36.5) gives as a possible reason for the eighth day of each month being sacred to Theseus the fact that Theseus first came from Troizen to Athens on the eighth day of a month.

50. Ferguson 1911, 122.

51. Mikalson 1975b.

52. Habicht 1956, 52; Jacoby on *FGrHist* 328 F 166.

53. Dinsmoor 1931, 8, line 42 (= *IG* II² 649 with a new fragment). See Dinsmoor, 15; Habicht 1956, 52.

the Athenians were happy then to be rid of the Dionysiac Demetrios, and the Demetrieia was abandoned.

In 291/0 Demetrios returned to Athens from Leukas and Cephallenia. The Athenians, according to Demetrios' enemy Demochares, received him with incense, wreaths, libations, processional dances, and ithyphallic poetry accompanied by dancing (*FGrHist* 75 F 2). One of these ithyphallic poems is summarized by Demochares and preserved by Duris of Samos (*FGrHist* 76 F 13).[54] This hymn, though often treated as a unique and uncharacteristic document in Athenian religious history, is a natural product of its immediate times. We have already noted that songs were sung about Demetrios in the symposia, and we learn from Philochoros (*FGrHist* 328 F 165) that the Athenians sang paeans "over" (ἐπί) Antigonos and Demetrios. A competition was held for the composers of such songs, and Hermippos of Cyzicus was judged the victor.[55] This recalls the prize the Athenians in 294/3 had decided to award the citizen giving the most lavish and costly hospitality to the Macedonian monarch (above, p. 92). If we take this song to be the song of Hermippos, which is not unlikely, then the poet was a foreigner as were most of the lyric poets writing in Athens at the time.

The opening lines of the hymn, containing probably an exhortation to begin the singing, are lost, but the rest seems complete:[56]

> 1   The greatest and the dearest of the gods
> are present for the city,
> for good fortune brought together here Demeter
> and Demetrios.
> 5   She comes to perform the sacred mysteries of Kore.
> He is present handsome, laughing, and cheerful,
> as a god ought to be.

---

54. Habicht (1979, 40) dates this hymn to the great Eleusinia of 291. The ithyphallic meter is characteristic of hymns and chants sung in the Dionysiac phallic processions. See Ehrenberg 1946, 180–81; West 1982, 148.

55. There is confusion in Athenaios' text (15.697A) about the poet's name. It may be Hermocles or Hermodotos. See Jacoby on *FGrHist* 328 F 165.

56. For detailed studies of the song, see Marcovich 1988, 8–19; Ehrenberg 1946, 179–98. For a recent account of it in relation to ruler cult and contemporary philosophy, see Green 1990, 55, 127, 398–99. Note also Weber 1995, 303–5.

I disagree with important claims of Ehrenberg, viz. that Dionysos was addressed in a portion of the lost beginning; that Demetrios was, in this song, assimilated to Dionysos and Demeter; and that the song represents in general an early syncretism of deities characteristic of late Hellenistic religion. Personally and in cult Demetrios sought, as we have seen, identification with Dionysos and association with Demeter in Athens, but the hymn unmistakably represents Demetrios as a separate, distinct deity.

It is a revered sight—his friends all in a circle,
himself in the middle,
10   as if his friends were stars, he the sun.
Hail, son of Poseidon, most powerful god, and of Aphrodite.
The other gods are either far distant,
or do not have ears,
or do not exist or pay no attention to us,
15   But we see you present, not made of stone or wood,
but real.
We pray to you:

First, dearest one, create peace, for you have
the authority.
20   And especially punish the Sphinx that tramples over
not Thebes but all Greece,
the Aetolian who sits on a rock, like the old Sphinx,
and snatches up and carries off all of us.
I am unable to fight him.
25   It is an Aetolian characteristic to rob neighbors,
but now they do it to those far away.
If you will not do it yourself, find some Oedipus
who will throw this Sphinx off a cliff or will
make it a pile of ashes.

Duris laments, as have several modern scholars, that the Athenians, those who two hundred years previously killed a man showing obeisance to the king of Persia and who slew countless Persians at Marathon, used to sing this song not only in public but also at home.

The song is, as Victor Ehrenberg notes, "not a specimen of high poetry." The Greek text is characterized by "simplicity and humdrum triviality" (1946, 180–81). Only the extended conceit of the Aetolians as the Sphinx gives it some life. Its primary interest to us is as a poetic expression of the attitude that at least some Athenians had developed toward the divine Demetrios over the past seventeen years. At points of emphasis, at the beginning of the song and immediately before the prayer, the actual, physical presence of the god Demetrios is emphasized, in contrast to the traditional gods who are (or whose statues are) made of wood and stone, who may or may not exist, and who, at best, are distant and pay no heed to us. Demetrios was there, in person, in Athens.[57]

The importance of Demeter (lines 3–5) to grain-starved Athens is self-

57. On Athenians, even in the classical period, not expecting epiphanies of their Olympian gods, see Mikalson 1991, 21, 64–65.

evident, and, as we have seen, Demetrios had courted association with her and her Mysteries. The friends who encircle Demetrios (8–10) are quite likely Adeimantos, Oxythemis, and Bourichos who, as new heroes, were like stars to the sun Demetrios. The solar imagery was characteristic of Demetrios' self-established role. In the theater of Dionysos he was represented as "riding on the world" (above, p. 92), and near the end of his career he was having a cloak woven for himself that would depict the entire cosmos and the heavenly bodies, a cloak that, according to Plutarch (*Dem.* 41.4–5), no later Macedonian king chose to wear.

The divine Demetrios is handsome, laughing, and cheerful (lines 6–7), probably real traits of Demetrios (e.g., Plut. *Dem.* 2.2–3) but also virtues of a symposiast and reminiscent of the "youthful" and "sweetest king" (above, p. 85 n. 26). In the symposia Eros and Aphrodite were his fellow deities, here Aphrodite is his mother, and the lover Demetrios had no doubt demonstrated mastery of his mother's art in the orgies in the Parthenon. In other ways too the song displays the playfulness of symposiastic literature. Two puns have been noted: the true god (ἀληθινόν) as opposed to the stone ones (λίθινον), and the Sphinx (Σφίγγα) made into an ash (σποδόν).[58] The mating of Poseidon and Aphrodite, unique to this poem, may be explained prosaically as uniting Demetrios' two areas of competence, the navy and sex,[59] but taken in light of the mythological tradition Poseidon and Aphrodite form a ludicrous pair. And, as we have seen, to be called the son of Poseidon was not necessarily a compliment (see chapter 1, p. 30). Such playfulness in the song, if we are not imagining it, recalls the similarly playful and sophisticated "heliomorphic" Demetrios of Phaleron, Demetrios Kataibates, and perhaps Demetrion, Demetrios' much-manipulated Mounichion. These and the Sphinx conceit should make us wary of attributing great religious seriousness to this song, however much it was performed publicly or privately. The song was quite probably composed by a foreigner, and the lack of specifically Athenian religious traditions and deities (apart from Demeter) in it is noteworthy and in this regard may be compared to Aristotle's hymn on Hermeias.[60]

---

58. Ferguson, 1911, 143 and Marcovich, 1988, 17. The text (σπεινον) is corrupt. Wilamowitz proposed σποδόν, Schweighauser σπίνον ("a tiny tit"), and Meineke σπίλον ("rock," "cliff"); the last was accepted, "with some misgivings," by Ehrenberg 1946, 179, and Marcovich, 19.

59. For Poseidon on (non-Athenian) coins of Demetrios, see Ehrenberg 1946, 185–86.

60. See above, chapter 2, pp. 48–49. Cf. Ehrenberg's comment (1986, 186): "The relationship between Demetrius and the two gods Poseidon and Aphrodite was little more than a kind of playful invention, and not primarily an expression of religion."

Critical to understanding the divine Demetrios, however, is the prayer of the song.[61] Here, as before, Demetrios is asked to provide for the Athenians what they themselves could not: peace and, more particularly, escape from harassment by the Aetolians to the north (lines 17–29). These Demetrios with his army and navy could, if he so chose, give. In fact, soon thereafter Demetrios mounted a successful expedition against these Aetolians.[62] The song to Demetrios did, in a primarily literary and perhaps playful way, raise pressing Athenian issues of life and death, issues that at that time could be addressed only by one greater and more powerful than themselves, only by a god more immanent and active than traditional gods.

That the "immanence" of the divine Demetrios was not just a literary cliché is suggested by the contemporary decree of Dromocleides.[63] In 340 the Athenians had remounted on the newly rebuilt temple of Apollo at Delphi their dedications of golden shields made from booty captured from the Persians at Plataea in 479. Now, in the late 290s, the Aetolians controlled Delphi and had removed or were planning to remove these prominent dedications. Normally in such a situation the Athenians would consult Apollo through the Pythia, and, in such a matter, Apollo's command would be decisive. But the Aetolians, hostile to Athens, controlled Delphi. The Athenians therefore turned to the new oracular god whom they had recently created: Demetrios. The decree of Dromocleides proposed that the Athenians elect a representative to go to Soter (Demetrios) and "ask him how most piously and best and most quickly the Demos could make the restoration of the dedications, and that the Demos do what he as an oracle bids ($\chi\rho\dot{\eta}\sigma\eta$) them to do" (Plut. *Dem.* 13.2). The language of the decree suits only the consultation of a deity, and Demetrios here, in 292/1, was given, and no doubt took on, the oracular role of Apollo Pythios.

Demetrios similarly took on the role of Apollo Pythios in the Pythia of 290/89. For centuries this festival had been celebrated quadrennially, in the third year of the Olympiad, in Delphi, in the god's honor. The festival included, in addition to customary sacrifices and processions, extensive and varied musical compositions featuring the hymn to the god. It had also a full range of athletic competitions modeled on the

61. That the hymn is in fact a prayer to Demetrios is itself noteworthy. It is clearly exceptional in that prayers (and votive offerings), both fundamental acts of Greek worship, are commonly *not* features of ruler cult. See Nock 1972, 833–46; Nilsson 1967–74, 2:182; Z. Stewart 1977, 567.

62. Plut. *Dem.* 41.1, *Pyrrh.* 7.3. See Shear 1978, 64 n. 185.

63. On all aspects of this decree, see Habicht 1979, 34–44.

Olympic games. Like all such festivals it was inextricably tied to one sanctuary and one god. Demosthenes, in the middle of the fourth century, calls it "the shared competition of the Greeks," and he is indignant that Philip, a Macedonian, is administering it. To Demosthenes that is an act of extreme *hybris* (9.32). In 290/89 the hated Aetolians controlled Delphi, and Demetrios and the Athenians apparently thought the Pythia was no longer accessible to them. Demetrios, according to Plutarch, chose to do a "very new and strange thing" (πρᾶγμα καινότα-τον), to hold the Pythia and its contests *in Athens*. He did so on the pretext that Apollo Pythios was especially "honored" in Athens as their "ancestral" (*patroös*) god and as the "founder of their race" (Plut. *Dem.* 40.4).

There were, indeed, cults in Athens of Apollo Patroös (in the Agora) and Apollo Pythios (near the Ilissos).[64] Apollo's close ties to Athens and his paternity of the Ionic peoples had been dramatized as early as Euripides' *Ion* in the late fifth century. Some Athenians regularly traveled to Delphi for the quadrennial Pythia, and we have seen that Lycourgos was among the ten *hieropoioi* who supervised the sending of a special delegation (Pythaïs) to Delphi in 326/5 (chapter 1, p. 34). What is, in Plutarch's judgment, most new and odd is for Athenians, at Demetrios' behest, to stage the Delphic festival in their own city. It was tantamount to stealing an old and prestigious festival from a god's own people. And, at the least, it indicates diminishing respect for the tie of such festivals to their gods, priesthoods, and places. Increasingly such agonistic festivals must be thought of in terms of international politics and entertainment, and this is the first unmistakable indication of a development that we shall see continuing throughout the Hellenistic period. There was still a bond between such a festival and the god's cult, and this bond remained throughout antiquity, but it was not as strong as it had once been.

Clearly the divine honors given to Demetrios and Antigonos initially, in 307/6, were widely and warmly accepted by many Athenians. Those after 307/6 were proposed and carried by the increasingly oligarchic and pro-Demetrian faction centered on Stratocles. We have seen opposition or reaction to them range over the years from barbs in comedy and, perhaps, playful wording and naming of these honors to occasional pub-

---

64. On the Athenian cults of Apollo Patroös and Pythios, closely related at this time, see Lambert 1993, 211–17; Hedrick 1988, esp. 200–210.

lic statements by individuals. Pythodoros, the Eleusinian *dādouchos*, unsuccessfully tried to stop the manipulation of the Mysteries, and in 303/2 Demochares in the Ekklesia spoke against the proposed honors and was exiled. According to Plutarch, even the gods expressed their displeasure:

> The Athenians had voted to have woven into the peplos figures of Demetrios and Antigonos along with Zeus and Athena, and as the peplos was being escorted through the Cerameicos a strong gust of wind fell upon it and tore it down the middle. And around the altars of Demetrios and Antigonos quantities of hemlock sprouted up, a plant which otherwise does not grow many places in the land. And on the day of the City Dionysia they disbanded the procession because an unseasonably heavy frost occurred. The freezing rain fell thick, and the cold not only burned the vines and all the fig trees but also destroyed most of the grain that was just turning green. And because of this Philippides, an enemy of Stratocles, wrote these lines against him in a comedy:

>> This man because of whom the freezing rain burned the vines,
>> because of whose impiety the *peplos* was torn down the middle,
>> the man who makes divine honors human,
>> these things, not comedy, destroy the Demos. (Plut. *Dem.* 12.2–4)

The ill-omened tearing of the *peplos* occurred probably during the quadrennial Panathenaia of 302/1, and in 299/8 Lysimachos, a Macedonian rival to Demetrios, sent to Athens a new mast and yard for the ship carrying the *peplos* in the Panathenaic procession, surely to replace those damaged three years earlier (*IG* II² 657).[65] This was a shrewd diplomatic maneuver by Lysimachos: a benefaction to Athens but also, perhaps, a warning to the Athenians in this period of neutrality and independence not to align themselves with those impiously honoring Demetrios.[66]

Lysimachos' sending of the equipment for the *peplos* was orchestrated by Philippides of Kephale (*APF* 14356), the comic poet who wrote the lines critical of Stratocles. In 283/2 Philippides was honored by the state for his *agōnothesia* and other contributions to the state:[67]

Whereas,

> Philippides has continually on every occasion shown his goodwill toward the Demos, and

---

65. On the ship-cart of the Panathenaic procession, see Robertson 1985, 290–95: Norman 1983.

66. On Lysimachos' sending of the mast and yard as part of his diplomacy, see Lund 1992, 85–87; Norman 1983.

67. On Philippides and *IG* II² 657, see Shear 1978, *passim* but esp. 94–95.

having gone to stay with king Lysimachos and beforehand having talked with the king, brought back to the Demos a gift of 10,000 *medimnoi* of grain that were distributed to all Athenians in the archonship of Euktemon (299/8), and

spoke (with the king) also about the yard and mast so that they might be given to the goddess for her *peplos* for the Panathenaia, and these things were brought in the archonship of Euktemon, and

when king Lysimachos won the battle at Ipsos against Antigonos and Demetrios (301), Philippides buried at his own expense those of our citizens who died in battle, and he indicated to the king those who were prisoners and secured release for them, and he arranged that those who wished to campaign be registered in military units, and those who chose to leave he clothed and from his own funds gave traveling money and sent each of them, more than 300, where each wished to go, and

he asked that those of the citizens who had been caught in Asia, restrained by Demetrios and Antigonos, also be released, and

he continues to help the Athenians he meets as each one asks him, and

after the Demos got its freedom he has continued saying and doing what is beneficial for the safety of the city, inviting the king to help with money and grain, so that the Demos may continue to be free and may recover Piraeus and the forts as quickly as possible, . . . and

he first prepared an additional contest for Demeter and Kore as a memorial [of the freedom] of the Demos, . . .

It has been decided to praise Philippides, son of Philocles, of Kephale because of the virtue and goodwill which he continues to have concerning the Demos of the Athenians, and to crown him with a gold crown in accordance with the law, and to announce the crown at the contest of the tragedies of the Great Dionysia, and to erect a bronze statue of him in the theater, and that he and his eldest descendant be given dining privileges in the Prytaneion and front seating in all the contests which the city holds. (*IG* II² 657.8–66)

These honors were voted for Philippides in 283/2, four years after the final ouster of Demetrios Poliorcetes and "the restoration of the democracy." The previous year (284/3) Philippides had taken on the *agōnothesia* (lines 38–50), and, apart from contributing his own money and administering the various contests of the dramatic and literary festivals, introduced a new contest, for Demeter and Kore, to celebrate the restoration of freedom.

IG II² 657, the honors of Philippides, well represents the nexus of religion, literature, and domestic and international politics in the period. The pro-democratic comic poet who, in his play, attacked Stratocles for impiously honoring Demetrios also courted, in exile, a Macedonian rival to the king—through him making a gesture, the sending of a new mast and yard for the Panathenaia, which, like his poetry, pointed to the impiety of the party serving Demetrios. The same man, after the ouster of Demetrios, used his *agōnothesia* to celebrate, in a religious setting, the ouster of Demetrios and the restoration of democracy. Religion was being used in a variety of ways for political purposes, but this certainly was not unique to this decade or to the Hellenistic age. Religion had been similarly manipulated both for and against Peisistratos in the sixth century and Pericles in the fifth. But now there was a new focus, the divine honors, clearly thought to be impious, awarded to Demetrios Poliorcetes, as well as new players, at an international level of competition. Foreign potentates were now attempting to manipulate Athenian cult.

In the overall judgment of the divine honors awarded to Demetrios, Plutarch's verdict is a good guide:

> For kings and potentates the worst evidence of the goodwill of the masses is excessive honors. The beauty of honors lies in the free choice of those who give them, but fear (of the kings and potentates) takes away trust in them. For people both in fear and in affection vote the same honors. Therefore sensible (kings) look not at statues and paintings and deifications but rather at their own deeds and activities and then either trust (in the awards) as honors or distrust them as the results of compulsion, because peoples, in the honors themselves, often hate those who receive them immoderately, ostentatiously, and from unwilling (givers). (Plut. *Dem*. 30.4–5)

The evidence, mostly from Plutarch, suggests that the Athenians willingly and enthusiastically gave such divine honors to Demetrios in 307/6. Thereafter, with the support of Stratocles and his party, Demetrios, it appears, did receive such honors "immoderately and ostentatiously" and began to act as the god he thought the Athenians had made him. We may suspect that the later honors to Demetrios, promoted by a small group of powerful partisans, were in fact ratified by many Athenians who were unwilling but afraid. The honors given to Demetrios became a travesty, in part because of Demetrios' immoderate reaction to them, in part because of his supporters' encouragement. The next government and the next Antigonid, Antigonos Gonatas, would react quite differently, and ruler cult would soon fade in importance in the religion of Hellenistic Athens.

The divine Demetrios understandably dominates the religious history of his period, but we must note also other developments of the time, most occasioned by actions of the human Demetrios. Alexander had given the neighboring Oropos and its sanctuary of the healing god Amphiaraos to Athens in 335, and in chapter 1 we surveyed the resulting burst of Athenian activity there in both a building and a festival program. After the Lamian War (322) Athens lost Oropos. In 304/3 Demetrios may have returned it to Athens, but, if so, Athens had lost it again by 287/6 and was not to regain control until the first century.[68] After 322 some Athenians, apparently closed off from Amphiaraos' neighboring sanctuary, founded at Rhamnous on the northeast coast of Attica their own Amphiaraion, with the new Amphiaraos eventually supplanting a preexisting Physician Hero (*iatros heros*).[69] For the Rhamnousian Amphiaraos there survive an altar (*SEG* 33.201) and private dedications (*SEG* 31.177; *IG* II² 4452 and perhaps 4426), as well as remains of the sanctuary, all dating to the late fourth and third centuries B.C. By the late third century the sanctuary was in disrepair: the "house" had lost its door and roof tiles were broken, part of the wall had collapsed and the god's "table" was broken, and the "stoa" was in danger of collapse. Then twenty-three Amphieraistai—all Athenians and many of them from Rhamnous, several of them military officers and soldiers stationed there—contributed money for the repairs and for sacrifices (*IG* II² 1322).[70] Around 300 this Ramnousian Amphiaraion was quite small and, apparently, not a great success. It could replace the Oropian Amphiaraion for only a small group of Athenians. The loss or the threatened loss of the Oropian Amphiaraion may at least partially explain renewed interest in Amphiaraos' rival healing deity, Asclepios. Also around 300 the central area of the City Asclepieion was remodeled with the construction of a new Doric stoa (*IG* II² 1685),[71] and, for the first time, a *kanēphoros* ("basket carrier") is attested for the Epidauria (*IG* II² 3457), a role henceforth often given to a relative of the priest.[72]

Conditions in and access to Piraeus must have varied considerably during these twenty years. For most of the time a Macedonian force

68. Ameling 1989; Robert 1960, 200–203.

69. On the various Attic Physician Heroes, see Kearns 1989, 14–21, 171–72.

70. On these texts and *IG* II² 1322 and on the sanctuary in general, see Petrakos 1981, 1983; Pouilloux 1954, 93–102, 144–47. See also chapter 5, p. 150.

71. On *IG* II² 1685 and the Doric stoa in the Asclepieion, see Aleshire 1989, 27, 34–35; 1991, 13–32. On these Amphieraistai, see chapter 5, p. 150.

72. On the Asclepian *kanēphoroi*, see Aleshire 1989, 90–92.

garrisoned the Mounichion Hill, and for many of the years, especially in times of hostility, Piraeus was no doubt closed off to Athenians from the city. That is reflected in the religious record. The only "state" religious event that survives on record for the period is a celebration of the Dionysia planned there in 307/6 (*IG* II² 456.32–33). Religious and political institutions in Piraeus must have taken a battering because from 307/6 until after ca. 261 the surviving inscriptions from the Piraeus record religious activities only of foreign, not state cults.[73]

The Citian *thiasōtai* (foreign members of a cult association)[74] of Aphrodite Ourania, whose cult was established, as we have seen in chapter 1, under Lycourgos in 333/2, continued to prosper, and in the years 302/1–300/299 they were able to stage a procession for their Adonia, to sacrifice regularly to their Aphrodite and other ancestral gods, to make a dedication to Demeter Homonoia ("Concord," an apt epithet, given the political circumstances), and to reward their fellow member Stephanos, the breastplate maker, with crowns and forty drachmas for a dedication for his services to the association (*IG* II² 1261). In 301/0 another Citian *thiasos*, that of Tynabos, honored its (Citian) *epimelētai* (*IG* II² 1262).[75] In 299/8 the *thiasōtai* of the Carian Zeus Labraundos, here first attested in Attica, were even able to complete the building of a colonnade and gable in their sanctuary, largely through the contributions of their treasurer Menis of Heracleia, himself in all likelihood a Carian (*IG* II² 1271). And, finally, in 300/299, a *thiasos* of an unknown deity, on the motion of a Cyprian from Salamis, honored the Olynthian Demetrios for his services (*IG* II² 1263). Each of these *thiasoi* had its own sanctuary, and each could employ Athenian formulaic language in its decrees, but there is no evidence that any had, as yet, Athenian members.[76] The turmoil in Piraeus, it would seem, did not affect foreign cults as much as it did the local, indigenous state cults.

Demetrios Poliorcetes and his Athenian partisans were responsible for the turmoil in some of the major cults of the state during these years, and in the next chapter we shall examine Athenian efforts in subsequent years to repair the damage. We close this chapter of Athenian religious

73. For the date of *IG* II² 1214, see Garland 1987, 227.
74. For the terms *thiasōtai* and *thiasos*, see chapter 5, pp. 141–42.
75. For the correct name—"Tynabos," not "Tynaros"—see Tracy 1995, 145–46.
76. For a more complete survey of these and other private religious associations in the period, see chapter 5.

history, however, with two events which marked the end of Demetrios' control over Athens in 288/7 and his departure thereafter. In accord with the times and the political situation, one has only local, the other international significance.

When in 287 Olympiodoros led the successful Athenian assault on Demetrios' Macedonian garrison on the Mouseion Hill, Leocritos, son of Protarchos (*PA* 9096) first scaled the fortifications but was soon killed in the battle. "Other honors came to him from the Athenians, and they dedicated his shield to Zeus Eleutherios, having inscribed on it Leocritos' name and his success" (Paus. 1.26.2). In 307/6 Demetrios had been welcomed to Athens and made a divine Soter in part because he brought *eleutheria* ("freedom") to the city. After years of oligarchy supported or caused by the same Demetrios, the Athenians dedicated to Zeus Eleutherios the shield of a hero who fell in the battle that freed the city Athens from his domination.[77]

On the international level the Epirote king Pyrrhos, coming at Athens' request in 287/6 with his army to assist against Demetrios, arrived just after the departure of Demetrios. He spent only one day in the city, and, according to Plutarch (*Pyrrh.* 12.4), he climbed the Acropolis and sacrificed to Athena Polias. This was, in religious terms, a wholly appropriate gesture to mark the end of the rule of Demetrios. The goddess whose cult he had so abused was, on his overthrow, at last given her due honor.

77. On the relationship of Demetrios Soter, Zeus Soter, and Zeus Eleutherios, see chapter 4, pp. 110–13.

4

The Calm between the Storms

From the ouster of Demetrios Poliorcetes in 287/6 to the outbreak of the Chremonidean War (ca. 267/6), the Athenians devoted attention to repairing and in some cases remodeling cults, deities, and festivals that had suffered under Demetrios. The divine Demetrios, with the help of his Athenian partisans, had insinuated himself into several major cults—for example, of Athena Polias, Dionysos Eleuthereus, and Demeter of Eleusis—and we shall see indications, primarily from epigraphical texts, that the Athenians worked to repair, to "de-Demetricize" these cults. The results were not, however, simply a restoration of the cults to their Lycourgan form. The twenty years of the divine Demetrios had their effect. Nor were reforms always immediate, in part because in 287/6 Demetrios surrendered only the city Athens: he retained control of Piraeus, Phyle, Panacton, Sounion, Rhamnous, Salamis, and Eleusis. Athens recovered Eleusis by 284/3, but Piraeus probably not until 229.[1] And, finally, the restoration of the cults was disrupted with the outbreak of the Chremonidean War ca. 267/6 and the resulting defeat and renewed subjugation to Macedonian power.

In 287/6 some cults must have been in shambles. Athena Polias had seen her sanctuary desecrated by Demetrios during his "residence" in

---

1. On Piraeus, see Garland 1987, 50–52; Habicht 1979, 95–112. For differing views on Athens' recovery of Piraeus in this period, see Gauthier 1979; Shear 1978, 79. For a full summary of the differing views of the date(s) of the recovery of Piraeus by the Athenians, see Taylor 1993, 214–26.

304/3 and her dedications stolen by Lachares in 295/4. The goddess had been ineffectual in protecting even her own property. Her sanctity had been violated and her cult, perhaps even her cult statue, stripped, all with apparent impunity. The Epirote king Pyrrhos, appropriately, commemorated the departure of Demetrios with a sacrifice to Athena Polias on the Acropolis, but this may mark not restoration but the beginning of a period of uncertainty and decline for her cult.

Demetrios had styled himself as Dionysos, and up to 288/7 the Demetrieia may have formed a major part of the City Dionysia in honor of Dionysos Eleuthereus. In 287/6 the status of the Eleusinian Mysteries, also once "patronized" by Demetrios, must have been quite uncertain. Eleusis was still garrisoned by Demetrios' hostile troops and access to the sanctuary was probably difficult if not impossible. Piraeus was also under Demetrios' control and after so many years of separation from the city was quite probably functioning almost as an independent city, especially in religious matters.[2] And, finally, the great festival of the Soteria, celebrated in honor of Demetrios and his father Antigonos, had to be dealt with. Was this festival to be continued or, more naturally, abolished?

Eleusis may provide an initial, straightforward correlation between religion and politics in the period. Not until after 285 was Demetrios' garrison, now obviously hostile to the Athenians, removed from Eleusis; and it may well be, as Shear (1978, 85) surmises, that before this the Athenians could celebrate neither the Mysteries nor the biennial Eleusinia. In 284/3 Philippides, as *agōnothetēs*, "from his own funds sacrificed the ancestral sacrifices to the gods on behalf of the Demos and [. . .] gave to all Athenians all the [contests], and first prepared an additional contest for Demeter and Kore as a memorial of the [freedom] of the Demos" (*IG* II² 657.40–45).[3] Philippides provided "*all* the contests"—including, no doubt, those of the biennial Eleusinia of 284—and to the contests of that festival he added a new one commemorating Eleusis' freedom from Demetrios.

And then, at the end of the period, in 267/6, just after the outbreak of the Chremonidean War between Athens and Antigonos II Gonatas, the son of Demetrios, the *epimelētai* of the Mysteries were honored by

<hr />

2. Garland 1987, 50. For the effects of isolation on Salamis at the time, see Taylor 1993, 226–44.

3. On *IG* II² 657 see above, chapter 3, pp. 99–101. Shear (1978, 85) notes that this decree honoring Philippides was passed the day before the Mysteries of 283 began.

the state for making sacrifices in the Mysteries at Agrai on behalf of the health and safety of the Boule, the Demos, and the friends of the Athenians; for sacrificing at the Mysteries; and for sacrificing, at their own expense, *sōtēria* to Demeter and Kore on behalf of the Boule and Demos (*IG* II² 661). These *sōtēria* were, quite possibly, in anticipation of the struggle against Antigonos Gonatas. Thus both Eleusis' liberation from Demetrios' forces and the war against Antigonos nearly twenty years later were signaled by religious rites in a sanctuary that had suffered and would suffer more in the future under Macedonian occupation.

In 283/2 the Boule recommended to the Ekklesia that the *astynomoi* ("city managers"), at the time of the procession of Aphrodite Pandemos, "make ready a dove for the purification of the sanctuary, anoint the altars, pitch the roofs, wash the statues, and prepare the purple dye" (*IG* II² 659). The *astynomoi*, who had various responsibilities concerning the cleanliness and repair of public buildings and roads, were to cleanse, ritually and literally, and spruce up the sanctuary in time for the goddess' annual festival. And they were to do this according to the "ancestral traditions." Aphrodite might seem, par excellence, the deity of the most private affairs, and in fact the majority of dedications to her in the fourth century (e.g., *IG* II² 4574–86, 4634, 4635) were made by private citizens.[4] The cult of Aphrodite Ourania in Piraeus, founded by the Citians in Lycourgos' time (above, chapter 1, pp. 30–31), remained, so far as we know, limited to Citians. But after Athens' liberation and the restoration of democracy, new interest in Aphrodite Pandemos, Aphrodite "of all the Demos," is not surprising.[5] Her sanctuary, shared with Peitho ("Persuasion"), was below and south of the Athena Nike bastion of the Acropolis;[6] it had been established, according to Pausanias (1.22.3), by Theseus when he united Attica. Another tradition, sufficiently well known that Philemon could allude to it in a comedy (frag. 3 KA), attributes the foundation to Solon from the proceeds of

4. Similar "private" offerings are attested in the recently discovered fourth-century treasury box of the city Aphrodite Ourania, into which Athenian girls were to deposit one drachma prior to their weddings (Tsakos 1990–91). But "public" was the statue made for Aphrodite by the demesmen of Halai Aixonides (*IG* II² 2820).

5. For a priestess of Aphrodite Pandemos from, perhaps, the late fourth century, see *IG* II² 4596. For his *Colax*, soon after 315, Menander apparently used as a setting a private, monthly (on the fourth day) banquet for Aphrodite Pandemos. Included were prayers, to all the Olympians, for "safety, health, many good things, and everyone's enjoyment of the good things available" (frag. 1 Sandbach, with Sandbach's commentary). On Aphrodite Pandemos see Pirenne-Delforge 1994, 26–34; Graf, 1985, 260–61; Sokolowski, 1964.

6. Pirenne-Delforge 1994, 26–28.

houses of prostitution.[7] The goddess thus had close ties to the unifier of Attica and a founding father of Athenian democracy, both of topical interest in the 280s. *IG* II² 659 would suggest that the Athenians were attempting, in 283/2, to reclaim for democratic and nationalistic purposes the deity whom, in 291/0, they had made the mother of Demetrios Poliorcetes (above, chapter 3, pp. 95–96). And we shall later see that she comes to the fore again when, in 229, the Athenians once again reclaim their independence.

The Panathenaia was the major festival of Athena Polias, celebrated annually at the end of the month Hecatombaion but every fourth year augmented (the Great Panathenaia) with the presentation of the embroidered *peplos* to the goddess and a full program of competitions. In the middle of the fourth century Demosthenes could claim that however chaotically they handled their other affairs, the Athenians always staged on time the Panathenaia and City Dionysia (4.35). In the decade after the ouster of Demetrios we should expect the Great Panathenaia to have been held in 286, 282, and 278. But in the decree which honored Callias of Sphettos (*PA* 7824) it is stated that "the Demos was about to make, [for the first time] from when the *asty* had been recovered, the Panathenaia for Archegetis" (*SEG* 28.60.64–66).[8] From the context and the nature of the arrangements it appears that plans were being laid for the Great Panathenaia of either 282 or 278.[9]

---

7. Ath. 13.569D–F and Harp. s.v. "Πάνδημος Ἀφροδίτη."

8. The restoration of πρῶτον (lines 64–65), suggested by Habicht, has been widely accepted (Shear 1978, 35). Very recently Dreyer 1996, who would have the first post-Demetrian Panathenaia in 286, has proposed the restoration τρίτον ("for the third time").

9. The dating of the first post-Demetrian Great Panathenaia is a complicated problem, hanging in part on the date of the first Ptolemaia celebrated by Ptolemy II in Alexandria. If the first Ptolemaia was held in 282, the Panathenaia may have followed that same year, as Habicht (1992a, 70 = 1994, 142) argues. If, however, the first Ptolemaia was in 279, then, as Shear claims (1978, 35–39), the first post-Demetrian Panathenaia was held in 278. Dreyer (1996) has recently treated in detail the chronology of events of this period, including the restoration of the Panathenaia. He argues that the Athenians would have reinstituted the Panathenaia as quickly as possible after establishing freedom from Demetrios, i.e., in 286, and proposes a new reading of the text of the Callias decree to accomplish this (see above, note 8). I do not find Dryer's arguments for a restoration of the Panathenaia in 286 compelling and will therefore leave the alternatives of 282 or 278.

The problems that Dreyer, Habicht, and Shear introduce about the two *agōnothetai* and the therefore likely celebration of the Panathenaia in 282 may be chimerical. The *athlothetai*, not the *agōnothetai*, were probably in charge of the Panathenaia in the 280s as they were still before 240 (*IG* II² 784). Cf. [Arist.] *Ath. Pol.* 60.1; Nagy 1978. The restoration of an *agōnothetēs* for the Panathenaia in 266/5 (*SEG* 25.186.3) is no more certain than that for the 220s (*SEG* 32.169.2).

The Great Panathenaia, thus, with the "ship-cart" procession and display of the *peplos* and the program of games, had not been held in 286 and perhaps not even in 282; the last celebration was probably in 290. We find, too, that Athena has a new epithet, Archegetis ("Founder").[10] And, further, Callias had negotiated with King Ptolemy of Egypt to provide the "equipment" (ὅπλα)[11] necessary for the *peplos* (66–70). All of this suggests some prior neglect and uncertainty concerning the cult which, at least in the age of Lycourgos, held the center position in state religion. The cost of the Great Panathenaia must have been very large,[12] but there were ways to economize and cost alone hardly seems a sufficient cause for missing one or two celebrations. If in fact the *peplos* was not woven for and presented to Athena during these years, that would be a break in ritual and would indicate a serious rupture in the state's relationship with its patroness. It may have taken the Athenians some years to recover from the *peplos* of 302, which bore, as may have those of succeeding quadrennia, the figures of Demetrios and Antigonos. And that the *peplos*-displaying cart had sat idle for eight or twelve years may explain the need for new equipment.

The new epithet, Archegetis, may also suggest that now the Athenians were searching for a new definition of their patroness.[13] Given the events of recent years, the epithet Polias ("City Protector") may have seemed inappropriate. Archegetis appears at this period linked to industry and the crafts. In 273/2 the prytanists sacrificed to her at the Chalkeia, the annual festival for the artisans of the city (*Agora* XV, #78.16–17).[14] The Athena Archegetis of the Chalkeia has now become the recipient of the Panathenaia. Archegetis and Polias were, of course,

10. On the relative rarity of this epithet, see Shear 1978, 36.

11. On the ὅπλα as hemp ropes used to support the mast of the ship-cart, see Shear 1978, 39–44.

12. The financing of the Panathenaia encountered a crisis ca. 354/3 (Dem. 24.26–29), and the festival's date near the beginning of the fiscal year may always have caused difficulties. Under Lycourgos the Athenians devoted revenues from Nea (wherever that might be) to the annual Panathenaia (Schwenk #17), but in 286/5 that piece of land may not have been accessible to the Athenians. If, as Robert claims (1960), Nea was in Oropos, the revenues would have been lost by 322, perhaps recovered, but then lost again by 286/5. On the financing of the Panathenaia, see Shear 1978, 38–39; Lewis 1959, 246–247.

13. The addition of τῆς πόλεως to Archegetis in *Agora* XV, #78.16–17 of 273/2 may be an indication that the epithet Archegetis is not yet widely known.

14. On the Chalkeia, see Jacoby on *FGrHist* 325 F 18. Jacoby has argued convincingly that the Chalkeia was not the festival of Athena Ergane as usually had been assumed. For the role of Athena Archegetis it may also be significant that centuries later the Roman market was dedicated to her (*IG* II² 3175). See Wycherley 1957, 190.

the same goddess,[15] but the choice of epithets may reveal a change of emphasis. Although Athena's temple continued to be known as that "of Polias" (*IG* II² 686 + 687.44, at outbreak of Chremonidean War), we find no cult document using the epithet Polias until ca. 250 (*IG* II² 776). After 287/6 the much battered Athena was to turn her attention to the industry, not the military defense, of the city. This is not to suggest that the traditional cult practices of Athena Polias were, after 287/6, significantly altered or even that the annual Panathenaia, the celebrations of her birthday, were not held. But now we shall see a new Athena, Soteira, emerging as a partner of Zeus Soter to take over the role of protecting the city as a whole. Clearly Polias had suffered damage under Demetrios and Lachares; for a time, her role in Athens was to be more limited.

There emerges in the city cult of Athens after 287/6 Athena Soteira, first attested in 273/2 (*IG* II² 676), always associated with Zeus Soter. Zeus is the senior in this partnership, and we must look first to his cult. V. J. Rosivach (1987) has, I think, properly sorted out the relationship of Zeus Soter, Athena Soteira, Demetrios and Antigonos as the Soteres, and the festival Soteria after the revolution of 288/7. For much that follows I am indebted to him, but I feel less certainty than he in assigning the texts of the earlier history of Zeus Soter's cult. Problems arise here because there were, at various times, two cults of Soter: one in the city, one in Piraeus.

The cult in Piraeus is well attested for the fourth century, and we have already discussed its nature in the age of Lycourgos (see chapter 1). When Zeus Soter emerges in the city he is certainly, as Rosivach has shown, the Zeus Eleutherios of the Stoa of Zeus in the Agora, whose cult dates at least to the early fifth century. But when did Zeus Eleutherios of the city acquire the epithet Soter? Which of our texts first unmistakably names the Zeus Soter of the city? Most of the fourth-century texts refer explicitly to Zeus Soter of Piraeus or are themselves from Piraeus.[16] Other inscriptions list him among other deities worshipped

---

15. Cf. *IG* II² 4318, which establishes the identity also of Athena Polias and Athena Ergane and casts doubt on DiVita's arguments (1952–54) that there was, from the late fifth century B.C., a *temenos* (and hence cult) of Ergane separate from that of Polias. Ergane seems to reflect an aspect of the goddess more of interest to individuals than to the state. The surviving dedications to her are all from individuals: *IG* I² 561, II² 2939 = 4339, 4318, 4328, 4329, 4334, 4338; *SEG* 25.220; *Hesp.* 9 (1940): 58–59, #7. The unusual and two-stage association of Athena Ergane with the Panathenaia on *IG* II² 4338 may, perhaps, be linked to the new orientation of the restored Panathenaia. On Athena Ergane, see also Ridgway 1992, 137–139.

16. *IG* II² 380, 1669, 4603, 4972. See above, chapter 1, pp. 38–39.

in Piraeus or elsewhere outside the city.[17] Most if not all of these prob-ably belong to Piraeus cult. The references in speeches (Lys. 26.6; Din. 1.36, 3.15) are too brief to locate the cult. But Isocrates indicates with-out question that there was a statue of Zeus Soter in the Agora by 394 (9.57), and this would certainly have stood in the sanctuary of Zeus Eleutherios.[18] There was thus early in the fourth century an identifica-tion, at some level, of Eleutherios and Soter, even though Zeus need not as yet have adopted Soter as an official epithet in the city.

Lycourgos in the *Leocrates* of 330 speaks of the joint sanctuary of Zeus Soter and Athena Soteira in Piraeus (17; cf. 136–37). Athena Soteira and Zeus Soter emerge together in the city cult first in the honors voted for their *epimelētai* in two successive years, 273/2 and 272/1 (*IG* II² 676; *SEG* 16.63). Together they receive a sacrifice, a lectisternium, and, in 272/1, a procession. There is only a single priest, a male, surely that of Zeus. About this time, perhaps also in 272/1, the priest of Zeus Soter was hon-ored by the state for sacrifices which he successfully made to Zeus Soter and Athena Soteira "for the health and safety of the Boule and Demos."[19] The priest had also, apparently, made the Boule's inaugural sacrifices (εἰσιτητήρια) for the safety of the Boule and Demos. That the priest sac-rificed for the "health and safety" of the Boule and Demos is not par-ticularly significant, because in this period, as we shall see, virtually all sacrifices in state cult were expressly for this purpose. If, however, the *eisitētēria* of *IG* II² 689 are those of the Boule, as it appears they are, then Zeus Soter has become very closely linked to this major institu-tion of Athenian democratic government.

We appear to have, then, a "new" or at least remodeled cult of Zeus Soter and Athena Soteira fully established in the city by 273/2, with its annual sacrifice and lectisternium overseen by elected *epimelētai* and with a procession. When did it emerge and why? Its origins are fairly clear. Already in the early fourth century Zeus Soter was identified, to some degree, with Zeus Eleutherios. The Piraeus cult in which Athena Soteira was associated with Zeus Soter would provide the model for bringing an Athena Soteira into the city Zeus Soter cult. As to the reason and the time, I share Rosivach's view that the "new" joint cult in the city

17. Schwenk #21.CEF 13; *IG* II² 410.18–19, 1496.88–89, 118–19. See above, chapter 1, note 79.

18. Cf. Harp. s.v. "ἐλευθέριος Ζεύς." It was beside this statue that a copy of *IG* II² 448, honoring a Sicyonian ally in the Lamian War, was to be erected in 323/2 and reerected 318/7.

19. *IG* II² 689. For the restoration of the date to 272/1, see *SEG* 16.64. Cf. *IG* II² 690.

probably resulted from Athenian attempts, after 287/6, to preserve the festival Soteria but to remove Demetrios and Antigonos from it. Zeus and Athena could now become the Soteres, and the festival could be celebrated in their honor.[20] Athena Polias had become Archegetis, and Athena Soteira along with her father could now assume the role of protecting the *eleutheria* ("freedom") of the city. Before 287/6 Athena Polias had not done this job particularly well, and through this remodeling of cults and festivals the Athenians could reorder the divine assignments. In her new role Athena would have the assistance of—or, better, she would assist—her powerful father, who, as Eleutherios, had always represented and championed Athenian freedom. In religious terms the safety (*sōtēria*) of Athens would no longer depend on Macedonian Soteres. Henceforth Zeus Soter and Athena Soteira of the city would be responsible for the freedom of the city. In a sense, with these developments the primary "state" cult of Athens moved from the Erechtheum to the sanctuary of Zeus Eleutherios, from the Acropolis to the Agora, and we may count this as one of the major religious changes occasioned by the actions, desecrations, and divine honors of Demetrios Poliorcetes.

The priest of Zeus Soter in, perhaps, 272/1 made what appear to be the year's inaugural sacrifices of the Boule (*IG* II² 689.20–23). If in fact Zeus Soter's cult was just coming into an era of new authority, the cults of the Boule were perhaps being modified to accommodate him. Already in the fifth century there was a sanctuary of Zeus Boulaios and Athena Boulaia in the Bouleuterion, and the members of the Boule prayed to them as they entered the building (Antiphon 6.45). Zeus' cult statue there was of wood.[21] Zeus Boulaios and Athena Boulaia, who are clearly a set pair, do not, however, appear amid the Boule's cultic activity from the time of Antiphon until the Roman period.[22] It is quite

20. If this reconstruction is correct, it would also allow the identification of the *Sōteres* in *Agora* XV, #111.4–5 of ca. 240 and #115.12–13 of 235/4 with Zeus and Athena, not Antigonos Monophthalmos and Demetrios Poliorcetes. There would then be no evidence of an Athenian cult of Antigonos and Demetrios as *Sōteres* after 287/6. See Rosivach 1987, 274.

21. Paus. 1.3.5. Pausanias saw in the Bouleuterion also statues of Apollo by Peisias and of Demos by Lyson. Both sculptors are, unfortunately, undatable, but the three statues may be a tableau of the history of the cults of the Boule, with Apollo joining and eventually dominating over Zeus, and with Demos added in the 220s (see chapter 6, pp. 172–78). We need not assume that these three deities shared the cult or were equally prominent throughout the classical and Hellenistic periods.

22. For the restoration of Zeus Boulaios and Athena Boulaia in a text of the second to first century B.C., see *Hesp.* 40 (1971): 96–100, #1. Artemis Boulaia is an equally possible restoration.

likely that in *IG* II² 689 the pair Zeus Boulaios and Athena Boulaia had become Zeus Soter and Athena Soteira; but if so, it was only a momentary phenomenon, not to be attested again for the Boule. Rather, in just this period, Apollo Prostaterios ("Protector") and his sister Artemis Boulaia begin to receive the sacrifices the prytanists made before the meetings of the Ekklesia and, no doubt, the Boule.²³

Agora XV, #78 of 273/2 is a well-preserved and early example of what becomes a long series of decrees in which the prytanists of a tribe or their officials receive a crown from the state for the excellent performance of their duties.²⁴ Such "prytany" decrees are an important source for the religious activities of this and following centuries, and for that reason, and because of its own importance, I offer a translation of *Agora* XV, #78:

In the archonship of Glaucippos (273/2), in the fourth prytany, that of the tribe Antiochis, for which Euthoinos son of [Euthycritos] of the deme Myrrhinous was secretary, on the twenty-ninth of Pyanopsion, [an Ekklesia]. Of the presiding officers Hegesilochos, son of Cephisodotos, of the deme Piraeus and his fellow officers brought the vote. The Demos decided. Euthymachos, son of Euthippos, of the deme Xypete made the proposal:
    Concerning what the prytanists of Antiochis report about the sacrifices which they were making before meetings of the Ekklesia to Apollo Prostaterios and the other gods to whom it was traditional to sacrifice, and they sacrificed also the Stenia at their own expense to Demeter and Kore on behalf of the [Boule] and the Demos, with good fortune it has been decided by the Demos:
        To accept the [good things] which they say occurred in the sacrifices which they were sacrificing for the health and safety of the Boule and Demos of the Athenians and of all others who are well intentioned to the Demos.

And since the prytanists [sacrificed] the appropriate sacrifices well and generously and took care of all the other things which the laws and decrees of the Demos assigned [them],
    To praise the prytanists of Antiochis and to crown them with a gold crown in accordance with the [law] because of their piety toward the gods and their generosity toward the Demos of the Athenians.

23. For an altar of Artemis Boulaia in the Agora near the Tholos, see Wycherley 1957, #118.
24. On these texts and their characteristics, see Dow 1937b and *Agora* XV. Such honors had been voted by the Ekklesia already in the fifth and fourth centuries, but only after 307/6 was the full decree, with descriptions of religious activities, inscribed on the stone. The better preserved examples of full decrees before *Agora* XV, #78 are #69 of 284/3 and #71 of 283/2.

And so that they may sacrifice also the Chalkeia to Athena Archegetis of the city and so that the relations [to the gods] may be good and pious for the Boule and the Demos, the Demos is to vote how much money it is necessary to dispense to them for the [administration of the sacrifice]. What the Demos decides to vote for, [the treasurer of the stratiotic fund] and those in charge of the administration are to dispense. And the revenue is to be from the money [spent for decrees] by the Boule. And [the secretary for the] prytany is to inscribe this [decree] on a stone stele and erect it [in the Prytaneion. And for the inscription] of the stele those in charge of the administration are to dispense [the expense that occurs].

For those still inclined to question the vivacity of Athenian state cult in the Hellenistic period, it is worth emphasizing how much importance is attributed to the religious duties and contributions of these fifty government officials in this, one of the first and best preserved of the prytany decrees. The language of the text was to become formulaic for centuries, but such is the nature of the Athenian official prose style for all subjects. The formulaic language should not, of itself, lead us to question the importance or significance of these activities now or later.

The sacrifices to Apollo Prostaterios and the other gods before legislative meetings are clearly already routine, and we shall return to these. Two provisions appear specific to these prytanists: that they sacrificed the Stenia to Demeter and Kore at their own expense, and that they be allocated funds to sacrifice the Chalkeia to Athena Archegetis. What little is known of the Stenia indicates that it was a women's festival, held at Eleusis on Pyanopsion 9 and featuring a night banquet characterized by the trading of insults.[25] It is known from the fifth century (Ar. *Thesm.* 834, of 411), appears in this text, and then first reappears in a probable restoration of a prytany decree of 140/39 (*Agora* XV, #240.9–10). There may have been local celebrations of the festival, as for the Thesmophoria, but the celebration at Eleusis—no doubt the major, state one—was quite probably impossible during the Macedonian occupation. *Agora* XV, #78, passed just twenty days after the festival, may suggest a time of revival for this festival at Eleusis, in part through the prytanists' generosity, after the recovery of Eleusis ca. 285. Presumably the prytanists paid for the victim that would, duly sacrificed, serve as the entrée for the women's banquet.[26]

25. Deubner 1932, 52–53.
26. If the restorations of *Agora* XV, #240.9 are correct, the victim in *Agora* XV, #78 was probably a cow ($\dot{\epsilon}\beta o \upsilon \theta \dot{\upsilon} \tau \eta \sigma a \nu$), an expensive offering worthy of mention in the decree.

Only one day after the decree was passed, on Pyanopsion 30, the Chalkeia was held. The timing indicates last minute and, since the budget for the festival was still undecided, somewhat chaotic preparation. The Chalkeia, too, was an established festival of the fifth century (Soph. frag. 760 Nauck) which, in 273/2, required some ad hoc financing. The role of the prytanists in this festival, here first securely attested,[27] may have continued. The festival has been restored in a prytany decree of 118/7 (*Agora* XV, #253.9–10; cf. *IG* II² 990).

That the Stenia and Chalkeia do not appear in prytany decrees from 273/2 until well into the second century B.C. probably results not from the temporary demise of these festivals but from their being subsumed under "the traditional sacrifices" that the prytanists of the month Pyanopsion made. In most years, unlike in 273/2, the prytanists' activity in regard to these festivals would have been routine. Only financial needs and extraordinary measures to meet them dictated their mention then.

In *Agora* XV, #78.6 of 273/2, Apollo Prostaterios first emerges as the deity who receives the prytanists' sacrifice before meetings of the Ekklesia. To him are added "the other gods to whom it was traditional to sacrifice." By 254/3 his sister Artemis, as Boulaia, has joined him in this role (*Agora* XV, #89.8), and henceforth they are regularly paired in the pyrtany decrees.[28] Apollo Prostaterios first appears in the Athenian tradition in a collection of oracles inserted into the text of the speech that Demosthenes prepared against Meidias in 348 (21.52–53). There are at least four oracles, coming from both Delphi and Dodona.[29] The second, seemingly from Delphi, orders the Athenians "for health to sacrifice and pray to Zeus Hypatos, Heracles, and Apollo Prostaterios; for good fortune to Apollo Agyieus, Leto, and Artemis."[30] Heracles was, of course, worshipped throughout Attica, and Zeus Hypatos received an annual sacrifice from the Marathonian Tetrapolis in the fourth century (*IG* II² 1358, col. 2.13). The oracle from Demosthenes, if genuine here, makes a fourth century B.C. cult of Apollo Prostaterios likely. Given the context and the source, it is probable that this Apollo Prostaterios was none other than Apollo Pythios, the Apollo of Delphi.

27. *Agora* XV, #70, which also records the prytanists' sacrifice of the Chalkeia, is dated ca. 290–275.

28. Dow 1937b, 8. Artemis Boulaia has been restored in *Agora* XV, #87.11 of mid–to late third century B.C. For an altar of Artemis Boulaia, ca. 220, see Wycherley 1957, #118.

29. On these oracles, see MacDowell 1990, 270–75; Fontenrose, 1978, 253.

30. Parts of these oracles may be abbreviated forms of the oracles given also in Dem. 43.66, which concern an unfavorable portent.

It is certainly possible that the prytanists had always, or at least since the fourth century, made such sacrifices to Apollo Prostaterios but that Apollo becomes known only when the prytanists first begin to record their sacrifices in the prytany decrees. Apollo may, however, have been given prominence first now, after the Athenians in 279 reconciled with the Aetolians and reestablished, after decades, ties to Delphi.[31] One may also assume that Zeus Boulaios/Athena Boulaia, Zeus Soter/Athena Soteira, and Apollo Prostaterios/Artemis Boulaia all maintained their own, somewhat distinctive roles in the cults of the Boule and Ekklesia throughout this period; another possibility, as I suggest, is that after a period of uncertainty and rivalry between the pairs, Apollo Prostaterios/ Artemis Boulaia emerge as the chief deities and the others fall into the category of "the other gods" who also receive sacrifices. If my suggestion is correct, this development would be a further indication of Athena's diminished importance in state cult. Athena has lost her role in the protection of the state as a whole to Zeus Soter and as Archegetis was tending primarily to industry and the handicrafts. In the cults of the Boule and Ekklesia her role of Boulaia/Soteria was lost to Artemis Boulaia, the junior partner of Apollo Prostaterios. If this development, admittedly hypothetical, is correctly proposed, it can be the result largely of the maltreatment of her cult by Demetrios Poliorcetes and his Athenian supporters and by the thug Lachares.

After 287/6 the Athenians also quickly removed Demetrian elements from the City Dionysia. Demetrieia, incorporated into the City Dionysia in 295/4 (chapter 3, pp. 92–94), disappears from the festival's name as early as 285/4 (*IG* II² 653.36–38, 654.41–43).[32] The City Dionysia is then attested or expected for 284/3 (*IG* II² 654.41–43), 283/2 (*IG* II² 657.61–63; *SEG* 25.89.12–13), 282/1 (*IG* II² 3079 + 668), 279/8 (*IG* II² 2853), 271/0 (*IG* II² 3083), 270/69 (*SEG* 28.60.92–94; *IG* II² 3081), and was doubtless held also in the intervening years.

But here too there may have been a change in the festival. Since the end of the fourth century it had been the practice to announce "in the competition of the tragedies" the honor of a crown given to an individual for some service or other. In the Callias decree of 270/69 (*SEG* 28.60.92–94) is the earliest appearance of the wording, "in the *new* competition of tragedies of the Great Dionysia."[33] In 385 the production of

---

31. On the reconciliation, see Habicht 1979, 87–94.
32. Habicht 1956, 53.
33. Peppas-Delmousou (1984) first recognized the significance of this phrase. τῶι καινῶι ἀγῶνι has been restored in *IG* II² 692.11–12 and 708.5–6, both from the first half of the

an old tragedy had been introduced into the City Dionysia, and the practice apparently became regular after 341.[34] The phrase "in the *new* competition of tragedies" has been taken to mean "in the competition of *new* tragedies," to distinguish it from the competition of *old* tragedies.[35] That may be correct, but it requires an awkward reading of the Greek. It may rather be that since 283/2, when honors were, as usual, to be announced "in the competition of the tragedies of the Great Dionysia" (*IG* II² 657.61–63),[36] a change had occurred. The Athenians either redesigned the competitions of the post-Demetrian Dionysia or, at the least, now first began in these texts to distinguish between the competitions of old and new tragedies. Henceforth that distinction is usually maintained.[37] In any case, "the new competition" suggests that changes, actual or conceptual, were made in the City Dionysia between 283/2 and 270/69, and this may have been the result of restructuring the festival after the removal of the "new" Dionysos, Demetrios Poliorcetes.

A further, major change occurred for the personnel of the City Dionysia by 278/7 when, for the first time, we learn of the existence of an Athenian guild or corporation of *technītai* ("artists" or "craftsmen") of Dionysos.[38] In *IG* II² 1132.1–39 the Amphictionic Council of Delphi guarantees to these *technītai* safe passage and freedom from taxes and military service as they travel the Greek world to participate in festivals.

At Athens in the early period of the City Dionysia the actors and choruses of tragedy and comedy, the choruses of the dithyramb, and virtually all the *chorēgoi* had been Athenian citizens. The poets too, except for the writers of dithyrambs, were Athenians. Apart from the musicians all the participants were Athenians, writing and performing for their fellow Athenians, celebrating the local festival of an Athenian Dionysos. And the plays themselves, at least in performance, were indissolubly bound to the city's Dionysiac festivals. Foreigners could and did attend the City Dionysia, however, and quite early the fame of

---

third century B.C. but not more closely dated. The phrase reappears first in *IG* II² 682.75–77 of ca. 255/4. Henry (1992) dates *IG* II² 682 to 259/8, but the matter is uncertain. For later examples of the phrase, see *IG* II² 1299.31; *SEG* 25.106.37–38; *IG* II² 983.2–3, 891.13–14; *SEG* 21.435.5–6; *IG* II² 1223.6, 957.19. See also Pickard-Cambridge 1988, 361–62.

34. Pickard-Cambridge 1988, 124.

35. It certainly appears to mean this in later times. Compare *IG* II² 956.33–34 of 161/0, 957.19 of 157/6, and 958.29–30 of 153/2. For the dates, see Bugh 1990.

36. Cf. *IG* II² 555.6–7 (ca. 305), 646.29–31 (of 295/4), 653.37–38 and 654.41–43 of 285/4.

37. See note 33 above.

38. On all matters of actors, guilds, and the City Dionysia, see Ghiron-Bistagne 1976 and Pickard-Cambridge 1988, 279–321, to both of which I am much indebted.

Athenian drama and dramatic poets drew international attention. The texts of some plays no doubt soon circulated far beyond Athens. Already ca. 476 Aeschylus visited the court of Hieron in Sicily, and in 456 he returned to Gela where he died. At the end of his career Euripides was enticed to the court of King Archelaos of Macedon where, in 406, he too died. We may also recall that the comic poet Philippides of Kephale was a guest and influential friend of King Lysimachos and in 283/2 was rewarded by the Athenians for his efforts on their behalf (chapter 3, pp. 99–101). During their various visits Aeschylus certainly and Euripides and Philippides probably wrote plays and assisted in staging productions. But none of this need have had much effect, except for the loss of talent, on the religious nature of the City Dionysia in Athens.

We may suspect, however, a change of atmosphere when the actors became to a degree divorced from the audience and the community, when they became thoroughly professional and, individually or in groups, traveled an international circuit, performing in festivals of other countries or even in purely secular productions. Henceforth for them the Athenian City Dionysia was just one, however important, stop on the circuit.[39] The increasing professionalism and cosmopolitanism of the poets and actors must have made the competitions of the City Dionysia, even more than they had been in the fifth century, a source of entertainment rather than of religious feeling for the assembled citizenry. Ordinary fellow citizens, neighbors, would no longer be performing and addressing the particular concerns of their state. Other changes may also have contributed to distancing the Athenian audience from the dramatic presentations. From the times of the reforms under Demetrios of Phaleron (317–307), only one Athenian each year, the *agōnothetēs*, took responsibility for the dramatic competitions; no longer were twenty-eight wealthy Athenians involved, financially and emo-

---

39. Because the Athenians did not give the demotics or ethnics on the lists of victorious actors in the City Dionysia or Lenaia, it is impossible to determine with certainty whether foreign actors regularly performed in these festivals as they did at those at Delphi and Delos. From the catalogue in Ghiron-Bistagne (1976, 301–64, see which for references), foreign actors known to have acted in the Athenian dramatic competitions are Mynniscos of Chalcis in the third quarter of the fifth century; Aristodemos of Metapontum, Neoptolemos of Scyros, Lycon of Scarpheia, Archias of Thurii, and Aristodemos of Scarpheia from the fourth century; and from the 270s Philonides of Zacynthos, Autolochos of Aetolia, Callicles of Boeotia, and Lyciscos of Cephallenia. Some of these foreign actors came from cities neighboring Athens or with close political ties to her, and many were probably metics or naturalized citizens whose primary residence was in Athens. See Ghiron-Bistagne 1976, 176–77.

tionally, in each year's productions. We might imagine the audience now less as participants (actual or psychological) than as spectators at an event presented by the *agōnothetēs* and the government. We also see that by the last quarter of the fourth century several of the prominent comic poets—for example, Alexis of Thurii and Philemon of Syracuse—were no longer born Athenians.[40]

At the end of the classical and throughout the Hellenistic period we can see tragedy and comedy progressing, if that is the word, from genres intimately tied to Athenian Dionysiac festivals to a form of entertainment suited to many occasions. At Athens it never reached the point at which it is found in Rome—where, for example, in the 160s Terence's *Hecyra* could be produced at the Ludi Megalenses, the funeral games of L. Aemilius Paullus, and the Ludi Romani, during which audiences were lost to a ropewalker and bear acts (prologue to Ter. *Hec.*). But, as such developments were occurring outside of Athens and Athenian actors were contributing to them, the effect was no doubt felt in Athens.

Macedon's influence was important, perhaps decisive also in this area of Athenian and Greek religion. Macedonian kings and nobility from early days clearly had a taste for Athenian drama and sought out poets, actors, and other performers. Euripides had left Athens for the court of Archelaos, and Philippides stayed with Lysimachos. By the middle of the fourth century the Athenian actors Neoptolemos, originally of Scyros (*PA* 10647), and Aristodemos, originally of Metapontum, were making extended stays at Philip's court and assisting Athens in her negotiations with him.[41] As actors they apparently had the right of safe passage (Dem. 5.6). After Philip took Olynthus in 348 he held an "Olympian" festival and provided *technītai* for the sacrifice and the night festival, himself crowning the victors. Demosthenes (19.192–95) reports that at a sym-

---

40. Foreign tragedians were common in the fifth century (Pratinas and his son Aristias of Phlius, Achaios of Syracuse, and Ion of Chios) but infrequent in the fourth (Dionysios the tyrant of Syracuse [a special case] and Phanostratos of Halicarnassos). No foreign tragic poet is recorded as winning a prize in the City Dionysia or Lenaia after 306.

All poets of Old Comedy were, apparently, Athenians, but numerous foreigners won prizes in Middle and New Comedy, including Anaxandrides of Rhodes (victories in Dionysia and Lenaia, 376–352); Alexis of Thurii (Dionysia, 347) and Philemon of Syracuse (Dionysia in 327, Lenaia in 306); from the 280s Diodoros of Sinope (Lenaia, 284) and Phoinicides of Megara (Lenaia, 285); and thereafter, in the City Dionysia of 254, Diodoros' brother Diphilos. At least some of these foreign poets (e.g., Philemon and Diodoros) were given Athenian citizenship.

For the careers of these poets and the sources, see Mette 1977, 200–204, 211–18; Austin 1974.

41. Dem. 5.6, 18.21, 19.12, 18, 94, 315; Aeschines 2.15–16.

posium on this occasion, the comic actor Satyros personally and successfully intervened with Philip on behalf of some girls captured at Olynthos.[42] Demosthenes treats the performance of actors in a non-Dionysiac, non-Athenian, ad hoc occasion at the request of the king of Macedon as routine. Later, in 336, the same Neoptolemos recited lines from tragedy at the festival Philip held in Aegae to celebrate the marriage of his daughter Cleopatra.[43] After his capture of Thebes in 335 Alexander held at Dion a nine-day festival, originally instituted by Archelaos, with dramatic competitions for Zeus and the Muses,[44] and did the same after taking Tyre in 332. In the Tyrian festival the actors Thettalos and Athenodoros participated.[45] To be there the Athenian Athenodoros had skipped his own City Dionysia. Thettalos, much to Alexander's dismay, was defeated by Athenodoros, but Alexander nonetheless paid the fine the Athenians levied on their fellow citizen for missing their festival (Plut. *Alex.* 29, *Mor.* 334D–E). Thettalos and Athenodoros as well as Aristocritos and the comic actors Lycon, Phormion, and Ariston also participated in the festival accompanying Alexander's wedding in Susa.[46]

These are but a few examples of a new type of "religious" festival, instituted by the Macedonians, which celebrated a military victory, a marriage, or another noteworthy occasion and contained, among other elements, musical and dramatic performances. Athenian actors, apparently still as freelancing individuals, participated widely, and Athens' measures to secure their services even for the City Dionysia were not always successful. Unlike the circulation of the plays and even of the poets, the international movement and experience of the actors would very likely have affected the atmosphere of the City Dionysia itself, changing it from the purely civic event it had once been.

By 278/7 actors and poets centered in Athens had organized themselves into a corporation. The Amphictiones of Delphi grant the Athenian *technītai* of Dionysos safe passage and safety for their property in times of war and peace, exemption from taxes and military service, for all time and among all Greeks, "so that the honors and sacrifices to which

42. Cf. Diod. 16.55.1–4.

43. Diod. 16.92.3–5; Stob. *Flor.* 98.70; Suet. *Calig.* 57.

44. Diod. 17.16.3–4; Arrian 1.11.1.

45. Presumably this is the Thettalos who won victories in the City Dionysia in the 340s (*IG* II² 2318.282, 315; *IG* II² 2319. 4, 9, 14, 27, 29; Pickard-Cambridge 1988, 120; Ghiron-Bistagne 1976, 330–31). Athenodoros won victories at the City Dionysia in the 340s also (*IG* II² 2318.291, 360; Ghiron-Bistagne 1976, 307).

46. Chares, cited in Ath. 12.538B–539A. Comic actors named Lycon and Phormion won victories at the Lenaia ca. 375 (*IG* II² 2325.195, 198), and the Lycon and Phormion of Ath. 12.539A may be their sons.

the *technītai* are assigned may be performed at the appropriate times" (*IG* II² 1132.15–17). The representatives of the guild to the Amphictiones were the Athenian tragic poet Astydamas and the tragic actor Neoptolemos. The text of the decree was to be set up at both Athens and Delphi, and copies of both happen to survive.[47] It is worth stressing that the avowed purpose of the decree is religious, to have *technītai* available for religious festivals and, more generally, "for the sake of piety toward the gods" (lines 32–33).

A Euboean decree of ca. 294–288 contains detailed provisions for a festival but makes no allusion to a guild of *technītai*.[48] The Athenian guild was thus probably formed in the years between the Euboean decree and 278/7. It then soon faced competition from a similar guild, the Isthmian-Nemean. The Amphictionic Council may have chosen this time to recognize the Athenian guild in order to secure its participation in the Soteria, a new Delphic festival commemorating victory over the Gauls. A guild of *technītai*, probably the Isthmian-Nemean, under the leadership of their priest Aristarchos of Hermione, "donated the *whole* competition to the god (Apollo) and the Amphictiones for the Soteria." This festival typically required sixty *technītai* of various specialties, including three teams each for tragedy and comedy. The inscriptions of the Amphictionic Soteria list 251 different artists, 29 of them from Athens.[49] It appears that the guild took full responsibility for the musical competitions, providing this component of the festival essentially prepackaged for their clients. The sacrifices would be the responsibility of the client. Presumably the occasion or even the deity would make little difference to the *technītai*. Given the availability of the competitions as a package, it is not surprising to find several new festivals appearing in the Greek world under the patronage of rich kings in the later third century. It is noteworthy, however, that there is no evidence of such guild activity or of the sudden appearance of such new festivals *in* Athens. The guild of Dionysiac *technītai* was an Athenian export. For the City Dionysia, the ultimate origin of such guilds, Athenians evidently secured the artists' participation on an individual basis. In this, as in other areas, Athenian state cult was conservative, lagging behind religious developments occurring elsewhere in the Greek world.[50]

---

47. *IG* II² 1132.1–39 and *FD* iii.2.#68, 61–94.

48. Pickard-Cambridge 1988, 281–82, 306–8.

49. Pickard-Cambridge 1988, 283–284.

50. It is also a conservative and nationalistic feature that, as Habicht has pointed out to me, membership in the Athenian guild of *technītai* was apparently limited to Athenian citizens.

Moreover, in approximately these years (278/7) the Athenians inscribed on a building in the theater records of victorious poets and actors in the Lenaia and City Dionysia from as far back as 485/4 (*IG* II²
2325).[51] Dina Peppas-Delmousou (1984) has associated these "historical" lists of victors, the "new competition of tragedies," and the appearance of the *technītai* of Dionysos in arguing, persuasively, that after the ouster of Demetrios Poliorcetes the Athenians gave to their
theater a new élan with an antiquarian flavor. As they perhaps formal-
ized a new structure to their festival, as they celebrated, with an inscriptional record, their glorious dramatic past, the Athenians were also
sending their actors in an organized troupe and individually to perform
tragedies and comedies at a wide variety of public and private occasions
throughout the Greek world. If Athens was, in international terms, weak
politically and economically, she could still reassert, for herself and other
Greeks, her literary and cultural predominance.

Itinerant actors not only circulated much of Athenian culture in the Hellenistic world; on their occasional visits to Athens they also surely
brought their experience of the royal courts and of the Hellenistic world
back to Athens. But in Athens of the late fourth and first half of the
third century, the true entry point of what we commonly consider Hellenistic culture was the schools of philosophy. Here we find an extensive international community producing and propounding elaborate
and innovative theories on the nature of the physical world, ethics, logic
and rhetoric, astronomy and astrology, and the history of philosophy.
From just before Athens' liberation from Demetrios Poliorcetes to just
after the Chremonidean War, the careers of major or founding figures
of the four philosophical schools in Athens came to an end: Theophrastos, the successor to Aristotle as the head of the Peripatos, died in 287/6;
Epicouros, the founder of the Garden, in 270; Zeno, the founder of
the Stoa, in 263; and Arcesilaos, a successor to Plato as head of the Academy and founder of the Middle Academy, in 242/1. It seems appropriate, therefore, to survey here the relationship of these philosophers to
the popular religion of their time.

These early Hellenistic philosophers practicing in Athens were concerned primarily with the physical sciences, rhetoric, and ethics, not with
religion and religious topics per se. Hundreds of titles of their books

---

51. See Pickard-Cambridge 1988, 112–20. See also Mette 1977, 159–88; Ghiron-Bistagne
1976, 53–62.

are preserved, primarily in Diogenes Laertios, and only a handful concern "the gods" or "piety."[52] The titles alone, of course, do not give a clear measure of their interests in religion; for example, the fragments indicate that in their books on "physics" they occasionally treated the nature of the gods. Remnants of their theories on the gods and piety do survive, and we find that the gods (or god) of the various philosophical schools differ markedly from one another but are all, like their early precursors in Xenophanes and like Plato's Forms, immortal, immaterial, and transcendent, products of the intellect rather than of the heart. The gods of the different schools stand in distinct contrast to the deities of private and state religion of the time. This is not the place to review the various theories on the gods developed by the four schools, but a few quotations will suffice to make the point. Let us take first the Stoics of Zeno:[53]

God is a living creature, immortal, reasoning, perfect or intelligent in happiness, not admitting of anything evil, concerned with the *kosmos* and the things in the *kosmos*. He is not, however, human in form. He is the maker (δημιουργόν) of the whole and, as it were, the father of all things, both in common and in that part of him that permeates all things. And that part is called, in accord with its powers, by many names. They say he is Dia because all things exist because of (διά) him; they call him Zeus in so far as he is responsible for life (ζῆν) or he pervades life; Athena in regard to the fact that his controlling element extends into the sky (αἰθέρα); Hera because it extends into the air (ἀέρα); Hephaistos because it extends into the creative fire; Poseidon for its extension into the moist; and Demeter for its extension into the earth. (D.L. 7.147)

God is one and *Nous* ("Mind") and fate and Zeus, and he is called many other names. In the beginning, being by himself, he changes all substance through air into water. And just as in generation the seed moves about, so also god, being seminal *logos* ("reason") of the *kosmos*, is left behind in the moist, making matter productive for himself for the generation of external things. Then first he begets the four elements: fire, water, air, and earth. (D.L. 7.135–36)

<hr/>

52. Of the 226 titles assigned to Theophrastos by Diogenes Laertios (5.42–50), three concern the gods, one piety, and one festivals. Of Epicouros' forty-one titles, one treats the gods, one holiness (10.27–28). None of Zeno's twenty titles suggests a religious topic (7.4). Arcesilaos, reportedly, "never so much as wrote a book" (4.32).

53. The fragments collected in Arnim 1903–24 give ample evidence that the theories propounded in these passages were originated or shared by Zeno himself: e.g., frags. 85, 87, 98, 102, 103, 107, 153–55, 157, 159–69, 171, 175, 176.

Epicouros' gods were completely remote from and disinterested in mankind, enjoying their own perfectly blessed and pleasurable life:[54]

First of all think the god is an imperishable and blessed creature, just as the common understanding of god was sketched out, and attach to him nothing foreign to imperishability and nothing alien to blessedness. Believe about him everything that is able to maintain his blessedness and his imperishability. For gods do exist because knowledge of them is clear. But they are not the type of gods that most people think, for most people do not even consistently maintain the types of gods they think of. It is not the person who does away with the gods of most people who is impious, but rather the person who attaches to the gods the beliefs that most people hold. For the statements of most people about the gods are not true preconceptions but false assumptions. (D.L. 10.123–24)

What is the life of the gods and what kind of life is spent by them? A life than which nothing can be imagined more blessed, more overflowing with all good things. For god does nothing, is involved in no occupations, works at no task, rejoices in his own wisdom and virtue, and knows for certain that he will always be in pleasures which are not only the greatest but also eternal. (Cic. *Nat. D.* 1.16.50–51 = frag. 352 Usener)

(The Epicureans) remove the divine into a life inactive and full of pleasures, as remote as possible from gratitude and anger and from concern for us. (Plut. *Pyrrh.* 20.3 = frag. 363 Usener)

God does not give kind services but is free from care and concern for us. Turned away from the world he does other things or, what seems to Epicouros the greatest blessedness, he does nothing, and kind services touch him no more than wrongs do. (Sen. *Ben.* 4.4.1 = frag. 364 Usener)

Noticeably lacking in these and other contemporary philosophical discussions of the gods, even in contrast to those of Plato and Aristotle, is reference to the polis. The god (or gods) of the philosophers is not only Panhellenic but cosmic. His interest, activities, and presence lie far beyond the bounds of the polis. These gods may be completely remote from man, enjoying their own pure blessedness (Epicouros), or god may be immanent in the world through Reason, in the order of the physical world and in the reason of each individual person (Zeno). The philosophers discuss their gods in terms of the universe and the

---

54. Numerous parallels to the following statements can be found in the collection of Epicurea by Usener (1887), esp. 103–4, 232–62. For Epicouros' views of the gods and the origins of the much later charges of atheism against him, see Obbink 1989. For possible Epicurean influences in the hymn to Demetrios Poliorcetes (chapter 3, pp. 94–95), see Green 1990, 618; Marcovich 1988, 13–17; Ehrenberg 1946, 188.

individual, not in terms of the city-state, which falls between these extremes. For these early Hellenistic philosophers in Athens, unlike for Plato and Aristotle, the polis has largely ceased to be a point of reference, in religion as well as in other matters. And that is, no doubt, in part because the polis has ceased to be a major point of reference in their own lives. Most of them, like Theophrastos, Zeno, and Arcesilaos, were foreigners who lived or had lived for decades in Athens. Only Epicouros was an Athenian by citizenship; he was born and raised on Samos but had served in the Athenian ephebe corps in 323/2–322/1. Thereupon he left Athens, to return fifteen years later, in 307/6.[55] The rather extensive records of these schools suggest that of the hundreds of students, as few as one in twenty was an Athenian.[56]

The deities of the philosophers differed fundamentally from those of ordinary citizens, but what of these philosophers' views of proper behavior in regard to traditional religious norms and customs? Little is known, but that little suggests that these philosophers were not led by their theories or their personal inclinations to disparage or violate all contemporary standards of religious behavior. They recommended some traditional cultic acts, but they redefined the purpose and recipient of these honors. The Stoics seemingly defined piety in traditional terms and approved of traditional religious acts, although with a characteristic emphasis on Reason:

Good men are god-respecting, for they are experienced in the traditional rites concerning the gods. Piety is the knowledge of the service (owed) to the gods. And furthermore good men will sacrifice to the gods and are religiously correct because they avoid offenses concerning the gods and the gods admire them. For they are holy and just toward the divine. And only the wise are priests because they have thought seriously about sacrifices, the foundings (of temples and dedications), purifications, and the other things related to the gods. (D.L. 7.119)

Epicouros recommended worship, sacrifice, and attendance at festivals —not to influence the gods but to show recognition of their supremely blessed nature.[57] There are, of course, in the writings of these philosophers statements and arguments contrary to contemporary practices.

---

55. On Epicouros' Athenian ties, see Green 1990, 58, 618 (but one can hardly call Epicouros "in essence, as Athenian as Socrates"). On these ties and on the possibility that Epicouros deposited his writings for safekeeping in the state archives, see Clay 1982.

56. Habicht 1988b, 3 = 1994, 233.

57. E.g., frags. 13, 30, 157, 169, 386, 387 Usener. For Epicouros' own participation in the Anthesteria and the Eleusinian Mysteries, see Rist 1972, 156–57. On the positive view

Theophrastos in his treatise "On Piety" made the case, with historical precedents, against animal sacrifice; Epicouros reportedly denied the usefulness of prayer and the validity of divination (e.g., frags. 27, 388, 395 Usener); and Zeno argued that cities should not erect temples and statues for the gods (frags. 146, 264–67 Arnim).

Such criticisms of religion by philosophers were hardly new in Athens, and these were quite mild compared to those of Diogenes of Sinope, the founder of Cynicism, in the third quarter of the fourth century. Diogenes, in the most public fora, wittily expressed his scorn for the most fundamental beliefs and practices of popular religion: for sacrifice, "it disturbed him that men sacrifice to the gods to ensure health but in the sacrifice itself feast to the detriment of health" (D.L. 6.28); for prayer, "Men ask for those things which seem to them good, not for those which are truly good" (42; cf. 37, 63); for purifications, "Unfortunate man, don't you know that just as you cannot get rid of errors of grammar by sprinklings, so you cannot get rid of errors in life?" (42; cf. 61); for votive offerings, "When someone was marveling at the votive offerings in Samothrace, he said, 'There would be many more, if also those who were not saved were setting up offerings'" (59); for divination, "When he saw interpreters of dreams and prophets and those who attended them . . . , he said he thought nothing more silly than man" (24; cf. 43); for cult officials, "When he saw the officials of a temple leading away someone who had stolen a *phialē* belonging to the treasurers, he said, 'The great thieves are leading away the little thief'" (45; cf. 72); for the Eleusinian Mysteries, "When the Athenians asked him to be initiated and told him that in Hades those who had been initiated enjoy front-row seating, 'It would be ridiculous,' he said, 'if Agesilaos and Epaminondas will spend their time in the mud but some worthless people, because they have been initiated, will be in the Isles of the Blessed'" (39); and, finally, for funerals, "Some say that when dying he ordered them to throw him out unburied so every beast might have a share of him, or to throw him into a ditch and sprinkle on a little dust. But according to others he ordered that they throw him into the Ilissos, in order that he be useful to his brothers" (79; cf. 52).

But of the philosophers only Diogenes seemed capable of maintaining his philosophical convictions in the face of illness and death. Even

---

of Epicureans about θεωρίαι in particular, see Obbink 1984. On Epicurean views of other forms of worship, see Obbink 1989; Clay 1986; Hadzsits 1908.

his student Bion of Borysthenes, as was recounted by the people of Chalcis, when he fell ill was persuaded to wear an amulet and to repent of his offenses against religion (D.L. 4.54).[58] Virtually all the philosophers whose last days or wills are known had or planned traditional funerals, with Epicouros, of all people, providing tomb offerings (ἐναγίσματα) for his father, mother, and brothers (10.18);[59] he, like Theophrastos (5.41) and Zeno (7.10–12), received an elaborate state funeral and tomb.

Diogenes called the performances at the City Dionysia "great spectacles for fools" (D.L. 6.24), but other philosophers found festivals at least an entertaining holiday. Epicouros, an Athenian, encouraged participation in them and claimed the wise man would take more delight than other men in state spectacles (10.120). Arcesilaos took the occasions of festivals to visit his close friend Hierocles, the Macedonian commandant of Piraeus and Mounichia (4.39).

This expatriate philosophic community, deprived of full participation in the social aspects of Athenian cult, developed their own monthly and annual celebrations. Halcyoneus, a son of Antigonos Gonatas, had received extensive philosophical education in Athens under the supervision of Zeno and his students, and after Halcyoneus' untimely death the philosophers of all schools assembled annually to celebrate his birthday, enjoying the largess of Antigonos (D.L. 4.41–42).[60] As we have seen (chapter 2, pp. 65–66), Plato was probably honored annually on his birthday, Thargelion 7. In his own will Epicouros endowed a variety of regular celebrations: annual ones of his own birthday (Gamelion 20), for his brothers (in Posideon), and for Polyainos (in Metageitnion), and monthly meetings of the school on the twentieth, in honor of himself and Metrodoros.[61] The latter continued well into the Roman period (D.L. 10.18). Such regular gatherings, no doubt accompanied by a banquet, would provide for these foreigners a quasi-religious substitute for the monthly and annual festival days of the citizens. Significantly, the philosophers in such recurrent celebrations rendered honor (τιμή) to deceased mortals, relatives, former philosophers, and friends; the citizens in their festivals honored deities.

58. On Bion of Borysthenes, see Green 1990, 142–43.

59. On this apparent contradiction between Epicouros' words and actions, on these offerings as the establishment of a type of hero cult appropriate to the Epicurean philosophy and for the Epicurean community, and on the possible early hero cult of Epicouros himself within the Epicurean community, see Clay 1986.

60. Habicht 1988b, 6 = 1994, 235.

61. On the religious nature of these celebrations, see Clay 1986.

The overall impression is that these foreign philosophers formed a lively, vibrant, but in some ways closed society within Athens—"nests of foreigners" as Ferguson puts it (1911, 215).[62] Many were wealthy, and some, like Theophrastos and Arcesilaos, lived extravagantly and ostentatiously. Zeno and Epicouros chose relatively simple lives but accumulated fortunes. At any given time a large group of students, numbering quite likely in the hundreds, usually young, wealthy, and foreign, attended the lectures and studied with these recognized philosophers; and they moved often from philosopher to philosopher, from school to school. In the very nationalistic, if not actively anti-Macedonian decades after 287/6, these philosophers and their students had close personal and financial ties to the Macedonian successors of Alexander: to Antigonos Gonatas, Ptolemy Soter, and other powerful kings of the Hellenistic world. Antigonos and his son were both students of Zeno, and many of the philosophers and their students lived and traveled for a time with the monarchs. Their expatriate status, their wealth, their lifestyles, and their politics all would tend to isolate them from the Athenian Demos. But this did not prevent the Demos from using some of these philosophers, no doubt because of their Macedonian connections and expertise in rhetoric, as ambassadors to the various Hellenistic kings,[63] nor rich and influential Athenians from dining and partying with them.

But how, then, did their philosophical theories and criticisms of religion affect Athenian popular religion? How did the Athenians react? The strongest and most outspoken critic, as we have seen, was the Cynic Diogenes. In the first half of the third century many of his criticisms were taken up by, for example, Bion of Borysthenes (ca. 325–255), who reportedly denied that the gods existed, refused even to look at temples, ridiculed soothsayers, and mocked men for sacrificing to deities (D.L. 2.135, 4.55–56). In the late fifth century sentiments similar to those of Diogenes and Bion had brought exile from Athens to Diagoras of Melos.[64] The charge of impiety against Aristotle in 322 was, as we have seen (chapter 2, pp. 48–49), for a much less blatant offense and was surely motivated in part by anti-Macedonian sentiments. The abortive attempt in 307/6 by the orator Sophocles to have the state regulate the

62. Cf. Habicht 1988b = 1994, 231–47.

63. For a list of such diplomatic activities and other honors, including citizenship, awarded by Athenians to philosophers, see Habicht 1994, 240–43.

64. Woodbury 1965.

schools of philosophy seems largely political, a reaction against the Peripatetics' close ties with Cassander and the deposed Demetrios of Phaleron.[65] Thereafter there is no known legal challenge to the philosophical schools on either political or religious grounds. The Athenians, in fact, seemed to have a certain affection for Diogenes (D.L. 6.43), in part, perhaps, because they were amused by his crankiness and bizarre lifestyle. One wonders if they would have shown similar tolerance for a fellow citizen. But there are also some indications that even a character such as Bion was aware of the dangers of expressing such criticisms outside philosophic circles.[66]

The evidence, mostly anecdotal and hardly conclusive, would suggest that many of the philosophers' and particularly the Cynics' criticisms of the gods and traditional religious practices were familiar to many Athenians, but there is no evidence that they affected, significantly or otherwise, popular belief and practice. Such criticisms had, we must remember, a long tradition in Greece, reaching back to Xenophanes in the late sixth century. Then, as in the third century, the criticisms influenced philosophical and, to a certain extent, literary thought and expression, but no impact on popular religion can be documented.

In sharp contrast to the philosophers who were mostly foreigners, almost all pro-Macedonian, and virtually isolated from Athenian religious cult stand the Atthidographers, "writers who," to give Jacoby's definition, "from the closing years of the fifth century B.C. down to the end of the Chremonidean War in 263/2 B.C. narrated the history of Athens and of Athens alone" (1949, 1).[67] They include Cleidemos, who pub-

65. For this incident and its causes, see Habicht 1988b, 7–9 = 1994, 236–37. In his speech in the case Demochares included, among a host of personal and political attacks on philosophers, also the charge of "impiety" (Ath. 11.508F–509B).

66. See D.L. (2.116–17) on Stilpo, the Megarian philosopher (ca. 380–300) who was one of Zeno's teachers: "They say that (Stilpo) asked some such question about the Athena (Parthenos) of Phidias, 'Is Athena, the daughter of Zeus, a god?' And when the other said 'Yes,' Stilpo said, 'She is not of Zeus but of Phidias.' And when the other agreed, Stilpo said, 'Then she is not a god.' For this he was summoned to the Areiopagos. He did not deny it but said that he had argued correctly, for Athena was not a god but a goddess. Nonetheless, the members of the Areiopagos ordered him to leave the city immediately. . . . And when Crates asked him whether the gods rejoice (χαίρουσι) in worship and prayers, they say that Stilpo said, 'Fool, don't ask about these things in the street but in private.' And Bion, when asked if the gods exist, said the same thing: 'Will you not scatter the crowd away from me?'"

67. On the Atthidographers, see F. Jacoby's *Atthis* (1949) and his commentary on the lives and fragments of these writers in the three volumes of *FGrHist* IIIB. For a very recent

lished between 354 (or 378/7) and 340; Androtion, after 344/3; Phanodemos, the contemporary and collaborator of Lycourgos, ca. 338/7–327/6; Demon and Melanthios, both probably late fourth century; and the most famous and best-preserved, Philochoros, whose *Atthis*, or history of Athens, ended shortly after the Chremonidean War. We treat them here because the Atthidographic tradition came to an end with the death of Philochoros, just after the Chremonidean War, and because, as a group, the Atthidographers represent an influence from within Athenian society counter to the religious theories and skepticism of the foreign philosophers.

Each of the six Atthidographers was an Athenian citizen. Some were actively engaged in politics. Androtion was a member of the Boule twice (after 378/7 and in 356/5). In 358/7 he served as governor of Arcesine on Amorgos and was praised by the locals for his virtue, justice, and goodwill (*IG* XII 7, no. 5). After a vigorous political career he was, late in life, exiled and wrote his *Atthis* in Megara.[68] Phanodemos served in the Boule, was honored for his excellent services, and proposed the dedication it made to Hephaistos and Athena Hephaistia in 343/2 (*IG* II²223).[69] Little is known of Philochoros' political views, but he must have somehow stood out as an anti-Macedonian: in the late 260s, he was executed by Antigonos Gonatas for having sided with Arsinoe, the wife of Ptolemy Philadelphos, against Macedonian interests. Philochoros and, apparently, all of these Atthidographers were pro-democratic.[70]

For our purposes the religious, not the political, activities of the Atthidographers are most relevant. Cleidemos, named by Pausanias (10.15.5) as the first Athenian to write a history of Athens, was an *exēgētēs*, an official expounder of sacred law, especially that concerning homicide, death, and pollution. He published, in addition to his *Atthis*, an *Exegetikon*, apparently a set of practical instructions based on exegetical laws that formerly were the exclusive domain of the aristocratic *exēgētai* (*FGrHist* 323 F 14).[71] Some time before 365/4 Androtion proposed a decree concerning an inventory of sacred property on the Acro-

---

account of them, and especially of Androtion and his writings, see Harding 1994. On those Athenian and other historians particularly interested in religious affairs, see Nilsson 1967–74, 2:51–54.

68. On Androtion's politics, see Harding 1994, *passim* but esp. 13–25, 178–80.

69. On Phanodemos, see Faraguna 1992, 217–18.

70. Harding 1994, *passim* but esp. 13, 24, 33–34, 49. On Kleidemos' pro-democratic stance and the general issue, see McInerney 1994.

71. On Cleidemos' *Exegetikon* and his writings in general, see McInerney 1994, esp. 22.

polis, including the statue of Athena Polias, processional equipment, and crowns.[72] Phanodemos was of the circle of Lycourgos, and we have already seen that in 331/0 he was honored for his legislation on the festivals and repair of the Amphiaraion; in 329/8 he was one of the ten men, including Lycourgos, overseeing the new quadrennial Amphiaraia. In 326/5, again with Lycourgos, he served on the official delegation to Delphi (chapter 1, pp. 33–34). Jacoby (1949, 78) rightly sees Phanodemos closely connected with Lycourgos' program for the revival of Athenian state cult. The fragments of his *Atthis* show him interested, as Lycourgos was, in the details and history of Athenian local cults and myths. As Lycourgos' use of such religious material in his speeches shows, the interest here was far more than antiquarian. Melanthios, perhaps as an *exēgētēs*, wrote a book *On the Eleusinian Mysteries* and Demon one *On Sacrifices*.

Philochoros brings the Atthidographic tradition to a culmination and an end. He was, in Jacoby's estimation, a true scholar and a religious conservative. Apart from his *Atthis*, in seventeen books, he wrote twenty-six monographs covering the range of Athenian history and religion. As a practicing prophet he wrote a study *On the Prophetic Art* and elsewhere described rather proudly his own success in the field (*FGrHist* 328 F 67; cf. F 135). He wrote books also *On Sacrifices, On Festivals, On the Days,*[73] *On Mysteries at Athens, On Purifications, On Dreams*, and on several literary figures and topics—virtually all, so far as we know, centered on Athens and her institutions and history. He also, it should be noted, in his *Atthis* attacked Demetrios Poliorcetes for his irregular initiation into the Eleusinian Mysteries (F69–70).[74]

Athenian religious history and institutions and local mythology played a significant role in most if not all of the *Atthides* and other writings of these Atthidographers from the fourth to the mid–third centuries B.C., with that interest apparently growing at the end of the period.[75] This would suggest that despite the ravages of Demetrios Poliorcetes and his Athenian supporters, and despite the presence of

72. *IG* II² 216/7 + 261 = Lewis 1954, 39–49. Cf. *FGrHist* 328 F 181.

73. The impression left by Green (1990, 597) that this work *On the Days* is an early example of astrology is wrong. So far as it can be determined, it dealt with which days were sacred in the calendar and why, and on one occasion (*FGrHist* 328 F 85) claims that if one were born on Heracles' day of the month, one's life might be one of service to others, as was Heracles'. This is a quite different matter from the much later personal horoscopes based on astrological schemes.

74. On Demetrios' initiation see above, chapter 3, pp. 89–90.

75. The fragments of the Atthidographers, collected and exhaustively discussed by Jacoby in *FGrHist* IIIB, suggest their interests. Of the 27 fragments of Cleidemos, 16

non-Athenian philosophers and their students, some of the spirit of the Lycourgan religious revolution, then exemplified by Phanodemos, was kept alive, perhaps finding its strongest exponent just before the Chremonidean War. And also, we should recall, at this same time the Athenians were celebrating their glorious literary past with the new inscriptional record in the theater of Dionysos (above, p. 122). In short, although some may judge that traditional Athenian religious beliefs and cults were being threatened from the philosophical quarter, these same beliefs and cults were receiving support, perhaps more effective because it was from Athenians for Athenians, from prominent pro-democratic citizens with experience in Athenian politics, society, and religion.

We have traced above the role of Demetrios Poliorcetes and his father Antigonos as *Sōtēres* and their festival the Soteria (see chapter 3), as well as the brief emergence, perhaps in their place, of Zeus Soter and Athena Soteira after 287/6. A survey of the Athenian sacrifices "for health and safety (*sōtēria*)" is appropriate at this juncture and reveals some trends of the period. Sacrifices expressly for "the health and safety of the Boule and Demos" are first attested for 343/2, and the Boule performed them (*IG* II² 223b.1–6). The proposal to honor the Boule for making such sacrifices apparently was made by none other than Phanodemos, whose role in religion and as an Atthidographer we have just examined and who was at the time a member of the Boule. In *IG* II² 410 of ca. 330, Dionysos, Poseidon Pelagios, Zeus Soter, and Ammon, all of Piraeus, were prayed to "for the health and safety of the Boule and the Demos of the Athenians and of the children, wives, and the other possessions of the Athenians" (see above, chapter 1, pp. 43–44). In Schwenk #40 of 332/1 the same Phanodemos proposed a crown for Amphiaraos for his concern for the health and safety of the Athenians. Amphiaraos and, later, Asclepios (Schwenk #54 of 328/7) understandably received offerings intended to promote the health and safety of the Athenian Demos. For the next forty years we find the phrase "for health and safety" in only one decree, proposed by Stratocles in 307/6, honoring the Athenian colonists at Colophon. The Colophonian ambas-

---

concern solely or importantly matters of Athenian religious and mythical history (1, 2, 4, 5, 9–12, 14, 18, 20, 22, 23, 25–27); likewise 9 of the 68 fragments of Androtion (1, 2, 16, 30, 36, 55, 56, 60, 62); 15 of the 27 of Phanodemos (1, 3, 4, 6, 8, 11, 12, 14–20, 27); 11 of the 21 of Demon (1–3, 6, 7, 9, 12, 16–18, 20); 3 of the 4 of Melanthios (2–4); and nearly half of the 226 fragments of Philochoros.

sadors had sacrificed "for the health and safety" of both peoples, and then made a dedication to Athena (Polias), likewise on behalf of both peoples (*IG* II² 456b.1–8).

From 307/6 to 287/6 Demetrios Poliorcetes was, at least officially, the Soter, and the numerous divine honors and festivals given to him were intended, no doubt, to recognize and promote his interest in the health and safety of the Athenians. We have seen above how, in his control of the food supply and of the military, he did, in fact, control just such areas of Athenian life (chapter 3, pp. 82–83). With the departure of Demetrios in 287/6 and the reestablishment of Athenian independence, sacrifices "for the Demos" and "for the health and safety of the Boule and Demos" reappear. In 284/3 the tribe Hippothontis honored a priest of Asclepios who, as was "befitting his office," sacrificed all the sacrifices "on behalf of the Demos" (*IG* II² 1163.1–8). The archon of 282/1 sacrificed to Dionysos "for the health and safety of the Boule and Demos of the Athenians and for all the crops in the land," surely as part of his management of the procession of the City Dionysia (*IG* II² 668). A prytany decree of 273/2 records sacrifices to Apollo Prostaterios and the other gods and the celebration of the Stenia for Demeter and Kore, all "for the health and safety of the Boule and Demos of the Athenians and of all others who are well intentioned to the Demos" (*Agora* XV, #78.4–11; above, pp. 113–14). This phrase, with minor variations, is already formulaic in such prytany decrees.[76] In, perhaps, 272/1 a priest is honored for his sacrifices to Zeus Soter and Athena Soteira "for the health and safety of the Boule and Demos" (*IG* II² 689). And, finally, in 267/6 the *epimelētai* of the Eleusinian Mysteries are honored for having made sacrifices at the Lesser Mysteries at Agrai for the same purpose. As we have seen, these *epimelētai* had also, on behalf of the Boule and Demos, sacrificed at their own expense the *sōtēria* to Demeter and Kore (*IG* II² 661). The Eleusinian deities, now after the recovery of Eleusis, receive both *sōtēria* and sacrifices on behalf of the whole Athenian Demos. And in the city itself, if the previous analyses of this chapter are correct, somewhat new deities—Apollo Prostaterios, Zeus Soter, and Athena Soteira, not Athena Polias—are entrusted with the nation's protection.

But, from the inscriptions, a new element also emerges. Beginning in 281/0 taxiarchs, the commanders of the tribal infantry units, are

76. Two other prytany decrees have been restored to give the same phrase in the 270s: *Agora* XV, #79, 80.

recorded as making, sometimes at their own expense, sacrifices "for the health and safety of the Boule and Demos." In 281/0 six taxiarchs were sent by the Athenians to participate in the Basileia at Lebadeia, and there they made sacrifice "for the health and safety of the Boule and Demos" (*SEG* 25.90). The taxiarchs of 275/4 were honored for making such sacrifices in Athens at their own expense, together with the generals (*SEG* 15.101). And, finally, the taxiarchs of 272/1 received similar honors for similar sacrifices with the generals (*SEG* 14.64). Such sacrifices had become, clearly, part of their job. These sacrifices for the national welfare by military officers may indicate attempts to establish or reaffirm, in religious terms, the tie of the army to the newly independent state. But, in more general terms, the independence gained by Athens in 287/6 clearly brought a resurgence of interest in sacrifices promoting the nation's overall welfare by a number of officials to a broad spectrum of deities.

On the international scene we have seen that prominent Athenian actors, poets, and philosophers participated, either as individuals or in guilds, in various festivals throughout the Greek world. It appears that first after their liberation in 287/6 the Athenians began again to be represented as a state in some of these. In 281/0 six Athenian taxiarchs attended the Basileia, the festival in honor of Zeus Basileus, in Lebadeia. And, apparently in 282, the Athenians sent a delegation, headed by Callias of Sphettos, to the Ptolemaia, a festival that Ptolemy II created, initially, as part of the funeral celebrations of his father Ptolemy I but then repeated at regular intervals.[77] It is assumed that Athens sent delegations for each celebration.[78] It was Ptolemy II who, it will be remembered, sent "equipment" necessary for the renewal of the quadrennial celebration of the Panathenaia in 282 or 278 (above, pp. 108–109).

A critical event in the period was the Galatian invasion of mainland Greece. The Galatians forced passage through Thermopylae, which was being defended by Aetolian, Athenian, and other Greek forces. The turning point came in 279/8 when, by a combination of military, meteorological, and supernatural events the Galatians were driven back with heavy losses from Delphi. The last contingent of Galatians was finally

---

77. *SEG* 28.60.55–64. For the date and origins of the Ptolemaia, see Habicht 1992a, 70 = 1994, 142.

78. Shear 1978, 45–46.

defeated in 277 by Antigonos Gonatas near Lysimacheia on the Thracian Chersonese.[79] The expulsion of the Galatians "freed" Delphi and all Greece from an immediate barbarian threat, and we find it marked in Athens by the dedication, to Zeus Eleutherios in the Stoa of Zeus, of the shield of the young Athenian warrior Cudias, who died probably in the battle at Thermopylae (Paus. 10.21.5–6).[80] To commemorate the victory at Delphi the Amphictionic League instituted, at Delphi, new games, the Soteria for Apollo Pythios and Zeus Soter,[81] and the Athenians undoubtedly sent an official delegation to participate in these. The victory over the Galatians and Athens' role in it apparently led to a reconciliation with the Aetolians and with Delphi. The emergence of Apollo Prostaterios in state cult may be related to these new ties with Delphi, and, in more general terms, Athenian pride in their role in the victory over the Galatians may have contributed to the surge in nationalistic religious activities we have seen in the mid-270s.

In sum, we may see the period of 287/6–267/6 as a time of cleansing, reestablishing, and reorganizing in Athenian religion. Most elements and vestiges of the "ruler cult" of Demetrios Poliorcetes were eliminated or redirected; only the two tribes, Demetrias and Antigonis, remained. In this period of independence there was a general movement back to the religious spirit of the age of Lycourgos; but, if the preceding analyses are correct, those deities who had previously failed the Athenians, like Athena Polias, lost prestige to other deities more suitable to the times, like Apollo Prostaterios and Zeus Soter. Concern and gratitude for *sōtēria*, in recent years the "gift" of the Macedonian king, were directed again to the gods.

Foreign influences on Athenian religion in this period are mixed and difficult to assess. Much of what we have seen is a conservative reaction, back to the time of Lycourgos, against the innovations both in cult and conception brought about by Macedonian monarchs and their Athenian partisans. The theories and criticisms of the philosophers,

79. On this Galatian invasion of Greece and on the Delphic Soteria commemorating Greek victory, see Nachtergael 1977.

80. A relative of Cudias, Cubernis of Halimous (*PA* 8918), about thirty years later proposed to the Athenians that they participate in the new Aetolian form of the Soteria at Delphi in honor of Zeus Soter and Apollo Pythios (*IG* II² 680). See Habicht 1985, 84–85; Nachtergael 1977, 192.

81. For Zeus Soter in the early, Amphictionic Soteria, see Nachtergael 1977, #1.30–33, from Cos.

which certainly stood at variance with basic popular religious concepts, appear not to have penetrated private belief or state cult. Here and in later chapters we shall see that changes in state cult, and the changes they imply for private belief, will be determined largely by diplomacy and on the battlefield, not in the lecture halls.

5

Again Domination,
Again Independence

By the 270s Athens had recovered all of her territory and forts in Attica—except for Piraeus. Apparently the desire to recover Piraeus and broader concerns about the "freedom" of Greek cities led the Athenians in 268/7 to make a formal treaty with Lacedaimon and her allies, Elis, the Achaean League, Tegea, Mantinea, Orchomenos, and others against those "attempting to destroy the laws and ancestral constitutions" of their cities (*IG* II² 686 + 687). Strong support was expected from Ptolemy II. This treaty, proposed by Chremonides, son of Eteocles, of the deme Aithalidai (*PA* 15572), prepared the stage for the Chremonidean War of Athens and her allies against Antigonos Gonatas. The war was disastrous for the independence and growing prosperity of Athens. After two sieges the city was finally surrendered, ca. 262/1, and Antigonos clamped down hard. He installed Macedonian garrisons on the Museion Hill, at Sounion, Salamis, Panacton, and Phyle. Through his military officers and appointees he took control of the government.[1]

In an essay titled "The End of the City State," A. W. Gomme marked 262 as a decisive date in Athens' history as a city-state: "the end of Athenian independence," the date at which, by the loss of the Chremonidean War, Athens ceased to operate in the Greek world as an independent military or economic power (1937, 204–48, esp. 223). The Athenian countryside and crops had been devastated by Antigonos' troops, the

---

1. Habicht 1979, 95–146.

forts were garrisoned by Macedonians, and some elected officials were replaced by appointees of the king. Chremonides and other democratic leaders fled to the court of Ptolemy II.[2]

Six years later, in 256/5, Antigonos relaxed his grip somewhat, removing his garrison from the Mouseion Hill and allowing the Athenians some domestic freedom. But the times were difficult. In 251/0 Alexander, the governor of Corinth, attacked Athens and Salamis but was repulsed. In 250/49 the Athenians bribed him not to attack again. In 242 Aratos, head of the Achaean League, marched through Attica and pillaged Salamis in an attempt to make Athens revolt from Antigonos. In 240/39 Antigonos Gonatas died and was succeeded by his son Demetrios II, and the Achaeans chose the moment to attack, though unsuccessfully, the Macedonian garrison in Piraeus. In the 230s Aratos returned several times to plunder much of Attica, including the Eleusinian and Athenian plains and several of the coastal towns.

Demetrios himself died in 229 and was succeeded by Antigonos III Doson. Eurycleides of Kephisia (*PA* 5966), a very rich and powerful politician, now took the lead in freeing Athens from Macedonian control, and he succeeded in this by bribing Diogenes, the Macedonian commandant in Athens, with 150 talents, a vast sum of money that Eurycleides had raised from friends both at home and abroad. With the departure of the Macedonian garrisons, Athens again, though now very weak, became free, with control over all her territory in Attica. Macedonian control of Athenian land was at last, after nearly a hundred years, over.

Athens' treaty with the Lacedaimonians and others that led to the Chremonidean War in 268/7 (*IG* II[2] 687) reveals how far Athenian independence and nationalism had progressed since 287/6.[3] The Athenians now were again prepared, at least mentally, to play a major, independent role in international affairs, and in the rhetoric of the treaty they hearkened back to their leadership against the Persians in the early decades of the fifth century. For their part, the Athenians swore allegiance to the terms of the treaty by Zeus, Ge, Helios, Ares, Athena Areia, and, as the text is restored, Poseidon and Demeter. Ares and Athena Areia were not peculiarly Athenian, but they did have a joint cult in Acharnai and they were the Athenian military deities par excellence.[4]

2. Habicht 1982b, 13–78.

3. For the text of the treaty, see Schmitt 1969, 129–33, #476.

4. Ares and Athena Areia are indisputably invoked also in contemporary oaths of treaties between the Aetolians and Boeotians ca. 292 (Schmitt 1969, #463a.8), Eumenes

The other invoked deities, as was common in international oaths, represent, in general terms, the sky (Zeus and Helios), the earth (Ge and Demeter), and the sea (Poseidon). This treaty and oath, ominously, are the last of their type to survive from Hellenistic Athens. It is also the last we are to hear of an Athenian Athena Areia until Roman times.[5] After the loss in the Chremonidean War Athens' role as a military force in international affairs was at last finished, and so too the need for her "offensive" military deities.

In a perverse sense, Athens was, as a result of the Chremonidean War, finally reunited, with one authority over all regions of Attica. For the first time since 294 Piraeus and city were again one, both equally garrisoned by Antigonos' Macedonian troops. One can imagine that this would have allowed more communication between the city and Piraeus, bringing Piraeus, after its years of isolation, a breath of fresh air. Several epigraphical texts from the late 260s give some support to these ideas.[6] In the archonship of Antipatros we find the devotees of Ammon having finished an addition to the sanctuary of their god and sacrificing to Amphiaraos (*IG* II² 1282). In contrast to the steady profusion of texts from the fourth century, only two dated cultic texts, both from private associations, come from Piraeus since 299/8: that of the *thiasōtai* of Zeus Labraundos of that year (*IG* II² 1271) and that of the cult of the Mother of the Gods in 272/1 (*IG* II² 1316). The last surviving mention of a public festival in Piraeus was from 307/6, of the Dionysia held there (*IG* II² 456.33). After 261 it was at the same festival that the demesmen of Piraeus announced special honors, including participation in many religious activities, for Callidamas of the deme Cholleidai (*IG* II² 1214).[7] This text gives the impression that Piraeus by this time had a full range of public sacrifices and festivals with the customary distributions of meat. We may, perhaps, assume that however difficult and limited Piraeus' circumstances, and without leaving a record on stone, much of its religious program had persisted through the deme's long isolation from the city.

I and his troops ca. 263–241 (Schmitt, #481.24, 52), and Smyrna and Magnesia on the Sipylos (Schmitt, #492.61, 70). On the cult of Ares and Athena Areia in Athens, see Graf 1985, 265–68.

5. Pausanias (1.28.5) reports an altar of Athena Areia, founded by Orestes, on the Areiopagos.

6. The dates of the archons and hence of the texts immediately after the Chremonidean War are mostly uncertain. See Habicht 1979, 113–46. Antipatros of *IG* II² 1282 was archon shortly before 260.

7. For the date of the announcement, see Garland 1987, 227.

The devotees of Bendis, a Thracian deity similar to Artemis, left the clearest record of attempts to reunite a cult sundered by the long separation of the city and the harbor town.[8] The cult had been founded in the fifth century in Piraeus, quite probably in the interest of Thracian traders and intended only for them. In the opening of the *Republic* (1.327A–328B) Plato has Socrates visiting Piraeus to see the first festival (ἑορτή) of Bendis, which is to consist of two processions (one of Athenians, one of Thracians), a sacrifice, a torch relay race on horseback, and a *pannychis*. Socrates has come "to pray to the goddess and to watch the new festival," but he is returning to the city after the procession. He is invited by friends to stay and watch the race and *pannychis*. In the *Republic* the festival, not the cult, is new. The cult must have been established some years before if it already has some Athenian members.[9] The "new festival" Plato describes is surely supported by the state, and such support is in fact attested in 334/3 (*IG* II² 1496.86).[10]

And thus, already in the classical period, the cult of Bendis had some Athenian members, its own festival, and a place in the state religious calendar. From our perspective, it is the grand doyen of foreign cults established in Attica in the historical period. Unlike its successors for many centuries, it won acceptance among the citizens and became part of established religion. Unlike traditional cults, however, it was not tied, by purpose or membership, to a social or political unit—to the deme, tribe, or family. It apparently consisted of citizens, in addition to the Thracians, who chose to become members and to pay the requisite dues. It thus created, for its no doubt relatively small citizen membership, a religious organization outside the traditional orders of Athenian society. As a cult of foreigners it was not unusual, but it was unique, to judge by the surviving records, in having citizen members in the classical period.[11]

8. On the cult of Bendis, see Garland 1992, 111–14; Simms 1988; Schwenk 1985, 63–67, 252–59; Ferguson 1944, 95–107, and 1949. For the Bendis cult on Salamis, see Taylor 1993, 133–34, 234–38.

9. Some of the deity's property was being stored on the Acropolis as early as 429/8 (*IG* I³ 383.143).

10. For a detailed study of problems of the chronology and nature of the classical cult of Bendis in Athens, see Simms 1988.

11. Because the *orgeōnes* of Bendis of *IG* II² 1283 and 1284 met on the eighth day of the month and crowned honorees with garlands of oak leaves, whereas those of *IG* II² 1324 and Schwenk #52 gave olive garlands and those of *IG* II² 1361 plan to meet on the second day of the month, scholars have widely accepted Wilhelm's theory, elaborated by Ferguson, that there were two sets of *orgeōnes* in Piraeus, and that one (*IG* II² 1283, 1284) was of Thracians, the other of Athenian citizens (*IG* II² 1324, 1361; Schwenk #13, 52). If in fact differences of meeting days and crowns are significant and not merely changes of practice, then there were indeed two sets of *orgeōnes* in Piraeus—but there is little reason

The members of Bendis' cult were termed *orgeōnes* ("sacrificers"), and it is necessary here to clarify the terminology that will be used for the various cults and their members in the following pages. From my analysis of the texts, Ferguson's statement, derived from ancient descriptions, seems correct (1944, 64): "The sacrifices offered by the *orgeones* were paid for by the *orgeones* themselves, not by the state, and the shrines in which they were offered were established by private, not by public, action." *Orgeōnes* belonged to *koina* ("associations") that were wholly or at least partially composed of citizens.[12] *Thiasōtai*, on the other hand, belonged to *thiasoi* ("religious groups") that were exclusively foreign and that also paid for their own sacrifices in cults established by themselves and not by the state. And, finally, a religious *koinon* might also, from an economic perspective, be termed an *eranos*, that is, a group of *eranistai* who jointly "contributed money" to the *koinon*. *Koinon* and *eranos* might, therefore, refer to the same private religious association—if foreign, made up of *thiasōtai*; if wholly or partially citizen, of *orgeōnes*. I offer these definitions here not as a prescription for determining the citizen status of the membership of the various groups to be studied but as conclusions drawn from the texts themselves. It is necessary to

---

to limit the one or the other to Thracians or Athenians. The only sure Athenians in all these records are the archons and, in Schwenk #13, Antiphanes and Nausiphilos, who may well be state and not cult officials. On the other hand, no individual in these texts can be assuredly identified as a Thracian. (One Thracian, Asclapon of Maroneia, would be sure if *IG* II² 2947 stems from the Bendis cult. On this see Ferguson 1949, 162–63.) In short, even if there were two sets of *orgeōnes* of Bendis in Piraeus, we need not conclude that one was exclusively Athenian and one exclusively Thracian. Both might be entirely Athenian or entirely Thracian. These distinctions are important. On Wilhelm's theory, we have Athenians adopting a foreign deity by establishing, exclusively for its own citizens, a cult mirroring and paralleling that of resident foreigners. The two groups would interact, presumably, only at the festival. If, on the other hand, there were two sets of *orgeōnes* and each had both citizen and Thracian members, then Athenians and foreigners were intermingling regularly in day-to-day cultic activity. Either option, parallel or shared cults, is, so far as we can judge, an innovation, but each suggests different attitudes about how the cult of a foreign deity should be treated. But we might also have two groups, both completely citizen or completely Thracian, with interaction between Thracians and citizens occurring only at the procession of the festival.

IG II² 1317 of 272/1, *SEG* 2.10 of 247/6, and *IG* II² 1317B are decrees of a separate, third *koinon* of Bendis, on Salamis, for which no citizen members are attested. On these Salaminian devotees of Bendis, see Taylor 1993, 133–34, 234–38. For a recent study of the Bendis texts and of the workings of the cult, see Simms 1988.

12. All known *orgeōnes* of the classical period were Athenian, and indeed membership in a *koinon* of *orgeōnes* would seemingly serve as proof of Athenian birth. If in fact they are Thracians, the devotees of Bendis in *IG* II² 1283 and 1284 of mid–to late third century B.C. would be the first non-Athenians designated *orgeōnes*. On *orgeōnes* in the classical period, see Lambert 1993, 74–77; Kearns 1989, 73–77.

give them now, somewhat prematurely, to facilitate the discussion. Occasional vagaries in the use of these terms will be noted as they occur.

The cult of Bendis in Piraeus was clearly prospering in the late fourth century. In *IG* II² 1361 it records financial arrangements for repair of the sanctuary and provisions and fees for nonmembers who wish to sacrifice or join the cult. For the annual sacrifice each member is to contribute two drachmas, and the *orgeōnes* are to meet on the second of each month. In 337/6 (Schwenk #13) they honored three *hieropoioi*, Antiphanes of Kytheros (*PA* 1237), Nausiphilos of Kephale (*PA* 10601), and Aristomenes, for other services and their administration of the procession and distribution of meat. If they are in fact cult members and not the state *hieropoioi*, then they are the first and only Athenian members of the cult attested.[13] In 329/8 (Schwenk #52) the *orgeōnes* honored two of their *epimelētai* with crowns worth 100 drachmas.

In the late 260s the *orgeōnes* of Bendis in Piraeus were accommodating to the new political circumstances. In *IG* II² 1283 they claim, correctly if all the claims are taken as one, that the Athenians had granted to the Thracians alone the right to own property and establish on it a sanctuary in accord with an oracle of Dodona *and* to hold a procession beginning at the Prytaneion. Here we learn, for the first time, that a branch of the cult had also been formed in the city, and had, probably during the Macedonian occupation of Piraeus, taken responsibility for the procession. Since the procession could now again go all the way from the Prytaneion in the city to the sanctuary on the Mounichion Hill, the two sets of *orgeōnes* (city and Piraeic) lay out detailed provisions for the responsibilities of each party in the new, reunited festival. All is to be done in accord with the traditions of the Thracians and the laws of the city, a provision that reflects the unique, twofold character of this cult and its membership. We may suspect that because of citizens' membership and the popularity of the festival,[14] the Athenians, when after 307 or 295 Mounichia and its Bendis sanctuary were no longer accessible, provided land and a sanctuary in the city and had the *orgeōnes* of Bendis there stage the festival as best they could.

The cult of the Mother of the Gods in the Piraeus with its festival of Attis, drums, and ritual begging seems, to judge from the large num-

---

13. See Schwenk 1985, 66–67.

14. From *IG* II² 1496, Ferguson (1944, 101) estimates that in 334/3 100–150 cattle were sacrificed for the festival and that all Athenians, members of the cult or not, shared in the resulting banquet.

ber of surviving reliefs, to have been popular in the fourth and third centuries, and it survived the Macedonian occupation.[15] In the earliest datable record of the cult, *IG* II² 1316 of 272/1, the goddess' *orgeōnes* honored Agathon of Phlya (?)[16] and his wife Zeuxion, the priestess, for their services and for contributing, as so many religious officials did in this period, their own funds for the maintenance of the cult. And sixty years later the same *orgeōnes* twice, in 213/2 and 211/0, honor their priestesses (*IG* II² 1314, 1315). These *orgeōnes* then continue to issue decrees throughout the second and first centuries (*IG* II² 1327–29, 1334). In the later third and second centuries the Piraeic cult of the Mother of the Gods appears wholly Athenian.[17] *IG* II² 1273, from 265/4,[18] evidently is the record of a separate, entirely foreign *thiasos* of the Mother of the Gods, also in the Piraeus. Here priests are featured, whereas in the texts of the other cult only priestesses are mentioned.

In Piraeus, then, the devotees of Ammon and of Bendis in this period were mending their cults, and the worshippers, now citizens, of the Mother of the Gods and Attis were maintaining theirs. The cult of the Mother of the Gods was to endure, but the last attestation of Bendis' cult in Piraeus is, at the latest, in the 230s (*IG* II² 1284).[19] After 260 Ammon in Piraeus also disappears. The cult of Aphrodite Ourania, founded and tended by Cyprians from Cition and very active in the last decade of the fourth century (chapter 3, p. 103), seems not to have survived the tribulations of Piraeus. The last sure inscription of her cult is *IG* II² 1261 of 300/299. There is no later record from the Piraeic Iseion, founded before 333/2 (chapter 1, pp. 30–31), but one could hardly expect Egyptian Greeks to have prospered or perhaps even been allowed in Macedonian-occupied Piraeus for much of this time. The record from Piraeus for 295–229 is at best scanty, but only one originally foreign cult, that of

15. On this cult, see Garland 1987, 128–31; Vermaseren 1982, 68–97.

16. The demotic has been restored and is, apart from the term *orgeōnes*, the only indication of citizen participation in the cult at this time.

17. Dedications and tombstones dated by letter form to the fourth century suggest that at the time there were both foreigners (*IG* II² 4563, 4609) and Athenians (*IG* II² 6288) participating in the cult of the Mother of the Gods in the Piraeus. This may explain why, in the earliest record of the Piraeus cult (*IG* II² 1316), the devotees are, anomalously, designated as both *thiasōtai* and *orgeōnes*. The dual designation may suggest that the cult was originally all foreign but then, probably like the Bendis cult, accepted some Athenian members.

18. For the date, see M. Osborne 1989, 230 n. 97.

19. For the date of the archon Lyceas of *IG* II² 1284, see Habicht 1979, 121–22, 144. The import of *SEG* 19.125 from the Agora is very uncertain.

the Mother of the Gods, appears to flourish and, after 260, few established ones survived.

In *Hellenistic Athens* and other of his writings W. S. Ferguson discussed and lamented as a feature of Athenian religion in the third century B.C. the development of private religious associations of the type I have been describing. He writes of a "new Athens with a narrower economy and narrower politics, with a loyalty divided between an anaemic state and hundreds of religious, professional and social organizations of a semi-public or private character" (1911, 232). Reflecting the ideals and predilections of his class and times, Ferguson sees as particularly decadent the religious "clubs." They were formed and maintained not by true Athenians of good families and good education, but by foreigners and, even worse, by what he calls "Atticans," people of uncertain heritage and background who lived in Athens as permanent residents but lacked the proper background of true Athenians.

Ferguson's assessment of the emergence and profusion of religious clubs in the third century contributes to his overall view of the decadence and, one might say, loss of "quality" of Athenian religion in the Hellenistic period. We have, in recent pages, been examining such *koina*, and this is the opportune moment to complete the survey and to reconsider Ferguson's judgment of them, a judgment that is widely accepted in the scholarly literature. Private religious associations *do* appear in the late fourth and third centuries B.C., but there are important questions beyond the fact of their existence: How many were there? Where were they located? Who, citizens or foreigners, participated in them? Did they affect the traditional state and private cults?

Let us first survey the private cults known to have been established or practiced from the beginning of the Hellenistic period to the end of the third century, taking them, generally, in the order of their first attestation.[20]

---

20. In 1953–54 was excavated, where now the statue of Harry S. Truman stands on Leophoros Basileos Constantinou, outside the city walls of ancient Athens, a sanctuary of Pancrates ("All Powerful"). Vikela has just published (1994) fifty-eight votive reliefs then excavated. They represent Pancrates in two forms: as an older bearded male, often with a horn of plenty, identified on the reliefs as Pancrates, Palaimon, or Pluton; and as a younger male, often beardless, called either Pancrates or Heracles Pancrates, and explicitly assimilated to Heracles by the lion skin and club. The reliefs are dedicated by both men and women, only one among them surely an Athenian (B 5). Vikela dates the reliefs from mid–fourth to mid–third century B.C. With extensive and complex arguments she sees the god(s) as chthonic, probably correctly, and draws connections to a wide variety of Phoenician and Cretan deities and cults. Numerous inscriptions were also excavated, a

1. The cult of Bendis was brought to Athens by Thracians in the second half of the fifth century, and by the end of the century it had a festival sponsored by the state. Bendis' initial and primary cult center was in Piraeus, but by the 260s a branch existed in Athens. Some Athenians participated in the cult—for example, in the procession of the festival—from as early as the late fifth century, but none can be surely identified from the cult's inscriptions. In all texts but *IG* II² 1317 and 1317B the members are termed *orgeōnes*. In *IG* II² 1317 and 1317B they are *thiasōtai*, and since these two inscriptions were found on Salamis, they are probably from a separate, perhaps wholly Thracian *koinon* of Bendis there. Nothing survives from the city Bendis cult after 260; nothing from the Piraeus cult after, at the latest, the 230s.

2. The Asclepiastai,[21] consisting of at least two groups, one being made up of citizens from the deme Prospalta, served cults of Asclepios. The Prospaltians, with sixteen members from no more than four families, called themselves *orgeōnes* and tended a local sanctuary (*IG* II² 2355).[22] The group named in *SEG* 18.33 styled itself a *koinon* and was centered, as was the state sanctuary of Asclepios, on the south slope of the Acropolis. All were Athenians, and their inscriptional records date from the late third and early second centuries (*IG* II² 2353; *SEG* 18.33).[23]

3. The *orgeōnes*, all Athenian, of Amynos, Asclepios, and Dexion tended as two *koina* two sanctuaries: one of Dexion; the other, of Amynos and Asclepios, in the valley between the Areopagos and the Pnyx (*IG* II² 1252 + 999 and 1253 of the mid–fourth century). In 313/2 they honored their two *histiātōres* ("banquet givers"), evidently the chief officials of the *koina* (*IG* II² 1259).

---

very few of which have been published or reported; they are conveniently collected in *SEG* 41.247. Proper analysis must await publication of these texts, but from reports the members of the cult identified themselves variously as *thiasōtai* (247C), *eranistai* (247B), and *orgeōnes* (247D). The one published text (247E of 300/299) is a dedication by cult officials, all foreigners, from Miletos, Thebes, and Heracleia. Of the dedicators of the votive reliefs, all but one (B 5) lack demotics and patronymics, and they are probably not Athenians. Seven Athenians reportedly occur in the unpublished and undated *SEG* 247D. This material, when fully published, promises to be a rich source for information on early Athenian interaction with what appears to be originally a foreign cult.

21. Aleshire 1989, 68–70.
22. Kearns 1989, 73.
23. For the dates, see Tracy 1990a, 49.

A series of fourth-century dedications survive from the Amyneion, most to Amynos alone (*IG* II² 4385–4387, 4424, 4435), one to Amynos and Asclepios together (*IG* II² 4365). Amynos, like and prior to Asclepios, was a healing deity, and Dexion ("Receiver") was probably involved in the "reception" of Asclepios in 420.[24] In quite early times the poet Sophocles was identified with Dexion (*Vita* 11; *Etym. M.* s.v. "Δεξίων"), and it is noteworthy that, ca. 50–20 B.C., the priest of Amynos, Asclepios, and Hygieia was a Sophocles, son of Philotas, of Sounion (*PA* 12836) (*IG* II² 4457).[25]

4. The Egyptian Ammon had already in the mid–fourth century a sanctuary in Piraeus and by 363/2 a substantial store of dedications made by the Athenian state (*SEG* 21.241; see chapter 1, pp. 37–38). In 333/2 he received a state sacrifice (*IG* II² 1496.96–97) and by ca. 330 his priest was an Athenian (*IG* II² 410.19). *IG* II² 1282 (above, p. 139) of the late 260s does not reveal whether the members of the association that repaired the sanctuary of Ammon were citizens or not, but no demotics are given. There is no evidence of citizen involvement after ca. 330, nor of the cult at all after 260.

5. In 342/1 the *hieropoioi* of Sabazios erected a monument in Piraeus (*IG* II² 2932). The Sabaziastai practiced a cult at the same site centuries later (*IG* II² 1335 of 103/2), and the latter group included both Athenian and foreign nationals. There is no evidence, however, that Athenians were members in 342/1 or that the history of the cult was continuous.

6. Before 333/2 Egyptians had founded a cult of Isis in Piraeus (chapter 1, pp. 30–31), but there is no further evidence for Isis in the Piraeus, nor in the city until the second century (*IG* II² 4692). Under Macedonian, anti-Egyptian domination of the Piraeus the Ammon cult probably suffered and perhaps lapsed; the Isis cult, with no citizen members, died.

7. In 333/2 Cyprian merchants from Cition formed a cult of Aphrodite Ourania in Piraeus (Schwenk #27; see above, chapter 1, pp. 30–31). They styled themselves *thiasōtai* and their group a

24. On all aspects of these cults, see Clinton 1994; Aleshire 1989, 9–11, and 1991, 235–39; Kearns 1989, 14–21, 147, 154–55; Ferguson 1944, 86–91.
25. On this family, see Aleshire 1991, 223–34.

koinon. In 302/1 and the two succeeding years they passed decrees honoring their own official, the breastplate maker Stephanos (*IG* II² 1261). Two dedications survive from Citian women (*IG* II² 4636 and 4637). No Athenians appear as members, and the last sure attestation is the decree of 300/29.[26]

8. In 307/6 the *orgeōnes* of Egretes, near the Hill of the Nymphs in Athens, rented out the wooded sanctuary of their hero for ten years, at 200 drachmas a year, with provisions made for their sacrifice and banquet there each Boedromion (*IG* II² 2499).[27]

9. In 301/0 the *thiasōtai* of Tynabos from Piraeus honor two of their *epimelētai*, both apparently named Dracon, both Citians no doubt resident in Athens (*IG* II² 1262). This cult may have some connection to the Citian cult of Aphrodite Ourania, but Tynabos is otherwise unknown.[28] One may wonder whether the philosopher Zeno, himself a Citian, patronized this or the Aphrodite Ourania cult.

10. In the late fourth century the *orgeōnes* of Hypodektes, like those of Egretes above, rented out the sanctuary of their deity in Athens for fifty drachmas a year, again with the provision that the sanctuary be available for their use one day a year, in this case on Boedromion 14 (*IG* II² 2501).[29]

11. In 300/299 the *thiasōtai* of an unknown deity in Piraeus honored their secretary, Demetrios of Olynthos. The decree was proposed by Cleon, son of Leocritos, of Cyprian Salamis (*IG* II² 1263).

12. *IG* II² 1271 of 299/8 is the first and only evidence for the *thiasōtai* of Zeus Labraundos,[30] among whom metics from Heracleia were prominent. This cult too was in Piraeus, and no Athenians are attested as members.

13. In the early third century two apparently amalgamated *koina*

26. The third-century altar of the *thiasos* of Homonoia (*IG* II² 4985) may also stem from this cult. *IG* II² 1290 is too fragmentary to be assigned to this cult with confidence.

27. On Egretes and his *orgeōnes*, see Ferguson 1944, 80–81; Kearns 1989, 157.

28. For the correct name, "Tynabos" and not "Tynaros," see Tracy 1995, 145–46. Tracy's very tentative suggestion that the cult is Egyptian seems unlikely given the Cyprian origin of the devotees.

29. On Hypodektes and his possible connection with Eleusinian cult, see Ferguson 1944, 81–82; Kearns 1989, 75, 202.

30. On Zeus Labraundos, see Plut. *Mor.* 301F–302A.

of Echelos and of the Heroines recorded debtors to their *koinon* and, more interestingly, inscribed earlier decrees that concerned their sacrifices to the Heroines and Echelos on Hecatombaion 17 and 18. Provisions are made for the distribution of meat to members; to their sons, wives, and daughters; and to female attendants. Here too the chief official was the *hestiātōr*. The one named member is an Athenian, and the inscription was found on the Areiopagos (*SEG* 21.530).[31]

14. Some apparently fourth-century dedications, from both Athenians and non-Athenians, survive from the Piraeic cult of the Mother of the Gods, but the first surely dated record is *IG* II² 1316 of 272/1, where the members are called both *orgeōnes* and *thiasōtai*. In the decrees of the late third century (*IG* II² 1314, 1315) and in the second and first centuries (*IG* II² 1327–29, 1334), the *koinon* seems wholly Athenian.[32] There was also in 265/4 an apparently separate, wholly foreign *thiasos* of the Mother of the Gods, also in the Piraeus (*IG* II² 1273).

15. Two decrees (*SEG* 2.10 of 247/6 and 2.9 of 241/0) record honors given to the *epimelētai* of a *thiasos* devoted to unidentified gods on Salamis. The association had, besides *epimelētai*, a secretary, treasurer, and priest. In 247/6 they met on Skirophorion 2; in 241/0, on Anthesterion 3. Twenty members are known, none with a demotic or patronymic and none probably an Athenian. This group may have been associated, in some way, with the Salaminian devotees of Bendis.[33]

16. *IG* II² 1297 of 237/6 records the honors that a *thiasos* of a goddess, probably located outside the Dipylon Gate, paid to its *archeranistēs* Sophron for his good services. The inscription lists *all* the members of the *thiasos*, thirty-eight men and twenty-one women. There are no demotics, a patronymic only for the priest, and several names suggest non-Athenian origins. Sophron himself had to provide the stele for the inscription, and in general the circumstances seem quite humble. The

31. On Echelos and these *orgeōnes*, see Ferguson 1944, 73–79, and 1949, 130–31; Kearns 1989, 165.

32. For the numerous sculpted, uninscribed reliefs from the cult of the Mother of the Gods in Piraeus, see Vermaseren 1982, 82–97.

33. On *SEG* 2.9 and 10, see Taylor 1993, 235–38. Her identification of *SEG* 2.10 with the Bendis cult and of *SEG* 2.9 as a separate cult, based solely on the different meeting days, is not convincing, however. *SEG* 2.9 and 2.10 clearly belong to the same cult.

goddess of *IG* II² 1297 is not identified, but quite probably is the Artemis named by perhaps the same *thiasos* in an honorary decree of 244/3 (*IG* II² 1298) found nearby. None of the twelve names on *IG* II² 1298 is the same as the fifty-nine on *IG* II² 1297 of seven years later, but several names suggest the same non-Athenian origins.

This *thiasos*, if it is in fact a single one, has been, wrongly I think, associated with an Athenian cult of Kalliste located in the same area.³⁴ Kalliste, associated with an Ariste, was apparently Artemis;³⁵ she had a cult also on the road from the Dipylon Gate to the Academy, first attested in 246/5 by a dedication of her priest Antibios of Phrearrhioi (*SEG* 18.87). In 235/4 Antidoros of Pergase, her priest chosen by lot for a one-year term, was honored by the state for the sacrifices he made to the goddess on behalf of the Boule and Demos and for dedicating a stone altar, at his own expense (*IG* II² 788; cf. *IG* II² 789). No doubt from the same sanctuary comes a series of private dedications to Kalliste, one by an Athenian man, Timasitheos of Plotheia (*IG* II² 4665), and three by women bearing noble, quite probably Athenian names: Hippostrate (*IG* II² 4667), Hippokleia (*IG* II² 4666), and Eukoline (*IG* II² 4668).³⁶

The *thiasos* of *IG* II² 1297 and 1298 is distinct, I think, from this citizen cult of Kalliste. To be sure, both have male priests of the goddess, which is unusual, and *IG* II² 1297, 1298, and 788 were found in the same general area, but the differences outweigh the similarities. There is nothing to indicate citizen membership in the *thiasos*. And, in particular, Antidoros of Pergase, who was to be Kalliste's priest in 235/4, is *not* listed among *all* the members of the *thiasos* in 237/6, nor are any of those who made private dedications. In short, the *thiasos* of *IG* II² 1297 and 1298 was devoted to Artemis and had foreign membership. The cult of Kalliste was practiced by citizens and sacrificed on behalf of the state. The *thiasos* disappears from the record after 237/6, but Pausanias in the second century A.D. saw not far from the Dipylon Gate the sanctuary of Artemis with its statues of Kalliste and Ariste (1.29.2).

17. In 238/7 a *thiasos* centered in Eleusis honored its treasurer

34. On the Kalliste cult, see Judeich 1931, 412; Wycherley 1957, 59.
35. Hesychios s.v. "Καλλίστη"; Paus. 1.29.2.
36. Cf. *Hesp.* 10 (1941): 242–43, #42.

Paidicos for his efforts during wartime and for the sacrifice that he made with other officials to Zeus Soter and Hygieia (*SEG* 24.156). On the side of the stele members, probably twenty-two originally, were listed, none with a demotic or patronymic.[37]

18. *IG* II² 1291, of unknown origin and dated by letter forms to the middle of the third century, records an honorary decree of a *koinon* of *eranistai* devoted to Zeus Soter, Heracles, and the Soteres. Among the honorees is Aischylion, son of Theon, who was an *isotelēs*, that is, a metic given exemption from the usual metic taxes.

19. The very fragmentary *IG* II² 1294, found in Athens, is a record of *orgeōnes* of Zeus and may date to the middle of the third century. Zeus' epithet is restored to "Epakrios," known also from the Erchia sacred calendar (*SEG* 21.541.V.60–64) and related to "mountain top" Zeuses such as Hymettios (Paus. 1.32.2).[38]

20. In the Amphieraistai of *IG* II² 1322 Jean Pouilloux sees a group of Athenians, styling themselves *eranistai*, who after 229 contributed to financing necessary repairs to the Amphiaraion at Rhamnous.[39] There Amphieraos, under the influence of the military garrisons, had displaced the local "Physician Hero" (ἥρως ἰατρός) (*SEG* 31.177), and among the *eranistai* of *IG* II² 1322 are several military officers and soldiers. This appears not to be a cult association so much as a group dedicated to the restoration and maintenance of a sanctuary important to them and their fellow soldiers.

21. In *IG* II² 1275, from Piraeus, the *thiasōtai* of an unknown deity make provisions for attendance at funerals of deceased members and for instances of injustice affecting the members. These are the kinds of support that, in particular, a noncitizen in Athens would require. By letter forms the text is dated to the third or early second century.[40]

37. For various restorations of this text, see Robert 1969, 14–23; Pouilloux 1969.

38. H. Schwabl, *RE*, s.v. "Zeus," col. 305; Wycherley 1964, 176. For an improved text of *IG* II² 1294, see Ferguson 1944, 93–94. On such mountain top sanctuaries in Attica, see Langdon 1976.

39. See above, chapter 3, p. 102; Pouilloux 1954, 93–102, 144–47; Petrakos 1981 and 1983.

40. For restorations of this text, see *SEG* 21.534.

22. Also in the third century in Piraeus *thiasōtai* of an unknown deity honor five members, one of whom is from Samaria (*IG* II² 2943).

23. Among the *koina* of *orgeōnes* of unknown deities, *AJA* 69 (1965): 104, #1 is a late-fourth-century cult table from Athens. *IG* II² 2947 of the third or second century from the area of the Academy records honors given to Asclapon of Maroneia. If Asclapon was a member of the *koinon*, he would be a rare example of a noncitizen among *orgeōnes*, but his membership is not assured.[41] In *IG* II² 1289, also from Athens, is recorded the outcome of a legal dispute involving *orgeōnes* of an unknown goddess.[42]

24. Two decrees (*IG* II² 1318 and 1319) of unknown provenance, both dated to the end of the third century, record honorary decrees of *thiasoi* of unknown deities.

    IG II² 1278 of 273/2, also of unknown provenance, records honors a *thiasos* gave to its officials.[43]

In evaluating the importance of these private *koina* to religion in Hellenistic Athens the important questions are, as stated above: How many were there? Where were they located? Who, citizens or foreigners, participated in them? We now are in a position to treat these questions.

Of the approximately twenty-five "private" cults for which the cult site or the provenance of the inscriptions is known,[44] eleven were located in Piraeus: the devotees of Bendis (#1), of Ammon (#4), and of Isis (#6); the Sabaziastai (#5); the *thiasōtai* of Aphrodite Ourania (#7), of Tynabos (#9), of Zeus Labraundos (#12); three *koina* of *thiasōtai* of unknown deities (#11, 21, 22), and the worshippers of the Mother of the Gods (#14).[45] Ten were situated in or very near the city Athens: the

41. Ferguson 1944, 94. It is also possible that *IG* II² 2947 stems from the Bendis cult (Ferguson 1949, 162–63).

42. Ferguson 1944, 84–86. Among other texts that might stem from *koina* of *orgeōnes* of the third century B.C. is *Hesp.* 10 (1941): 56–57, #20 (Ferguson 1944, 82–83); *SEG* 17.36.

43. Also restored as belonging to *thiasoi* of the period are *SEG* 21.532 of 227/6, 21.533, 17.36.

44. I exclude the Amphieraistai (#20) as not being a true cult association. The *koinon* of Amynos and Asclepios shared activities with that of Dexion (#3) as the *koinon* of Echelos did with that of the Heroines (#13), and for statistical purposes I treat them as four separate *koina*.

45. On both foreign and citizen cults of the Piraeus, see Garland 1987, 101–38, 228–41.

devotees of Bendis (#1); the Asclepiastai (#2); *koina* of *orgeōnes* of Amynos, Asclepios, and Dexion (#3), of Egretes (#8), of Hypodektes (#10), of Echelos and the Heroines (#13), and of Zeus Epakrios (#19); and a *thiasos* of Artemis (#16). The *thiasos* of Zeus Soter and Hygieia was in Eleusis (#17), and a separate *thiasos* of Bendis and another of unknown gods were on Salamis (#1, 15).

The private cults may be divided quite evenly between the city and Piraeus, but the nature and membership of the cults were significantly different. The attributable Piraeic cults were all devoted to foreign deities, some of whom were taken up by citizens (Bendis, Ammon, and Mother of the Gods), while the others had only foreign membership (Isis, Sabazios, Aphrodite Ourania, Tynabos, Zeus Labraundos). Bendis was established as a state deity by the end of the fifth century, Ammon by the middle of the fourth. The Mother of the Gods had long since been established in the Agora as a part of state cult, although her relationship, if any, to the Piraeic Mother is uncertain.[46] Only the Bendis cult, recognized as unusual in this regard by Socrates (Pl. *Rep.* 1.327A), certainly had simultaneously both citizen and foreign members. In Piraeus then we have citizen members in cults accepted by the state (Bendis, Ammon, and, perhaps, Mother of the Gods) but wholly foreign cults devoted to Isis, Sabazios, Mother of the Gods, Tynabos, and Zeus Labraundos.

In the city the majority of private cults were *koina* of *orgeōnes*, devoted to Bendis, Amynos and Asclepios, Dexion, Egretes, Hypodektes, Echelos and the Heroines, and Zeus Epakrios. Bendis, Asclepios, Amynos, Dexion, and Hypodektes all apparently had classical origins, and the *koina* dedicated to them probably are survivals from the classical period.[47] The same is probably true of Egretes, Echelos and the Heroines, and Zeus Epakrios. With the exception of Bendis,[48] these "orgeonic" *koina* had only Athenians as members, and many, perhaps most, of them featured an annual sacrifice and formal banquet. The only non-Athenian *koinon* attested for the city was that of Artemis outside the Dipylon Gate (#16).

46. See Garland 1987, 129–31. On the citizen cult of the Mother of the Gods in the Agora, and on the possibility that the building usually termed "The Old Bouleuterion" was in fact from its beginnings the Metroön, see Miller 1995b. For criticisms of Miller's argument and for more on the history of the Mother of the Gods of the Agora, see Shear 1995.

47. On the classical *orgeōnes*, see Ferguson 1944; Kearns 1989, 73–75.

48. On the uncertainties of the membership in the various Bendis cults, see above, pp. 140–42.

The division between the city and Piraeus could not be more clear. Private cults in the city were dedicated to classical deities and had exclusively citizen membership. Private cults in Piraeus probably all began as cults of foreigners. Some of them attracted citizen members and gained state recognition (Bendis, Ammon) or even became wholly Athenian (Mother of the Gods). Most noteworthy is how few of the Piraeic foreign cults (only Bendis) penetrated the city. One would expect, in the normal course of religious development in the Hellenistic period, that some foreign cults, once introduced, would spread throughout the population. That there are relatively few new foreign cults in Piraeus in this period and that they did not penetrate the city are quite probably owed in part to the long periods in which Piraeus, the port of entry and incubator for such cults, was isolated from the city. This may be one key to explaining what appears to be the religious conservatism of Athenian religion in the Hellenistic period.

In terms of membership, the devotees of the Bendis cult (#1), the Asclepiastai (#2), the worshippers of Amynos, Asclepios, and Dexion (#3), of Egretes (#8), of Hypodektes (#10), of Echelos and the Heroines (#13), one cult of the Mother of the Gods (#14), the devotees of Zeus Epakrios (#19), and members of three *koina* of unknown deities (#23) all explicitly termed themselves *orgeōnes*. They were all Athenian citizens, albeit few in number. The Asclepiastai of Prospalta (#2) were sixteen, and the cult table of a similar *koinon* (*AJA* 69 [1965]: 104) suggests a similar size. These citizen *koina* may have been small, but, as Ferguson concluded (1944, 104), the members in the third century were "quite respectable Athenians, preponderantly persons of the propertied classes."

The Salaminian devotees of Bendis (#1), the other Salaminian *koinon* (#15), the Citian worshippers of Aphrodite Ourania (#7) and Tynabos (#9), the members of the cult of Zeus Labraundos (#12), some devotees of the Mother of the Gods (#14), the worshippers of Artemis in the city (#16), and members of three *koina* from Piraeus (#11, 21, 22), of one from Eleusis (#17), and of two of unknown location (#24) designated themselves as *thiasōtai* or their *koina* as *thiasoi*. Apart from the complicated cult of Mother of the Gods, none of these *thiasōtai* is surely an Athenian and many among them are designated as foreigners. They too, like the *koina* of *orgeōnes*, were small, with that of Artemis (#16) recording thirty-eight male and twenty-one female members and that in Eleusis (#17) having twenty-two members.

Particularly significant here is the clear separation between *koina* of

citizens (*orgeōnes*) and of foreigners (*thiasōtai*). In this period and before, the distinction between *orgeōnes* and *thiasōtai* holds for all but two
cults, of Bendis and the Mother of the Gods, those two Piraeic cults
that began foreign but eventually became partially if not wholly Athenian. Clearly even in the third century, with rare exception, Athenian citizens were *not* participating in foreign cults, certainly not in those of
recent origin.

And, finally, the subsequent history of the foreign cults would suggest that they were not only small but weak. Most are attested by only
one inscriptional text (#5, 6, 9, 10, 11, 12, 17, 18, 21, 22, 23, 24). The disappearance of the wholly foreign *koina*, even of Isis, is not surprising,
but the loss of the state deities Ammon (after 260) and Bendis (after,
at the latest, 230) is noteworthy. The one foreign cult that was to thrive,
probably because it had become wholly citizen, was that of the Mother
of the Gods. Also noteworthy is the virtual disappearance from the
record hereafter of the citizen cults of *orgeōnes* of traditional deities—
for example, those of Asclepios, Amynos, Dexion, Egretes, Hypodektes, and Echelos—many or all of which dated back to the classical period.

I save for last *IG* II² 1277 from 278/7, which, because it is complete,
offers some insight into the activities and purposes of the foreign *thiasoi*. It fills out details preserved only in fragments in the *thiasos* texts
considered thus far. The goddess is unknown, but her cult center may
have been in the city, near the Pnyx.

In the archonship of Democles (278/7), on the seventeenth of Mounichion,
at an authoritative meeting. Noumenias proposed:

> Whereas the *epimelētai* and secretary put in office by the *koinon* in the ar-
> chonship of Democles took care of the sanctuary well and generously;
> and made all the sacrifices according to ancestral traditions; and adorned
> (ἐπεκόσμησαν) the goddess and built from scratch the altar; and for these
> things contributed 65 drachmas of their own funds; and, having had a
> silver cup weighing 57 1/2 drachmas made at their own expense, dedi-
> cated it to the goddess; and in a good and generous manner took care
> of those who died; and have given an accounting and audit of every-
> thing they have administered,

it was voted, with good fortune, by the *thiasōtai* to praise these *epimelētai*,
Eucles, Thallos, and Zeno, and the secretary Ctesias, and to crown each of
them with an olive crown because of their virtue and generosity toward the
koinon and because of their piety toward the goddess. Their crowns and
praise are to be proclaimed at each sacrifice together with the other benefactors. And they are to receive from the *koinon* whatever other good they
seem to be deserving, so that all those who enter into the office of *epimelētēs*

may be generous toward the goddess and the *koinon*, knowing that they will receive worthwhile returns. And the *epimelētai* (in the year) after Democles are to inscribe this decree on a stone tablet and erect it in the sanctuary.

The members of this *koinon* are given neither patronymics nor demotics, and hence are probably not Athenian citizens. The elected *epimelētai* had major responsibilities for the sanctuary, sacrifices, building program, and dedications of the cult. The three men spent, as was the custom of the time, from their own funds: 65 drachmas for the sacrifice, adornment of the goddess, and the building of the altar, and money for the silver cup weighing 57 1/2 drachmas—altogether rather modest sums. Among their good services was proper tendance of those *thiasōtai* who had died during the year.[49] For all Greeks funeral responsibilities fell upon family members, but family may well not have been present for many foreign nationals residing in Athens, and *koina* such as this could provide this valuable service. That some foreign *koina* took on the responsibilities of burial of their members indicates nothing, of course, about the status of the Athenian families of the time. Athenian citizens no doubt provided as they always had for their deceased members.

In sum, there were some private religious "clubs" or associations in early Hellenistic Athens. Those of citizens were predominantly in the city, dedicated to traditional deities and tended by prosperous individuals. Those in Piraeus were made up largely of foreigners worshipping their native gods. Most of these were relatively small and short-lived. Athenian citizens apparently participated in or took over two of them (Bendis and the Mother of the Gods), and these had a somewhat longer life. But compared to native Athenian cults, there were only a handful of foreign cults and they had only a handful of members. If, as Ferguson claims (1911, 225), each citizen, foreign or Athenian, who joined such associations "struck a blow at the ancient national religion," then the blows were few and weak, and there is no reason to assume that private *koina*, citizen or foreign, significantly affected the strength or "quality" of Athenian religion in this period.[50]

Of a completely different order were the religious associations of Athenian soldiers stationed in the forts of Attica. In 240/39 Antigonos Go-

49. Cf. *IG* II² 1275 (#21 above), 1278.2–4 (#24).

50. Strabo (10.3.18) claims that the Athenians, as in other things, were especially "foreign loving" (φιλοξενοῦντες) about the gods because they accepted many of the foreign cults. His sources are exclusively literary, apparently, and he can offer as examples only the cults of Bendis and Sabazios.

natas died and was succeeded by his son, Demetrios II. For the previous five years Aratos, head of the Achaean League, had been trying to detach Athens from Antigonos and gain her support for his league. In 242 he had marched through a corner of Attica and pillaged Salamis. In 240 he attempted a direct assault on Piraeus, which was still held by the Macedonians. In 233 the Athenians celebrated a false report of Aratos' capture or death, but Aratos again this year entered Attica. In the midst of these events, in 236/5, the demesmen of Rhamnous, the important coastal deme, town, harbor, and fortress,[51] honored Dicaiarchos and his father Apollonios of the deme Thria (*SEG* 25.155). Dicaiarchos and his father had been put in charge of the garrisons at various forts by Antigonos.[52] They were Athenians, appointed by Macedonian kings but commanding garrisons made up at least in part from Athenian citizens, defending Attica against foreign, now Achaean attacks.

In addition to his other good services, Dicaiarchos had contributed "victims for the sacrifice of the Nemesia and the king,[53] from his own funds, since these sacrifices had lapsed because of the war, so that relations with the goddesses[54] might be good for the Rhamnousians" (lines 27–30). The Nemesia was the annual festival of Nemesis, in the Attic religious tradition a peculiarly Rhamnousian deity, perhaps kindred to Artemis.[55] One may speculate about the goddess' functions from her name,[56] but virtually nothing is known of the cult. Her association with the victory over the hubristic Persians at Marathon (Paus. 1.33.2), however, makes her a particularly appropriate goddess at the important coastal fort of Rhamnous, whatever her origins and early nature may have been. Her annual festival would naturally be a concern to the military commander and his troops there.

51. On the fort of Rhamnous and its history, see Pouilloux 1954; Petrakos 1981, 1983.
52. On this family, see Habicht 1982b, 52, 57.
53. On the "sacrifices of the king," see below, p. 160.
54. The "goddesses" here are Nemesis and Themis. Cf. *SEG* 41.90.10; *IG* II² 2869.
55. From *SEG* 41.75.7–9 the gymnastic contest of the Great Nemesia was celebrated in Rhamnous on Hecatombaion 19. In a famous statue Phidias had represented Nemesis with a crown of deer and small Nikai, an apple bough in her left hand, a *phialē* in her right. On the base Phidias had, among other figures, Helen being led off by Leda to her mother Nemesis (Paus. 1.33.2–8). This statue, at least by Pausanias' time, was associated with the Athenian victory over the Persians at Marathon in 490. Substantial fragments of this statue and its base have been recovered, and for drawings of the restorations, see Petrakos 1986. For attribution of the statue to Agoracritos, or a second statue of Nemesis, see Pliny *NH* 36.17. On other representations of Nemesis, see Palagia 1994.
56. Nemesis may, if we are not misled by homonyms, be particularly associated with the dead. Cf. Dem. 41.11; Soph. *El.* 792.

We have seen previously taxiarchs assuming a religious role and surmised from that the increasing importance of the military (chapter 4, pp. 133–34). Now commanders of garrisons come to the fore and intervene in religious affairs. In *SEG* 25.155 they interact with, essentially, three groups: the Demos of the Athenians, the demesmen of Rhamnous, and the *koinon* of Athenian soldiers stationed in the fort at Rhamnous. The Athenian people and the demesmen of Rhamnous had, traditionally, their own religious programs, but in this period there is a new concern for the *koina* of Athenian soldiers who were stationed in forts throughout the year, possibly for several years. These soldiers, uprooted from their homes and family and deme cults, needed to be provided with some religious activities, and we see the commanders doing this and being praised for having done so.[57]

At Rhamnous it appears that, initially, as in *SEG* 25.155, the commander supported or revived established cults of the community. In 236/5 Dicaiarchos with his own funds restored the Nemesia, to the benefit of all, including his own soldiers. Earlier, ca. 255, Callisthenes of Prospalta (*PA* 8104a), as general for the coastal region, had erected a dedication at Rhamnous to Dionysos Lenaios, a deity already established there (*IG* II² 2854).[58] But after the independence of Athens and the departure of the Macedonians in 229, a new cult emerges at Rhamnous, that of Zeus Soter and Athena Soteira; henceforth this cult, no doubt commemorating Athens' independence, becomes the focus of the generals' and soldiers' attention.[59] In or shortly after 229 the soldiers themselves honored for his piety their commander, Demostratos of Phlya (*PA* 3631), who had sacrificed to Zeus Soter and Athena Soteira, put on a torch race, and honored the other gods (*SEG* 15.111).[60] At about the same time they honored the general Aischron of Phyle, who had made sacrifices to the same gods and perhaps staged a javelin and archery contest (*SEG* 22.128).[61] In 225/4 the Rhamnousians, those of the citizens living in Rhamnous, and in particular his sailors honored the trierarch Menandros of Eitea. Among his services he "had sacrificed to

---

57. Soldiers stationed at Rhamnous in the mid–fourth century, as a group, made dedications there, in honor of their officers (*SEG* 40.145). On the makeup of these garrisons and on the term of service of the soldiers, see Lauter 1989, 29–32.

58. Cf. *SEG* 23.122.16, 25.155.40.

59. On this cult at Rhamnous, see Petrakos 1992, 20–21.

60. For the date, see Pouilloux 1956, 61–63. The torch race is probably that of the Nemesia, in which the ephebes had participated in the late 330s (*IG* II² 3105 + *SEG* 31.162).

61. For new text and date, see Garlan 1978.

Zeus Soter and Athena Soteira for the health, safety, and concord (ὁμονοίας) of his fellow sailors so that they might be in concord, be saved, and hereafter be useful to the Demos" (*SEG* 15.112.9–12). We have here the clearest expression of how Zeus Soter and Athena Soteira were thought responsible, after the establishment of independence, for *both* physical safety *and* political harmony. When Menandros was in Rhamnous he also sacrificed, with the general and religious officials, to Nemesis and contributed victims and wine (16–19). It may have been partially for this that the Rhamnousians and residents there joined the sailors in honoring him.

This Rhamnousian cult of Zeus Soter and Athena Soteira, which first appears after 229, belonged, perhaps, primarily to the armed forces, whereas Nemesis was the community's deity.[62] The Rhamnousian cult of Zeus and Athena—established, if the above reconstruction is correct, on the model of the state cult but for the soldiers of the garrison—then apparently persisted until at least 99/8.[63] About this time may also have been founded at Rhamnous the cult of Aphrodite Hegemone, to whom, in 222/1, the general Nichomachos of Paiania set up a dedication and to whom he sacrificed on leaving office, inviting all those stationed at Rhamnous and nearby Aphidna (*SEG* 41.90). She too, located inside the fort, may have been a deity primarily for the garrison troops.

In a similar manner troops stationed at Sounion in 298/7, the earliest such association attested, honored their commander (ἐξεταστής), Cephisodotos of Acharnae (*PA* 8327) (*IG* II² 1270; cf. *IG* II² 1309). The inscription recording these honors was to be erected, as were other decrees of the Sounion garrison (*IG* II² 1300), in the major sanctuary there, that of Poseidon (lines 18–19). In 220/19 these troops honored the general, Theomnestos of Xypete (*PA* 6970), because, among other things, he "built in addition to (προσκατεσκεύαζε) the existing sanctuaries there a temple and sanctuary of Asclepios" (*IG* II² 1302.6–8).[64] Theomnestos was clearly, as a general, contributing to the health of his troops and community.

The troops stationed at Eleusis, Panacton, Phyle, and near the city had a *koinon* separate from those posted at Rhamnous and Sounion. In

---

62. Ca. 200 the Rhamnousians and soldiers jointly honored the Phocian Sopolis and erected the honorific stele in the sanctuary of Nemesis (*SEG* 31.112). Cf. *IG* II² 1312; *SEG* 41.86.

63. *IG* II² 2869; *SEG* 41.162, 164–65, 248F.

64. *SEG* 16.177, a dedication to Asclepios by a private citizen, is quite likely from this sanctuary.

or shortly after 236/5 this *koinon* and the deme of Eleusis honored, in separate decrees, the general Aristophanes of Leukonoion (*PA* 2092) (*IG* II² 1299). He had sacrificed, at the Eleusinian festival of the Haloa, "to Demeter, Kore, and the other gods to whom it was traditional (to sacrifice), on behalf of the Demos of the Athenians, King Demetrios, his queen Phthia, and their children.[65] He invited all the citizens to the sacrifice,[66] thinking they should share in the good things occurring in the rites, and he spent his own funds" (lines 9–13). For these and many other good services Aristophanes was to receive a crown and a statue to be erected in the courtyard of the sanctuary at Eleusis. The crown and statue were to be announced "at the ancestral contest of the Haloa,[67] at the sacrifice of the Apatouria in Panacton, at Phyle at the sacrifice to Artemis Agrotera," and in Athens at the City Dionysia (28–32).

These soldiers, unlike those at Rhamnous, seem not to have developed their own cults but utilized, for their purposes, cults in their various regions: that of Demeter and Kore at Eleusis,[68] of Artemis Agrotera at Phyle, and the festival of the Apatouria, a local celebration of which was probably held at or near the deme centered at Panacton (cf. *IG* II² 1285.22). Aristophanes evidently opened up the celebration of the Haloa, usually and perhaps mistakenly thought to be exclusively a women's festival, to all the citizens and, no doubt, provided them a fine banquet, all at his own expense. This was surely welcome to the soldiers stationed there, perhaps more so than to the demesmen of Eleusis, who make no mention of it.

The decrees of these three associations of soldiers, one centered at Rhamnous, one at Sounion, and one at Eleusis, reveal two trends. First, units of now full-time, year-round soldiers provided for themselves a religious program of sorts, either through a new cult (e.g., of Zeus Soter and Athena Soteira or of Aphrodite Hegemone at Rhamnous), or by participation in some of the cults of the region in which they happened to be stationed, or by both. Second, the military commanders naturally played a role in developing and promoting such religious activities of these units, so far even as contributing funds for the sacrifices. By and large the religious activities of these permanent garrisons of Athenians

65. On such sacrifices for King Demetrios and his family, see below, pp. 160–61.

66. By "the citizens" here Habicht (1961, 134 = 1994, 31) understands "citizen soldiers" in contrast to "foreign soldiers."

67. Cf. *IG* II² 1304B.14–15 of 269/8, 1304.45–47 of 211/0.

68. Cf. the dedication to Demeter and Kore of *IG* II² 2971, redated by Tracy 1995, 43–44, 171–74, to ca. 250 B.C.

were integrated into those of the local community. It is also noteworthy that foreign mercenaries, although they served in these garrisons and might even contribute financially to the honors of the commanders (*IG* II² 1299.11–14, 93–117), were not invited to and quite assuredly did not participate in the religious activities of their Athenian counterparts.

From the end of the Chremonidean War (261) to his death (240/39) Antigonos Gonatas, through his agents and garrisons, maintained close control over Athens, relaxing it somewhat after 256/5. It has been previously been assumed, quite reasonably from the lack of explicit evidence, that unlike his predecessor Demetrios Poliorcetes, Antigonos had neither sought nor received divine honors from the Athenians.[69] The very recently discovered *SEG* 41.75 from Rhamnous reveals, however, that the Athenian state, surely after the Chremonidean War, honored Antigonos with "godlike honors" as *Sōtēr* of the Demos and benefactor. The Rhamnousians then in this decree instituted a sacrifice to Antigonos as part of their Nemesia on Hecatombaion 19.[70] This is surely the sacrifice "of the king" revived by Dicaiarchos at Rhamnous, as described in *SEG* 25.155 of 236/5. It is noteworthy that all the evidence for Antigonos' divine cult comes from the fort whose commander was appointed by the reigning Macedonian. The limited range and duration of this "ruler cult" may, however, be explained by Antigonos' personal dislike for such honors.[71]

But for honoring Antigonos the Athenians turned also to a new and quite different religious device, one that was to have a long history. In the third century the Athenians had begun to introduce "all those who are well-intentioned to the Demos" into the list (including Boule, Demos, and, often, children and wives) of those for whose "health and safety" public sacrifices were made.[72] Now, after Antigonos had granted them "freedom" in 256/5, the Athenians specified these friends of the Demos: namely, Antigonos and his family. The first securely dated example is *IG* II² 780 of 249/8, in which the *agōnothetēs* Agathaios of Prospalta (*PA* 24) was honored for making sacrifices to Dionysos and

69. F. Walbank 1987, 375; *CAH* 7.1:92; Tarn 1913, 250–51, 435; Ferguson 1911, 190–91 (for lack of ruler cult in Macedonia).

70. On this text, see Petrakos 1992, 31–34.

71. See Green 1990, 141–43, 199–200, 406, for discussion of reasons why Antigonos Gonatas, as a Macedonian and a Stoic, would have disapproved of divine cult for himself.

72. *Agora* XV, #78.9–11, of 273/2 (above, chapter 3, pp. 113–14) is the first example dated with certainty. *IG* II² 661, of 267/6, records such sacrifices by the *epimelētai* of the Eleusinian Mysteries at the Mysteries at Agrai. Cf. *IG* II² 807; *Agora* XV, #79, 80.

the other ancestral gods "for the health and safety of the Boule, the Demos of the Athenians, their children and wives, and on behalf of King Antigonos" and, presumably, his queen and children (lines 6–11).[73] In *SEG* 33.115 of 246/5 Timocrite, priestess of Aglauros, is recorded as having made sacrifices to Aglauros, Ares, Helios, Horai, Apollo, and the other gods "for the health and safety of the Boule, the Demos of the Athenians, their children and wives, and on behalf of ($\acute{v}\pi\acute{\epsilon}\rho$) King Antigonos and his queen Phile and their children" (lines 9–25). In 245/4 for the same beneficiaries the *epimelētai* of the Eleusinian Mysteries made sacrifices to Demeter, Kore, and the other gods (*IG* II² 683). From about the same years, records survive of similar sacrifices to Asclepios, Hygieia, and the other gods by the priest of Asclepios (*SEG* 18.19) and to Athena Polias by her priestess (*IG* II² 776). All of these sacrifices are not "to" Antigonos but "for" him,[74] and presumably Antigonos and his family would benefit in the same manner as would Athenian men, women, and children. Inclusion among the citizen beneficiaries is a mark of honor and distinction, but not of cult.

We see here, I think, an important transitional time in the Athenian handling of "honors" for their rulers. The Rhamnousian texts, from a Macedonian stronghold, show continuance of the system of "godlike honors" and sacrifices "to" the king, a system begun in earnest for Antigonos Monophthalmos and Demetrios Poliorcetes. For this there is no evidence after 236/5.[75] The inclusion of the ruling king and his family among the citizen beneficiaries of sacrifices is a retreat from ruler cult. The two systems overlapped, at least from 249/8 to 236/5, but soon the "godlike honors" and sacrifices to rulers were eliminated and the kings and benefactors again became men, not deities. And so they were to remain in Athens in the Hellenistic period.[76]

The number and names of the deities who received these sacrifices "on behalf of Antigonos and his family" suggest that by the mid-240s, many traditional elements of Athenian state cult were again prospering.

73. The same phrase should probably be restored in the erasure of *Agora* XV, #89.11–12, 29 of 254/3 B.C.

74. On the significance of this difference, see F. Walbank 1987, 366; Nilsson 1967–74, 2:182.

75. After Antigonos' death, his son Demetrios II and his family received the honor of being beneficiaries in the sacrifices of the demesmen of Eleusis and the soldiers garrisoned there, sacrifices made to Demeter, Kore, and the other gods (*IG* II² 1299.9–11, after 236/5).

76. For the Soteres of *Agora* XV, #111.4–5, 115.12–13, being Zeus Soter and Athena Soteira, not Antigonos Monophthalmos and Demetrios Poliorcetes, see above, chapter 4, note 20.

Athens recovered Eleusis after 285, but the next twenty years offer little epigraphical record of activities in Eleusis, especially compared to the voluminous record of the fourth century. In 267/6, however, the state honored two *epimelētai* of the Mysteries for their sacrifice at the Mysteries at Agrai, for their tendance of the sacrifice at Great Mysteries, and for their sacrifice of the *sōtēria*, presumably at the Eleusinia, at their own expense (*IG* II² 661). This annually elected board of overseers of the Mysteries had probably been established in the mid–fourth century,[77] was active in the late fourth century,[78] but then virtually disappears from the record until 267/6. It may well not have been able to function until Eleusis was reunited with Athens after 285. An individual who also held generalships was honored for his service as *epimelētēs* in the 250s (*IG* II² 3460), and in 245/4 it was this board that oversaw the sacrifice to Demeter and Kore for, in addition to others, Antigonos and his family (*IG* II² 683). The impression is left that by the middle of the third century, Eleusis is again operating fully, with the Mysteries and Lesser Mysteries, and with superintendence by the state. *IG* II² 1299 of ca. 236/5, decrees of troops stationed in Eleusis and of the demesmen themselves (see above, pp. 158–59), confirms this and attests to the celebration also of the "ancestral contest of the Haloa" and the invitation of "all the citizens" to it (lines 9–13). For that celebration the honoree of the decrees, the general Aristophanes of Leukonoion, contributed his own funds.

For the fifteen years after 285/4 the City Dionysia is attested as occurring or being expected almost every other year, and celebrations were surely held also in the intervening years (chapter 4, pp. 116–17). The last year in the sequence was 270/69 (*SEG* 28.60.92–94; *IG* II² 3081); the next attested celebration is ca. 255/4 or later (*IG* II² 682.75–77, 793.6).[79] A notice of victors in dramatic contests of the 250s survives (*SEG* 26.208), and in the City Dionysia of 249/8 the *agōnothetēs* made the sacrifices "for the health and safety of the Boule, the Demos of the Athenians, their children and wives, and on behalf of King Antigonos" (*IG* II² 780.6–11). The City Dionysia is then next attested for 247/6 (*SEG* 32.117.26–28). The next record, after 236/5, contains the usual request to proclaim an individual's honors "at the new contest of tragedies of the Dionysia in the city," but adds, unusually, "when the Demos first puts

77. [Arist.] *Ath.Pol.* 57.1; Develin 1989, 12–13.
78. E.g., *IG* II² 1191, 2840, 2841 of 321/0 or 318/7.
79. Henry (1992) dates *IG* II² 682 to 259/8, but the date remains problematic.

on the Dionysia," which may suggest that the City Dionysia was not necessarily being held every year (*IG* II² 1299.31–32). Whatever may have been the situation at the end of the period, it appears that the City Dionysia and *agōnothesia* were functioning in their traditional ways in the mid-240s. It is also noteworthy that in this period, for the first time since 307/6 (*IG* II² 456.33), the Dionysia in Piraeus is attested (*IG* II² 1214.19–25).

In the 240s a priest of Asclepios was honored for making sacrifices to Asclepios and Hygieia "for the health and safety of the Boule and Demos, children and women, and on behalf of King Antigonos" and his family (*SEG* 18.19).[80] He had made the sacrifices, adorned a "table" (lectisternium), and put on the all-night festival (*pannychis*) (lines 16–20; cf. *IG* II² 704). The cult was prospering to the extent that an inventory of recent dedications to the god was assembled in 244/3 (Aleshire, Inv. V), the first such inventory to survive since 274/3 (Aleshire, Inv. IV). As to the purpose of the inventory, I quote Sara Aleshire, its most recent editor: "The priest of 244/3 . . . saw that the City Asklepieion was in need of cleaning and refurbishing, much like Leonides Phyleus some one hundred and Diokles Diokleous Kephisieus the younger some two hundred years later, and set about persuading the boule and demos to aid him in this task. Inventory V preserves the results in part" (1989, 301).[81]

Similar inventorying of the dedications on the Acropolis was done in the archonship of Alcibiades, probably in the 250s (Pollux 10.126), and from Alcibiades' year also survives a decree (*IG* II² 776) honoring the priestess of Athena Polias. The priestess had successfully sacrificed "for the health and safety of the Boule and Demos, children and women, and of King Antigonos, his queen, and his descendants" (lines 5–10). She held a lectisternium for the goddess and did all else assigned to her by the laws and decrees of the Demos (10–14). She made dedications at her own expense and contributed 100 drachmas to the Praxiergidai for the traditional sacrifice (16–20). Her husband, Archestratos of Amphitrope (*PA* 2419), was also honored (26–30). This is the first significant cult activity attested for Athena Polias since King Pyrrhos' sacrifice in 287/6 (chapter 4, pp. 108–10), and it, together with the in-

---

80. For the dates, nature, and circumstances of these decrees, see Habicht 1982b, 75–77; Lewis 1985a.

81. For a sacrifice by the public physicians to Asclepios and Hygieia, probably from ca. 250, see *SEG* 25.96.

ventory described by Pollux, suggests renewed interest in Athens' Acropolis cults.[82]

The Panathenaia, the festival of Athena Polias, was also apparently renewed in this period—perhaps in 254, the first year of the Great Panathenaia after Antigonos' relaxation of control.[83] The agent of renewal was Heracleitos, son of Asclepiades, of the deme Athmonon (*PA* 6496), the man Antigonos had put in charge, as general, of the Piraeic garrisons (*IG* II² 1225). If the restorations of *IG* II² 677 are not misleading, the Athenians renewed the sacrifice and contests of the Panathenaia, and Heracleitos repaired the Panathenaic Stadium built under Lycourgos. Heracleitos also dedicated to Athena Nike paintings showing Antigonos' victories "over the barbarians, for the sake of the safety of the Greeks" (lines 3–6). Heracleitos' honors are to be announced in the gymnastic contest of the Panathenaia (14–16). Later, in the year of the archon Athenodoros, probably in the 250s, the *athlothetai* were honored for administering the Panathenaia and its music, gymnastic, and equestrian events (*IG* II² 784).[84] In 247/6 the Great Panathenaia of the next year was being anticipated (*SEG* 32.117.28–29).[85]

In Athenaios (4.167E–F) is preserved an anecdote, attributed to Hegesander, that casts a flicker of precious light on one aspect of the Mysteries and Panathenaia of this period. Demetrios of Phaleron (*APF* 3453), grandson of the tyrant, was rich, like his notorious grandfather enjoyed without compunction the good life, and for his outspoken defense of his lifestyle was appointed *thesmothetēs* by Antigonos. Once, at the Panathenaia, as *hipparchos*, he built for his Corinthian *hetaira* a platform "rising above the Herms" for her viewing of the procession. For the Mysteries, probably as general of the region (*IG* II² 1285), he placed a seat for her immediately next to the *anaktoron*. Both acts were considered scandalous and probably impious.[86]

The recent publication of a decree in honor of Timocrite, the priestess of Aglauros, of 246/5 has expanded significantly our understanding of this cult and helps confirm its continued existence in the third cen-

---

82. Cf. the roughly contemporary honors of Penteteris, another priestess of Athena Polias (*IG* II² 928). For the date, see Tracy 1990a, 259.

83. Shear 1978, 11 n. 11. Cf. *IG* II² 682.75–78.

84. For this being the Great Panathenaia, see Habicht 1979, 137–38.

85. SEG 32.169 records an *athlothetēs* of the Panathenaia, Micion the brother of Eurycleides, for some year in the period 230–222. The year was probably 226/5 or 222/1, years of the Great Panathenaia (Habicht 1982b, 46). On the date, see also Tracy 1988b, 315.

86. Habicht 1961, 137–38 = 1994, 33–34.

tury (*SEG* 33.115).[87] We have previously seen that Aglauros, whose sanctuary now is known to have been beneath the east slope of the Acropolis,[88] was the prime witness to the oath of the ephebes cited by Lycourgos in the *Leocrates* (76; see above, chapter 1, pp. 16–17). Fellow witnesses there were Hestia, Enyo, Enyalios, Ares and Athena Areia, Zeus, Thallo, Auxo, Hegemone, Heracles, the territory of the fatherland, the wheat, barley, vines, olive trees, and fig trees. From her company Aglauros may be seen to be integrally related to the welfare, in both military and agricultural terms, of the city and its citizens. In *SEG* 33.115 Timocrite is honored, in a decree perhaps proposed by her husband,[89] for sacrificing the *eisitētēria* to Aglauros, Ares, Helios, the Horai, Apollo, and the other traditional gods, sacrifices intended "for the health and safety of the Boule, the Demos of the Athenians, their children and wives, and on behalf of King Antigonos, his queen Phila, and their descendants." She also watched over "good order" in the all-night festival and adorned a table for the goddess.

The differences in the figures associated with Aglauros in the ephebic decree of the fourth century and the decree of 246/5 may be instructive. Their omission in the decree suggest, as was already quite apparent, that the land and crops of Attica were not imagined as cult deities in the oath but as symbolically appropriate witnesses to it. Heracles found a place in the oath, but not in the state sacrifices, because of his association with the ephebes. For the role of the Horai (Thallo, Auxo, and Hegemone) in the cult of Aglauros and their appearance in the oath, see chapter 6 below (pp. 174–77). Of the war deities in the oath — Enyo, Enyalios, Ares, and Athena Areia — only Ares, Aglauros' husband, persists, and it is quite probable that the others have lost cultic importance.[90] Zeus was in the oath perhaps only as Zeus Horkios ("of Oaths"), but it is significant that Apollo appears in the decree. If our reconstruction of the relations of Zeus Boulaios and Apollo Prostaterios in the third century is correct (chapter 4, pp. 115–16), Apollo may have been the cur-

87. Dontas 1983, 48–63. Cf. *IG* II² 3459, a dedication of Pheidostrate, sister of Chremonides and priestess of Aglauros, dated to the beginning of the third century B.C. See Dontas 1983, 54. Robertson (1984, 392 n. 47) has shown how *SEG* 33.115 makes it likely that *IG* II² 948 of ca. 190 (for date, see Tracy 1990a, 84) also stems from the Aglauros cult. On the Aglauros cult, see also Merkelbach 1972; Brulé 1987, esp. 33–34; Kearns 1989, 23–27, 57–63, 139–40; and below, chapter 6, pp. 175–76.

88. Dontas 1983, 48–63.

89. Lewis 1983.

90. On Athena Areia, see above, pp. 138–39. On the relationships of Enyalios, Enyo, and Ares, see Graf 1985, 265–68.

rent recipient of *eisitētēria* on behalf of the Boule and Demos in 247/6. Helios, who appears here for the first time in an Athenian state cult, was not to have a significant future in Hellenistic Athens.[91] Even if we take into account the different purposes of the oath and of the sacrifice recorded in the decree, some changes appear, changes that seem to reflect a de-emphasis of the military deities, a promotion of Apollo, and a single but characteristically unsuccessful introduction of a new cult figure (Helios).

The above inscriptions, all of which record sacrifice on behalf of King Antigonos and his family, indicate that at least by the 240s, several of the most traditional Athenian state cults were again functioning in their traditional ways; the Mysteries, City Dionysia, and the Panathenaia were being celebrated, and priestly families, priests, priestesses, and traditional boards of overseers were fulfilling their traditional responsibilities. The mid-240s also provide the first evidence, since the 270s, of Athenian participation in international religious activities. In 246/5 the Aetolian League reorganized, in Panhellenic, quadrennial form, the Soteria in honor of Zeus Soter and Apollo Pythios, to be held in Delphi, "in memory of the battle (in 279/8) against the barbarians who campaigned against the Greeks and the shared Greek sanctuary of Apollo" (*IG* II² 680).[92] To this international festival the Aetolians invited, along with several other Greek states,[93] the Athenians. The Athenians had contributed to this victory against the Galatians (*IG* II² 680.11–13), and they undoubtedly accepted the invitation to the music, athletic, and equestrian games of this festival. Just as the Athenians had rejoined the larger Greek world in international religious activities after their escape from Demetrios Poliorcetes in 287/6, so they did in the 240s after regaining some "freedom" under Antigonos Gonatas in 256/5.

It is probable that the functioning of many state cults had been disrupted by the Chremonidean War and its aftermath, but, as we have seen before, the resilient state cults of Athens quickly reestablished themselves. The appearance of Athena Polias and Aglauros may even suggest that the 240s found, to some degree, the completion of the restora-

91. On Helios in the classical period, see Mikalson 1989, 97–98. For dedication to Helios in the third century, see *IG* II² 4678; for a sacrifice, perhaps in the second century, *IG* II² 4962.19–21.

92. On the Soteria at Delphi, see Nachtergael 1977, esp. 328–73, and above, chapter 4, pp. 134–35.

93. Nachtergael 1977, #22–25.

tion after Demetrios Poliorcetes, the restoration begun in 287/6 and interrupted but not aborted by the Chremonidean War. We may be seeing the Acropolis cults reasserting themselves vis-à-vis the Agora cults and a return, however partial, to the cult dynamics of the age of Lycourgos. But all of these developments looked to the past. Soon after the Athenians regained their independence in domestic affairs in 229, they devised a new state cult to look to the future.

6

Demos and the Charites

The Athenians at last, in 229 B.C., established their freedom from Macedonian domination. Before turning to the political and
religious events of the newly free Athenian state, we pause for a moment to introduce a contemporary account, however brief and garbled,
of life in Athens at about this time, as viewed by a foreign traveler. The
geographer Heracleides of Crete wrote accounts of several Greek cities
and here describes Athens as he found it, probably in mid–to late third
century B.C.:[1]

From (Eleusis) one goes to the city of the Athenians. The road is pleasant, and (the land around) all is farmed and has a humane look. But the
city as a whole is dry, not well-watered, and because of its antiquity the
streets are badly arranged. Most of the houses are cheap but a few are ser-
viceable. Strangers, when they first see it, would doubt whether this is the
renowned city of the Athenians, but they would quickly come to believe
it. Here is what is most beautiful in the world. The theater is worth noting, large and wonderful. Athena's temple, the so-called Parthenon, is expensive, visible from afar, and worth seeing, sitting above the theater. It
creates great wonderment for those who see it. The Olympieion is only half
finished, but the floor plan of the building causes wonder, and, if it had
been finished, it would be the best (temple in the world). There are three
gymnasia, the Academy, the Lyceum, and Cynosarges, all with woods and
grass. There are all kinds of festivals, and there are diversions and recreations

1. On this Heracleides and on the text, its date, and the tradition in which it was written, see Pfister 1951.

for the mind from all kinds of philosophers, many leisure-time activities, and continuous spectacles.

All the agricultural products are inestimable, some outstanding in taste but rather sparse. The ever-present diversions, well suited to the desires of foreigners, distract their attention to what is pleasing and make them forget the hunger of the city. Because of the festivals and leisure-time activities, the (widespread) hunger is not perceived by the common people, because they cause one not to think of the provision of food. But for travelers with their own supplies there is no city like Athens for pleasure. The city has also many other pleasant things, for the neighboring cities are really suburbs of the Athenians. . . . The inhabitants are good at creating a great reputation for craftsmen because they heap fame on even ordinary ones. The city is a wonderful place to study statuary of all types.

Some of the inhabitants are "Atticans," some Athenians. The Atticans are meddlesome in their talk, deceitful, swindling, and lie in wait for foreigners. But the Athenians themselves have a grandeur of spirit, are simple in their ways, and are genuine guardians of friendship. Some lawyers run around the city, shaking down temporary residents and wealthy visitors. Whenever the Athenian state catches them, it imposes harsh punishments. The pure Athenians are a harsh audience of the arts and are constant festival goers. In general, to the degree that other cities surpass their rural areas in providing pleasure and proper guidance of life, to that degree the city of the Athenians surpasses other cities. But one must especially watch out for the courtesans, or one may, without realizing it, perish—but quite pleasantly. And there is a poem of Lysippos:

> If you have not seen Athens, you are a log.
> If you have seen it but not been captivated, you are an ass.
> If happily you leave it, you are a mule. (Pfister 1951, #1)

From Heracleides' account one imagines the city as crowded, relatively poor, struggling to feed its population. The many festivals that we have been chronicling were a distinctive feature of the city and served even to distract the urban poor from their miseries. That population was mixed, with many foreign residents ("Atticans") pestering the rich traveler at the city's tourist attractions. The Athenians themselves were clearly distinguishable, by manners and character that are reminiscent of the fifth century. Heracleides, no less than the modern tourist, is interested primarily in seeing the monuments of the city: the theater, the Parthenon, the Olympieion, and the sculpture. Unlike Pausanias he has no interest in religious traditions and cults, and such was, no doubt, the attitude of most foreigners, even those living in Athens. At this time, as for most of her religious history, it was the Athenians to whom Athenian religion had meaning, as was no doubt true also for other Greek cities. Foreigners, by and large, could not share in the religion of the city which they visited or in which they lived, and to them Athenian temples and religious sculpture were only architectural and artistic marvels. But, as we shall see, to the Athenians themselves they remained elements of a living religion.

In 229 B.C. the Athenians won their freedom from Macedonian domination by convincing, with 150 talents of cash, the Macedonian commandant Diogenes to withdraw all the remaining garrisons. Eurycleides, son of Micion I, of the deme Kephisia (*PA* 5966), who had served as treasurer of the military fund in 244/3 and as eponymous archon in 240/39, orchestrated this arrangement and the collection of money from both local and international sources. For the next several years he and his brother Micion II directed Athenian political affairs,[2] leading a national revival not unlike that of Lycourgos after the battle of Chaeroneia in 338. A cornerstone of this Eurycleidean revival was a firm policy of neutrality in the disputes between Macedon, the Aetolian League, the Achaean League, and their various allies and opponents. In these contentious times support was needed even to maintain neutrality, and for this the Athenians turned to the Ptolemies of Egypt. Major tests of their neutrality were the Social War (220–217) with the Aetolians, Spartans, and Eleans against Philip V of Macedon and his allies, and the First Macedonian War (211–205) of the Aetolians and Romans against Philip. The Athenians successfully avoided entanglement in both these affairs.[3]

In 200 the Athenians, after thirty years, broke their neutrality as a direct result of a sacrilege committed at Eleusis and its aftermath, and they joined Rhodes and Attalos I of Pergamon in declaring war on Philip. Athens, Rhodes, and Attalos were joined by Rome and the Aetolian League, all against Philip, the Boeotian League of Thebes, Euboea, Corinth, and Megara, and the Achaean League for the Second Macedonian War (200–197). After Philip's defeat at Cynoscephalae in 197, the victor in the battle, the Roman proconsul Titus Quinctius Flamininus, declared the Greek states "free" at the Isthmian Games of 196. Twenty-five years later Athens joined Rome in the Third Macedonian War (171–168) against Philip's son Perseus. Perseus was defeated at the battle of Pydna in 168, and, as fruits of victory, Athens was given

2. On the family and policies of Eurycleides, see Habicht 1982b, 179–82; MacKendrick 1969, 39–43.

3. Habicht 1982b, 79–142.

Haliartos in Boeotia and island properties she had lost, in some cases centuries ago: Lemnos, Imbros, Scyros, and, most important, Delos.

These developments in the international arena found expression in Athenian domestic religion. The last true foreign benefactors to Athens had been Antigonos I Monophthalmos and his son Demetrios Poliorcetes in 307, and we have seen the honors, both secular and divine, the Athenians awarded them: statues next to Harmodios and Aristogeiton, crowns, a cult and festival as *Sōtēres*, and status as eponymous heroes for two new tribes. The subsequent extension and perversion of these honors led to sacrilege and debasement of some state cults, but this was owed largely to the character of Demetrios and to a faction of his supporters within Athens (see chapter 3). After nearly one hundred years the memories of this debacle must have faded because, once again, the Athenians began to use similar secular and divine honors to express their gratitude to foreign benefactors. It is during this period that some religious honors given at the end of the fourth century in an innovative and ad hoc manner become standard and routine. Up to this period Attic festivals and religious practices served, quite occasionally and haphazardly, international political purposes. But after 229 the Athenians, now independent, seem systematically to be employing their religious structures to promote diplomatic goals, and the Hellenistic potentates apparently welcomed their overtures.

Diogenes, the Macedonian commandant who in 229 led his garrison troops out of Athens for 150 talents, was not the typical commander of an occupying force. Reportedly he used the money to pay his troops, and he was immediately and for centuries afterward treated as a "benefactor" by the Athenians.[4] He probably had been given Athenian citizenship before 229 and eventually married into the Eteobutadai, the prominent Athenian family who boasted of the statesman Lycourgos. A dedication by, probably, Diogenes' granddaughter reflects Athenian sentiments toward him in the last third of the second century:

> Near your temple, Pallas (Athena), Archegetis of the Erechtheidai,
> this statue of your priestess Philtera was erected.
> She is from the bloodline of the Eteobutadai. Her father
> was Pausimachos, five times a general of the army.
> Her ancestors flourished among the Aegeidai: Lycourgos

4. On the role of Diogenes as "benefactor" and on his cult, see Le Bohec 1993, 165–72, 264; Habicht 1982b, 79–84; M. Osborne 1982, 187–88; Oikonomides 1982.

and the Diogenes held in honor in the Attic land.
Lycourgos delighted in oratory, but by Diogenes' deeds
our fatherland achieved its ancient freedom.

(*IG* II² 3474)

Philtera was an Eteobutad and priestess of Athena Polias,[5] and it was
in this family, famous for its long association with Athena's Acropolis
cult and for Lycourgos' accomplishments, that the foreigner Diogenes
found his place. In later times, at least before 107/6, Diogenes received
sacrifices from the ephebes, had a festival (the Diogeneia), and his eldest male descendant had a special seat in the theater (*proedria*).[6] The
Diogeneion, a gymnasion or, more probably, a palaestra, was built in
his honor.[7] The sacrifices, with or without attestation of a priest, and
the festival presume a divine cult. Habicht has argued that these religious honors followed soon after and from his "liberation" of Athens
in 229 (1982b, 83–84). That may be, but we should also note that his
cult was centered in and, so far as we know, was limited to the corps of
ephebes. Critical to his cult must have been the construction of the Diogeneion, the center of ephebic activity thereafter, which provided both
the site and probably the motive for the cult. The precinct's encircling
wall was already ramshackle in 107/6 (*IG* II² 1011.41) and thus should
be dated well before this, perhaps as early as the 220s. Diogenes was
viewed, like the legendary Aglauros, as having made a significant contribution to the "freeing" of Athens, and hence perhaps as a suitable
model and recipient of sacrifice by the ephebes. The festival, which may
have been limited to the ephebes, never attained the stature of the major festivals in Athens.

Certainly before 211 B.C., probably before ca. 215,[8] and quite likely in
the 220s the Athenians created a new state cult, that of Demos and the
Charites.[9] They chose a site prominent for those who like the foreigner

5. Cf. *IG* II² 3870. On Pausimachos and the family, see M. Osborne 1981–82, 2:187–88.

6. Inscribed seat in the theater: *IG* II² 5080; sacrifices of two bulls by ephebes, *IG* II²
1011.14–15 (107/6), 1028.23–24 (101/0), 1029.14 (99/8), 1039.55–57, 1040.2, 1043.48–49; festival Diogeneia, *IG* II² 1029.14, 1039.55–57, 1040.2, 1043.48–49.

7. For the recent argument that the Diogeneion was a palaestra adjoining the gymnasion of Ptolemy and for its location and close association with the ephebes, see Miller
1995a. See also Frantz 1979, 201–3; Dow 1960, 408.

8. 211 B.C.: *IG* II² 844.32–43. Ca. 215: *IG* II² 834.25–26, for the text and date of which
see Habicht 1982b, 118–27.

9. On this cult see Habicht 1982b, 84–93; Rocchi 1980; Maass 1972, 109; Oliver 1960,
106–17; Wycherley 1957, ##125–31.

Heracleides entered the Agora from the Dipylon, on the north slope of Colonos Agoraios, behind the Stoa of Zeus Eleutherios, facing to the north a street leading to the Sacred Gate. The close proximity to the Stoa of Zeus Eleutherios may be significant.[10] Quite probably Eurycleides served as the cult's first priest, his son Micion III (*PA* 10186) succeeded him in this office, and the priesthood remained thereafter in their family.[11] Hereafter and in the second century, foreigners who showed "goodwill toward the Demos of the Athenians" were given honors or statues to be displayed in this sanctuary.[12] The cult flourished, and after 127/6 and probably much earlier the priest of Demos and the Charites attended the inaugural sacrifices of the ephebes each year at the sacred hearth of the Prytaneion.[13]

The cult of Demos and the Charites is a major innovation in Athenian state cult. We have seen how in previous years Athenians had remodeled and reorganized existing cults, but this may be the first entirely new state cult since that of Demetrios Poliorcetes. Immediately noteworthy is the absence of Olympian deities—in particular Athena Polias, Zeus Soter, Zeus Eleutherios, and the like.[14] The Demos itself, not Demokratia, is a cult figure, but this may not be significant. In Athenian political terms, oligarchy, monarchy, tyranny, and foreign oppression were expressed as limitations on and enslavement of the Demos. The Athenians conceived of the removal of the Macedonians in 229 as the "freeing of the Demos" and the "restoration of the ancestral constitution."[15] Hence Demos and Demokratia were virtually synonymous, and presumably the now divine Demos represented the freedom of the Demos, that is, democracy.

The divine Demos of this new post-Macedonian cult brings to mind the noble, older, bearded personification of Demos that appeared on several reliefs accompanying public documents in the fourth century just prior to the Macedonian occupation.[16] This figure, most appropriately being crowned by Athena on the law against tyranny (Schwenk, #6) of

10. See H. Thompson's remarks in Habicht 1982b, 92–93 n. 73.

11. *IG* II² 4676 (Eurycleides), 2798 (Micion III). See Habicht 1982b, 84 n. 32.

12. *IG* II² 844 (of 212/1), 908, 909, 987, 1236; Josephus *AJ* 14.153 of 106/5.

13. E.g. *SEG* 15.104.5–8. For other examples, see Pélékidis 1962, 217 n. 3; and below, chapter 8, p. 254.

14. Nilsson 1967–74, I.144.

15. Habicht 1982b, 81–82.

16. On the personification and development of Demos, see Lawton 1995, 55–58. For representations of Demos on the document reliefs of the fourth century, see Lawton, #38 (the antityranny law of 337/6), 49, 54, 117, 126, 133, 149, 150, 167, 172, 176.

337/6 B.C., has characteristics of Zeus, Asclepios, and a typical elderly Athenian citizen, but he is consistently larger than human in scale. In this "pre-Macedonian period" he appears still simply a personification in artistic expression, but after 229, when the Demos of the Athenians has at last recovered its freedom, he is deified in cult.

The divine Demos is thus a new deity, but are the Charites also new? Χάριτες can mean simply "thanks," and the new cult of Demos and the Charites could be thought, from its deities, to be an expression of gratitude by the Athenian Demos to those foreigners and Athenians who contributed money to the freeing of the Demos in 229 and who afterwards made efforts on Athens' behalf. Christian Habicht (1982b, 87–92) has surveyed the role of Charites in Athens and elsewhere in the Greek world and, following a suggestion by Homer Thompson, he sees in Aristotle *EN* 5.1133a2 proof that some Greek states erected cults of Charites for this purpose. This would explain nicely why hereafter honors to helpful foreigners were erected in this sanctuary.[17]

Yet such an expression of gratitude, through a cult of abstract personifications, would be unusual in Athenian religious history, and I suspect that the nature of this cult, and in particular of the Charites, is more complex, more in accord with Athenian traditions. I follow a line of interpretation begun by Habicht (1982b, 87–90) but carry it somewhat further. It involves the nexus of Charites, agricultural prosperity, peace, and the ephebes, and it looks to the domestic purposes of the cult.

According to Pausanias (9.35.1–2), the Athenians from ancient times worshipped *two* Charites, Auxo and Hegemone, and likewise *two* Horai, Carpo and Thallo. Here Pausanias seems to be correcting the view that made the Athenian Carpo a Charis, not a Hora. Soon thereafter, however, Pausanias adds (9.35.3) that *three* Charites stood before the entrance to the Acropolis and that there the Athenians performed rites secret from most people.[18] Habicht has reviewed the long-standing scholarly dispute about how many Athenian Charites there were and what their names were, and he finds this the most reasonable solution: originally Auxo and Hegemone were the Attic Charites but then, when the number of Charites was canonically accepted as three throughout the

17. Above, n. 12. The statue of Eumaridas of Cydonia was moved from the Acropolis to this sanctuary on the recommendation of Eurycleides and Micion in 212/1 (*IG* II² 844.33–43). On links with Ptolemy III Euergetes in *IG* II² 4676, see below, pp. 178–79.

18. On this cult of the Charites and a votive reliefs from it, see Palagia 1989–90.

Greek world, Thallo was added, and she, Auxo, and Hegemone were the recipients of the cult on the Acropolis (1982b, 89). Carpo seems to have lost out—but, as we shall see later, perhaps not.

The Demos of this new cult was in origin a personification, and it is noteworthy that the Charites/Horai were personifications as well, the most obvious and abundant of the previous Athenian religious tradition. Auxo ("Growth"), Thallo ("Blossoming"), and Carpo ("Harvest") all point to agricultural fertility. Hegemone ("Leader") is of a different order but like the others is a descriptive name, pointing to a function. Pausanias claims that Thallo, a Hora, was associated with Pandrosos ("All-Dewy"), one of the daughters of ancient King Cecrops (9.35.1–2). Aglauros ("Shining") was another daughter of Cecrops, and we have previously encountered Auxo, Hegemone, and Thallo among the witnesses whom the ephebes in the fourth century invoked for their oath in the sanctuary of Aglauros (chapter 1, 16–17). In 246/5 the priestess of Aglauros sacrificed to, among others, Aglauros and the Horai "for the health and safety of the Boule, the Demos of the Athenians, their children and wives, and on behalf of King Antigonos, his queen Phila, and their descendants."[19]

Pandrosos, with her Hora Thallo, had her sanctuary on the Acropolis, directly to the west of the Erechtheum. Aglauros, with her Charites Auxo, Hegemone, and perhaps later Thallo, had hers at the base of the east slope of the Acropolis. Together Pandrosos and Aglauros were major players in the etiological myth of the Arrephoria, secret rites performed by women and lying at the core of the earliest Athenian state cult—a cult that was, to judge by the names of the deities and their attendants, intended, at least in part, to promote agricultural fertility.[20]

We have seen the link between the Charites and agricultural fertility, and between them and the ephebes. A similar link, reaching back at least to the fifth century, exists between the Charites, Horai, and peace. In 421 Aristophanes produced his *Peace*, and in lines 456–57 he has his main character, Trygaios, and the leader of the chorus discuss which gods they should invoke to help them recover Peace:

Trygaios: Hermes, Charites, Horai, Aphrodite, Pothos. And Ares?
Choros: No! No!

19. *SEG* 33.115. See chapter 5, pp. 164–65.
20. On the role of the daughters of Cecrops in the Arrephoria and on varying interpretations of the significance of the ritual, see Kearns 1989, 23–27; Brulé 1987, 79–98; Robertson 1983; Burkert 1966.

Trygaios: Not Enyalios either?
Choros: No!

To recover Peace this comic character appeals to Hermes and to the Charites, Horai, and Aphrodite and Pothos ("Longing"). Hermes is understandable because of his role in the play and as "the warder-off of evils" (422). The others are figures with whom, at least in the fifth century, one could naturally associate Peace. The rejected Ares and Enyalios were war gods. In the fourth century, when the Athenians were still capable of undertaking wars and inclined to do so, gods of both war and peace served as witnesses to the ephebes' oath. In 246/5 Ares, probably as Aglauros' husband, and the Horai still both received the sacrifices of the priestess of Aglauros (*SEG* 33.115), but after 229 the Athenians said "No!" to Ares. The new cult of Demos and the Charites promoted, for all the Demos and especially for the ephebes, only peace.

Among his "peaceful" deities Aristophanes included Aphrodite, and she too, for a time, found a place in the cult of the Demos and Charites. In 194/3, after the Athenians had had another taste of battle in the Second Macedonian War (200–197), the Boule, in the priesthood of Eurycleides' son Micion III, dedicated a magnificent altar to Aphrodite Hegemone of the Demos and the Charites (*IG* II² 2798).[21] Aphrodite "Leader of the Demos" is truly remarkable—it appears that she now is the mistress of Athens. But this can hardly be the import of the title. Aphrodite Hegemone is here, I suggest, the product of an attempt to incorporate *all* the Charites/Horai into the cult. As the Athenians tried to unite their four Charites/Horai (Auxo, Hegemone, Thallo, and Carpo) into a single cult of the Charites, they felt compelled, by the canonical number of three Charites, to omit one. Hegemone, by her name, had always stood somewhat apart, and on this altar, I think, an effort was made to include her. Aphrodite was identified with her (hence Aphrodite Hegemone) and the three unnamed Charites then would have been Auxo, Thallo, and Carpo. A place was found for each of the four, but the solution was not a lasting one. This altar is the only evidence for this grouping, and neither

21. For the identification of a larger than life-size statue, found in the Agora, as this Aphrodite Hegemone, see E. Harrison 1990.

22. For the role of Aphrodite here Judith Binder has suggested to me a simpler and more elegant, hence perhaps more attractive possibility: that the new cult of Demos and the Graces was founded in the venerable sanctuary of the Athenian Aphrodite Ourania

Aphrodite nor Hegemone found a permanent place in the cult of the Demos and the Charites.[22]

Finally, can this nexus of the Demos, peace, agricultural prosperity, and the youth be related to Eurycleides' personal and political interests in such a way as to make understandable his founding of the cult? His concern to establish Athenian neutrality and maintain peace is well documented and even criticized in the sources.[23] *IG* II² 834, of ca. 215, relates honors that the Athenians gave to their now aging politician for his services, and included among them are that "when the land was lying idle and unsown because of the wars, he was responsible for it being worked and sown by providing money, and he with his brother Micion established freedom for the city." Eurycleides worked for renewed agricultural fertility of Attica and for the freedom of the Demos: both, I would claim, reflected in the cult of Demos and the Charites.

For Athenians the cult of Demos and the Charites would thus have been founded not simply as a memorial but, in accord with very old Athenian religious practices and traditions, as a means of furthering the related interests of democracy, peace, and agricultural prosperity. And what better way to promote those interests than to involve the leaders of the next generation, the ephebes, and to position the sanctuary in the civic center, the Agora, adjoining the sanctuary of Zeus Eleutherios?

For foreigners not familiar with the role of the Charites in Athenian state and agricultural cult, the Charites could, however, easily be taken to mean "thanks," and in association with Demos, "thanks from the Demos of the Athenians." For external purposes, therefore, this sanctuary was a logical place for Athenians to express their gratitude to foreigners.[24] But

---

(on whom see above, pp. 107–108), that this makes explicable Aphrodite Hegemone of the Demos on the altar of 194/3, and that the Charites of that altar are simply the usual attendants of Aphrodite and are not and need not be given individual names.

Further complicating the situation is, however, the recent discovery of a naiskos of Aphrodite Hegemone *in* the fort at Rhamnous and particularly patronized by the commander of the garrison (*SEG* 41.90; see above chapter 5, p. 158). How this Rhamnousian Aphrodite Hegemone of 222/1 relates to the Aphrodite Hegemone "of the Demos" of 194/3 remains uncertain. The simultaneous or prior existence of a Rhamnousian Aphrodite Hegemone may, however, explain why Aphrodite Hegemone of the state cult needed the further definition "of the Demos." Whether either the Ramnousian or Agora Aphrodite should be associated with the Aphrodite who "led" Theseus on his mission to Crete (Plut. *Thes.* 18) is equally uncertain. On this Rhamnousian Aphrodite Hegemone, see Pirenne-Delforge 1994, 39–40.

23. Polyb. 5.106.6–8, on which see Habicht 1982a, 93–105.

24. It is noteworthy that honors for citizens were apparently not displayed there.

the cult was to flourish in the coming centuries not because it memori-
alized past favors, but because it served the greater needs of Athenians
themselves for democracy, peace, and food.

The peace and prosperity sought by Eurycleides and promoted by the
cult of Demos and the Charites were to prevail until 200 when Athens
declared war on Philip V of Macedon. Athenian troops continued, however, to patrol border areas, and the *koina* of soldiers stationed at
Sounion, Rhamnous, and Eleusis continued to honor their commanders
for both religious and secular services.[25] As we have already seen (above,
chapter 5, pp. 157–58), the *koinon* of soldiers at Rhamnous may have
marked the liberation of Athens in 229 with a new cult of Zeus Soter
and Athena Soteira (*SEG* 15.111, 112; 22.128). That cult then continued
until at least 99/8.[26] At Sounion in 220/19 the garrison general Theomnestos of Xypete built a temple of Asclepios (*IG* II² 1302.6–8). Among
the services that Demainetos, son of Hermocles, of Athmonon (*PA* 3269)
provided in his years of generalship at Eleusis (219/8, 215/4, and 211/0)
were to sacrifice to the goddesses at the Great Eleusinia for the safety
(*sōtēria*) of the Demos and to oversee each year the celebration of the
Mysteries and keep it safe (*IG* II² 1304.24–29). For us this text, which
dates to 211/0 or shortly thereafter, marks the end of the record of such
koina, for religious and secular purposes, of soldiers on garrison duty
in the Attic forts. As an institution they may well have been brought to
an end by the invasion of Philip and the Acarnanians in 200 B.C.

Such soldiers and garrisons, however, played a small role in Athenian safety after 229. Athens' greatest risk was not from the occasional
raid but from being forced to give up her neutrality and becoming en-
tangled in the hostilities among Philip V, the Aetolian League, the
Achaean League, and the Boeotian League. Athens' "savior" and "benefactor" here was Ptolemy III Euergetes, who evidently gave assurances
to Athens that he would protect her. Only some such action on his part
would explain the great honors, unparalleled since the time of Demetrios Poliorcetes, that the Athenians awarded him in 224.[27] As they
had for Demetrios and his father, for Ptolemy the Athenians created a

25. Sounion: *IG* II² 1300 (from 220s, for Eurycleides as general of the hoplites), 1302
(of 220/19). Rhamnous: *SEG* 15.111 (ca. 229/8), 112 (225/4), and 22.128 (after 229). Eleusis:
SEG 25.157 of ca. 217/6, *IG* II² 1304 (after 211). See above, chapter 5, pp. 155–60.
    26. *IG* II² 2869; *SEG* 41.162, 164–65, 248F.
    27. On these honors, their date and occasion, see Habicht 1982a, 105–17, and 1992a,
74–75. Pausanias (10.10.2) claims that the Athenians dedicated at Delphi a statue of Ptolemy

new tribe, the thirteenth, Ptolemais. Ptolemy then became an eponymous hero, and his wife Berenice, in a new type of honor, was made
the eponym of a new deme. One priest served them both. About this
time the priest of Demos and the Charites, surely a member of Eurycleides' family if not Eurycleides himself, dedicated a bench in the theater of Dionysos to be shared by himself, the priest of Demokratia, and
the priest of Ptolemy and Berenice (*IG* II² 4676).[28] Ptolemy's importance to the newly free Demos could hardly have been made more clear.
Also in 224/3 the gymnasiarch Theophrastos, "following the policy of
the Demos to 'honor' the king," added new agonistic contests "for those
of the young men wishing to compete" (*SEG* 25.157.9–12). These were,
or were a prototype for, the Ptolemaia, a new agonistic festival that
quickly attained the stature of the City Dionysia, the Panathenaia, and
the Eleusinia. The Ptolemaia was then celebrated or expected more or
less regularly for over a century, at least until ca. 98/7 B.C.[29]

To be associated with these honors is the gymnasion (Ptolemaion)
which, ca. 224, Ptolemy donated to the city of Athens.[30] According to
Pausanias (1.17.2) it lay not far from the Roman Agora, on the lower north
slope of the Acropolis. It included lecture halls and a library and became
a center of philosophical study for centuries to come.[31] Beginning in 117/6
the ephebe classes contributed books to its library (*IG* II² 1009.7–8,
1029.25–26, 1043.50). If the restorations of *SEG* 21.522 are correct, the
Ptolemaion was *not* the cult center of the Ptolemais tribe. We may suspect, in fact, that Ptolemy's cult as hero of the tribe was purely honorific,
for this decree of the Ptolemais tribe was to be erected not in the Ptolemaion but in the sanctuary, in the Agora, of Ajax's son Eurysakes.[32] The
cult served by the priest of Ptolemy and Berenice was probably of the
state as a whole, not of one tribe.

---

among their eponymous and other heroes because of their "goodwill" (εὐνοίᾳ) toward
him. The statues of Demetrios Poliorcetes and his father they dedicated "in fear" (δέει).

28. On the restoration and use of *IG* II² 4676, see Maass 1972, 108–18.

29. Habicht 1992a, 83–84 = 1994, 155–56. The last securely dated expectation of the
Ptolemaia is from an ephebic decree of 101/0 (*IG* II² 1028.100–101), but the festival has
been reasonably restored also in *IG* II² 1029.32 of 98/7. Thereafter it disappears and may
well have been among the casualties of Sulla's sack in 86 B.C.

30. For evidence, see Wycherley 1957, #456–63. For the probable location, on the lower
north slope of the Acropolis, see Miller 1995a. On the possibility that the gymnasion was
built not by Ptolemy III but by Ptolemy VI in the second quarter of the second century
B.C., see Miller 1995a, 230.

31. E.g., Apollodoros, *FGrHist* 244 F 59; *IG* II² 1006.19–20; Cic. *de Fin.* 5.1.

32. On the Eurysakeion, see Kearns 1989, 165: Wycherley 1957, #246–55.

The honors to and the gift from Ptolemy III Euergetes in 224/3 are indicative of the nature of the national restoration, both religious and secular, after 229. To reward their benefactors Athenians reached back to the type of honors they had given years earlier, the creation of a new tribe and cult. Here they extended honor even to the king's queen, which, given the importance of the Ptolemaic queens, is understandable. Unlike in 307 the benefactions might now be just promises of support and not immediate, personal intervention in Attica. The festival in the new deity's honor also now, for the first time, became a major and lasting agonistic contest of the type favored by Hellenistic monarchs, completely independent from preexisting Athenian cults and religious traditions. And, finally, the honoree financed for Athens a major public building—here, in the Ptolemaic tradition, a building dedicated to the training of both mind and body. It was the first major construction since the Lycourgan period and, unlike work undertaken then, it was paid for by a foreigner.

Previously Hellenistic culture in general terms had come to Athens primarily through philosophers, who were in many ways apart from Athenian society, and from dramatic poets, who tended to become Atticized. We now see additional elements of Hellenistic culture, especially from Egypt, penetrating Athens. In the religious realm the first unmistakable sign of this is the importation, from Egypt, of a cult of Sarapis, a deity transformed and Hellenized by the early Ptolemies to serve as their national cult.[33] Ptolemy I Soter had called upon two Athenians, Timotheos and the exiled former tyrant Demetrios of Phaleron, to develop the mythology, ritual, and liturgical hymns for Sarapis.[34] An Athenian may have sculpted the cult statue.[35] As early as Menander (frag. 151A Edmunds) the Athenians had known of Sarapis, but the first evidence for cultic activity is a decree from 215/4 of the Sarapiastai, a non-Athenian *koinon* devoted to this deity.[36] The cult is by then already firmly

33. On Sarapis in Athens, see Dunand 1973, 1.45–66 and 2.4–17, 144–53; Dow 1937a.

34. Plut. *Mor.* 362A; Tac. *Hist.* 4.83; D.L. 5.76. See also chapters 7, pp. 229–31, and 8, pp. 275–77.

35. Dow 1937a, 186.

36. Dow placed the birth of the first Athenian attested to have the name Sarapion ca. 250. The text honoring his son (*SEG* 18.20) is now known to have been inscribed by a letter-cutter working from 179/8 to 161/0, and it is not impossible that the birth of the senior Sarapion should be dated somewhat later, to the time of the great Athenian interest in Ptolemy in 224. See Tracy 1990a, 134; Dow 1937a, 221–22. Other Athenians named Sarapion (see list in M. Osborne and Byrne, 1994, 393) can all be dated to the late third century, the second century, or later.

established with probably about fifty to eighty members.[37] The willingness of the Athenian state to permit the establishment of a sanctuary and cult of this deity for foreigners surely represents pro-Ptolemaic sentiments of the period. Here, with the Ptolemaia and Sarapis, the influence of international politics and the Hellenistic world at large on Athenian state religion is clear. For the cult of Sarapis among the Athenians, however, these are just the beginnings, and in chapters 7 and 8 we shall see a surge of interest in this cult after Athenians assumed management of his sanctuaries on Delos.[38]

Such are the major innovative elements in Athenian religion from the establishment of freedom in 229 to the outbreak of the First Macedonian War in 200. During this prolonged period of peace the routine of Athenian Hellenistic state religion was maintained. The prytanists of these years before each Ekklesia sacrificed to Apollo Prostaterios and Artemis Boulaia and the other ancestral gods "for the health and safety of the Boule, the Demos, and the children and women."[39] The Panathenaia were expected for 225/4 (*SEG* 25.106.38), 203/2 (*SEG* 26.98.35), and 202/1 (*IG* II² 2313.8–15), and were quite certainly celebrated every year.[40] Likewise the city Dionysia were expected for 226/5 (*SEG* 25.106.37–38) and 204/3 (*SEG* 26.98.34–35) and were doubtless held each year.[41]

In what is necessarily a predominantly diachronic study we shall take advantage here of the fortuitous survival of several inscriptional records for one year (215/4) to direct attention to the amount, variety, and vigor of state religious activity. These texts offer a record which, though far from complete, is still the most complete that we have for any one year of Athenian religious history. These records include an honorary decree for the ephebes of that year (*SEG* 29.116);[42] an honorary decree for the *epimelētai* of the Eleusinian Mysteries (*IG* II² 847); a similar decree for Demainetos, the general over the region including Eleusis (*IG* II² 1304);

---

37. *IG* II² 1292, on which see Dow 1937a, 188–97.

38. For Dow's dating of an Athenian priest of Sarapis to 226/5–222/1 from *IG* II² 4692, see chapter 8, note 94.

39. *Agora* XV, #120.9–13 of 228/7; #121.7–9 of 226/5; #128.9–12 of 223/2; #130.6–9 of 220/19; #135.7–10 of 214/3; #129.7–10 of 212/1; and #147.1–4 of 203/2. Cf. #134, 138.

40. Cf. *IG* II² 851, 3145, 3146; *SEG* 25.108.10–11. For the date of *IG* II² 2313, see Tracy and Habicht 1991, 218 = Habicht 1994, 102.

41. *IG* II² 836.20–21, 851.12–13, 861.19–20; *SEG* 25.108.10.

42. On *SEG* 29.116, see Tracy 1979, 174–78.

and, finally, an inventory of dedications to Asclepios (Aleshire, Inv. VII), all recording events and activities of 215/4.

In the last third of the fourth century the *ephēbeia* was a compulsory, two-year course of service and training for as many as five hundred young Athenian males (see chapter 1). During the rule or after the expulsion of Demetrios of Phaleron in 307 service was reduced to one year, and membership was restricted to the higher economic classes and was consequently significantly smaller.[43] After 229 the ephebes, now probably only twenty to fifty in number,[44] all probably from the privileged classes, become prominently involved in state cult, participating in the processions and contests of major festivals and undertaking a broad range of other religious responsibilities. This would appear to be the beginning of what we might term a "youth movement" in Athenian religion, a movement even more in evidence in later years (see chapter 8). The ephebes of 215/4 served at the Mysteries, obeying the orders of the archon basileus and the *epimelētai*. In the agonistic contests they "escorted" the processions and ran the torch races. They made sacrifices and took omens in accordance with the laws and decrees of the state. On Salamis they escorted the procession for Demokratia, participated in the Aianteia, and ran the race for the eponymous hero, just as the laws assigned (*SEG* 29.116). The twenty-nine ephebes of 205/4, in addition to the services listed above, participated in the inaugural sacrifices "from the hearth" in the Prytaneion; escorted the processions of the Semnai Theai and of Iacchos; put on a display, in armor, at the Epitaphia; and served in the Hephaistion (*SEG* 26.98.7–17).[45]

The two *epimelētai* of the Mysteries of 215/4, for their part, sacrificed "on behalf of the Boule, Demos, children and women" the traditional sacrifices to Demeter, Kore, and the other gods. They also performed the sacrifices preliminary to the Mysteries, at their own expense provided a team of oxen to convey the *hiera* to Athens, oversaw the procession to the sea, supervised the reception of Iacchos (and the procession of initiates) at Eleusis, celebrated the Mysteries at Agrai twice because of the Eleusinia, sent a bull as a sacrificial victim to the Eleusinia and distributed the meat to the 650 members of the Boule, rendered their accounts in accordance with the laws, and spent, from their own

---

43. Tracy 1995, 40; Habicht 1992b = 1994, 248–50; Gauthier 1985a, 161–63; Reinmuth 1971, 101–15.

44. Tracy 1979, 177–78; 1982a, 158–59.

45. On *SEG* 26.98, see Gauthier 1985a.

funds, all else necessary for the sacrifices (*IG* II² 847). Also in this year, Demainetos, as general of the region, joined the Eleusinians in sacrificing "for the safety of the Demos" at the Great Eleusinia and oversaw the celebration of the Mysteries, as he also did in 219/8 and 211/0, to ensure safety (*IG* II² 1304.24–29).

The two inscriptions from Eleusis (*IG* II² 847, 1304) indicate that the full program of the religious activities there—the Mysteries themselves, the Mysteries at Agrai, and the biennial Eleusinia—was flourishing. The ephebes participated in the procession and contests of the Eleusinia, and the Boule, 650 strong, was present for the sacrifice and the banquet. Crowds at the Eleusinia or other circumstances necessitated a second celebration of the Mysteries at Agrai. The gods, as usual, were asked to provide "health and safety," and the general, in a more earthly way, assured this safety for initiates at the Mysteries. Also as was customary in the period, the annual, elected *epimelētai* made a substantial financial contribution to the success of the activities they superintended.

The list of religious activities thus far described for 215/4 is a salutary reminder of the limits of our knowledge of even the basic program of Athenian state religion in this or any other period. The Eleusinian Mysteries, the Mysteries at Agrai, and the Eleusinia are familiar and well-known since the classical period. But several elements, treated as traditional or routine in the two ephebic decrees, are in fact first attested here. These include the Aianteia and the procession for Demokratia, both on Salamis, as well as the sacrifice "from the hearth" in the Prytaneion, the procession of the Semnai Theai, the Epitaphia, and the ephebes' service at the Hephaistion. The last is not attested again, and nothing is known of it. But we have later record of the sacrifice in the Prytaneion, the Aianteia, and the Epitaphia.[46]

The attestation now of the procession for Demokratia and the Aianteia on Salamis may well be related to the reunification and independence of Athenian territory, including Salamis, after 229. The cult of Ajax on Salamis had surely long existed.[47] Ajax's home was Salamis, and on the day of the famous sea battle there in 480 the Athenians had invoked him and other members of his family to aid them (Hdt. 8.64, 121). No doubt victory in this battle brought renewed interest in his Salaminian cult. The temple and its ebony statue (Paus. 1.35.3–4) may

46. For the later evidence, see below, chapter 8, pp. 243–54.

47. Ajax's cult as eponymous hero of the Aiantis tribe was centered in the shrine of his son Eurysakes in Athens. On the two cults of Ajax, see Kearns 1989, 81–82, 141–42. On the Aianteia, see Culley 1977, 294–296; Deubner 1932, 228.

well have been built after this victory. The major events of the Aianteia, after 215/4 celebrated for more than a hundred years, included a regatta, a "long race," a torch race, a procession, and a sacrifice to Ajax.[48] For their participation in the Aianteia the ephebes and their officials were regularly honored with gold crowns. From at least 127/6 the ephebes also sailed, on two ships, to the trophy monument for the battle of Salamis and made an offering there to Zeus Tropaios.[49] Although separate from the Aianteia, it and the Aianteia together would be suitable memorials of the great Athenian naval victory. The Aianteia surely existed, in some form, after the battle of Salamis, but that it could have survived the expulsion of the Salaminians in 304 (Paus. 1.35.2), the Athenians' later loss of her harbors and navy, and the other misadventures under Macedonian domination is unlikely. In the ephebic documents after 215/4 we probably have an Aianteia reestablished as a sign of Athenian independence, nationalism, and renewed control of Salamis. A statue of Demokratia on Salamis (*IG* II² 1011.62) and the procession for this Demokratia (*SEG* 29.116.18) of 215/4 suggest the 220s as the time for the revival of the cults on Salamis. The "race for the eponymous hero" of *SEG* 29.116.19, also held on Salamis, is unknown elsewhere and is, perhaps, just an early attempt to describe Ajax and the Aianteia.

The Epitaphia was similarly militaristic and nationalistic. By 123/2 and probably much earlier, it included a torch race, a footrace in armor, and, for the Boule, a parade in armor, all performed by the ephebes. The race began at the *polyandreion*, the state tomb of the war dead in the Cerameicos.[50] The Epitaphia performed by the ephebes may well have been a continuation or revival of the fourth-century "contest" administered by the polemarch "for those having died in war."[51] The Epitaphia of the fourth century evidently included gymnastic, equestrian, and literary contests. Its purpose was "to honor" the war dead, and each year the city as a whole performed for them the ritual that individual families

---

48. *SEG* 29.116.17–20; 15.104.21–23, 130–31 of 127/6; *IG* II² 1006.30–32, 72–74 of 122/1; 1008.22–24, 75–77 of 118/7; 1011.16–18, 53–55 of 106/5; 1028.24–27 of 101/0; 1029.14–16 of 98/7; 1030.24–26. While at the Aianteia the ephebes might also sacrifice to Asclepios (*SEG* 15.104.23; *IG* II² 1011.17, 55).

49. This event is always listed separately from the Aianteia and should not be considered part of the same festival: *SEG* 15.104.22; *IG* II² 1006.28–29; 1008.17–18; 1028.27–28; 1032.8.

50. For later ephebic celebrations of the Epitaphia: *IG* II² 1006.22–23, 77–78; 1008.16–17; 1009.4; 1011.9–10; 1028.19–20; 1029.12–13; 1030.9, 18–19.

51. [Arist.] *Ath. Pol.* 58.1. On the Epitaphia, see Deubner 1932, 230–31.

customarily performed for their own dead (Pl. *Menex.* 249B). After 205/4 at the latest, the small band of ephebes displayed their newly acquired military skills at this festival. Whether now being revived or being given new emphasis, the Aianteia and Epitaphia suggest that after winning their independence peaceably in 229 the Athenians, however much they craved and courted peace, still recognized that on previous occasions freedom had been maintained by war and by the sacrifices of their soldiers and sailors.

I have left for last perhaps the most surprising activity of the ephebes of 205/4, the procession of the Semnai Theai (*SEG* 26.98.9–10). The Semnai were last attested in 362/1, as recipients of a vow along with Zeus Olympios, Athena Polias, Demeter and Kore, and the twelve gods in the record of a treaty made with several Peloponnesian states (*IG* II² 112.6–9; cf. *IG* II² 114.6–8). The Semnai are those deities portrayed as rehabilitated Erinyes in Aeschylus' *Eumenides* of 458,[52] and the procession of the ephebes may have had a classical antecedent on which Aeschylus modeled, to some degree, the end of his play. The ephebes of 172/1 and 128/7 also served the Semnai Theai, but these ephebic decrees are the only and last evidence that this venerable cult was practiced in the Hellenistic period.[53] In the fifth century the cult was particularly associated with murder trials held on the Areiopagos and, perhaps more generally, with the maintenance of oaths.

The last text from 215/4 is a record from the Asclepieion on the south slope of the Acropolis of various small private dedications that the Athenians were having recast into larger, more impressive ones (Aleshire, Inv. VII).[54] Three Athenians and two members of the Areiopagos Council were selected to oversee the procedure, along with Asclepios' priest and various other state officials. Six years earlier one of the members of this commission, the Areopagite Theognis of Kydathenaion (*PA* 6742), had served on a similar commission to purge and recast silver models of body parts dedicated to the Hero Iatros ("Physician Hero") "in town" (*IG* II² 839).[55] As a result the Hero's sanctuary was adorned

52. Lardinois 1992, 315–22; Mikalson 1991, 214–17.

53. *Hesp.* 15 (1946): 198, #40.16–17; *SEG* 15.104.26. The ephebic procession for the Semnai Theai may be that described by Polemon (frag. 49 Preller) and Apollodoros (*FGrHist* 244 F 101). Pausanias in the second century A.D. saw as part of an apparently still-living cult the altars and statues of the Semnai on the Areiopagos (1.28.6, 7.25.1–2).

54. For text, commentary, and discussion, see Aleshire 1989, 345–50.

55. On *IG* II² 839 see Dow 1985. On Hero Iatros, see Kearns 1989, 20–21, 171–72; Wycherley 1957, #340, 347.

with a new silver oenochoe weighing 183 1/2 drachmas. In both cases the inscribed list of dedications to be melted down and of their donors would, as it stood in the sanctuary, in a sense replace the original dedications and preserve the memory of the donors as well as serve as accounts of the commissioners.[56] Such inventorying and repair or replacement of dedications suggest a period of renewed concern for and some prosperity of these state cults, and with them we close our account of the year 215/4 B.C.

We have seen that in the period 229–205 Demeter's sanctuary at Eleusis was busy and prosperous, and there is a certain irony that a sacrilege perpetrated by foreigners at the Mysteries there in 201 was to change the direction of Athenian foreign policy and to lead, quite quickly, to new destruction of her countryside and rural sanctuaries. Our only account of the incident is from Livy who, like his source Polybius, was hostile to Athens:

> The Athenians entered into the war with Philip for no worthy reason, at a time when they kept nothing of their old prosperity except high spirits. On the days of the Mysteries two Acarnanian young men who had not been initiated, not thinking of the religious import, entered the sanctuary of Demeter with the rest of the crowd. Their talk easily betrayed them because they asked some foolish questions. They were led off to the officials of the sanctuary, and, although it was obvious they had entered the sanctuary by mistake, they were put to death as if they had committed an unspeakable crime.
>
> The Acarnanians reported to Philip what had been done in such a foul and hostile way, and they obtained permission from him to attack the Athenians with the Macedonian forces they had been given. This army first devastated Attica with sword and fire and then returned to Acarnania with every kind of booty. This was the first provocation of Athenian feelings. Later a real war was made by proclamation with decrees of the state. (Livy 31.14.6–11)

In response to Philip's support of the Acarnanian invasion the Athenians eliminated their two "Macedonian" tribes, Demetrias and Antigonis, which they had created in 307/6 to honor two of Philip's ancestors, Demetrios Poliorcetes and Antigonos Monophthalmos (above, chapter 3, p. 81).[57] Since they had introduced the Ptolemais tribe in 224, the

---

56. Cf. *IG* II² 840, a later record of a similar procedure for the Hero Iatros. For other contemporary inventories or records of repairs of dedications, see *IG* II² 841, 842; Aleshire, Inv. VI, VIII, IX; *SEG* 26.139.

57. On this and on other events and the chronology of the period, see Habicht, 1982b, 142–58.

Athenians now had, for a short time, eleven tribes; in their new hatred of Philip, they began again the process of de-Macedonizing their governmental and religious life.

Soon after the Athenians had joined Attalos and the Rhodians in this, the Second Macedonian War, the Macedonian king sent Philocles with 2000 infantry and 200 cavalry to devastate further the Athenian countryside (Livy 31.16.1–2). And then, in 199, when they saw their allies taking control of the sea, or perhaps earlier, in 201, when they eliminated the two Macedonian tribes, the Athenians took what revenge they could on Philip:[58]

But then the Demos of the Athenians, whose hatred of Philip had so long been tempered by fear, in the expectation of immediate help poured out this hatred. And nowhere in Athens are there lacking tongues ready to stir up the common people. Orators are supported by the favor of the common people in all free states and especially in Athens where oratory has the greatest power. The orators immediately proposed a decree and the Demos approved it, to the effect that all statues and representations of Philip and their inscriptions, and likewise those of all his ancestors, male and female alike, should be removed and destroyed; that the religious festivals, sacrifices, and priesthoods which had been introduced to honor him and his ancestors should be deconsecrated; that the places in which anything had been placed or inscribed in Philip's honor should be put under a curse, and that nothing which, by religious law, must be placed or dedicated in a "pure" place be put or dedicated hereafter in these places; and that the state priests, every time they prayed for the Athenian Demos and its allies, armies, and fleets, curse and execrate Philip, his children and kingdom, his land and sea forces, and the whole race and name of the Macedonians. They added to the decree that if hereafter anyone proposed a measure for the disgrace or ignominy of Philip, the Athenian Demos would approve of it, but whoever killed a man who had spoken or acted against Philip's ignominy or for his honor would commit that murder lawfully. And lastly it was added that all the provisions which once had been decreed against the sons of Peisistratos should be maintained in the case of Philip. The Athenians were waging war against Philip with decrees and words, the only areas in which they have strength. (Livy 31.44)

The violation of the Mysteries by Acarnanian youths led to the attack of the Acarnanians, and Acarnanian and Athenian hostilities over the event, because the Acarnanians were allies of Philip, brought Athens into war with Philip. Religion could determine the course of interna-

---

58. Habicht (1982b, 142–50) argues that Livy's chronology is mistaken here, and that this decree should be dated, like the elimination of the two tribes, to late 201.

tional events no less now than it had in the sacred wars of the archaic and classical periods. Athens, using for retaliation what means it had at its disposal, eliminated the tribes honoring the Macedonians and instituted a *damnatio memoriae* of Philip, his family, and his ancestors. The names of Philip, Antigonos Doson, Antigonos Gonatas, Demetrios Poliorcetes, and Antigonos Monophthalmos and their family members were systematically erased from epigraphical records of the previous one hundred years.[59] Festivals, sacrifices, and priesthoods in honor of Philip and his ancestors were to be abolished, but we may well ask what these were by 200 B.C. No such festivals are attested for the period (see above, chapter 4, pp. 111–12). The sacrifices and priesthoods would seem to be only those of the tribes Demetrias and Antigonis, and this would support Habicht's argument that this decree was in fact passed not in 199, as Livy asserts, but in 201, at the same time that those two tribes were eliminated.

The curses on the places that once had served to honor Philip and on Philip, his family, his race, and his armed forces may well ultimately have stemmed from the Eleusinian priesthood, which traditionally punished in this manner those who committed sacrileges against their sanctuary.[60] The original sacrilege had been committed by the two Acarnanian young men, but in a real sense the Acarnanian people and Philip were accessories after the fact.[61] The common prayer before the Ekklesia for the health and safety of Athenian allies and benefactors was made into a curse against their enemies.

And now, in 201 or 199, all the religious honors awarded to Macedonian benefactors since 307/6 had not only been eliminated in one fell swoop but had in fact been turned against them. The Macedonian component of Athenian state religion was obliterated, but the effect on the religious mentality of the Athenians from their century-long attempts to honor and accommodate the Macedonians remained. We see this, immediately, in the response that the Athenians gave to a new benefactor, Attalos I of Pergamon, in these very times. Attalos and the Rhodians were already at war with Philip, and in spring 200, they came to Athens to meet Roman ambassadors there and to urge the Athenians to join them against Philip:

59. For examples, see Habicht 1982b, 148 n. 137; Dow 1937b, 48–50.
60. Cf. the Eleusinian reaction against Alcibiades, Diagoras the Melian, and Andocides (Clinton 1974, 15–16, 70; Mylonas 1961, 224–25).
61. Attalos may well have making a political statement as well as fulfilling personal needs when he had himself initiated into the Eleusinian Mysteries in 199 (Livy 31.47).

When the Demos of the Athenians learned that Attalos would be in Athens, they voted a generous sum for the reception and all the entertainment of the king. After he sailed into Piraeus, Attalos spent the first day negotiating with the ambassadors from Rome, and he was overjoyed when he saw that they remembered their previous joint ventures with him and were ready for the war against Philip. On the next day, amid great pomp, he went from Piraeus to the city, accompanied by the Romans and the archons of the Athenians. Not only the officials and the cavalrymen were receiving them, but also all the citizens along with their children and wives. And when they met, there could not have been more goodwill (φιλανθρω-πία) on the part of the common people toward the Romans and still more toward Attalos. When Attalos was entering the city by the Dipylon, the Athenians stationed the priestesses and priests on each side of the road and then opened all the temples, and, having placed offerings on all the altars, they asked him to sacrifice. And finally they voted for Attalos honors of a type and magnitude which they had hastily voted for no one of their previous benefactors. In addition to other honors they named a tribe after him and put him among the eponymous heroes. (Polyb. 16.25.3–9)[62]

This reception of Attalos in 200 is reminiscent of that of Demetrios Poliorcetes in 307/6 (on Demetrios, see chapter 3): the willing participation of the citizens, the presence of the state's governmental and religious officials, and the honor of a new tribe and the status of eponymous hero. The invitation to a non-Athenian to sacrifice in public cult recalls the sacrifice made by Pyrrhos on a similarly joyous occasion, the liberation of Athens from Demetrios in 287/6. The Athenians had, however, after the fiasco with Demetrios' divination, given up making their benefactors gods,[63] and there is no evidence that Attalos became anything more than an eponymous hero for his good services.[64] The brief period of eleven tribes ended, and with the addition of Attalis they became twelve. So they were to remain. Attalis and Attalos were to be the last instances of new tribes and new eponymous heroes and of this particular type of divine honor in Athens until the time of Hadrian.

The coalition of Attalos, the Rhodians, the Romans, and the Athenians was eventually to win the Second Macedonian War with the victory over Philip at Cynocephalae in 197. But in the interim Athens and her countryside suffered more devastating invasions by Philip or his representatives. While the Roman ambassadors were still in Athens, Nica-

62. Cf. Livy 31.14.11–15.7.
63. For the divine honors paid to Antigonos Gonatas, see chapter 5, pp. 160–61.
64. Attalos' wife Apollonis was made the eponym of a new deme, Apollonieis, as had been Ptolemy's wife Berenice in 224 (Whitehead 1986, 20).

nor led Macedonian troops up to the Academy but was convinced to withdraw by the Romans (Polyb. 16.27.1–5). Later Philip himself brought an army against the city. Diodorus Siculus, writing in the first century B.C., describes this invasion in the context of an unfavorable comparison of Philip to the "just and pious" Romans. On previous occasions Philip had put his friends to death without trials and had razed the tombs of the dead and many sanctuaries (28.3). After detailing instances of such behavior at home and abroad, Diodorus describes Philip's invasion of Attica (28.7): "After Philip the Macedonian came to Athens, he encamped at Cynosarges. After that he put to the torch the Academy and he razed the tombs, and in addition he maltreated the sanctuaries of the gods. He indulged his anger, as if he were sinning against Athens and not against the divine. He had long had a bad reputation among men, but then he was totally hated. But he quickly received the appropriate punishment from the gods." According to Livy (31.24.1–25.2) the Athenians repulsed Philip's attack at the Dipylon, but Philip in his rage—"for he was more hostile to no other Greek state"— set fire to Cynosarges, the Lyceum, and whatever was sacred or pleasant around the city. "Not only buildings but also tombs were razed, and nothing of divine or human use was saved in the face of his uncontrollable anger." Philip then turned on the sanctuary and fort at Eleusis but found them well guarded and withdrew to Megara. Shortly thereafter, still in 200, Philip himself and his general Philocles again plundered Attica and made unsuccessful attacks on Eleusis, Piraeus, and Athens itself (31.26). Livy describes Philip's parting blows:

Philip set out again to pillage the countryside. Although he had previously pillaged by destroying the tombs around the city, now, so that he might leave nothing unviolated, he ordered that the sanctuaries of the gods which the Athenians had consecrated in the countryside be destroyed and burned. And the Attic countryside, which was exceptionally well ornamented by such works because of the abundance of local marble and the talents of the craftsmen, provided much material for this madness. And Philip did not think it enough only to destroy the sanctuaries and overturn the statues; he ordered that even the individual blocks of stone be broken so that they might not form a pile of undamaged blocks. And afterward, when he had not so much satisfied his anger as run out of material on which to exercise it, he withdrew into Boeotia and accomplished nothing else worth remembering in Greece. (Livy 31.26.9–13)

A short time later, after Philip's departure, the Athenians had occasion at a council of the Aetolians to describe the destruction:

The Athenians, who had suffered foul things and were able more justly to attack the cruelty and savagery of King Philip, were introduced. They deplored the lamentable devastation and despoiling of their land; they did not complain that they had suffered enemy actions at the hand of an enemy, for there were laws of war that it was right to suffer what it was right to do. That fields were burned, buildings torn down, and booty of men and animals taken were lamentable rather than undeserved for the one who experienced them. But they did complain that the man who called the Romans aliens and barbarians so polluted all human and divine laws that in his first pillaging he waged an unspeakable war against the gods of the underworld, in his second against the gods of the upperworld. All the tombs and monuments in their territory had been destroyed. The shades of all the dead were laid bare and no one's bones were covered with earth. They had shrines which once their ancestors, dwelling in those small forts and villages, had consecrated and had not even abandoned when they joined together into one city. Philip cast hateful fire about all these sanctuaries. The statues of the gods, half burned and mutilated, lay among the fallen doors of the temples. What Philip had made Attica, once ornate and rich, so he would, if permitted, make all Aetolia and Greece. Their city itself, if the Romans had not come to help, would have suffered the same mutilation. For Philip would have sought with the same wickedness the gods who tended the city and Athena who presided over the citadel as he did the temple of Demeter at Eleusis and Zeus and Athena in Piraeus. Driven away from their temples and walls by force of arms, Philip turned his savagery on those sanctuaries which were protected only by religious reverence. The Athenians thus begged and pleaded with the Aetolians to have pity on the Athenians and to take up this war, with, as their leaders, the immortal gods and the Romans who had power second only to the gods. (Livy 31.30)

The destruction of the Athenian countryside wrought in this short period was truly staggering. Philip may have intended to destroy everything in a scorched earth policy, and then it would be pointless to inquire after the motives of individual targets. But the sources (Diodorus, Livy, and his source Polybius) distinguish among them, and their distinctions are worth noting. The Athenians understood that it was in the nature of war that crops be destroyed, secular buildings be razed, and booty be taken. The burnings of the gymnasia of Cynosarges, the Academy, and the Lyceum were attacks on perhaps the only still current Athenian claim to international prominence, the study and teaching of philosophy.

The destruction, intentionally made irreparable, of the rural sanctuaries, temples, and statues and dedications of the gods was gross impiety, but one that had become not uncommon during Philip's war against the Aetolians and their allies in the Social War of the previous decades. Livy indicates the nature of the destruction but can hardly depict the scale. To grasp this we look at our best record of religious activity sponsored by the rural demes, the sacred calendar of the deme Erchia from the fourth century.[65] In the Erchia calendar thirty-four separate local deities received sacrifices at, minimally, fifteen different cult centers, several of which had multiple sanctuaries. Erchia was somewhat larger than most demes, providing seven of the five hundred members of the Boule at the time. If, for the purposes of a most general estimate, we assume the same correlation between population and number of deities and sanctuaries for the other demes, and if we exclude the demes not affected by Philip's attack (Eleusis, Piraeus, and the 5 demes within the city's wall, with altogether around fifty *bouleutai*), the remaining 132 demes, at least in the fourth century, may have had as many as 2,200 deities (many sharing names and functions, of course, but worshipped separately) and 965 centers of cult.[66] These would have been the victims of Philip's fury.

And, in fact, the destruction may have affected most of them. There is scarcely a dedication, decree, or any other piece of inscriptional evidence from any rural sanctuaries after 200 B.C.[67] There is nothing in the record to disprove or even weaken the claims made in the sources of the widespread and permanent destruction by Philip of the religious sanctuaries and cults of Attica.[68] We may imagine, I think, that apart from Eleusis, Piraeus, and the city, most state cults and deme cults in the rural areas virtually ceased to exist after 200 B.C. This once rich area of Athenian religious life[69] had, since the late fourth century, no doubt been taking a battering from the various invading and occupying

---

65. For the text of which see Daux 1963. For the locations and bouleutic quotas of the demes used here, see Traill 1975.

66. These numbers are obtained by assuming that Erchia provided 7 *bouleutai* in the fourth century and that the demes later destroyed by Philip provided 450. The ratio of 7:450 is then applied to the number of local Erchian deities (34) and cult sites (15).

67. The exceptions are from the fort at Rhamnous: the Nemesia of 187/6 (*SEG* 21.435.24) and sacrifices to Zeus Soter, Athena Soteira, and sometimes Themis and Nemesis at the end of the second and the beginning of the first centuries (*IG* II² 2869; *SEG* 41.162, 164–65, 248F).

68. For archaeological evidence of the destruction of rural temples, see H. Thompson 1981, 352–54. The extensive reclamation, cleansing, restoration, and reconsecration of ca. 80 shrines and sanctuaries in the last quarter of the first century B.C. (*SEG* 26.121) concerned almost exclusively sites on Salamis, in Piraeus, between Athens and Piraeus, and in Athens. Only one other sanctuary, "near Hymettos" (line 58) is included. Many of these sanctuaries had probably been damaged in the Roman attacks of 87/6 (Sulla) and 48 (Calenus).

69. Parker 1987; Whitehead 1986, 176–222; Mikalson 1977.

armies. We know little of how vital the rural sanctuaries were in 201 or in the last half of the third century, but clearly most no longer had the resources to erect dedications or inscriptional records of activities. Many may have been, as the sources hint, mere relics of much earlier settlement and religious patterns. But both the healthy and the moribund suffered a death blow from Philip. Individuals still living in the countryside would, of course, have continued to practice their domestic cults, and a few local cults quite likely escaped or were revived; but, by and large, public cult henceforth was largely limited to Athens, Eleusis, and Piraeus, and the once-prominent deme cults disappear.

Philip had, if not so systematically, destroyed sanctuaries in other Greek cities,[70] but he showed his particular hatred for Athens by the demolition of funeral monuments and, apparently, even the opening of graves. Such actions would have been so shocking to the religious sensibilities of both Greeks and non-Greeks that one can hardly dismiss them as acts of random vandalism. Philip may have ordered it as an appropriate (in his eyes) retribution for the *damnatio memoriae* that the Athenians had voted and enacted against him and his ancestors. So too he executed a *damnatio memoriae* against those Athenians within his grasp. Whatever reason Philip had for ordering or allowing it, it was a horrific sacrilege against Greek religious traditions.[71]

---

70. For this Philip is consistently condemned by Polybius: e.g., 5.9–12, 7.14.3, 11.7.2–3, 16.1. See F. Walbank 1957–79, 1.517.

71. Polybius (5.10.1–8), writing less than a century later, after describing the impious pillaging of Thermon by Philip V, introduces for comparison Philip II and Alexander the Great:

> Philip II, who first enlarged the (Macedonian) empire and led the adornment of the royal house, after he defeated the Athenians in the battle at Chaeroneia, accomplished more through his reasonableness and humaneness than through weapons. For by the war and weapons he defeated and gained authority over those who faced him on the battlefield, but by his considerateness and moderation he won over all the Athenians and their city, not, in anger, adding to what already was being done, but competing and warring only until he had the opportunity to show his gentleness and goodness. Therefore he returned prisoners of war without a ransom, provided funeral rites for the Athenian dead and delivered their bones to Antipater, and provided clothing for most of those released. And thus at little expense because of his shrewdness he accomplished a great deal. . . .

> And what of Alexander? He was so angry at the Thebans that he enslaved the inhabitants and razed the city to the ground, but in the taking of the city he did not neglect piety toward the gods. He took the greatest care that not even an involuntary sin be committed about the temples and the sanctuaries in general. And even when he crossed into Asia and was punishing the Persians' impieties against the Greeks, he tried to take from men a deserved punishment for what they had done, but he held off from everything consecrated to the gods, even though the Persians especially in this regard had sinned in the Greek lands.

The violence and destruction brought on by their punishment of two sacrilegious foreigners at Eleusis in 201 had caused, by 198, extensive and irreparable damage to the Athenian religious structure. The effect must have been shock and dismay comparable to that caused by the deification and resulting impieties of another Macedonian, Demetrios Poliorcetes, after 307/6. We hear of no program to rebuild or repair the rural sanctuaries at this time, and most were probably left in ruins.[72]

After Cynocephalae Rome, because it had other concerns to pursue, gave Philip lenient terms. He lost his navy and much of the territory he had captured or controlled outside Macedonia, but he was left to rule Macedonia and to rebuild its finances and other resources. There was no mention made of his sacrileges at Athens or elsewhere. And, as the conclusion to this series of events, at the Isthmian Games of 196 the Roman proconsul Titus Quinctius Flamininus, victor at Cynocephalae, declared the Greek states "free, without garrisons, liable to no tribute, and subject to the laws of their own state."[73] Following this proclamation the Roman commissioners assigned the spheres of influence of the various Greek leagues and cities as they saw fit.

For the next thirty years, although in the Greek world there was occasional turbulence among the Romans, the Macedonians, the Aetolians, Antiochos of Syria, and others, Athens' domestic situation was comparatively calm and peaceful. The prevailing party in Athens, the successors of Eurycleides and Micion, remained staunchly pro-Roman. When Perseus succeeded his father Philip in 179, Athens refused invitations to join his coalition against the Romans. When in 171 the Romans declared what came to be known as the Third Macedonian War on Perseus, Athens volunteered to send a small force and was required to provide a large amount of grain. But after the Romans ended the war with their victory over Perseus at Pydna in 168, the Athenians received their reward from the Romans: the territory of the Boeotian city Haliartos, and the islands Lemnos, Imbros, Scyros, and Delos.

The epigraphical record, though comparatively slight, suggests that during these thirty years much of the routine of urban state religion continued and that there was little significant innovation. Before the meetings of the Ekklesia the prytanists made their traditional augural

---

72. In the early third century one deme had undertaken repair of sacred buildings and dedications that had been damaged, probably in warfare (*IG* II² 1215).

73. On the proclamation and on Greek antecedents for it, see Gruen 1984, 132–57.

sacrifices to Apollo Prostaterios, Artemis Boulaia, and the other deities.[74] A notable addition is Artemis Phosphoros ("Light Bringer") who first makes an appearance in 182/1 as a separate entry among the prytany sacrifices, is omitted in 181/0 and 178/7, but from 175/4 on is usually grouped with the now traditional Apollo Prostaterios and Artemis Boulaia.[75] This Artemis Phosphoros may well be a revitalized form of the Mounichian Artemis who, with her moonlight, was thought to have assisted the Greeks at Salamis in 480;[76] explicitly as Phosphoros, she was also thought to have supported the democratic faction under Thrasyboulos with her "light" in the civil war at the end of the fifth century.[77] Athens had by now recovered Mounichia, and the pro-Athenian and pro-democratic stance of Artemis Phosphoros, as well as the Boule's occasional practice now of meeting in her sanctuary (*Agora* XV, #240.39), may help to explain her appearance now as the recipient of sacrifices of the prytanists.

The sanctuary of Demos and the Charites remained an appropriate site to honor foreigners (*IG* II² 1236.5, 908.19–20, 909.22–23). There are scattered attestations of the Nemesia at Rhamnous (*SEG* 21.435.24 of 187/6) and the Chalkeia (*IG* II² 930.3, 990.2). In this period the Hermaia, an agonistic festival in honor of Hermes with torch and other races, also appears (*IG* II² 2980, 895.5 of 188/7). It may have been held on Salamis because, in 131/0, the cleruchs of Salamis honored the gymnasiarch who staged the festival there (*IG* II² 1227). *IG* II² 1227 is, however, the last record of the Hermaia in Athens.[78]

74. The prytanists' sacrifices are recorded for 196/5 (*Agora* XV, #166), 195/4 (#165), 193/2 (#186), 192/1 (#187), 190/89 (#171, 172), 189/8 (#173), 188/7 (#174), 185/4 (#179), 184/3 (#180), 182/1 (#183, 184), 181/0 (#167), 178/7 (#194), 175/4 (#199, 200), 174/3 (# 202), 173/2 (#206), and 169/8 (#212).

75. On the epigraphical evidence for Artemis Phosphoros, see Wycherley 1957, 56–57. On her cult in Athens see Palaiokrassa 1991, 37–38. On her cult in Athens and the rest of the Greek world and her associations with stability after a period of severe crisis, see Graf 1985, 228–36.

76. Garland 1992, 72.

77. Clement of Alexandria (*Strom.* 1.24.163) reports an altar of Artemis Phosphoros at Mounichia, where a fire in the sky at night had led Thrasyboulos from Phyle. See Garland 1987, 35–36. A private dedication to her, dating perhaps from the fourth or third century B.C., was found on the south slope of the Acropolis (*IG* II² 4659).

78. The Hermaia attested for Athens in the fourth century (Pl. *Lysis* 206D; Aeschines 1.10) may have been highly localized, celebrated at each gymnasion. If *IG* II² 2971 refers to the Athenian Hermaia, ca. 250 B.C. it also included a chariot race (on the date see Tracy 1995, 43–44, 171–74). On the Hermaia, see Habicht 1961, 140 = 1994, 37. The Eleutheria of *SEG* 21.458 is probably the Plataean festival attested in *IG* II² 3149a. On the latter see also *SEG* 38.178. On the Plataean Eleutheria, see Robertson 1986.

Celebrations of the annual Panathenaia were expected for 187/6 (*IG* II² 891.14), 187/6 or 186/5 (*SEG* 21.435.6), and 183/2 (*IG* II² 900.10). For the quadrennial Panathenaia we have a wealth of information from the recent publication of a new set of victory lists of this period, together with the restudy of previously known such lists (*IG* II² 2313–17) by Tracy and Habicht (1991).[79] Their studies make possible a survey of the structure, development, and participants in this festival for the whole first half of the second century. The main day of the festival, Athena's birthday, was Hecatombaion 28, in August. Completing the athletic and equestrian events probably took five full days. The athletic contests were divided into separate divisions for boys, youth, and adult men. The men had footraces of one stade (ca. 220 yds.), two stades, four stades, and twelve stades, a race in armor, wrestling, boxing, *pankration* (a combination of boxing and wrestling), and a pentathlon consisting of the long jump, a footrace, discus throw, javelin throw, and wrestling. The boys had all the above except for the four-stade race, the race in armor, and the pentathlon. The youth lacked the boys' long race and two-stade race but had a pentathlon. All these events were presumably held in the Panathenaic Stadium built by Lycourgos 150 years previously, and probably required two days.

The third day was devoted to equestrian events for citizens only, held, apparently, on the stretch (ca. 770 yds.) of the Panathenaic Way between the Dipylon and the Eleusinion, running through the Agora. There were six chariot races of various types and lengths, two of which involved dismounting and mounting a moving chariot. These were followed by three types of horse races, one with the rider in armor. The triad of horses race was held once for the twelve phylarchs and once for the cavalrymen. The horses used in these citizen equestrian events were the usual cavalry horses, not those bred for racing. It is very likely that the owners in these "citizen" competitions rode and drove their own horses.

On the fourth day a series of fourteen to sixteen equestrian events was held in the hippodrome. The first set was an open competition in which horses and riders sponsored by dignitaries and kings from throughout Greece and Asia Minor participated. There were races for horses, for two-horse chariots, and for four-horse chariots, with separate divisions for young and mature horses. These animals were all bred for racing, and their riders and drivers were professionals. All attested winning sponsors were non-Athenians. These events were followed by

79. Tracy and Habicht 1991 = Habicht 1994, 73–139; see also Tracy 1991.

eight to ten races for horses and chariots, and here the competitors had to be citizens or individuals, like the Ptolemies and Attalids, who had been given Athenian citizenship. This second part of the hippodrome competition, for citizens only, first appears in 178.

In addition to these grand athletic and equestrian events there were also elaborate musical contests, torch races, a contest of "manliness," the "sham horse fight," and recitations of Homeric poetry. The winners in all competitions received crowns, and, in addition, those in the athletic and equestrian contests were awarded olive oil in the prize Panathenaic amphoras. Winning musicians, in addition to their crowns, received cash prizes.

Among the victorious sponsors in the open equestrian competitions of 170/69, 166/5, and 162/1 were King Ptolemy VI Philometor, his wife and sister Cleopatra II,[80] King Eumenes II and Prince Attalos of Pergamon, and a host of high officials, both men and women, from the Ptolemaic and Seleucid empires, and especially from Cilicia. Throughout this period of the second century, foreign monarchs, officials, and wealthy citizens regularly entered chariots into the Panathenaic open competitions.[81] But, as we have seen, foreign interest, if not actual participation, in the Panathenaia by kings was of long standing. The Macedonian king Lysimachos had sent a new mast for the procession of 298 B.C., and Ptolemy II had provided similar equipment for the renewal of the Panathenaia in 282 or 278 (chapters 3, pp. 99–101, and 4, pp. 108–109). But by the second century foreign entries into the competitions had apparently so dominated them that the Athenians had introduced two citizen-only events: the races in the Agora and the special, closing set in the hippodrome.

A surprising entry at the end of the victors list for 162/1 records that Zeuxis, presumably the *agōnothetēs*, put on also dramatic contests (τοὺς δὲ σκηνικοὺς ἀγῶνας, line 39). The text is fragmentary and does not itself allow the determination whether Zeuxis first staged such contests at the Panathenaia or did so in an especially notable way.[82] In this

80. Here it is noteworthy that in 169 there was an Athenian delegation, headed by the *pankratistēs* Callias, in the court of Ptolemy VI on some matter concerning the Panathenaia. There was also a separate Athenian delegation there about the Eleusinian Mysteries (Polyb. 28.19–20).

81. For a list of victors associated with the Ptolemies, see Habicht 1992a, 78–79 = 1994, 150–51; and for all foreigners on these lists, Tracy and Habicht 1991, 213–17, 229–33 = Habicht 1994, 108–14, 130–36.

82. Tracy and Habicht 1991, 203–4 = Habicht 1994, 95–97. Cf. D.L. 3.56; Pickard-Cambridge 1988, 56.

regard it is noteworthy that during this period the City Dionysia was also changing. After 200 the festival is recorded as expected or held in 187/6 or 186/5 (*SEG* 21.435.5–6), 186/5 (held, *IG* II² 896), 184/3 (*IG* II² 900.9), and 175/4 (held, *IG* II² 3088). Victors in the comedies are recorded for 189/8, 186/5, 184/3, 182/1, 170/69, and 168/7, but the comedy competition was *not* held in 188/7, 187/6, 185/4, 183/2, and 169/8 as also in at least occasional years before (*IG* II² 2319–2323.141–218; see also *SEG* 38.162). The presentation of the comedies was also irregular after 165, not being held in 164/3, 163/2, 162/1, held in 161/0 and 158/7, not held in 157/6 and 156/5, and held in 155/4 (*IG* II² 2319–2323.99–245).[83]

Hitherto we have seen, since the Lycourgan period, the gradual accretion of new elements and competitions to the major festivals, and such had no doubt been the pattern of development from their beginnings. Here, on the contrary, we see unmistakable evidence of a loss, at least in certain years, of a major and early component of a festival, the comedies of the City Dionysia. The Panathenaia during these years was apparently still growing, adding new events just for citizens and dramatic contests and enjoying international participation. The City Dionysia, however, may have been weakening and, within the century, dramatic competitions may have ended entirely.

IG II² 896 of 186/5 gives us a glimpse into the administration of the City Dionysia in this period. On Elaphebolion 21, probably just a day or two after the festival, the Ekklesia passed two decrees as it met in the sanctuary of Dionysos. The first, apparently at his own urging, honored the archon Zopyros of Melite (*PA* 6268) because he had his own daughter Timothea carry the sacred basket "for the god in the ancestral way," had brought the best victim he could, and had taken care of (ἐπιμεμελῆσθαι) all his other duties in regard to the procession well and generously. He was to receive a crown of ivy because of his piety toward the gods and generosity toward the Demos of the Athenians. In the second decree the Demos honored, by name, the twenty-four *epimelētai* of the same festival, all Athenians. They had been elected, made the sacrifices to the traditional gods, and, with the archon, put on the procession as generously as they were able. They were to receive gold crowns because of their piety toward the gods and generosity toward the Boule and Demos. Both decrees were to be inscribed on stone and erected in the sanctuary of Dionysos.

---

83. See Pickard-Cambridge 1988, 108–11. I list only those references to the City Dionysia that can be securely dated.

These decrees suggest both the old and new in the City Dionysia of the early second century. If Zopyros the archon is also the father of Timothea, as seems likely,[84] then the eponymous archon retained, as he had since at least the fifth century, responsibility for the procession. The comedy and other competitions of this year (cf. *IG* II² 2319–2323.146) are not mentioned in these texts because they would have been the responsibility of the *agōnothetēs*, not of the archon or *epimelētai*. Both Zopyros and the *epimelētai* performed their duties well and generously, the latter indicating that they contributed their own money. The most sacred parts of the festival, the procession and sacrifices, remained entirely Athenian affairs, paid for and performed by them. The new elements of the age are the archon's selection of his daughter to serve as basket carrier, the archon being honored for that, and the large number of *epimelētai*.

Beginning in this period and expanding in the next there is an interest among the Athenians to honor their daughters for performing religious services. Since the classical period two Athenian girls, called *arrēphoroi* ("carriers of the sacred things" or, perhaps, "carriers of the basket"), had participated in the cult of Athena Polias in the Arrephoria and as weavers of the *peplos* presented to Athena at the Panathenaia.[85] In 220/19 (*IG* II² 3461) begins a long series of inscriptions erected by fathers and other family members to honor their daughters who served as *errēphoroi*, as they were now called.[86] Customarily the father, mother, and brothers honored the *errēphoros* with a statue upon completion of her year of service.[87] As with the increasing role of the ephebes, we may see this as another sign of the growing "youth movement" in Athenian state religion.

The increase of the number of *epimelētai* of the City Dionysia from the ten of the fourth century to twenty-four is also the sign of a new

---

84. The accusative τὸν πατέρα of line 9 suggests that Zopyros the archon and Zopyros the father of Timothea were separate individuals, but the rest of the text would indicate otherwise. Perhaps in line 9 we have a simple grammatical error, with an accusative for a nominative.

85. For the various current theories on the Arrephoria and the nature of the service of the *arrēphoroi*, see Robertson 1983; Brulé 1987, 79–98; Burkert 1983, 150–54.

86. For honors of *errēphoroi*: *IG* II² 3465 by father and mother; 3470 by father, mother, and uncle; 3471 and 3472 by fathers; 3473 by father, mother, and brothers; 3482 by father; 3486 by father and mother; 3488 and 3497 by father, mother, and brothers; and 3496 by grandfather (cf. 3461, 3466). On ἐρρήφορος vs. ἀρρήφορος, see Brulé 1987, 79–82; Burkert 1966, 3–6.

87. *IG* II² 3488, 3497. In *IG* II² 3473 the *errēphoros* appears still to be in office.

development.[88] We shall soon be seeing several such large, and even considerably larger, committees managing state festivals in Athens. This was intended, perhaps, to ease the financial burden of individuals, but it also would give more individuals the opportunity to share in the honor of such services. For whatever reasons, larger committees and the greater involvement, or at least recognition, of the youth in the state religious affairs are both characteristic of late Hellenistic religion in Athens.

The Olympieion, the grand temple of Zeus Olympios, was and remains one of the greatest attractions for visitors to Athens. The "half-finished" Olympieion that Heracleides saw at the end of the third century comprised probably the foundations and perhaps some columns of the monumental building planned and begun by the Peisistratids in the last third of the sixth century. After their ouster construction was stopped and the partial building was left unfinished, perhaps as a symbol of the hated tyranny. Now, in 174, the Seleucid king Antiochos IV Epiphanes financed for the Athenians a new, equally grand temple on the site and employed for its design the Roman architect D. Cossutius.[89] Construction of the new temple, now in Corinthian style, at least in some places reached the cornice before Antiochos' death in 164. Then, again, work was halted. The temple was eventually finished by Hadrian in A.D. 132, but the imposing remains standing today are generally thought to be those of Antiochos' construction. In the democratic times after the Peisistratids the cult as well as the temple of Zeus Olympios may have languished.[90] The Athenians seem to have directed their state's attention more to the Zeus Eleutherios of the Agora. However, Zeus Olympios still had property that needed to be stored in 429/8 (*IG* I^3 383.78–79, 269–70, 276–77, 325–26, 348–49), rented out in 343/2 (*Agora* XIX, #66.74–85, 146), and repaired or remade under Lycourgos in 335/4 (Schwenk #21.CEF 15). A member of the Boule served as *hieropoios* for his sacrifice in 324/3 (Schwenk #77). His festival, the Olympieia on Mounichion 19 with its equestrian procession and contests, is attested

---

88. According to [Arist.] *Ath. Pol.* (56.4) of the late fourth century, earlier the ten *epimelētai* had been elected and contributed to the expenses of the procession, but in the late fourth century they were selected by lot and received 10,000 drachmas from the state for expenses.

89. On the Antiochean Olympieion, see Polyb. 26.1.11; Livy 41.20.8; Strabo 9.936; Vitr. *de Arch.* 7.praef.15; Vell. Pat. 1.10.1; *IG* II^2 4009. For modern studies, see Tölle-Kastenbein 1994; Abramson 1975; Travlos 1971, 402–3; Wycherley 1964; Dinsmoor 1950, 280–82; Welter 1923.

90. For a differing view of the later prosperity of the cult, see Wycherley 1964.

for 334/3, 333/2, 319/8, 282/1, and once again in the early third century.[91] After that it disappears until Roman times, when the cult was totally remodeled by Hadrian.[92] The lack of dedications, of records of cult officials, and of participation in sacrifices and festivals suggests that after the mid–third century, if not earlier, the cult may have been suffering some neglect. Antiochos, who had, in William Dinsmoor's words, a "mania for showing lavish honors to Zeus Olympios" (1950, 280),[93] may have been trying to rectify this situation with the construction of the grandiose temple, but the continuing silence of the sources would suggest that he met with little success. Despite its grand quarters the cult of Zeus Olympios would continue to languish until Roman times.

Among the rich stores of Hellenistic poetry in the *Palatine Anthology* there are, unfortunately, few poems that unmistakably treat Athenian religious topics,[94] but these few seem to cluster in just this period after Athens' freedom from the Macedonians. Two, undated and unattributed, compliment the widely recognized magnificence of Antiochos' Olympieion:

> This is a building worthy of Zeus himself.
> Not even Olympos would fault Zeus
> if he came down here from the sky.
>
> > (*Anth. Pal.* 9.701)

> The descendants of Cecrops built this home for Zeus
> so that, when he came to earth from Olympos,
> he might have another Olympos.
>
> > (*Anth. Pal.* 9.702)

In contrast to the generic, witty, noncultic nature of these stand two epigrams composed by Phaidimos of Amastris, epigrams that derive from cult and have considerable value as personal expressions of religious sentiment:

---

91. *IG* II² 1496.82–83, 113–114; Plut. *Phoc.* 37.1; *IG* II² 3079.5–6; *Hesp.* 9 (1940): 111–12, #21. On the Olympieia, see Parke 1977, 144–45; Deubner 1932, 177.

92. On the nature of the Hadrianic cult of Zeus Olympios, see Benjamin 1963.

93. Cf. Green 1990, 437–38, 505, 526; A. Stewart 1979, 47.

94. For poems concerning Athens and the city's limited importance in this collection, see Hartigan 1979, 104–6.

For you, Artemis, (Leon) the son of Cichesias dedicated these sandals
    and Themistodice these folded robes
because you came, Mistress, without your bow
    and gently held your two hands over her bed of childbirth.
Artemis, grant to Leon that he see his son, now a baby,
    as a growing young man.

(Anth. Pal. 6.271)

Callistratos dedicated to you, messenger of Zeus,
a statue that shares the form of his own age.
The boy is from Kephisia. Taking pleasure in this statue,
lord, protect the child and homeland of Apollodoros.

(Anth. Pal. 13.2)[95]

The Leon II of Aixone (*PA* 9108) who with his wife made the dedication and prayer to Artemis was a member of "one of the most influential families in the Hellenistic period."[96] His prayer for his son Cichesias was answered, and this Cichesias went on to have his own son,
Leon III, in the 190s and to propose a decree in the Boule in 187/6 (*SEG*
21.435). Because both epigrams were composed by Phaidimos, Callistratos' dedication to Hermes must date to approximately the same period. The deities, the occasions, the purposes, and the language of
Phaidimos' epigrams for Leon's and Callistratos' dedications are virtually indistinguishable from those of the fifth and fourth centuries.
Artemis is thanked for her help in childbirth and is asked that the child
prosper. If her cult were still thriving, she might well be Artemis Brauronia; alternatively, she might be Artemis Mounichia. Hermes, now patron of ephebes, is asked to protect a young man. These two dedications, uncommonly revealing for documents of this period, indicate that
in some important areas of religious belief and practice, little had
changed since the classical period.

Of the private religious *koina* of the period we have noted the appearance of the Sarapiastai in 215/4, initially a group of fifty to eighty foreigners devoted to Sarapis. Of the over twenty private cults surveyed

95. On Phaidimos, his origins and career, and on the texts and problems of these two
epigrams, see Gow and Page 1965, 2:452–55.

96. Habicht 1961, 130 = 1994, 26. On the family and especially on the pro-Roman activities of Leon II, see Habicht 1982b, 194–97.

in chapter 5, only that of the Mother of the Gods, now wholly citizen, seems to have survived and prospered.[97] Her sanctuary, located in Piraeus, escaped the destruction of Philip V, and the decrees from before (*IG* II² 1314 of 213/2 and 1315 of 211/0) and after (*IG* II² 1328.1–20 of 183/2, 1327 of 178/7, and 1328.21–44 and 1329, both of 175/4) Philip show considerable continuity. The *orgeōnes* of the Mother of the Gods had a sanctuary with a temple, a priestess selected annually by lot, a female *zakoros* ("attendant") usually appointed annually from among former priestesses by the current priestess (1328.1–20) but with one in 175/4 appointed for life (1328.21–44), a treasurer (1327), and a secretary (1329). Elements of their religious program included a sacrifice to the goddess in the month Mounichion, during which they apparently held an annual business meeting (1329.26–27), two celebrations of the Attideia, the festival lamenting the death of Attis (1315.9–10), and a double lectisternium (1328.1–10). The deities were the Mother and Attis, sometimes with the mother alone designated as ἡ θεά (1314.7, 1328.27), sometimes with both designated as οἱ θεοί or αἱ θεαί (1315.14, 1327.5, 1329.25).[98] The officers, including the priestess, regularly contributed their own funds for the support of the cult. In 183/2 provisions were made that the priestesses, who complained of the expenses, were henceforth to pay only for the two lectisternia and for silver jewelry for the *phialophoroi* ("*phialē* carriers") and other female attendants of the goddess when they participated in the *agermos*, presumably a ritualistic begging in the community (1328.8–11). The treasurer Hermaios of Paionidai in 178/7 was honored for, among other contributions, giving money for the burial of some members when the association's fund failed. The purpose was to maintain "decorum" for the deceased (εὐσχημονεῖν, 1327.10–12).

The begging, the almsgiving, and the burial fund are all here for the first time attested for a cult of Athenian citizens. Presumably these were characteristic of the cult from its beginnings, with citizen participation perhaps as early as 272/1 (*IG* II² 1316; above, chapter 5, pp. 142–43), certainly by 213/2 (*IG* II² 1314). In a sense this cult would, for its members,

97. On the Piraeic cult of the Mother of the Gods, see Garland 1987, 129–31; Vermaseren 1982, 68–97; Ferguson 1944, 107–15, 137–40; and above, chapter 5, pp. 142–43. The lack of a demotic and patronymic for Ergasion, listed among the *epimelētai* of the cult (*IG* II² 1327.33), may indicate that he was not a citizen (Ferguson 1944, 111, 113). If so, he would be the first surely attested noncitizen member in a cult association of *orgeōnes*.

98. The designation of a male and female deity together as αἱ θεαί (*IG* II² 1315.14, 1329.25) is certainly odd but may be done to suggest the prominence of the Mother. It seems better to assume this than to introduce another goddess into the cult.

have taken on the traditional familial responsibilities of the care of the dead and of the indigent.[99] Cults with such practices were common in the Hellenistic world, but only now, in the late third and second century B.C. and in Piraeus, do we find unmistakable evidence that Athenian citizens participated in them.

From the activities and concerns of the Piraeic cult of the Mother of the Gods in the second century one might imagine that its members, all citizens, were of the lower economic and social classes. But of the eleven individuals identifiable in these texts, three belonged to families that at least later had some prominence. A descendant of Dionysodoros of Alopeke (*PA* 4290) of *IG* II² 1315 served as the chief presiding officer of the Ekklesia in 118/7 (*IG* II² 1008.3). Descendants of Chaireas of Athmonon (*PA* 15097), the secretary honored in *IG* II² 1329, served as a gymnasiarch in 55/4 (*IG* II² 2993) and as a prytanist late in the Roman period (*IG* II² 1794.50). Also about that time a descendant of Paramonos of Epieikidai (*PA* 11619) of *IG* II² 1314 was an ephebe (*IG* II² 2052.91).

Most interesting among the members of the Mother cult, however, is Simon, son of Simon, of the deme Poros (*PA* 12705). He proposed the first decree of *IG* II² 1328 in 183/2, and in 178/7 was serving as an *epimelētēs* (*IG* II² 1327). But in the same period, in 185/4, he was one of fifteen members of a quite different Piraeic private cult, that of the Dionysiastai.[100] The *orgeōnes* of this cult, listed on *IG* II² 1325, were even more distinguished: Apollodoros of Lamptrai (*PA* 1427, 1428) was a *thesmothetēs* in 214/3 (*IG* II² 1706.114), Andron of Hamaxanteia (*PA* 920) was a *thesmothetēs* in 213/2 (1706.128), and Dionysogenes of Paiania (*PA* 4277) contributed to a statewide fund-raising effort in 183/2 (*IG* II² 2332.133). A fellow contributor was Dionysios, son of Agathocles, of Marathon (2332.306–7), whose family founded, patronized, and controlled the cult.

This Dionysios of Marathon (*PA* 4213) is the focus of the three surviving documents of the cult: *IG* II² 2948 records a poem, no doubt commissioned by Dionysios, describing his establishment of the temple, sanctuary, and cult statue; *IG* II² 1325 of 185/4 is a decree of the Dionysiastai, honoring Dionysios for his services; and *IG* II² 1326 of 176/5 pays tribute to the recently deceased Dionysios and makes Agathocles II, his eldest surviving son, the new priest of Dionysos.[101] From these sources we can piece together the early history of the cult. This

---

99. The cult's concern for funerals of the dead would be easily explicable if some members, such as Ergasion of *IG* II² 1327.33, were foreigners. See above, note 97.

100. On the cult of the Dionysiastai, see Garland 1987, 124; Ferguson 1944, 115–19.

101. For the family tree of Dionysios, see *PA* 4213.

private but citizen cult of Dionysos was founded by Dionysios or perhaps cofounded by him and his father Agathocles I. Agathocles probably served as the first priest; on his death he was heroized and a statue
of him was set beside the cult statue of Dionysos. Dionysios probably
served as the first treasurer, a particularly important role in this cult
whose members designated themselves as "those making the contribution to the god" (τοὺς τὴν σύνοδον φέροντας τῷ θεῷ, *IG* II² 1326.5–6). It
was most likely as treasurer that Dionysios built the temple, contributed 1,000 drachmas to endow the association's traditional (κατὰ
τὰ πάτρια) monthly sacrifices, contributed an additional 500 drachmas
for the cult statue and had it erected in accordance with an oracle, and
provided various gold and silver cultic implements and dedications.[102]
The reasons for these benefactions Dionysios had set in poetry:

> Lord, Dionysios dedicated here this temple for you
> and a fragrant sanctuary and a cult statue[103] like you,
> and everything. He did not think, Bacchos, that he would increase
> the wealth of silver in his home but the reverence for your cult
>   practices.[104]
> In return, Dionysos, please be appeased and provide safety for his
>   house, his family, and your whole *thiasos*.

When Dionysios I was priest, his eldest son Callicrates joined the association, and, after Callicrates' death, Dionysios' second son, Agathocles II,
was inducted. It was he who, in 176/5, was made priest in his father's place,
and he promised to continue serving as treasurer as well. Agathocles also
brought into the association his younger brother, Dionysios II. We hear
nothing more of this cult, but members of Dionysios' family continued
to be prominent statewide in Athens for the rest of the century.[105]

The Dionysiastai of Piraeus were thus a well-to-do group, contributing to the maintenance of the cult and enjoying the endowed
monthly sacrifices and banquets. Business meetings they apparently held
in Posideon. The founding, leadership, and much of the support of the
cult lay, however, in the hands of one family, and we may imagine that

---

102. Excavations at the site where these inscriptions were found seem to reveal a large
house (of Dionysios ?) with a very large attached and colonnaded courtyard where Dionysios' temple of Dionysos may have stood. For description and plans, see Rider 1916, 222–24;
Dörpfeld 1884. The complex was probably destroyed in the sack of Sulla in 86 B.C. (Oeconomides-Caramessini 1976).

103. The plural ξόανα (line 2) is probably poetic license.

104. The syntax of this line is muddled, but the sense seems clear.

105. *IG* II² 958.87–88, 93–94; 964.23–26; 2452.19.

the members of this family invited a rather select group of friends to join. From the formal records of the inscriptions the cult has more the flavor of a men's club than of an orgiastic or otherworld Bacchic cult. Here one would not expect begging female devotees or burial funds. For its purpose, however, we should take seriously Dionysios' dedicatory poem: it was not to increase his family's wealth (which was probably already considerable), but to show reverence for Dionysos, in the hope that Dionysos might provide safety (σῴζοις) for Dionysios' family, descendants, and fellow members of the association.

With the Dionysiastai and the *orgeōnes* of the Mother of the Gods we have, for the first time, clear evidence of private religious associations of citizens—private cults standing apart from state, local, and domestic cults. We still have only two, both in Piraeus and quite small, but composed at least in part of prominent citizens. There were at this time quite probably several other such which left no records on stone. But it is first now, in the first half of the second century B.C., that one can claim to find some impact of such private cults on the religious lives of Athenian citizens, some indication that some Athenians were reaching beyond the traditional structures of state, local, and domestic cults to fulfill their religious needs.

In the previous chapter (pp. 163–64) we saw signs of an apparent reinvigoration of the cult of Athena Polias on the Acropolis after 250 B.C., and now, as we approach the decisive year 167/6, we note that this cult central to Athenian state religion appears to continue to flourish. In this chapter, we have observed the prosperity and international appeal of the quadrennial Panathenaia in this period and the current fashion of fathers to honor their daughters who served as *errēphoroi*. The Athena Polias of this period probably remained concerned primarily with the economic, not military, safety of Athens. In the poem on the base of the statue of Philtera, priestess of Athena Polias, an Eteobutad and proud descendant of Lycourgos, Athena is addressed in the opening line as both Pallas and Archegetis, the latter, as I argued previously, particularly associated with the goddess' function of promoting economic welfare (*IG* II² 3474).[106]

Ferguson, in his general summary of Athenian culture of the third century down to the occupation of Delos, continues his lament over Athenian religious conservatism:

---

106. See chapters 4, pp. 109–10, and 6, 171–72. For celebrations of the Chalkeia in the second century, see *IG* II² 930.3, 990.2. For private dedications to Athena, *IG* II² 4339a, b.

The spirit which brooded over Attica during the third century B.C. was that of Lycourgos of Butadae, whose pietism and fanaticism for archaising had created an artificial glow of sentiment on behalf of the ancient order. In Athens there was no emancipation of women, no enthusiasm for a religion of redemption.

The great movement of social and religious change which set in from the East at the end of the fourth century B.C. was met in Athens by a fierce counter-movement which aimed to preserve, together with the city-state, its old usages and its old deities and cults. (Ferguson 1911, 308)

Despite his negative characterization of the spirit of Lycourgos and of the motives behind Athenian religious conservatives, Ferguson has correctly assessed the facts. The cult of Athena Polias, the cult promoted by Lycourgos in the fourth century and still under the control of his family, had reemerged after various dislocations occasioned by Macedonian kings and overlords. By 168 the rural cults of Attica had probably been devastated, but, despite occasional additions, the state cults of urban Athens, Piraeus, and Eleusis were probably little changed from those revived by Lycourgos. Even as late as 168 private and foreign cults, which were mechanisms for religious change in so many cities, had scarcely made an inroad into Athens and were certainly not greeted with enthusiasm.

Yet the persistent return to the spirit and cults of the age of Lycourgos cannot be explained by mere archaizing. We see it recur at each moment when the Athenians recover some measure of freedom from an oppressive foreign power. In a sense it is as characteristically Athenian as the persistent attempts of Athenians, when newly free, to reestablish the power of the Demos and the democratic institutions. When the Athenians had the opportunity to reassert themselves, they did so both politically and religiously. In both areas they sought τὰ πάτρια that had served their fathers, grandfathers, and ancestors so well. This is a fundamental characteristic of religion in Athens from earliest times, and the attitude is not one of archaizing or of stubborn, unreasonable conservatism. Respect for and dependence on ancestral traditions are the foundation of Athenian and Greek religious behavior. What requires explanation in Greek religious history is not tradition but change, for it is change that is contrary to the Greek religious spirit.

We have thus far noted some changes in religion in Athens. They have been, I would argue, relatively minor, and they have virtually all been occasioned by foreign political and military powers. We shall now see how, with their occupation of Delos, the Athenians themselves become agents of change; and because these changes were introduced to Athenians by Athenians, they took greater hold.

7

Athens and Delos

In return for her loyal support, the Romans, after their victory over the Macedonian king Perseus at Pydna in 168, gave to Athens the island of Delos to administer as a free port. The Athenians expelled the Delians from their island and themselves took over the secular and sacred management of all Delian state cults and of the sacred treasury. For the religious history of Hellenistic Athens the assumption of control of the Delian cults is an important, perhaps decisive, moment. We now have Athenian citizens, men and women of social and political prominence, not only aware of but participating in and serving as priests and other officials in non-Athenian, sometimes non-Greek, cults. This inevitably had an impact both on the individuals themselves and on the Athenian society to which they returned after their years on Delos. And, furthermore, what happened to the religious cult structure of Delos illustrates in macrocosm, as what happened back in Athens illustrates in microcosm, what I think to be the primary cause of lasting change in religion in the Hellenistic period: namely, the dislocation, voluntary or otherwise, of citizens from their homelands and the resulting long-term exposure to alien religious cults, whether Greek or not. When the Delians were expelled and Athenians seized control of Delian cults, the new masters, living in a new country, were less limited by their own Athenian religious traditions and even less restricted by Delian traditions. The Athenians had a relatively free hand, psychologically as well as practically, to innovate in religious matters on Delos, and this chapter will first examine how this freedom dramatically changed Delian re-

208

ligion and then describe the religious activities, at home and abroad, of some Athenians who participated in the process.

Delian Cults prior to 168/7

Delos was, of course, an international religious center, enjoying its fame as Apollo's and Artemis' birthplace. Over time the whole island had become, in a sense, sacred, for in the Hellenistic period neither birth, death or burial, nor war was permitted on it.[1] For centuries various Greek and foreign states had sent, in acknowledgment of Apollo's power, first-fruit offerings, choruses, and dedications to Delos. But despite the international appeal of the cult and despite the regular presence of foreigners on the island, the Delians had maintained their religious institutions and traditions and had excluded foreign influences no less tenaciously than had the Athenians. So long as Delians retained control of their own religion, Delian institutions were upheld. What these institutions were and what the Athenians found on Delos when they arrived in 167/6 can be summarized from the superb and highly detailed study of Philippe Bruneau, *Recherches sur les cultes de Délos à l'époque hellénistique et à l'époque impériale* (1970).

On Delos the myth and cults of Apollo, his sister Artemis, his mother Leto, and the birth goddess Eileithyia predominated. The sanctuary of Apollo had three temples, with the "Great Temple" finally nearly completed ca. 280 and replacing the archaic poros temple as "the" temple of Apollo (52–54).[2] The sanctuary had its great altar of goat horns (Κερατών), founded by Apollo himself (19–29). His festival, the Apollonia, was celebrated annually with sacrifices, athletic contests, choral songs, literary and musical productions, and, as at the City Dionysia in Athens, the awarding of crowns to individuals for meritorious civic service (65–81). At the Apollonia a chorus of Delian women (Deliades) performed, a chorus that the Delians, unlike the Athenians, maintained throughout the year to perform at a multitude of religious occasions, often at night, under torchlight, to the accompaniment of a flutist (35–38). Also throughout the year

---

1. Bruneau 1970, 48–52.

2. Page references here and on the following pages are to Bruneau 1970. For the primary sources, see Bruneau. For briefer accounts of many of these topics, see Bruneau and Ducat 1983.

Apollo received *theōriai* (religious embassies) bearing first-fruit offerings from cities such as Calymna, Cnidos, Rhodes, Alexandria, and Athens, and the Deliades regularly performed on these occasions (93–114).

Artemis' sanctuary adjoined Apollo's to the northwest. Her archaic temple remained in service until it was replaced by a new Artemision in extensive remodeling after 179. In her sanctuary was the tomb (σῆμα) of the Hyperborean Maidens Laodice and Hyperoche (172–74). Artemis was also honored by the Delians on adjacent islands: the Artemision "on the island" with a temple, altar, bronze cult statue, and dining room, and another sanctuary for her as Artemis Ortygia with a "house" (οἶκος) and a spring (176–91). As the myth has it, Artemis, the firstborn, had assisted in the birth of her twin brother, and hence was appropriately revered by women as Artemis Lochia ("of Childbirth") on the east slope of Mount Cynthos. Her sanctuary there, on a long terrace, included an altar and a temple (191–95). The Letoön, the sanctuary of Apollo's mother Leto, was just north of her son's sanctuary and included an archaic temple, altar, wood cult statue, and the sacred date palm to which Leto clung in the agonies of childbirth (207–12). Within the sanctuary of Apollo was a temple of Eileithyia, goddess of childbirth, who enjoyed unusual prominence at Delos because of her role in Apollo's birth myth (212–19). Both Leto and Eileithyia had annual festivals.

The myths and cults of this Delian triad, Apollo, Artemis, and Leto, together with Eileithyia, gave Delos its international prominence and its raison d'être as a religious center, but the Delian people, like peoples of other Greek states, had also a coterie of deities to serve their local needs. Zeus Cynthios, the major figure, shared with Athena Cynthia on the summit of Mount Cynthos a large sanctuary, the Cynthion, which was remodeled and improved in the century before 270. The sanctuary was the site of banquets, armed processions, and torch races (221–32). The cult may have served as the Delian equivalent of an Olympian acropolis cult, like that of Athena Polias in Athens, at least in spatial terms. The Delian Athena Polias, known from the sixth century, was associated with and probably subordinate to a Zeus Polieus. In the third century first appear Zeus Soter and Athena Soteira (233–38). After 166 the Athenians had one priest serve all four. Apollo was, of course, "the" god of Delos, and it is not surprising that, unlike in Athens, the cults of the Poliades and Soteres developed little. No temple for them is known, and the one surviving altar, of Zeus Polieus from the third century, stood in Apollo's sanctuary.

Delos was famed for *not* having earthquakes (Hdt. 6.98), and credit for that no doubt should be given to Poseidon, because at his festival, the Posideia, he was honored as Asphaleios ("Securer") and Orthosios ("Uprighter"). The festival featured contests and a banquet, and from the records of expenditures (520 drachmas in ca. 180 B.C.) for the banquet, Bruneau has calculated, at 1 1/2 obols per banqueter, about 2,000 participants, consuming about 1,600 quarts of wine. The banquet quite likely served most of the male, adult citizenry of Delos, and those few who missed it received their 1 1/2 obols in cash (257–67).

The women of Delos celebrated, as Greek women everywhere, the Thesmophoria for Demeter, Kore, and the Zeus Eubouleus common in the Cyclades. The Thesmophorion had altars for each, a temple for Demeter and perhaps one for Kore, a stoa, megaron, treasury, and statues of Demeter and Kore (269–90). As part of this cult the Delian women performed annually a separate, idiosyncratic ritual, the Nyktophylaxia ("Guard of the Night"), which involved, among other events, digging through a certain door, perhaps of the megaron, and walling it up again after the festival (290–93).

Although no Dionysion is attested, choregic monuments survive from the late fourth century and an altar for Dionysos was built in 281 near the Letoön. The Delians held annual Dionysia, surely in the theater, and this festival featured a phallic procession and competitions in tragedy, comedy, and boys' choruses (295–326). The Delian month name "Lenaion" also presumes a Dionysiac Lenaia like the Lenaia in Athens. The Dioscouroi, as protectors of travelers, received a sacrifice on Delos as early as 301, and their sanctuary, the Dioscourion, included a temple, a hero cult–type altar (ἐσχάρα), and a dining hall where *theoxenia* was probably held (379–94). Hestia's cult, as in Athens, was located in the Prytaneion where a continual fire was maintained. She served as patroness of the archons, who regularly made dedications to her (441–44).

To these traditional deities we may add the hero Anios, whose role is analogous to that of Erechtheus in Athens. He was the son of Apollo and Rhoio, was king of Delos at the time of the Trojan War, and served as priest of Apollo and as a *mantis*. His sons were Andros, Myconos, and Thasos, eponyms of nearby islands. His daughters, the Oinotrophoi Oino, Spermo, and Elaïs, had the power to transform whatever they touched into, respectively, wine, grain, and olive oil, a gift no doubt of their great-great-grandfather Dionysos. Anios' sanctuary included a colonnaded courtyard, "houses," and an ἐσχάρα. By the Delians he was called simply Basileus ("King") or Archegetes ("Founder"), and they alone could enter his sanctuary (413–30).

The Delians were as if not more hesitant than the Athenians to introduce foreign cults and accept them into state cult. Asclepios appears first at the end of the fourth century, one hundred years later than in Athens. His temple was still under construction in 297, and his sanctuary eventually had also, among other buildings, a gateway, colonnade, and dining room. As at Athens and everywhere, he was a god of healing and his cult, once founded, prospered (355–77). The cults of non-Delian gods, when introduced, were placed distant from the civic and cult center of the island; thus the Asclepieion was on the north coastline of the Bay of Fourni. The Cabeireion (later called the Samothrakeion), the sanctuary of the Cabeiroi, protectors of sailors, was founded in the first half of the fourth century on the left bank of the Inopos River (379–99).[3] The Egyptian cults, attested as early as 332/1 in Athens, first appear on Delos in the first half of the third century along the Inopos. The earliest Sarapieion (A) was privately founded by the Egyptian priest Apollonios from Memphis, and after his death at the age of ninety-seven the priesthood remained in his family. The largest Sarapieion (C), a monumental complex above the reservoir of the Inopos, was the only one to become a state cult, and that not until ca. 180 B.C. (457–66). Sarapis, Isis, Anoubis, and Harpocrates were, at this period, primarily "saviors," "healers," and protectors of sailors. The needs of foreign sailors and merchants passing through or based on Delos are probably sufficient to explain the introduction of these cults, as they are for the foreign cults in Piraeus, and the Delians themselves seem little more inclined than the Athenians to participate in them.

Within the sanctuary of Apollo, Aphrodite had a state cult, by legend founded by Theseus on a stop on his return to Athens from Crete. Her festival, the Aphrodisia, included among other events a performance by the Deliades. Near the theater there was another Aphrodision, a private sanctuary founded by the Delian Stesileos, with a temple, altar, "houses," and a marble cult statue. Stesileos, who served as archon in 305 and as a *chorēgos* for the Apollonia in 284 and the Dionysia in 280, also provides an example of a religious institution, common at Delos but not at Athens, that allowed the Delians to cope with some of the religious and political pressures of the times. Stesileos in 302 donated a considerable sum of money, a fund to be held by the state and administered by the state *hieropoioi*, to endow the Stesileia, an annual sacrifice, banquet, and dedicatory vase for Apollo and Aphrodite. Though

3. See also Cole 1984, 77–80.

named after the donor, this "festival" and others like it on Delos were to give divine honors to the deities, not to the founders. Years later Stesileios' daughter Echenice followed her father's example and endowed, with 3,000 drachmas, the Echenikeia for the same deities (331–44).

This particular type of "festival," named after the donor but intended to honor the deity, perhaps derived from the embassies (*theōriai*) sent to Delos by cities with sacrifices, choruses, and dedications to honor Apollo. Whatever its origins, it became the format according to which, in the third century, the Ptolemies, Antigonids, and Attalids made their primary contribution to Delian religious life. In Athens, as we have seen, benevolent Hellenistic monarchs might be rewarded with divine honors and large public festivals in *their* honor. But on Delos these same monarchs received from the Delian state itself no such honors. Rather, the kings or members of their families or staff contributed sums of money, probably rather modest by their standards, and from the interest each year a sacrifice was performed, the Deliades sang, and a vase was made and inscribed to commemorate the event. The celebration was named after the monarch, whether Ptolemaieia, Antigoneia, or Attaleia, but the recipient of the honors was Apollo, not the monarch. In addition to endowing such festivals the Hellenistic monarchs also occasionally made dedications of precious objects or, less frequently, of buildings (515–83).

The Confederation of Island States, however — made up of Delos, Myconos, Cynthos, Ceos, Ios, Andros, Naxos, Amorgos, and Paros and based on Delos — at the end of the fourth century gave, as Athens did, divine honors to Antigonos Monophthalmos and Demetrios Poliorcetes in festivals of alternating years, the Antigoneia and Demetrieia.[4] These festivals included sacrifices, contests, artistic performances, and singing by the Deliades (564–68). As political fortunes changed, the Confederation apparently abandoned the Antigoneia and Demetrieia and established ca. 287/6 a cult for Ptolemy I Soter. Soon after his death in 283 "the Savior" was honored "with godlike honors" (τὸν σωτῆρα Πτολεμαῖον ἰσοθέοις τιμαῖς) for having "liberated" their cities. The Confederation erected an altar for Ptolemy on Delos and celebrated a festival, the Ptolemaieia, for him there. The festival included a tragedy competition. Delians, as did citizens from the other islands, no doubt participated in these festivals, but the celebrations were not *their* state festivals (531–33). The Delians may also have participated in the cult of Arsinoe Philade-

4. On this confederation, see Billows 1990, 220–25. On the cults see also Habicht 1956, 58–61, 111–13; 1970, 256, 258–59.

phos privately founded by the Egyptian admiral Hermias in 268 (543–45). Another exception to the usual practice on Delos was Antigonos Gonatas' foundation, in 245, of the Panaia, a festival of the Macedonian Pan (561).

Such is a rough summary of the pre-168 B.C. major Delian cults, deities, and festivals. Though offering only a bare-bones survey of the detailed study of Bruneau and of the complex and beautiful site of Delos, it does give in outline the religious structure the Athenians found on their arrival. This structure was traditionally Delian and probably little changed, except for architectural improvements, from that of the fourth and fifth centuries B.C. The relative newcomer Asclepios the Athenians knew well. Sarapis had by now at least one state cult on Delos, but the Athenians knew of him and Isis only from one or two small, private non-Athenian cults in their own city. The cult of the Cabeiroi, though probably still private on Delos, the Athenians no doubt knew only by reputation. Although the Delian state itself had not established divine cults for Antigonids and Ptolemies, Delian citizens surely participated in the Confederation's Ptolemaieia and, earlier, in its Antigoneia and Demetrieia that were not dissimilar to those once held in Athens. But, all in all, the religion of Delos in 168 was conventional and traditional, classical in structure. The Delians, as Bruneau says in summary (657–58), were attached to the religious traditions of their island, were hostile to establishing new foreign cults, and allowed the private foundation of some Egyptian cults but were slow to make them "official." All these traits they shared with the Athenians.

Delos and Athens before 167/6

In the fifth century, after 478/7, Athens had designated Delos the financial center of the Delian League and sent her own officials, the *hellēnotamiai*, to Delos to administer League funds. When the treasury was transferred to Athens in 454/3 and the League even more transparently became the Athenian empire, Delos remained subject to Athens, but not paying tribute. In 426/5 Athens "purified" Delos and established there the quadrennial Delia. Thucydides describes both events and their antecedents from an Athenian point of view:

During the same winter (426/5) the Athenians also purified Delos on the basis of some oracle. Peisistratos the tyrant had also purified it before, not all of it but that part of the island which was visible from the sanctuary. But then (in 426/5) the whole island was purified in the following manner: they took up all the tombs of the dead on Delos, and they made a proclamation that henceforth no one was to die or bear a child on the island but such people were to be transferred to Rheneia. Rheneia is so close to Delos that Polycrates, the tyrant of the Samians, when he had for some time been strong with a naval force and had gotten control of the other islands, took Rheneia and dedicated it to Delian Apollo, binding it with a chain to Delos. And then (in 426/5) first after the purification the Athenians put on the quadrennial Delia.

And once also long ago there was a great gathering of Ionians and surrounding islanders on Delos. For they were coming as religious pilgrims (ἐθεώρουν) with their wives and children, just as the Ionians now go (to Ephesos) for the Ephesia. Athletic and musical contests were held there, and the cities used to provide choruses. In these lines from the Hymn to Apollo Homer reveals that there were such things:

> But when you, Phoebus, especially delighted in your heart in
>   Delos,
> where the chiton-trailing Ionians gather for you
> into your street with their children and wives.
> There, when they make their contests, they remember you
> and delight you with boxing, dance, and song.

And in the following lines which are from the same hymn, Homer reveals that there was also a contest of the musical arts and that people used to come to compete. For after having sung of the Delian chorus of women he ended his praise in these lines in which he mentioned also himself:

> But come now, may Apollo with Artemis be appeased.
> And hail, all you women. And hereafter also
> remember me, whenever some other wretched mortal man
> comes and asks, "O girls, who, in your view, is
> the best of the poets to come here and in whom do you
> you especially find pleasure?" And then all in order answer well,
> "A blind man, and he lives on craggy Chios."

Such evidence Homer gave that also once long ago there was a great assembly and festival on Delos, but later the islanders and the Athenians used to send choruses and sacrifices. But the contests and most other things had been dissolved, because of misfortunes it seems, before the Athenians then made their contest and horse races. There had not been horse races before. (Thuc. 3.104)

The Athenian removal of Delian tombs in 426 was apparently quite complete and scarcely a tomb has been found there. The Athenian edict that forbade death and birth on the whole island also remained in effect for the subsequent history of Delos as a religious sanctuary.[5] Thucydides treats the quadrennial Delia, with its games, sacrifices, and chorus, as an Athenian replacement for an ancient but lapsed Panionian festival on the island. This Delia founded by Athens apparently continued to be celebrated until 314, when Athens lost control of the island. After that the festival, which in a sense symbolized Athenian domination of Delos and the Aegean area in general, probably came to an end,[6] but the Athenians no doubt continued, as other states did, to send an occasional *theōria* to Delian Apollo. We shall see that the Athenians reinstituted or enhanced the Delia after they regained control of the island.

Athens controlled Delos, to greater or lesser degrees, from ca. 478/7 to 314, with that control interrupted only by her defeat in the Peloponnesian War. Early in the fourth century Athens regained the island, and then Athenian officials (*amphictiones*) again "managed" Delian sacred funds, but only as financial administrators. In 314, following the decree of Antigonos Monophthalmos "liberating" all Greeks and Athenian losses in trying to put down Lemnian attempts to claim this independence,[7] Athens lost her authority over Delos and did not regain it until 167/6. The description of the deities and cults of Delos with which this chapter opened is for the period of Delian independence, from 314–168, and it was that religious structure which the Athenians remodeled. But the Athenians had had a long involvement and familiarity with Delos and her cults, and it was no doubt that which made them aware of the possibilities there.

Athenian Innovation in Delian Religious Cult

From 158/7 survives on stone a list, in apparent hierarchical order, of Athenians then serving on Delos as priests of Delian cults (*ID* 2605). We begin our study of Athenian participation in and remodeling of Delian cults with this list because it provides not only an overview of the situation but also gives entrée to the new structure of individual cults.

---

5. Bruneau 1970, 48–51.

6. If the Delia recorded on *IG* II² 2971 is this same festival, the general Demetrios of Phaleron won a chariot victory there ca. 250 B.C. For the date see Tracy 1995, 43–44, 171–74.

7. Ferguson 1911, 49–51. On the decree of Antigonos Monophthalmos, see Diod. 19.61.3–4.

1. Priest of Apollo on Delos: [- - -]s, son of Philoxenos, of Oion

2. Priest of Hestia, Demos, and Roma: [- - -g]oras, son of Nicocles, of Kropidai

3. Priest of Zeus Cynthios and Athena Cynthia: Micion, son of Acrisias, of Semachidai

4. Priest of Zeus Soter, Athena Soteira, Zeus Polieus, and Athena Polias: Ephoros, son of Nicanor, of Ptelea

5. Priest of Artemis "on the island": Athenagoras, son of Athenagoras, of Melite

6. Priest of the Theoi Megaloi, Dioscouroi, and the Cabeiroi: Seleucos, son of Diocles, of Pergase

7. Priest of Dionysos, Hermes, and Pan: Eumenes, son of Eumenes, of Oinoe

8. Priest of Asclepios: Echos, son of Straton, of Sounion

9. Priest of Sarapis: Philocrates, son of Philocrates, of Hamaxanteia

10. Priest of Anios: Noumenios, son of Euthias, of Phyle

To the list of priests in *ID* 2605 were added also the sacred herald, Dionysios, son of Demanthes, of Lamptrai; the *mantis*, Olympiodoros, son of Cromachos, of Pallene; a flute player, Perigenes, son of Phocion, of Eupyridai; and the *kleidouchos* ("key bearer"), Nymphodoros, son of Nymphodoros, of Marathon.

The establishment of ten priesthoods by itself suggests the extent of systematization the Athenians employed.[8] Among the annual ten priests of 158/7 at least seven tribes are represented. At least one tribe has two priests (Ephoros and Noumenios are both from Oineis), and the sequence of some priests in some periods follows the canonical order of tribes.[9] The annual terms, the number ten, the distribution among the tribes, and some arranging according to the canonical order of tribes all indicate that the Athenians were bringing to bear on this religious remodeling their long-standing governmental and bureaucratic systems.

8. That the Athenians considered the Delian priests as a specific "group" is suggested by *ID* 1499 of 153/2, in which the Athenian state honored with a crown nine of the ten priests for "having made all the appropriate sacrifices on behalf of the Boule and Demos of the Athenians and their children and wives and on behalf of the Demos of the Romans and of the Athenians dwelling on Delos" (2–8).

9. The complete list of priests of Sarapis from 137/6–110/09 (*ID* 2610) follows almost perfectly the canonical order of tribes and establishes beyond doubt that this was one of

This may serve as our first indication that Athenian involvement in Delian cults was tied more to administrative than to religious purposes.

To have only ten priests, some of the Delian cults had to be combined. Zeus Cynthios and Athena may already have had a combined cult, and, as we have seen (above, p. 210), the Soteriad and Poliad deities may well already have been identified, but first under the Athenians do we have attested one cult and one priest for them. Also first under the Athenians are Hermes and Pan united with Dionysos, and the Dioscouroi and Cabeiroi joined with the Theoi Megaloi ("Great Gods") of Samothrace. The latter consolidation in particular is our earliest clear example of what will become common on Delos and what is taken to be a characteristic of Hellenistic religion: that is, syncretism, the blending of deities of quite different origins but of similar functions into one cult.

Our investigation of Athenian Delos is greatly facilitated by Pierre Roussel's excellent study *Délos colonie Athénienne* (1916) and by Philippe Bruneau's work (1970). With them as our guides we now survey, in the hierarchical order of the priesthoods, changes that Athenians made to the cults they "inherited" on Delos. I also add the results of our own study of the dedications made to the various gods in order to indicate the amount and nature of Athenian participation in these cults.

1. *DELIAN APOLLO* (ROUSSEL, 206–15; BRUNEAU, 15–114)

Apart from installing their own fellow citizens as the annual priests for Delian Apollo, the Athenians probably continued many of the traditional practices of this most prestigious and profitable cult. They managed the annual celebration of the Apollonia, but now, for the first time, we have attested for it participation of resident foreigners and of foreign religious associations. In a sense all the inhabitants of Delos were now foreigners (i.e., non-Delians), and the Athenians could hardly stage a major festival with only their fellow citizens. Necessity thus promoted foreign participation, but it is also characteristic of the Athenians on Delos that in religious affairs they welcomed foreigners, even into cults that had once been exclusive to the Delians. For

---

the fundamental criteria for the selection of priests of some cults. On priests of this and other cults and on the tribal order, see Ferguson 1932, 155–71; Roussel 1916b, 347–50.

obvious reasons the Athenians were less inclined to maintain the exclusivity of Delian cults than they were to maintain that of their own cults back home. The model for the new Apollonia was probably the Athenian Panathenaia, which was designed to include and provide roles for all members of the community. The Athenians essentially made the Apollonia a Panapollonia.

By 158/7 the Athenians had also appended an Athenaia to the Apollonia. The new Athenaia, probably held concurrently with the Apollonia, included a sacrifice and a torch race, and it is indicative of Athenian attempts throughout Delian cult to promote *their* patroness, a deity who had been, as we have seen, of limited importance to the Delians themselves.

For Apollo himself the Athenians also reestablished the Delia, which they had instituted in 426 but which had since probably lapsed. The new, now annual Delia included contests and the horse race that had been part of the original Delia. Athenian *theōroi*, called Deliastai, traveled from Athens to Delos to participate. The renewed festival would recall the glory of classical Athens and was surely intended, at least in part, to reassert what the Athenians no doubt thought to be their traditional suzerainty over the island.[10]

During the Athenian period Apollo, as head of the Delian triad of Apollo, Artemis, and Leto, received hundreds, probably thousands of dedications. On a dedication he alone might be named or he might be joined with his sister and mother. Many, if not most, of these dedications were statues.[11] The dedicators erected statues of the humans they wished to honor and dedicated them to Apollo or the Delian triad.

Among the honorees were kings of Egypt, Syria, Pontus, Pergamon, members of their families and staff, and friends, and these dedications were usually made by the royalty themselves, their staff, and friends.[12] On these "royal" dedications Athenians infrequently appear as dedicators: Areios, son of Pamphilos (*PA* 1589), for a member of the Ptolemaic court (*ID* 1525); Stolos, son of Theon (*PA* 12909), a Ptolemaic official, honoring and being honored by a friend (1533, 1534); an Athen-

---

10. In the middle of the second century, at least, the Athenians could put it this way: "The Demos through the Romans reacquired (ἀνεκτήσατο) the island" (*ID* 2589.4–5).

11. I omit the dedications of ephebes, gymnasiarchs, *agōnothetai*, and athletic victors (*ID* 1922–61) because they were made to Apollo in association with Hermes and Heracles as patron of the gymnasion, a role somewhat distinct from the Delian Apollo associated with Artemis and Leto.

12. *ID* 1525–31, 1533–35, 1540–42, 1544–49, 1551, 1553, 1544.

ian honoring Antiochos IV (1541); an Athenian satrap of Demetrios I or II for his son (1544; cf. 1545); and an Athenian for Seleucos VI (1553). Athenians themselves are three times recipients of the honor: Himeros, son of Zenon (*PA* 7579), from a Cleopatra (1537); Apollonides, son of Theophilos, a naturalized citizen, from Attalos II (1554); and Dionysios, son of Boethos (*PA* 4118), from, probably, a member of the court of Mithridates V (1559). Similarly with a bronze plaque dedicated to the Delian triad, the Demos of the Athenians honored Stratonice, daughter of King Ariarathes IV of Cappadocia, for "her virtue and goodwill toward it" (1575).

By such statues dedicated to Apollo Athenians commonly honored also their own officials on the island: for example, *epimelētai* who held the highest administrative position,[13] *epimelētai* of the market, *agoranomoi*, and, quite naturally, a priest of Apollo.[14] We find also statue dedications by family members for sons who served as *kleidouchoi* in Apollo's cult and for daughters who were *kanēphoroi* and subpriestesses of Artemis.[15] These dedications have been occasioned by some secular or religious office held by the honoree. There are, in addition, numerous statues of apparently ordinary but no doubt prosperous Athenians dedicated to Apollo by family members. One *exedra* in Apollo's sanctuary held statues of the two sons of Artemidoros, son of Hephaistion (*PA* 2272), and of himself, his father, and his wife, all dedicated to Apollo by Artemidoros or his sons (*ID* 1962). Such statuary dedications of multiple family members by Athenians are common,[16] and to them can be added numerous single Athenian dedications: by sons for fathers, by a father for a son, by a wife for her husband, by a mother for a son, by an uncle for a nephew, and by nephews for an uncle.[17] Athenians also used this means to honor friends and acquaintances.[18]

The dedications to Apollo also give a taste of the religious cosmopolitanism of Delos in the period. For example, the Poseidoniastai were a *koinon* of merchants and shipowners devoted to the worship of Poseidon, Astarte, and Echmoun, the triad of deities of their native

---

13. On the dates, role, and social positions of the *epimelētai*, see Habicht 1991 = 1994, 264–86; Roussel 1916b, 97–125.

14. *Epimelētai* of island: *ID* 1618, 1619, 1643, 1646, 1650, 1654, 1657, 1658, 1664–66; of the market, 1647; *agoranomoi*, 1648, 1649; priest of Apollo, 1656.

15. For sons, *ID* 1830, 1875, 1876; for daughters, 1867–73, 1963.

16. *ID* 1963–64, 1966, 1968–70, 1973–75.

17. Sons for fathers, *ID* 1979, 1980, 1982, 1983, 1985; father for son, 1544; wife for husband, 1987; mother for son, 1988; uncle for nephew, 1993; nephews for uncle, 1994.

18. *ID* 1533, 1843, 1845, 1999, 2000, 2006, 2012.

Beirut.[19] The members of this foreign cult, however, in 122/1 made a large public dedication to Apollo honoring the Demos of the Athenians for "virtue and goodwill toward them" (*ID* 1777). And, as perhaps the best example, the banker Philostratos of Ascalon made dedications of altars to, quite naturally, Astarte (1719) and Poseidon (1720, 1721) of Ascalon for the sake of himself, his family, and his city. But, on another occasion, he presented dedications "to Apollo and the Italians" (1717, 1718). The same Philostratos was, in turn, honored by Romans with a statue dedicated to Apollo (1722, 1724) and, on another occasion, by a fellow Ascalonite, his nephew, with a statue dedicated to Zeus Cynthios and Athena Cynthia (1723), all ca. 100 B.C.[20] What we have here is the participation of foreigners in both their national and the Delian cults. But we shall see that as private citizens Athenians, with a few major exceptions, limited themselves to Greek, Delian cults.

The dedications to Delian Apollo are the most numerous set of dedications in the Athenian period, but, in comparison to those of other cults, they seem most devoid of religious content. That these statues, plaques, and other objects were dedicated to Apollo probably meant little more than that they were to be erected in Apollo's sanctuary and were to become part of Apollo's sacred and inviolable property.

On some (e.g., *ID* 1645, 1651, 1652, 1663) even the god's name was omitted. Among the deities Apollo was probably selected when honor was being sought generally among the whole Delian community and when neither the dedicator nor the honoree had close ties with another cult. In this time and in this place, the dedication, though made to Apollo, seemingly was intended primarily to honor the human represented by the sculpture or praised in the text, not the god.[21] We shall see, however, in other cults on Delos in this period some signs of religious devotion to the deities themselves.

2. *HESTIA, DEMOS, AND ROMA* (ROUSSEL, 221–23; BRUNEAU, 441–46)

Hestia had been worshipped, alone, by the Delians in their Prytaneion, and the Athenian remodeling of her cult gives one of our best examples of cult being used symbolically to represent changed

---

19. Bruneau 1970, 622–30. For the chronology of the cult of this *koinon*, see Meyer 1988.

20. On the career of Philostratos, see Leiwo, 1989.

21. Cf. A. Stewart's (1979, 75) comment on the style of the portrait sculpture of these dedications: "on Delos the portrait was simply a form of glorified advertisement, and surface realism was thus the major desideratum."

political circumstances. Athens had gained control of Delos by Roman intervention, and the new cult—of the Delian Hestia, the Athenian Demos, and the goddess Roma, all elevated to the second level of importance just behind Apollo—perfectly reflects political realities. A later reality appears in 103/2 and thereafter when the priest is listed only as the Priest of Roma (*SEG* 32.218.40, 127–28, 264–65). The Demos of this triad recalls the cult of Demos and the Charites founded in Athens in the 220s and prospering in this period (above, chapter 6, pp. 172–78). In an Athenian context, however, the goddess Roma is new. The Delian Romaia was held as early as 167/6 (*ID* 1950) and was probably founded, as were other Athenian "political" festivals, in genuine gratitude to powerful benefactors. The Athenians on Delos apparently participated vigorously in the Romaia, in 127/6 providing eighteen of the twenty-one *hieropoioi* for the festival (*ID* 2596); but, to judge from the surviving inscriptions, they did little else in these cults of Hestia, Demos, and Roma.[22] Only the priest of 129/8 erected a dedication (*ID* 1877). Most dedications were to Roma, and these only from foreign associations and usually in their own sanctuaries (*ID* 1763, 1778, 1779, 2484).

3. *ZEUS CYNTHIOS AND ATHENA CYNTHIA* (ROUSSEL, 223–28; BRUNEAU, 222–32)

At the Cynthion on the summit of Mount Cynthos, before 166, Zeus Cynthios predominated, but even the nomenclature of the first attested Athenian priest suggests that from the very beginning the Athenians gave to Athena in this cult the increased prominence she was later to enjoy. The sanctuary was considerably enlarged and embellished in the second half of the second century with new terraces, entrance, *exedra*, and temple. Also, between 156/5 and 145/4, a single bronze statue (no doubt of Zeus) was replaced by two bronze statues of Zeus and Athena. The torch race ending at the altar of the Cynthion may also, in the Athenian period, have been that of the new Athenaia (above, p. 219).

Forty dedications attest to the prosperity of the cult in the Athenian period before the sack of Sulla, particularly at the end of the second century and the beginning of the first.[23] At least nineteen of these are

---

22. For the argument that *IG* II² 1938 of 149/8 refers to the Delian Romaia, not the Athenian, see below, chapter 8, pp. 274–75.

23. *ID* 1442.A.82, 1532, 1723, 1817, 1878–93, 1895–97, 2074, 2104, 2418–30; and two reported by Bruneau 1970, 223.

made by former priests, *kleidouchoi*, or other officials of the cult. One priest, Charmicos, son of Ainesias (*PA* 15516), dedicated a cult statue (*ID* 1881) and, on behalf of the Demos of the Athenians and the Demos of the Romans, a temple (1880). Another priest, Dionysios, son of Menias (*PA* 4229), dedicated two altars, one at his own expense on behalf of the Athenians and Romans (1882, 1883). Diophantos, son of Parnasos (*PA* 4431), contributed an *exedra* in 96/5 (1878), and the former *epimelētēs* of 97/6, Aristion, son of Socrates (*PA* 1749), at his own expense had several buildings built in the sanctuary (1817). A significant number of dedications come from foreigners: from Italy (*ID* 1893), Alexandria (1532), Ascalon (1723), Laodicea (2420), Seleucia on the Tigris (2429), and Gerrha (1442.A.82).

The Athenians again opened up to foreigners a cult once limited to Delian males. Some results of such inclusion may be seen in two dedications, both found in Sarapieion C: one by an Athenian (2074) to Zeus Cynthios, Athena Cynthia, Sarapis, and Isis; the other (2104) of 92/1 to Zeus Cynthios, Sarapis, and Isis. We have in these two dedications our first instance of *l'orientalisation* of two purely Greek deities in the cosmopolitan Delian society. Here, seemingly, devotees of the Egyptian gods have assimilated Zeus Cynthios to Sarapis and Athena Cynthia to Isis. As further evidence of this development Bruneau (231) notes the oriental style of a statue dedicated to Zeus Cynthios and Athena Cynthia (*ID* 2428), the formula κατὰ πρόσταγμα ("according to [the god's] command"), characteristic of oriental dedications (2104, 2424), and the Egyptian structure (with priest, *zakoros*, and *kleidouchos*) of the cult personnel. The datable oriental features are relatively late, all after ca. 125 B.C. Zeus Cynthios as a "summit" deity may well have appealed also to the oriental worshippers of Ba'al, who had neighboring sanctuaries on Mount Cynthos. The process on Delos was thus not only the acceptance of foreign cults by Athenians but also a transformation of the understanding of a Greek deity under the influence of foreign cults, even for some Athenians there (*ID* 2074).[24]

A cult regulation (*ID* 2529), unfortunately of uncertain date but at least fifty years after the Athenians occupied Delos, may give tangible evidence of this *orientalisation* of Zeus Cynthios and Athena Cynthia. It is the reissue of a former ordinance, produced κατὰ πρόσταγμα, by the priest of the two deities, that orders that those entering "the sanc-

24. For a detailed study of this reciprocal process—i.e., the Hellenization of oriental gods and the orientalization of Greek gods on Delos in this period—see Baslez 1977. On Zeus Cynthios in particular, see 89–90, 117–20, 222–23.

tuary be with pure hands and soul ($\psi\nu\chi\hat{\eta}$ $\kappa\alpha\theta\alpha\rho\hat{\alpha}$), wear white garments and no shoes, be pure ($\dot{\alpha}\gamma\nu\epsilon\dot{\nu}o\nu\tau\alpha\varsigma$) of a woman and meat, and carry with them no key, or iron finger-ring, or belt, or purse, or military weapons, and do nothing other of the things forbidden but perform their sacrifices and seek omens in their sacrifices ($\kappa\alpha\lambda\lambda\iota\epsilon\rho\epsilon\hat{\iota}\nu$) in the ancestral ways." The provisions for strict physical purity, the dress code, and especially the demand for moral purity, the first we have met in this study, suggest that a strong oriental influence has had its effect on this cult.[25]

4. *ZEUS SOTER, ATHENA SOTEIRA, ZEUS POLIEUS, ATHENA POLIAS* (ROUSSEL, 228–29; BRUNEAU, 233–38)

The pairs Zeus Soter / Athena Soteira and Zeus Polieus / Athena Polias are first unmistakably associated in one cult in the priest list of 158/7. In origin the Poliades were quite probably civil gods whereas the Soteres may have been linked more to specific instances of "saving" in international political affairs (cf. *IG* XI 559). The Poliades appear earlier (sixth century B.C.), and the Soteres are not attested until 280 (*IG* XI 559), about the time when Athena Soteira emerges as a partner to Zeus Soter in Athenian city cult (above, chapter 5, pp. 110–13). The Poliad deities of the Delian state may have been of slight interest to the Athenians, and by the end of the second century the priest can be denoted simply as "of Zeus Soter and Athena Soteira" (*ID* 2608), the pair more familiar to the Athenians from their homeland. A major task of this priest must have been the staging of a procession, and for this he selected as many as thirty young Athenian males as *pompostoloi* ("conductors of the procession"; *ID* 2607, 2608).[26] No dedications by Athenian officials or laymen survive, and cult activity seems similar in pattern to that of Hestia, Demos, and Roma.

5. *ARTEMIS "ON THE ISLAND"* (ROUSSEL, 215–21; BRUNEAU, 176–88, 197–201)

Before 166 this cult was probably served by a priestess who was assisted by a male *neōkoros* ("warden"). One would expect a priest-

25. For such provisions in other, non-Delian and non-Athenian cults, see Nilsson 1967–74, 2:74.

26. First in the list of *pompostoloi* of *ID* 2608 is the priest's son.

ess for Artemis,[27] and it is probably an indication of the bureaucratic (vs. religious) orientation of the Athenian reorganization that a male priest was chosen for this service. Neither the site nor much else is known of this cult, and only one dedication survives from the Athenian period; it is not by an Athenian (*ID* 2374).

6. *THEOI MEGALOI, DIOSCOUROI, CABEIROI* (ROUSSEL, 229–33; BRUNEAU, 379–99)

At the time of the Athenian occupation of Delos there was a Dioscourion, with its own annual ritual, and a separate sanctuary of the Theoi Megaloi and the Cabeiroi.[28] These cults, at least in this form, had not been established in Athens, and we can see here how the Athenians coped with them. The Athenians had at home several well-established cults of the Dioscouroi and knew them as protectors of sailors from their own literature,[29] and on Delos they combined their cult with the Samothracian Theoi Megaloi and the Cabeiroi, who had a similar function. The Athenians may have united the cults at the sanctuary of the Theoi Megaloi, which they called the Samothrakeion, and may have virtually abandoned the Dioscourion. Under the Athenians the Samothrakeion was enlarged and remodeled in the third quarter of the second century. The Dioscourion has not yet been positively identified; but in contrast to the Samothrakeion, it must have fallen into some disrepair, for near the beginning of the first century, a priest, Athenobios, probably not an Athenian, prided himself on restoring the statues of the Dioscouroi on the porch of the temple, on renewing the lapsed annual procession, and on giving the gods their traditional honors (*ID* 2548).[30] Rituals there as well as artifacts needed restoration.

27. Athenian subpriestesses (ὑφιέρειαι) were appointed to serve Artemis' cult in the sanctuary of Apollo on Delos itself (Bruneau 1970, 196).

28. On the Samothracian Theoi Megaloi on Delos and their relationship to the Dioscouroi and the Cabeiroi, see Cole 1984, esp. 77–80.

29. E.g., Eur. *El.* 990–93, 1347–56; *Or.* 1636–37. Cf. Mikalson 1991, 252 n. 215. For the several Athenian cults of the Anakes, usually identified with the Dioscouroi, see *IG* I³ 133, 258.6; II² 1425.182–85, 4981; *SEG* 21.779, 785; and the Erchia and Thorikos sacred calendars. See also Kearns 1989, 148; Wycherley 1957, 61–65. *IG* I³ 133 associates the Anakes with seafaring. The last securely dated attestations of the Anakes in pre-Roman Athens are Dem. 45.80 of the mid–fourth century and a list of hydriai dedicated to them in an inventory of 368/7 (*IG* II² 1425.182–85). Dem. 19.158 (pace Kearns) is referring to a sanctuary in Pherai, and the Anakeion of *IG* II² 968.48 of 144/3 is restored.

30. On the identification of the Dioscourion, on *ID* 2548 and the possibility it may derive from the Samothrakeion, see Bruneau 1987, 313–19.

In this cult complex we can see, perhaps better than elsewhere, the Hellenistic process of assimilation of deities (syncretism) and an Athenian contribution to it. By 166 the Samothracian Theoi Megaloi and the Cabeiroi were probably already assimilated, but the Dioscouroi were distinct. The Athenians then, in public cult, brought the Dioscouroi into the group, and among the now heterogeneous gods gave precedence to the Theoi Megaloi. In the nomenclature of the priest, the Theoi Megaloi always occur and always come first. In organizing this priesthood the Athenians had to decide which cults to combine, which deities should have priority, and, presumably, which of the sanctuaries should form the cult center. The selected sanctuary would profit from state support, and the others could be neglected. The result was an idiosyncratic cult because only on Delos were these sets of deities combined in just this fashion.

As *epimelētēs* of the island in 120/19 Polemon, son of Patron (*PA* 11891), dedicated a building in the Samothrakeion to the Theoi Megaloi and Heracles (*ID* 1808; cf. 1809). In this sanctuary the Athenian priests of the Theoi Megaloi regularly erected dedications throughout the Athenian period (1898–905, 1981). One of the priests, Helianax, son of Apollodoros (*PA* 6403), was exceptionally active. He may have been a naturalized citizen; if so, he was the only such among the Delian priests. As priest in 102/1 he dedicated a temple and accoutrements "to the gods for whom he served as priest and to King Mithridates . . . on behalf of the Demos of the Athenians and the Demos of the Romans" (*SEG* 40.657). On this "monument of Mithridates"[31] Helianax dedicated a number of statues: to Antiochos VIII (1552), to Mithridates and members of his court (1563, 1569, 1574), to Ariarathes VII (1576), and to other kings (1581, 1582). He also erected a statue of his own father (1903; cf. 1902). Apart from Polemon, the *epimelētēs* of the island, all other Athenians erected dedications to the Theoi Megaloi as priests of the cult.[32]

7. DIONYSOS, HERMES, AND PAN (ROUSSEL, 233–37; BRUNEAU, 295–328, 349–54, 435–38)

Before 166 Dionysos had altars and choregic monuments on Delos but, apparently, no Dionysion. The Athenians combined his

---

31. On this building, a virtual temple for Mithridates, see Bruneau 1970, 576–77.

32. It is also noteworthy that, until the second century A.D., no Athenians are attested as initiates of or *theōroi* to the Samothracian sanctuary of the Theoi Megaloi (Cole 1984, 43–44; 49–51).

cult with that of Hermes and Pan and constructed for the unified cult a new sanctuary near the theater. It included a gateway, an altar, a stoa, and both a larger and smaller temple. In 146/5 the Athenians, interestingly, purchased from sacred funds a new garment for Artemis and gave to the cult statue of Dionysos the goddess' old garment (*ID* 1442.B.54–56, 1444.Aa.38). In cultic terms such a move is unprecedented and scarcely conceivable, but it has the flavor of a purely bureaucratic maneuver to provide low-cost adornment for a relatively new cult. The Athenians continued to celebrate on Delos the Dionysia and the Lenaia, both probably with dramatic competitions.[33] One priest of the cult (*ID* 1907), a priest of Sarapis (2061), and other Athenians (1870, 1873) honored their daughters, as was the fashion also in Athens (above, chapter 6, pp. 198–99), for their service as *kanēphoroi* in these festivals. The priest of Dionysos also selected Athenian young men as *pompostoloi* for the festivals (*ID* 2609). The Athenians may well have introduced into the Delian Dionysia their own practice of announcing crowns for civic services (*ID* 1505.18–21, 1507.21–23). Dionysos also received dedications from the *epimelētēs* of 111/0, who had won victories in a dramatic competition (*ID* 1959), and from the *epimelētēs* of 110/09.[34]

Before 166 Hermes was one of the patrons of the Delian gymnasia, and he remained that throughout the Athenian period. In 156/5 forty-one marble herms stood in the gymnasion (*ID* 1417.A.I.146–47), and Hermes shared with Apollo and sometimes Heracles dedications erected by winners of torch races at the Romaia (*ID* 1950), Theseia (1951, 1952), and Athenaia (1953), most of them ephebes.[35] He was particularly associated with the ephebes and ephebic training, and the Hermaia as an agonistic festival included a torch race for young men from both Athens and elsewhere. For this festival in the late second century ten young men from one palaestra, again both Athenians and non-Athenians, were designated as "priests" and no doubt assisted in the sacrifice.[36] Private, non-Athenian commercial associations made dedications to Hermes as, probably, the Roman Mercurius, often joined with Apollo and Heracles,[37]

---

33. For tragedy and satyr play competitions, probably at the Delian Dionysia, see *ID* 1959.

34. *ID* 1812. This *epimelētēs*, Dionysios, son of Nicon (*PA* 4237), also patronized the Aphrodision, giving a temple and a statue from his own funds (1810, 1811; cf. 2221, 2627). He also dedicated statues to Zeus Hikesios (1813) and Zeus Herkeios (1814) and was, in turn, honored by his wife with a statue (1815).

35. Cf. *ID* 1948, 1949, 1954. On the differing nature of the dedications in the gymnasion before and after the Athenian takeover of Delos, see Jacquemin 1981.

36. *ID* 2595 (cf. 1947). On the Hermaia in Athens, see above, chapter 6, p. 195.

37. *ID* 1709, 1711, 1713, 1714, 1731–33.

but only one Athenian, a Dionysios, made a private dedication, on behalf of Dionysios his "professor" and his fellow students (*ID* 1801).

Pan shared with the Nymphs a Nymphaion near the theater from as
early as the fourth century, and in 115/4 Ptolemaios, son of Ptolemaios
(*PA* 11880), who was put in charge of the Nymphaion, dedicated from
his own funds an arch and doorway, "on behalf of the Demos of the
Athenians" (*ID* 1839). After 166 Pan's state cult was probably centered
in the new Athenian sanctuary administered by the priest of Dionysos,
Hermes, and Pan. One dedication to these three gods, from 98/7, survives (*ID* 2400). Pan's specific function in the Delian pantheon is not
known, nor are there any obvious religious reasons for uniting Dionysos, Hermes, and Pan into one cult. Their priest, of all the Athenian
priests, seems to have had the responsibility for the most heterogeneous
cult.

8. *ASCLEPIOS* (ROUSSEL, 237–39; BRUNEAU, 355–77)

After its founding in the late fourth century and initial
burst of construction, Asclepios' cult developed little. Under the Athenians there was no new construction, and, as it had under the Delians,
the treasury grew slowly. An inventory (*ID* 1417.B.I.102–50) of 156/5
gives a good contemporary picture of this treasury as the Athenians "inherited" it: a gold ring; numerous silver *phialai* and cups; two censors;
the gold crown worn by the cult statue; coins; a lancet; a brazier; a marble table; statues, including three Asclepioi, one marble Apollo, one
Apollo holding a bow, a centaur holding torches, and three children;
an ivory pyxis; and ninety-seven votive tablets. The inventory, if it lists
all dedications of the past 150 years, is rather small, and it grew very
little in the following decade. The Athenians had at home their own
cult and annual priesthood of Asclepios, and this priesthood on Delos
would have probably been the most familiar and least challenging for
an Athenian. But given Athenian familiarity with Asclepios and the magnificence of his sanctuary, it is surprising that no Athenian dedications
made simply to him in his sanctuary survive. A priest of Asclepios even
made his dedication to Artemis Soteira (*ID* 1909), and another was honored by a statue dedicated to Apollo (1834). The most detailed Athenian dedication to Asclepios and gods related to him was erected in Sarapieion C (2387). The Athenians clearly turned elsewhere than the
Asclepieion for their healing.

9. *SARAPIS* (ROUSSEL, 249–52; BRUNEAU, 457–66)

By contrast to that of Asclepios, the priesthood of Sarapis must have required the most ingenuity and open-mindedness on the part of its new Athenian priest.[38] For him the deities (Sarapis, Isis, Anoubis, and, later, Harpocrates) were probably known only by name, the rituals were quite alien, and the devotees were non-Athenians.[39] But it seems also to be the Delian cult into which the Athenian priests threw themselves most wholeheartedly and which enjoyed, under the Athenians, the most prosperity.

Sarapis and Isis were imagined as more immanent in human life than their Olympian counterparts. They are often, in dedications, addressed as "hearing" (ἐπηκόος) and "appearing" (ἐπιφανής) deities. Dedications and buildings were often given to them "as ordered" (κατὰ πρόσταγμα)—that is, presumably, as the deities commanded in a dream.[40] Both served as healers, which may suggest a reason for the slow growth of the Asclepios cult on Delos, and Isis protected sailors. For the former role Isis was associated with Hygieia (*ID* 2060) and for the latter Sarapis and Isis were linked to the Dioscouroi (*ID* 2123). Isis, as elsewhere

38. *ID* 1510 of 164 illustrates one type of problem the Athenians encountered. They wished to prevent Demetrios "of Rheneia" from serving (θεραπεύειν) Sarapieion A as he had done in the past. Demetrios protested to the Roman Senate, and the Senate passed a *consultum* in Demetrios' favor. The Athenian Boule discussed the *Senatus consultum* and then ordered the *epimelētēs* of Delos to restore Demetrios to his former office. On the episode, see Tracy 1982a, 156–57.

39. On the (foreign) cult of Sarapis in Athens in 215/4, see chapter 6, pp. 180–81. There was, however, one direct Athenian connection to the ritual of Sarapis. In 298/7 Demetrios of Phaleron, in flight from Athens, took up residence in Alexandria, quite probably at the invitation of King Ptolemy I Soter. During his lengthy stay there he suffered an eye disease and, healed by Sarapis, wrote hymns in his honor. These hymns continued to be sung for Sarapis still in the third century A.D. (D.L. 5.76). We do not know whether Demetrios composed these hymns at the request or urging of Ptolemy, but they must have contributed to the Hellenization of this god whom Ptolemy was promoting among both the native and Greek populations of Egypt. These hymns, in Greek by a Greek, surely eased the later reception of Sarapis in many parts of the Greek world. Demetrios also made a collection, in five books, of dreams involving Sarapis (Artem. *Oneir.* 2.44). On the cults of Sarapis and Isis on Delos and elsewhere, see also Baslez 1977; Dunand 1973; Stambaugh 1972; Vidman 1969, 1970; Dow 1937a.

40. *ID* 2047, 2059, 2080, 2098–15. Only two such "orders" were given to Athenians, both priests (2047, 2059). On the nature and later history of such "commands" by a deity, see Pleket 1981, 158–59; Nock 1972, 45–48. Although such commands in dreams were given predominately by Asclepios and the oriental deities, they were not limited to them. See Straten 1976, esp. 12–27.

in the Hellenistic world, took on many epithets and roles. On Delos she was praised as "just" (δικαία), "savior" (σώτειρα), and "good" (χρηστή). She was linked with Aphrodite, the Mother of the Gods, Astarte, Nemesis, Nike, and Hygieia. In Sarapieion C, which Roussel (251) nicely terms "un véritable pandémonium," stood dedications to Ammon, Boubastis, Osiris, Zeus Ourios, Demeter Eleusinia, Kore, Hermes, Heracles, Apallaxikakos, Asclepios, Hygieia, the Dioscouroi, and even Apollo.[41]

The cult structure, even under the Athenians, had the oriental form: a (Athenian) priest, (often Athenian) subpriest (ὑφιερεύς), *kleidouchos, zakoros* ("attendant"), females serving as *kanēphoros* and dream interpreter, lamp bearers, and aretologists. Of the hundreds of donors to special projects in Sarapieion C at the end of the second century (*ID* 2614–25), only a handful, all officials, can be identified as Athenians (e.g., 2616.I.3–10, 2619.6–10). Most of the donors bear Greek names, a substantial minority are Roman, and many were quite likely freedmen and slaves. In this cult, more than in any other of the original ten priesthoods, the Athenians found themselves participating in and leading foreign religious activities of a very mixed and cosmopolitan congregation.

The Demos of the Athenians itself also dedicated several temples and buildings in Sarapieion C: one before 135 and others in 135/4, 130/29, and ca. 90 (*ID* 2041–43, 2045). The state also erected a large statue of Isis in 128/7 (2044).[42] Athenian priests of the cult also contributed significantly:

Athenagoras, son of Athenagoras (*PA* 217), of 126/5, "as ordered": a *megaron* (*ID* 2047; cf. 2048)

Staseas, son of Philocles (*PA* 12875), of 118/7: *exedrai* and a statue (2053, 2054)

Hipponicos, son of Hipponicos (*PA* 7665), of 117/6 and his *kanēphoros*, Mystion, daughter of Heracleides (*PA* 10515): vaults, altars, and steps (2055, 2056)

Dionysios, son of Dionysios (*PA* 4249), of 116/5: a spring house (2057)

41. On the relationships of these various deities to Sarapis, Isis, Anoubis, and Harpocrates, see Baslez 1977, *passim*, esp. 35–65. For surviving dedications from Sarapieion A, all by non-Athenians, see *ID* 2116, 2117, 2135, 2180–82.

42. On the Athenian preference for Isis over Sarapis, see Baslez 1977, 51.

Sosion, son of Eumenes (*PA* 13302), of 110/09: temple and statue of Isis Nemesis along with other dedications (2038, 2062–64)

Dionysios, son of Zenon (*PA* 4190), of 109/8: a gateway and pavement (2065)

Dicaios, son of Dicaios (*PA* 3784), of ca. 94/3: a building, on behalf of the Athenians, Romans, Mithridates, and his own mother and father (2039; cf. 2040)

Other priests of Sarapis also made dedications to the Egyptian gods and were in turn honored by members of the cult or by their own relatives for their service.[43]

Eight of the nearly 130 surviving private dedications to the Egyptian deities can also be attributed to Athenians.[44] In 111/0 a father erected, for the sake of himself, his wife, and his children, a statue of his daughter who had served as a *kanēphoros* (*ID* 2125). In 92/1 the brother of a priest erected a dedication for Isis Aphrodite Dikaia (2158). In the late second century an Athenian dedicated an altar to Isis Euploia (2153), and a former *epimelētēs* and a priest made cash contributions (2165–66). Athenagoras, son of Athenagoras, was, as we have seen, priest in 126/5, and members of his family thereafter made gifts to the Egyptian deities (2152, 2179). This level of state, priestly, and private participation by Athenians is unparalleled among the cults of Delos, and it reflects the favor that Sarapis, Isis, and their entourage quickly found among the new masters of the island.

10. *ANIOS* (ROUSSEL, 239–40; BRUNEAU, 413–30)

The Athenians, despite assigning him a priest, showed little interest in the purely Delian hero Anios. To the Delians he was Archegetes ("Founder") and his sanctuary was the Archegesion. The Athenians had, of course, their own Founder, Athena Archegetis, and they designated the Delian hero's sanctuary as only "that of Anios" (*ID*

43. Priests of Sarapis making dedications to the Egyptian gods: *ID* 2048–52, 2059 (to Isis Nike), 2060 (to Isis Hygieia), 2066, 2068 (to Artemis Hagia), 2069, and 2079 (to Isis Dikaiosyne). Priests honored by members of the cult: *ID* 2075–78; no Athenians are found among the *melanophoroi* ("wearers of black") or *therapeutai* of this cult in, e.g., 2085–88. Priests honored by their own relatives: 2058, 2067.

44. *ID* 2125, 2147, 2152, 2153, 2158, 2165, 2166, 2179.

1417.A.I.117–18). Only three dedications survive from the Athenian period, two of them by the priests of Anios (*ID* 1910, 1911). In the great
inventory of 156/5 the only dedication listed for the sanctuary is an archaic bronze statue of Apollo, Anios' father (*ID* 1417.A.I.117–18). Clearly,
to the Athenians, this cult deserved its last place in the hierarchy.

Our survey of the cults of the ten priesthoods the Athenians established
in the first years of their control of Delos indicates their initial orientation toward these non-Athenian cults. They followed their own governmental and bureaucratic systems, with annual priesthoods distributed among the tribes and occasionally rotated on the cycle of the
canonical order of tribes. They maintained the major Delian cults—
Apollo, Artemis, Zeus Cynthios and Athena Cynthia—but wherever
possible "Atticized" them by the introduction or emphasis of Athena.
The purely Delian, as Anios, was de-emphasized. The lesser deities in
the Delian pantheon they grouped, the Soteres and Poliades together,
Pan and Hermes with Dionysos. The cult of Delian Hestia they significantly politicized, linking it with Athenian Demos and the Roman
Roma and then giving it second rank. Asclepios they maintained as he
was but did not promote, and the foreign Theoi Megaloi and Cabeiroi
they combined with the more familiar Dioscouroi. Initially they probably mistook the importance of the cult of Isis and Sarapis, of negligible importance back in Athens, and gave it only the ninth rank, but they
quickly moved to promote this cult when they saw the support it had
in the local community.

Most notable, as we attempt to assess the Athenian religious commit-
ment to the Delian cults they administered, is the lack of Athenian private dedications to these gods, apart from the cult of Sarapis. There are,
for example, no such dedications to Artemis "on the island," the Samothracian gods or the Dioscouroi, Hestia, Demos, and Roma, the Soteres
or Poliades, or Anios. Asclepios received only one (*ID* 2387), and that in
Sarapieion C. The only Athenian private dedication to Zeus Cynthios and
Athena Cynthia was also erected in the Sarapieion (2074). The dedications to Delian Apollo, while numerous, were intended primarily to honor
the humans, not the god. The Athenians on Delos, it appears, for private
cult turned more to Sarapis and, as we shall see, to Aphrodite Hagne.

The receptiveness the Athenians showed to the Delian Sarapis and Isis
cult is atypical of the attitude they had had in their own country, but it
is characteristic of their handling of Delian cults. The Athenians on Delos soon took to the Syrian cult of Atargatis and Hadad of the Hi-

eropolitans.[45] Initially the priest was himself a Hieropolitan, and in 128/7 Achaios, the Hieropolitan priest, dedicated a temple, some altars, and an οἶκος. By 112/1 at the latest, Athenians had assumed the priesthood. The Athenians identified Atargatis with Aphrodite, who was given a specifying epithet, Hagne ("Pure"). Hadad, Atargatis' paramour, became Zeus Hadatos. The assignment of Olympian names, however, could only be superficial; and for Athenians at least, the cult, despite the Olympian names, must have remained very alien. The divine pair, with the prominent female and her inferior male paramour, could hardly be fully assimilated to Athenian conceptions of Aphrodite and Zeus. The cult structure was also, even in the period of Athenian priests, oriental: a priest, a *kleidouchos*, a female *kanēphoros* (all Athenian), a non-Athenian *zakoros*, and a slave. The cult of Atargatis and Hadad prospered quickly, and soon the sanctuary, next to Sarapieion C, included a courtyard with temples, a stoa, banquet halls, a theater seating six to seven hundred, cisterns, and many smaller structures. Much of this monumental construction is dated to the time of the early Athenian priests, from 113/2 to 105/4.[46]

The numerous dedications from 128/7 to ca. 90 are very revealing. In the earliest (*ID* 2226 of 128/7) a Syrian from Hieropolis named Achaios, son of Apollonios, the elected priest, dedicated "to his ancestral gods" Hadatos and Atargatis, on behalf of "himself, his wife, his children, and his brothers," a temple, an adjoining οἶκος, and some altars. By 112/1 the priest had become an Athenian: "Theodoros, son of Theodoros, of Aithalidai (*PA* 6850), priest in the year of the archonship of Dionysios, and the *therapeutai* ("devotees"), on behalf of the Demos of the Athenians, dedicated the vaults to Aphrodite Hagne" (*ID* 2229). Here Atargatis has been given a Greek name, and the dedication is "on behalf of the Demos of the Athenians." Sometime between 128/7 and 112/1—the date is usually given as 118/7—Athenians had assumed the priesthood and control of the cult. Until that time Hieropolitans served as priests.[47] The Hieropolitans, however, all maintained the Syrian names of the deities. Aphrodite Hagne appears first in the first dedication by an Athenian priest, and we may suspect that it was the Athenians who changed her name.[48]

---

45. Will 1985; Baslez 1977, *passim*, esp. 67–97; Bruneau 1970, 466–73; Roussel 1916b, 252–270. Will dates the beginnings of the cult to the early second century (99, 103).

46. Will 1985, 105.

47. *ID* 2226, 2247, 2257–59, 2280, 2282, 2283.

48. Syrians from Hieropolis, Antioch, and Laodicea continued, even under Athenian priests, to use the name "Atargatis" or "Hagne Theos": e.g., *ID* 2224, 2261, 2263, 2264, 2285. Only once in these texts do we find "Aphrodite" (*SEG* 31.731).

As in the cult of Sarapis, the Athenian priests of Aphrodite Hagne, despite being only annual and appointed from Athens, seem wholeheartedly to have become involved in the cult. And, also notably, Athenians with no official capacity were participating. Even under a Hieropolitan priest, an Athenian Cleostratides, son of Apollonios (*PA* 8619), offered a *charistērion* ("a gift of gratitude") to Hadatos and Atargatis (*ID* 2258). In 108/7 the same Cleostratides, "on behalf of the Athenians, the Romans, and the *therapeutai*," gave a "throne," now to Aphrodite Hagne as a *charistērion* (2250). This year he dedicated also Erotes and pilasters, both no doubt for the sanctuary's theater (2251, 2252). The Athenian priests of Aphrodite Hagne in these years showed an interest well beyond that of fulfilling administrative assignments. In 110/09 Demonicos, son of Heuremon (*PA* 3564), added to the usual beneficiaries (the Demos of the Athenians and the Demos of the Romans) himself, his nephew, his wife, and the *therapeutai* when he dedicated an Ionic colonnade (2230). The same Demonicos gave to the sanctuary, from his own funds, another building and "furniture" (2231). Also in Demonicos' year the *epimelētēs* of Delos, the chief Athenian official on the island, and his wife dedicated "for themselves, their children, and the Demos of the Athenians" a temple and pronaos (2221). In 107/6 the priest Aischrion, son of Aischrion (*PA* 387), from his own funds dedicated altars (2232, 2233; cf. *SEG* 36.740). And, as a final example, Philocles, son of Zenon (*PA* 14561), was priest in 100/99 and dedicated a temple and doors (*ID* 2237), a statue of the *kanēphoros* Nympho (2238), and an altar (2239).[49] Among the dedications made privately by Athenians are a statue of a son erected by his mother (2246), Cleostratides' four contributions (2250–52, 2258), and Phormion's for himself, his wife, his children, Philippos (a cult official), and the *therapeutai* (2274). A few Athenians, including Cleostratides and the priest, are also listed among the many contributors to the sanctuary's theater in 108/7 (2628.I.18 ff.). But this list and the many other dedications also serve to remind us that the large majority of *therapeutai* were non-Athenians, coming from places such as Antioch, Laodicea, Hieropolis, Rome, Alexandria, Ascalon, Seleucia, Ephesos, and Damascus.

In the Delian cult of Atargatis, more than in any other of the Hellenistic period, we have good evidence for Athenian private and official participation in a truly exotic, foreign, and highly cosmopolitan cult. In

---

49. For more dedications by Athenian priests, see *ID* 2228, 2229, 2235, 2236, 2240; *SEG* 35.887.

the Delian context Atargatis / Aphrodite Hagne seems to promote "healing" and "immanence" amid secret, mystery-type rituals requiring temporary purity from certain foods (including fish and pork), sex, childbirth, and miscarriage (*ID* 2530). In the many *charistēria* to this goddess on behalf of the Demos of the Athenians, the Demos of the Romans, the givers and their family and friends, one sees the same striving, on the political and personal level, for "health and safety" that we have seen, in Athens, in the Olympian cults. Here, living on an island a day's voyage from their homeland, some Athenians found, as they did in Sarapis and Isis, a new provider of health and safety. That these effects were felt also back in Athens is best suggested by one dedication to the goddess by the Demos of the Athenians itself, made κατὰ προστάγματα, that is, "at the commands" of the goddess herself (*ID* 2220). The Athenian Demos, in Athens, had voted in 110/09 to honor the requests of a Syrian deity.

Athenians on Delos seem particularly attracted to the cults of Sarapis and Atargatis, but they also allowed, more readily than had their Delian predecessors, foreigners to found sanctuaries for the worship of their native gods. By ca. 100 B.C. there were on Delos sanctuaries of (1) Zeus Hypsistos = Ba'al (*ID* 2306); (2) of Astarte of Ascalon (1719, 2305); and (3) of Heracles (= Ba'al) and Hauronas, gods of the Palestinian city Iamneia (2308). There was also a Jewish synagogue of Theos Hypsistos (2328–33). A number of other "oriental" sanctuaries have also been identified in which foreign deities were honored under Greek names such as Megistos Ares Ouranios (2312) and Theoi Protoi (2310).[50] In addition to these, there were various private cult associations of merchants and sailors such as the Roman Competaliastai (1760–71), the Heracleistai of Tyre (1519), and the Poseidoniastai of Beirut (1520, 1772–96, 2323–27, 2611).[51]

Although the Athenians did not participate in these various cults as either officials or laymen, they must have approved for them the purchase of land and hence the permanent establishment of the cults.[52] The result was that, by ca. 100 B.C., as Bruneau (1970, 1) puts it, "here, more than elsewhere in Greece, the confrontation of Greek deities and of

50. On these oriental deities, see Baslez 1977; Bruneau 1970, 240–41, 474–78, 480–93.

51. Baslez 1977; Bruneau 1970, 615–38.

52. In 153/2 the Heracleistai of Tyre honored a fellow member, Patron, son of Dorotheos, who, among other services, "encouraged the *koinon* to send an embassy to the Demos of the Athenians so that a piece of land (τόπος) might be granted to them where they would build a *temenos* of Heracles who was responsible for most goods for men and was founder (ἀρχηγοῦ) of their fatherland." As the ambassador to the Boule and Ekklesia, Patron sailed to Athens and successfully completed his mission (*ID* 1519).

foreign deities was multiplied by a real encounter among their devotees." Within two generations the Athenians, in part by participation
and in part by tolerance, neither of which they exhibited at home, had
turned the religiously conservative Delos into a mixing pot of a bewil-
dering variety of Greek and foreign cults. They did this, I think, because as newcomers themselves to Delos they were inhibited by neither
Athenian nor Delian religious traditions. With much less constraint than
they felt at home, they were able to innovate with and participate in the
new religious movements flooding Asia Minor and the Aegean.

We have thus far been examining, from epigraphical texts, the externals
of the Delian cult structure and the changes effected by the Athenians.
But the same inscriptions allow us to see more clearly than does any other
evidence from the Hellenistic period the participation in religious cults
by Athenian individuals and families, both as officials and as laymen. It
immediately becomes apparent that individuals and families participated
in a wide variety of quite different types of cults. There is virtually no
evidence for exclusive devotion to one cult, even for the devotees of the
Egyptian or Syrian deities. We shall also see how members of individual families—fathers, brothers, sisters, sons, and daughters—played
roles in various cults and how sacred offices were passed around among
a rather large group of prominent families. And, we shall see, many of
these families maintained their ties with traditional cults back at Athens.

Euboulos, son of Demetrios, of Marathon (*PA* 5364) is among the
earliest attested Athenian priests on Delos, and his priestly career is unparalleled not in the number (three) of priesthoods he held,[53] but because he held them in successive years. In 159/8 Euboulos was praised
for his services by the Ekklesia of the Athenian cleruchs on Delos:

Chosen as *archetheōros*, with his son and fellow *theōroi*, he administered
(βραβεύσας) all things well and properly, and he brought it about that for
the first time at the Panathenaia the Demos of the Athenians on Delos was

---

53. Several Athenians held two priesthoods: Demetrios of Anaphlystos (*PA* 3385), of
Apollo and Sarapis; Philocrates of Hamaxanteia, of Theoi Megaloi and Sarapis; Theomnestos of Kydathenaion (*PA* 6968), of Artemis and Sarapis; Diophantos of Marathon
(*PA* 4433), of Zeus Cynthios and Aphrodite Hagne; Athenagoras of Melite (*PA* 217) of
Artemis and Sarapis; Eumenes of Oinoe (*PA* 5824), of Asclepios and Dionysos; Dionysios of Paiania (*PA* 4229), of Zeus Cynthios and Sarapis; and Philoxenos of Sounion (*PA*
14710), of Sarapis and Aphrodite Hagne. The following each held three priesthoods: Gaios
of Acharnai (*PA* 2937), of Theoi Megaloi, Sarapis, and Aphrodite Hagne; and Theobios
of Acharnai (*PA* 6674), of Zeus Cynthios, Sarapis, and Aphrodite Hagne. If our epigraphical record were more complete, there would be surely many more examples of such
multiple priesthoods.

honored with a gold crown that was announced in the theater (in Athens), and having been an ambassador and having spoken zealously many times he brought about many of the useful things for Athenians on Delos. He was priest of the Theoi Megaloi, and again of Asclepios, and again, chosen by the Demos and having won the lot, of Dionysos. From his private funds he paid for and performed all the processions and sacrifices on behalf of the Athenians and Romans well and in ways befitting sacred rites (ἱεροπρεπῶς). (*ID* 1498.8–22)

From this we conclude that Euboulos was priest of the Theoi Megaloi, the Cabeiroi, and the Dioscouroi in 161/0, of Asclepios in 160/59, and of Dionysos, Hermes, and Pan in 159/8. His brother Demetrios (*PA* 3422) also resided on Delos, and Euboulos' son, Demetrios II (*PA* 3423), was a *theōros* and like his father served as an ambassador to Athens. This son set up in the Samothrakeion a statue honoring his father and dedicated to the Theoi Megaloi (*ID* 1981). We see here, in our first and earliest example, elements characteristic of the Athenian role in Delian religion: multiple priesthoods, each of a year's term, held by one person; the priest's contribution of his own funds; the rather high social and political status of the priest (suggested by the ambassadorships); and the involvement of whole families, not just individuals. The multiple priesthoods of Euboulos, like those of the other Athenian priests, reveal no particular pattern. There is no religious tie, for example, between the cults of Dionysos and Asclepios, nor is there any apparent *cursus honorum*. In the hierarchical ranking of *ID* 2605 Euboulos' first priesthood, of the Theoi Megaloi, was sixth; his second, of Asclepios, was eighth; and his last, of Dionysos, was seventh. The multiple priesthoods, the rotation of some on the tribal cycle, and the annual tenure suggest that from the very beginning, these priesthoods were largely administrative in nature. For some cults, as we have seen for Sarapis and Aphrodite Hagne, the priesthoods may, for some priests, have become considerably more; but for most they did not.

Euboulos' successor, in 158/7, as priest of Dionysos was Eumenes of Oinoe (*PA* 5824). In 144/3 Eumenes was among a large group of prominent Athenians who served as *hieropoioi* for the annual Delian Apollonia. As commonly happened on Delos, Eumenes' son Sosion (*PA* 13302) later held a priesthood, that of Sarapis in 110/09, and dedicated a temple and a statue to Isis Nemesis.[54] A few years earlier, in 113/2,

---

54. Other Athenian sons who served, as their fathers had, as priests of Delian gods were Diophantos, son of Diophantos, of Marathon, as priest of the Theoi Megaloi, whose father (*PA* 4433) had been priest of Zeus Cynthios and of Aphrodite Hagne and had been

Sosion's daughter Hedea had served as a *kanēphoros* for the island's Dionysia. A descendant of Eumenes also served as priest of Asclepios.[55]

The family of Athenagoras II of Melite (*PA* 217), the priest of Artemis in 158/7, had a long and constant involvement in the cults of both Athens and Delos. His daughter Soteira served as *kanēphoros* for Asclepios in Athens when her cousin Leonides (II) was the *kleidouchos* and her uncle Zenon (I) was priest. On Delos in the last half of the second century members of Athenagoras' family served as priest of Sarapis in 126/5, as *kleidouchos* and *pythaïstēs* to Delphi, and as subpriestess of Artemis and *kanēphoros* for the Delian Pythaïs to Delphi. They patronized especially the Sarapieion, giving a *megaron*, altar, gateways, and a door, in addition to five statues of family members. These dedications were primarily for Sarapis, Isis, and Anoubis, but some named also Zeus Sarapis, Zeus Ourios, and Artemis Hekate. Outside the Sarapieion they dedicated statues of family members to Apollo and to Zeus Cynthios and Athena Cynthia.[56]

Gaios, son of Gaios, of Acharnai (*PA* 2937), who shared with his father a Roman name, was priest of the Theoi Megaloi in 128/7, of Sarapis in 115/4, and of Aphrodite Hagne in 98/7. He seems one of those priests who became involved in the cults he was serving, making dedications to Isis Dikaiosyne, the Theoi Megaloi, and Aphrodite Hagne. In his priesthood of the latter he had his daughter Nicopolis as *kanēphoros*, and they together with the *therapeutai* offered a *charistērion* to Aphrodite Hagne. It is most interesting, however, that about this time, perhaps somewhat earlier, Gaios' daughter Nicopolis also served in Athens as one of the many *ergastīnai* ("workeresses") who, at least nominally, wove the *peplos* for Athena Polias. Service to the most traditional cult of Athens was apparently not incompatible with service in one of the most exotic cults in the Athenian realm.[57]

The priesthood of Apollo was first in the hierarchical rankings, and the record of three brothers from Anaphlystos suggests that it may have been reserved for men of the first rank. Dionysios (III) (*PA* 4152) first

---

coadministrator of the island's religious affairs (*ID* 1709, 1887–89, 1904, 2235, 2236, 2245); and Echedemos of Sounion in the late second century B.C., as priest of Asclepios, as his father Echos had been in 158/7 (*ID* 1834, 2605.22–23).

55. *ID* 1958, 2038, 2061–64, 2126, 2322, 2593.7, 2605.20–21, 2610.35.

56. *ID* 1871, 1891, 1994, 2047, 2048, 2092–94, 2147, 2152, 2179, 2207, 2215, 2343, 2352, 2375, 2376, 2605.16–17, 2630.17; *IG* II² 4456.

57. *IG* II²1942; *SEG* 32.218.237–38; *ID* 1900, 2072, 2073, 2079, 2091, 2240, 2610.29.

served as priest of Apollo, then as *epimēlētēs* of the island in 111/0. That same year his brother Demetrios (III) (*PA* 3385) was priest of Sarapis. Later, in 100/99, Demetrios too held the priesthood of Apollo. In the interim, in 107/6, their brother Ammonios (IV) (*PA* 722) was *epimelētēs*. Their uncle Ammonios (II) (*PA* 721) also had been *epimelētēs* for two years, ca. 128. The *epimelētēs* was first rank in the secular administration, as was Apollo's priest among the other priests.[58]

We first meet Theodotos, son of Diodoros, of Sounion (*PA* 6803) as the priest of Aphrodite Hagne shortly before 110/09. In the year of his priesthood his two sons, Cleophanes and Apollonios, contributed funds for some construction in the sanctuary. The same Apollonios served as *kleidouchos* of the cult during his father's priesthood. A few years after his priesthood Theodotos, "on behalf of the Demos of the Athenians, the Demos of the Romans, his wife, and his son Apollonios," gave, at his own expense, a stoa to the goddess as a *charistērion*. Theodotos then returned to Athens and in 106/5 proposed two decrees: one honoring John Hyrcanos, high priest of the Jews; the other honoring the ephebes of 107/6, among whom was another son, Timocrates. In 104/3 he proposed a decree honoring the pyrtanists. Then Theodotos went back to Delos where he held the highest position, *epimelētēs*, in 102/1.[59] Clearly Theodotos was a man of wealth and high political position who moved easily to and from Delos.[60]

As the last of our examples of Athenians participating in Delian religious cults I offer Medeios, son of Medeios, of Piraeus (*PA* 10098).[61] Around 120–110 his mother and father erected on Delos, in an *exedra*, statues of Medeios for his service as a member of the Athenian embassy to Delos for the Delia; of his sister Philippe, who had been both *kanēphoros* for the Delia and a subpriestess (ὑφιέρεια) of Artemis; and of another sister, Laodameia, who had been a *kanēphoros* for both the Delia and the Apollonia (*ID* 1869). These statues were all dedicated to

---

58. *SEG* 32.218.147–49; *ID* 1531, 1959, 2070, 2125, 2610.34. For a stemma of the family see Roussel 1916b, 104. Cf. Anticrates, son of Philiscos, of Epikephisia (*PA* 1082) who was priest of Apollo in 101/0 and polemarch in Athens in 98/7 (*SEG* 32.218.121–22, 249).

59. *IG* II² 1011.5, 33, 99; Josephos *A.J.* 14.153; *SEG* 40.657; *Agora* XV, #254.7; *ID* 1800, 2228, 2261, 2285, 2626. Theodotos' father was apparently one of the few Athenian members of a large *koinon* in Athens headed by an individual from Antioch (*IG* II² 2358.22).

60. For the extensive Delian activities, domestic and religious, of the Athenian family of Dioscourides of Myrrhinoutta, a less prominent but still prosperous family, see Kreeb 1985. Kreeb is in error, I think, in seeing the prominently placed statues of Dioscourides and his wife Cleopatra as the result of a "private divination."

61. On the career and family of Medeios, see Tracy 1982a, 159–64.

Apollo, Artemis, and Leto. As archon in Athens in 101/0 Medeios himself contributed probably 100 drachmas to the annual collection for the Pythaïs to Delphi. In 99/8 he gave far more for the Pythaïs: 250 drachmas as *epimelētēs* of Delos; 200 drachmas as general "for the weapons" in Athens; 250 drachmas as *agōnothetēs* of the Panathenaia; 250 drachmas as *agōnothetēs* of the Delia on Delos; and, finally, another 200 drachmas as magistrate "for the public bank" on Delos.[62] Apart from indicating great wealth, Medeios' contributions as the simultaneous holder of five offices in one year suggest that his religious role now was symbolic or, better, merely financial. He no doubt gave his funds, but little more, for the celebration of the Panathenaia and the Delia. It is noteworthy, however, that like many other *epimelētai* and prominent political figures of the time he is not attested to have held a priesthood on Delos.[63] A priesthood would probably have required residence on the island for the year or at least regular visits.

As leader of the oligarchic faction in power in the troubled years of the late 90s, Medeios served as archon for three successive years, from 91/0–89/8 (*IG* II² 1713.9–11), until he, along with other pro-Romans, fled when the pro-Mithridaic faction took control of Athens. He or his son would eventually return, with the army of Sulla, in 86. But in the religious activities of Medeios, one element stands out, an element that will take us back over two hundred years to the beginning of this study. Medeios was, however distant, a descendant of the fourth-century statesman Lycourgos, a member of the Eteobutad family. We find Medeios, like generations of Eteobutadai, like Lycourgos himself, assuming the priesthood of Poseidon-Erechtheus, the deity of the most venerable cult on the Athenian Acropolis.[64] And Medeios' sister, the same Philippe who had been a *kanēphoros* at the Delia and a subpriestess of the Delian Artemis, served, as an Eteobutad, as the priestess of Athena Polias ([Plut.] *X Orat.* 843B).[65] After so many generations,

---

62. *SEG* 32.218.94, 164–65, 182–89. On Medeios as *epimelētēs* of Delos, for which he received two statues, see *ID* 1711, 1757, 1761, 1816, 1929, 2400.

63. E.g., Sarapion, son of Sarapion (*PA* 12564), *epimelētēs* of Delos in 100/99, held the *agōnothesia* of the Eleusinia, Panathenaia, Delia, and one other festival in 98/7 (*SEG* 32.218.207–14). One daughter, Sosandra, was on Delos *kanēphoros* at the Lenaia and Dionysia and subpriestess of Artemis (*ID* 1870); two others, Apollodora and Theodora, were *kanēphoroi* at Delphi in 98/7. A son Diocles was *kleidouchos* the year his father was *epimelētēs* (2364). On Sarapion, see Tracy 1982a, 159–64.

64. On Lycourgos and this priesthood, see chapter 1, p. 22.

65. In earlier times the two branches of the Eteobutad family had separately held the priesthood of Poseidon-Erechtheus and that of Athena Polias. By Medeios' time the branches

after so much political upheaval, after sixty years of experience on Delos — still, less than three years before Sulla's devastation of Athens, the Eteobutadai, Lycourgos' family, maintained its authority over the cult central to Athenian state religion.[66] Despite everything, the most venerable of Athenian cults was still tended according to traditions that reached back into the classical and archaic periods.

We have examined what, in religious terms, the Athenians found on Delos when they took it over in 167/6, how they reorganized some cults and "Atticized" others, and how they themselves as officials or as private individuals participated in them. We leave Delos somewhat reluctantly, because the abundant sources there give us our best information on Athenian individuals and families practicing their religion in the Hellenistic period, in fact in all of Athenian history; but it remains now to be seen what, in religious terms, was going on back home in Athens and what impact the Delian experience had there.

---

must have merged to allow Medeios and his sister to hold both offices (Davies 1971, 348). On Philippe and the other attested priestesses of Athena Polias, see Lewis 1955, 7–12.

66. On the religious and other activities of other Eteoboutadai in this period, see MacKendrick 1969, 50–52.

8

Indian Summer

From when the Athenians established their independence
from the Macedonians in 229, they had fairly successfully navigated the
perils of international diplomacy.[1] They avoided involvement in the First
Macedonian War (211–205); sided with Rome, Rhodes, and Pergamon,
the victors of the Second Macedonian War (200–197); and in 168 re-
joiced with Rome in the victory over Perseus in the Third Macedonian
War (171–168). Athens' most serious loss in the period was the devastation of the countryside by Philip V in 200 B.C. (see chapter 6). But as
her spoils from the Roman victory in 168 Athens received Delos, and
control over Delos ushered in for Athenians a new period of international activity. The peace and prosperity begun in 229 continued
throughout the second century. It came to an end for Athenians both
on Delos and in the homeland itself only when they became involved
in the hostilities between Rome and Mithridates VI Eupator. The result was destruction—the sack of Delos by Mithridates' forces in 88 and
the pillaging of much of Athens by Sulla's army on March 1, 86. In the
period we now treat, 168–86 B.C., those disasters occur only at the end,
and so we shall examine them at the end of this chapter in relation to
their effect on the religion of Athens at the time.

Here I first describe religion in the prospering Athens after 168, including the maintenance of many cults and practices reaching back to

---

1. I take the title of this chapter from MacKendrick (1969), who, a fellow Wiscon-
sonite, appreciates the beauty and respite, however brief, of an "Indian summer."

the classical period, the occasional innovation, and, in particular, what effect contemporaneous Athenian experience on Delos was having back in Athens. Only after that shall we turn to religious aspects and causes of the destruction resulting from the Athenian encounter with Mithridates.

The best record for the activities of state cult in this period, in fact for any period of Athenian history, is a set of decrees, ranging from 127/6 to 98/7 B.C., in which the Athenians honored the previous year's ephebes and their officials.[2] These texts provide a valuable continuum with the ephebic decree of 214/3 (SEG 29.116), which we considered in chapter 6 (pp. 181–85). In 215/4 about thirty young men served as ephebes. In the late second century there were from 100–150 ephebes each year, a few of them foreigners.[3] These decrees honoring the ephebes and their officials are very similar, almost formulaic, and I offer here a translation of one (IG II² 1006.1–43 of 122/1) with supplements from the others. The supplements are in parentheses, with the relevant text cited.

In the archonship of Nicodemos, in the third prytany, that of the tribe Aegeis, for which Epigenes, son of Epigenes, of Oinoe was secretary, on the eighth, intercalated day of Boedromion according to the archon, on the ninth day according to the moon, on the ninth day of the prytany, the Ekklesia Kyria met in the theater. Of the *proedroi* Timon, son of Theopompos, of Paiania and his fellow *proedroi* presided. It was approved by the Boule and the Demos. Aphrodisios, son of Aphrodisios, of Azenia proposed:

Whereas the ephebes in the archonship of Demetrios (123/2)

- (#1) sacrificed (the *eisitētēria*, 1011.5) at their registration in the Prytaneion on the public hearth of the Demos (and sought good omens, 1008.6), with the *kosmētēs*, the priest of Demos and the Charites, and the *exēgētai* in accordance with the laws and decrees of the Demos,[4] and put on the procession for Artemis Agrotera;
- (#2) and (in armor, 1008.8) met the sacrificial victims and escorted them, and did the same for Iacchos;
- (#3) and lifted up (in manly fashion, 1006.78) the cattle (at the Mysteries, 1008.8–9 and SEG 15.104.12) in Eleusis at the sacrifice

2. The major texts, chronologically arranged, are SEG 15.104 of 127/6; IG II² 1006 of 122/1 (on which see also SEG 19.108, 38.114); 1008 of 118/7 (on which see SEG 16.101, 21.477); 1009 of 116/5 (on which see SEG 38.116); 1011 of 106/5; 1028 of 101/0; 1029 of 98/7. IG II² 1030 dates ca. 105 (Tracy 1990a, 198). Similar texts, but from after (?) the sack of Sulla, are IG II² 1032, 1039–43.

3. See Tracy 1979, 177–78; 1988a, 252.

4. In 107/6 and 102/1 the *kosmētēs* paid for these sacrifices (IG II² 1011.35, 1028.73).

and at the Proerosia and those in the other sanctuaries and gymnasia, and performed the races;

(#4) and also participated in the processions and ran the appropriate torch races;

(#5) and joined (with the *gennētai*, 1011.11) in leading Pallas to Phaleron and back again from there under torchlight in all good order;

(#6) and brought Dionysos from the *escharā* into the theater under torchlight and at the Dionysia sent a bull worthy of the god—a bull which they also sacrificed in the sanctuary at the procession. And for this they received a crown from the Demos;

(#7) and, when the sacrifice was being performed for Athena Nike, they joined in the procession well and in an orderly manner, escorting the cow which they also sacrificed on the Acropolis to the goddess;

(#8) and they joined in performing also the other appropriate sacrifices to the gods and to the benefactors (including Diogenes, 1011.14–15) in accordance with the laws and decrees;[5]

(#9) and through the whole year they continually were at the gymnasia and obeyed the *kosmētēs*, and, having thought it most important and most necessary to maintain good order in the lessons assigned by the Demos, they were always without reproach and obeyed the pronouncements of the *kosmētēs* and their teachers;

(#10) and through the whole year they persevered in studying with Zenodotos in the Ptolemaion and the Lyceum,[6] and likewise with all the other philosophers in the Lyceum and the Academy;

(#11) and also they sat in good order in weapons in the meetings of the Ekklesia;

(#12) and through the whole year they met Roman friends, (allies, 1006.75) and benefactors who arrived;

(#13) and at the Epitaphia they made the race in weapons from the public tomb and the other appropriate races;

(#14) and they made a display (for the Boule, 1006.77) in weapons at the Theseia and the Epitaphia;

(#15) (and they sacrificed to the Mother of the Gods at the Galaxia, 1011.13) and they contributed seventy drachmas to the fund established for this purpose according to the decree of the Demos for the *phialē* for the Mother of the Gods, and they dedicated a second (silver, 1006.80) *phialē* (as a *charistērion* in the Mysteries, 1028.30) (for Demeter and Kore, 1009.7) in the sanctuary in Eleusis;

(#16) and they went out to the boundaries of Attica in weapons and became experienced in the land and roads, and they were

5. In 117/6 these sacrifices were paid for by the *kosmētēs* himself (*IG* II² 1009.36–37).

6. On Zenodotos the Stoic philosopher, see D.L. 7.30; Dorandi 1989.

present [. . .] at the sanctuaries in the countryside, and in these they continually sacrificed and sought good omens on behalf of the Demos;

(#17) and coming to the public tomb at Marathon they put a crown on it and made an offering (ἐνήγισαν) to those having died in war for freedom's sake;

(#18) and they went to the Amphiaraion and they inquired into the proprietary rights over the sanctuary which were established from ancient times by their ancestors, and, having sacrificed, they returned on the same day to their own land;

(#19) and they sailed to the trophy monument and they sacrificed to Zeus Tropaios;

(#20) and in the procession of the Theoi Megaloi they made the contest of the ships;

(#21) and at the Mounichia they sailed in a race into the harbor at Mounichia (and sacrificed to the goddess, 1028.21), and likewise at the Diisoteria (for Zeus Soter and Athena Soteira, 1008.21–22);

(#22) and they sailed also to the Aianteia, and, after having made the contest of the ships there, the procession, and the sacrifice to Ajax (and to Asclepios, 1011.17 and 55 and *SEG* 15.104.23), they were praised by the Demos of the Salaminians and received a gold crown because they had made their stay in an orderly and seemly manner;

(#23) and in the whole year they preserved harmony and friendship with one another, with no discord, in accordance with the policy of the *kosmētēs;*

(#24) and, (at the end of their term, 1028.41–42), they made also the appropriate display for the Boule in accordance with the law;

(#25) and showing a love for all good and beautiful things, and wishing to act, in accordance with the policy of the *kosmētēs*, for the benefit of the state and for their own seemliness, from their own funds they serviced one of the old, stone-throwing catapults, repaired the defective parts, and restored, after several years, the use of and instruction in the weapon, [. . .] and they practiced with it;

(#26) and in other matters they continually were free from reproach in their activities [. . .];

in order that the Boule and Demos may appear honoring those from their earliest youth worthy and obeying the laws, decrees, and *kosmētēs,*

with good fortune, the Boule has resolved that those selected by lot *proedroi* for the coming Ekklesia treat this matter and report to the Demos the opinion of the Boule, that the Boule resolves to praise the ephebes of the archonship of Demetrios and to crown them with a gold crown because of their piety toward the gods, because of the good order which they have maintained in the whole year, and because of their generosity toward the

Boule and Demos, and to announce this crown at the new tragedies of the City Dionysia and at the athletic contests of the Panathenaia and Eleusinia.

We know from the other ephebic texts that the ephebes in these years also served the Semnai Theai and participated in the Pythaïs to Delphi (*SEG* 15.104.26, 85–86), escorted and sacrificed two cows at the Eleusinia, sacrificed a bull and gave a *phialē* to Dionysos in Piraeus, and sacrificed two bulls at the Diogeneia (*IG* II² 1011.12–13, 1028.15–16, 23–24).

In their year of service the ephebes received, under the direction of the *kosmētēs* and his assistants, a full curriculum of training in military weapons, local geography, philosophy, government, and religion. A reading of the whole text of *IG* II² 1006 suggests the importance, relative to the other activities, that Athenians even at this late date were giving to religion in the education of their youth. The ephebes participated in most of the city's major cults and festivals, and the large majority of these remained, even in the late second century B.C., very traditional, with roots reaching back to at least the classical period.

The ephebes of 123/2, like those of 215/4, devoted considerable time to the Eleusinian cults of Demeter and Kore. At the Mysteries they participated in the procession to Eleusis (#2) and in the sacrifice in the sanctuary (#3). They also dedicated a *phialē* as a *charistērion* to the goddesses (#15). At other times of the year they assisted at the sacrifice of the Proerosia (#3), a plowing festival, and no doubt competed in the games of the Eleusinia where, the next year, their honors were to be announced. All elements of this Eleusinian program, with the possible exception of the dedication of the *phialē*, appear virtually unchanged from the classical period. Since the *phialē* dedication is attested for the Mysteries only in these ephebic documents, we cannot know whether it was a traditional practice at Eleusis or an innovation of the second century.

Similar questions bedevil our understanding of many elements of these ephebic texts. For example, the ephebes in the procession of the City Dionysia led and then sacrificed in the sanctuary a bull, both familiar elements of the festival. But these ephebes also "brought Dionysos from the *escharā* ("hearth altar") into the theater under torchlight" (#6). This is the first and only evidence for this "introduction" (εἰσαγωγή) of Dionysos preliminary to the festival, a nocturnal doublet of the daytime procession, presumably bringing Dionysos from the temple near the Academy to his theater on the south slope of the Acropolis.[7] The ques-

---

7. On which see Pickard-Cambridge 1988, 59–61.

tion arises whether this nighttime εἰσαγωγή, first mentioned in 127/6 (*SEG* 15.104.15), is a traditional element of the City Dionysia—that is, whether it or something very like it was part of the festival also in the fifth century. In this case it is usually judged traditional, as by Arthur Pickard-Cambridge: "The reenactment of the god's advent does not look like an afterthought and probably goes back to the earliest days of the festival" (1988, 60).

A similar question arises about some old festivals and rituals that are now again attested after centuries of silence. They would include the Eleusinian Proerosia (#3);[8] the taking of Pallas Athena to Phaleron (#5);[9] the Mounichia for Artemis Mounichia (#21);[10] and the Galaxia for the Mother of the Gods (#15).[11] When a festival or ritual, as often happens, is attested, say, in 325 and then not again until 127/6, we would very much like to know whether (1) it was celebrated continuously throughout the period and just happens not to turn up on the inscriptions, or (2) it lapsed for a period of time and then was revived. Here evidence fails us and we must depend on probability.

Of these festivals and rituals, those which required free and open ac-

8. The Proerosia of Eleusis on Pyanopsion 6 was last attested in the Eleusinian Sacred Calendar of ca. 330–270 (*IG* II² 1363.1–7 as reedited by Dow and Healey 1965). On this festival see Dow and Healey, 14–20. The Eleusinian Proerosia should be distinguished from similar rituals at Myrrhinous (*IG* II² 1183.32–35), in the city and at Skiron (Plut. *Mor.* 144A–B), in Piraeus (*IG* II² 1177.9), and in Thorikos (*SEG* 33.147.5).

9. Burkert (1970) distinguished this ephebic procession from the Plynteria, which involved the washing of the *peplos* of Athena, also in the sea at Phaleron. He has the ephebes escort what the Athenians claimed to be the ancient Palladion of Troy, now kept in the Palladion Court. Nagy (1991) has the Pallas being escorted be the *xoanon* of Athena Polias of the Erechtheum, in a reenactment of the evacuation and reinstallment of the statue in 480 B.C.

On the Plynteria see Nagy 1991, 300–302; Parker 1983, 26–29; Burkert 1970. In our period the Plynteria may possibly appear ca. 250 B.C. (in the archonship of Alcibiades), in a sacrifice made by the Praxiergidai and financed by the priestess of Athena (*IG* II² 776.18–20).

10. In chapter 2, pp. 52–53, it was suggested that the cult of Artemis on the Mounichion Hill may have been a victim of the Macedonian garrison quartered nearby after 322. The last datable attestation of her cult is Dem. 18.107 of 330 B.C. According to Plutarch (*Mor.* 349F), on the day of her festival, Mounichion 16, she, as a full moon, appeared to the Greeks as they defeated the Persians in the bay of Salamis. The Mounichia probably became as much a celebration of this victory as a festival for Artemis, and the regatta of the ephebes may have been understood in the same way. On the Mounichia, see Palaiokrassa 1991, 28–29, 34–36; Garland 1987, 113–14; Deubner 1932, 204–7.

11. The Galaxia, an offering by the prytanists of a milk and barley porridge to the Mother of the Gods, presumably at the Metroön in the Agora, is first attested in 319 (Theophr. *Char.* 21.11) and reappears only in these ephebic texts. On the Galaxia, see Deubner 1932, 216.

cess to the countryside probably lapsed for considerable periods of time when the Macedonians garrisoned Attica (322–229). The Macedonian fort on the Mounichion Hill almost certainly prevented the Athenian celebration of the Mounichia for Artemis Mounichia, and *IG* II² 1006 of 122/1 may be the first indication of its revival.[12] Similar problems probably prevented the procession carrying Pallas Athena to and from Phaleron and the plowing, at the Proerosia, of the Rarian Field in the open country of Eleusis. Under the Macedonians most of the festivals and rituals that required leaving the city for the countryside must have suffered some lapses, in some cases of several years. But the Galaxia of the Mother of the Gods was held in the city, and presumably it would have been interrupted only by severe economic or social turmoil. Thus some of the festivals and rituals may have been restored, while others may have been continually celebrated. For those occurring in the countryside, the most likely time for revival is shortly after 229, when the Athenians had reestablished control over Attica. But they were quite probably disrupted again by the devastation caused by Philip. In any case, when these old festivals and rituals reappear in the record, they seem to have their traditional forms.

The ephebes of 127/6 and following years also continued religious activities that commemorated the Athenian victory over the Persians in the early years of the fifth century:[13] the Aianteia on Salamis (#22), the offering to Zeus Tropaios (#19),[14] the offering at the tomb of the war dead of the battle of Marathon (#17), and the procession for Artemis Agrotera (#1) on the occasion of the annual sacrifice vowed at that same battle.[15] The Mounichia (#21) also looked back to the battle of Salamis.[16] The Epitaphia (#13, 14) and the ephebes' own Diogeneia (#8) also appear intended to honor those who won or died fighting for the freedom of the state.[17] All of these festivals and rituals celebrated, in various ways, Athenian victories and sacrifices in the cause of freedom,[18]

12. If, as seems likely, Artemis Phosphoros is or is associated with Artemis Mounichia, then the cult of Artemis Mounichia reappears in 182/1 (*Agora* XV, #183, 184). See above, chapter 6, p. 195.

13. Nagy 1991, 303–4.

14. On the Aianteia and the offering to Zeus Tropaios, see chapter 6, pp. 184–85.

15. The sacrifices to Artemis Agrotera in the fourth century were performed by the polemarch ([Arist.] *Ath. Pol.* 58.1). Cf. Xen. *An.* 3.2.12; Plut. *Mor.* 862A; Aelian *VH* 2.25; and scholia to Ar. *Eq.* 660.

16. Above, note 10.

17. On the Epitaphia and Diogeneia, see above, chapter 6, pp. 171–72, 184–85.

18. To this list should be added the ephebes' escorting of Pallas Athena to and from Phaleron (#5) if Nagy (1991, 299–306) is correct in associating it with the evacuation of the *xoanon* of Athena Polias before the battle of Salamis and the reinstallation of it immediately thereafter.

and each—down to the sack of Sulla in 86 and even afterward—was thought to be an appropriate venue for the worship, sacrifices, and demonstration of athletic skills by the future leaders of Athens. Clearly religion was contributing much to keeping alive, at least for the elite youth of Athens, the Athenian ideals of freedom and glories of military victory and sacrifice, however remote in history they may have been. Most of these festivals, in addition to being expressions of nationalism, required easy access to the countryside and even the sea, and it is most probable, for both reasons, that they were instituted, or remodeled and reinstituted, after 229 B.C.

A similar nationalistic thrust is evident in the ephebes' one-day trip to the Amphiaraion in Oropos (#18). We have seen that in 335 Athens was given Oropos and the sanctuary, and that the state repaired and remodeled the buildings, established a quadrennial festival (chapter 1, pp. 30, 33), but lost the territory and the sanctuary in 322 after the debacle of the Lamian War. Athens had recovered Oropos in 304 but then lost it again by 287/6. The indoctrination of the city's ephebes into their "ancestral" but denied rights of ownership of the sanctuary is first attested here in 122/1, and, like many of their other religious activities, it looks to reestablish the city's more glorious past.

For several hundred years Athens had had few if any occasions to be grateful to Athena Nike. What military successes Athens had or shared she owed largely to foreign kings, and usually they, not Athena Nike, received the honors.[19] We may perhaps take the procession and sacrifice for Athena Nike in which the ephebes participated (#7) as another indication of revived national pride. A sacrifice to her had probably been a part of the Panathenaia since the fifth century and is attested for 336/5 (Schwenk #17B.20–23). *IG* II² 677 suggests Nike was still associated with the Panathenaia in the 250s. But these ephebic decrees after 122/1 appear to record a separate, distinct procession and sacrifice not elsewhere attested.[20] This festival for Athena Nike may be an innovation to celebrate independence after 229 and to refocus attention on a once prominent but now perhaps somewhat neglected Acropolis cult.

In 476/5 the Athenian general Cimon recovered the bones of Theseus from the island Scyros and returned them to Athens, thereby estab-

---

19. For an example of both Antigonos Gonatas and Athena Nike being honored, see *IG* II² 667.

20. The activities of the ephebes in the Panathenaia are nowhere explicitly described in these decrees but are surely included in their participation in various sacrifices and athletic contests (#3, 4, 8).

lishing or reinvigorating the hero's cult there. On his return Theseus received both a major sanctuary, the Theseion, east of the Agora and on the lower north slope of the Acropolis, and a festival, the Theseia, celebrated in the days just before his great sacrifice on Pyanopsion 8.[21] In 332/1 and 331/0 the Theseia was still a major festival, rivaling the annual Panathenaia in number of sacrificial victims (*IG* II² 1496.134–35, 143), but then the Theseia disappears from the record until the middle of the second century.

Theseus was also linked legendarily and etiologically with several major Athenian festivals of the classical period, including the Pyanopsia, Oschophoria, Delphinia, and Synoikia. Most of these myths involve Theseus' expedition to Crete to kill the Minotaur, and in his life of Theseus Plutarch draws from the Atthidographers and other sources to weave these tales together, as in this passage treating the Pyanopsia and Oschophoria:

> As they were approaching Attica, Theseus and his pilot both, in their joy, forgot to raise the sail by which they were to make known to Aigeus their safety. Aigeus in despair hurled himself down from the rock and perished. After Theseus landed, he himself was sacrificing the sacrifices which he had vowed to the gods at Phaleron when he was departing, and he sent a herald to the city to report his safe return. The herald came upon many people who were bewailing the death of their king and upon others who were rejoicing, as was natural, and were eager to embrace and garland him for (his good news of) the safe return. The herald accepted the garlands and put them on his herald's staff. When he returned to the sea, he waited outside (the sanctuary) since Theseus had not yet made the libations and the herald did not wish to disturb the sacrifice. But after the libations were made, the herald announced the death of Aigeus. And then, hastening amid weeping and confusion, they went up into the city. As a result still even now, they say, in the Oschophoria not the herald but his staff is garlanded and in the libations those present cry out "Eleleu! Iou! Iou!" The first of these cries those make who are hurrying and singing a victory song. But "Iou" is a sign of astonishment and confusion.

After he buried his father, Theseus repaid to Apollo his vow, on the seventh day of the month Pyanopsion, because on this day, safe, they went up to the city. The boiling of the pulse (on this day) is said to occur because Theseus and his men, saved, mixed into one pot the remnants of their pro-

---

21. Plut. *Thes.* 36.1–4, *Cim.* 8.3–6. On the calendar date of the festival, see Tracy 1990a, 185. On Theseus in Athenian cult and myth, see Garland 1992, 82–98; Kearns 1989, 117–24, 168–69; Herter 1939, 244–326. On the location and nature of the Theseion, see Miller 1995a, 209–10, 233–35.

visions and, after having boiled them in one common pot, feasted and dined together. And (the Athenians) bring out the *eiresiōnē*, an olive branch garlanded with wool, just as the suppliant bough then, and full of all kinds of first-fruit offerings, because (Theseus and his companions) had brought to an end their lack of provisions, and (the Athenians) sing,

> The *eiresiōnē* brings figs and rich breads,
> and honey in a cup, and olive oil to wash with,
> and a cup of unmixed wine, so that, getting drunk, a woman may
> sleep well. . . .

Until the time of Demetrios of Phaleron the Athenians preserved the boat on which Theseus sailed and returned safely with the young men. They removed the old wood and put in other, strong pieces and fitted them together. And so the boat served as a model for philosophers on the uncertain question of "growth." Some philosophers said that it remained the same boat, others said not.

And (the Athenians) also celebrate the festival of the Oschophoria as Theseus established it. For he did not take with him (to Crete) all the maidens who then were selected by lot, but (in place of two) he put two of his young male companions who looked fresh and girlish but were manly and eager in their hearts. He changed their appearance as much as possible by warm baths, by keeping them away from the sun, by jewelry, and by unguents for their hair and for the smoothness of their skin and for their complexion. He taught them to become like, as much as possible, maidens in their voice, dress, and gait. He then put them among the maidens, and no one noticed. And, after he returned, he and the young men held a procession dressed as now they dress (in the festival), carrying the *ōschoi* ("vine branches"). They carry those to show their gratitude to Dionysos and Ariadne because of (their role in) the story, or else because Theseus and his companions returned when the (grape) harvest was being collected. And the *deipnophoroi* ("dinner carriers") are taken along (in the procession) and share in the sacrifice, imitating the mothers of those young people who were selected by lot (to go to Crete). Their mothers had come bringing meat and provisions for them. And stories are told (at the festival) because then those mothers told stories to their children to encourage and inspire them. Demon has written a study of these matters. A sanctuary was set aside for Theseus, and Theseus ordered that members of the families who provided the tribute (to the Minotaur) contribute for the sacrifice to himself. The Phytalidai oversee the sacrifice, (an honor) which Theseus gave to them in return for their hospitality. (Plut. *Thes*. 22.1–23.3)

By myths such as these Plutarch and others, using fourth-century sources, associated Theseus not only with the Pyanopsia and Oschophoria, but also with the Delphinia and the festival of Athenian unification, the Synoikia.[22] These festivals, however, like the Theseia and the maintenance of Theseus' ship, were all apparently discontinued after the fourth century. The Oschophoria is last found in the decree of the Salaminioi of 363/2, the Pyanopsia in the calendars of the demes Thorikos (ca. 430–420) and Eleusis (ca. 330–270).[23] There are no attestations after the fifth century for the Delphinia or for what should be a particularly important festival, the Synoikia.

Theseus was the *synoikistēs* of Attica and, in some traditions, the founder of Athenian democracy,[24] and the disappearance of him, the Synoikia, and of other festivals particularly associated with him may, in fact, be owed to the political and geographical *dis*unity of Attica after the fourth century. Apart from the physical difficulties of celebrating these mostly rural festivals at these times, the Athenians may have felt little inclined, when their countryside was under foreign control, to honor the hero who had once unified this territory. It is not coincidental that in 165/4 or 161/0, after the Athenians had regained control of her territory and even of previously subject states, the Theseia reemerges. We have, beginning then, a series of decrees honoring the *agōnothetēs* of a major quadrennial festival for Theseus: a festival that included a procession and sacrifice, competitions for trumpeters and heralds,[25] reviews of the troops and ephebes, torch races, and a host of other athletic, equestrian, and military contests rivaling those of the Panathenaia.[26] This is a new festival, and the first of these decrees, *IG* II² 956 of 161/0, records the second celebration of the festival. The first celebration was held in 165/4 to mark Athens' recovery, along with Delos, of Scyros, the island from which Theseus' bones had been retrieved in 476/5.[27] From the ephebic inscriptions we know that there must have also been annual Theseia in the years between the quadrennial "Great"

22. For Theseus' association with the Delphinia and with the Synoikia, see Thuc. 2.15.2; Plut. *Thes.* 18.1–2, 24.4. For descriptions of these and the other festivals, see Parke 1977; Deubner 1932.

23. Salaminioi, *SEG* 21.527.21; Thorikos, *SEG* 33.147.27; and Eleusis, *IG* II² 1363.8–19 as reedited by Dow and Healey 1965.

24. E.g., Eur. *Supp.* 403–8; Plut. *Thes.* 24. See also Garland 1992, 88.

25. Cf. the important role of the herald in the Oschophoria (Plut. *Thes.* 22.1–3).

26. *IG* II² 956 of 161/0, 957 of 157/6, 958 of 153/2, and 959 + 1014 of 109/8 (for the last, see Tracy 1990a, 183–85). Undatable but probably later than the above are the following honors of *agōnothetai* and victory lists of the Theseia: *IG* II² 960–65. On these texts and the second-century festival of the Theseia, see Bugh 1990.

27. Bugh 1990; Pélékidis 1962, 229–30. On the return of Scyros and Imbros, see Bugh 1990, 25.

Theseia.[28] This festival, once begun, was then held down into the Roman period.[29]

The new Theseia after 165/4 would thus celebrate, virtually, the second *synoikismos* of Athens, in a sense a reestablishment, in geographical terms at least, of pre-Macedonian Athens.[30] Public and ephebic participation in this and in other festivals we have seen in the ephebic decrees point to a national interest—whether it be labeled nostalgic or not—to celebrate great events (Marathon and Salamis) and great figures (Theseus and the war dead) of the Athenian past, and to do this through religious festivals and rituals. These activities all must be associated with Athens' newly won independence and reestablishment of its own territories after 229. We have seen, throughout this study, smaller attempts to reassert Athenian traditions in other moments of independence, but the closest parallel to this range of nationalistic activities after 229 are those led by Lycourgos after Chaeroneia in 338. Athens then was more wealthy, more democratic, and more free, but the instincts and the direction were the same. And here, with the Theseia, we see second-century Athenians reestablishing a festival of their national hero and returning it to the status that it had last had in the Lycourgan period.

All the religious activities of the ephebes in 123/2 that we have surveyed are, in some sense, traditional. In the order in which they occur in the decree, the procession for Artemis Agrotera (#1), the Eleusinian festivals and rituals (#2, 3, 15), the taking of the Palladion to Phaleron (#5), the City Dionysia (#6), the Epitaphia (#13, 14), the Theseia (#14), the Galaxia (#15), and the Mounichia (#21) all existed in the classical period and either were celebrated more or less continuously from then or were reintroduced, perhaps with some changes, after significant interruptions. By 123/2 the Aianteia (#22) had been part of the ephebic program for nearly a hundred years and had classical antecedents, as probably did also the offerings to the Marathon dead (#17) and to Zeus Tropaios

---

28. *SEG* 15.104.17 for 128/7; *IG* II[2] 1006.23 for 123/2, 1008.17 for 119/8, 1029.13 for 99/8.

29. For further evidence of Theseus in the second century, see *IG* II[2] 2865, a dedication to Theseus by his priest, Apollonides of Rhamnous (*PA* 1501), and a sacrifice to Theseus, in 140/39, by the prytanists (*Agora* XV, #240). The same prytanists also dedicated an *eiresiōnē* to Apollo (line 12), which suggests a revival of the Pyanopsia. See Meritt 1963; Stanley 1961. On the *eiresiōnē*, see Robertson 1985, 388–95.

30. For a celebration of a Theseia on Delos in 154/3 and 148/7, see *ID* 1951–52. Cf. *ID* 1955.

(#19) (above, chapter 6, pp. 183–85). The cult of Demos and the Charites (#1) and the ephebes' own festival, the Diogeneia (#8), dated back to the 220s (above, chapter 6, pp. 172–78). Even the sacrifice to Athena Nike (#7), if in fact it was, as I have suggested, relatively new, was part of one of the older state cults of Athens. Thus even in this late period to its participants state cult would have appeared to be, and in fact was, solidly based on long traditions, most reaching back to the classical period.

In the whole list of ephebic activity the one festival that would probably have appeared new was the procession and regatta for the Theoi Megaloi, presumably the "Great Gods" of Samothrace (#20), and here we have our first clear evidence of the influence of the Delian experience. In Athens itself the Theoi Megaloi are first attested for 123/2 (*IG* II² 1006.29), and they, their procession, and their regatta are almost certainly imports from Delos. We have already seen how, on Delos after 166, the Athenians assigned a priest to them and combined their cult with that of the Dioscouroi and Cabeiroi, other protectors of sailors. It was precisely at this time, in the third quarter of the second century, that their sanctuary on Delos, the Samothrakeion, was being remodeled and enlarged, and in 120/19 the Athenian *epimelētēs* of the island contributed a building to this project (*ID* 1808). The festival of the Theoi Megaloi in Athens was apparently short-lived, attested only for 123/2, 118/7, and 117/6,[31] either because it did not find general favor or, perhaps, as the dedications made by the priest Helianax on Delos indicate (chapter 7, pp. 225–26), the cult could become a vehicle to promote Mithridates.[32]

But the most significant innovation, in both religious and social terms, is the enrollment of foreign youth in the Athenian corps of ephebes. In 123/2 there were ca. 127 ephebes, 14 of them foreigners and 4 of these Romans (*IG* II² 1006). In 107/6, 24 of the 140 ephebes were foreigners, 5 Roman (1011). And, finally, in 102/1 there were 141 ephebes, of whom 40 were foreigners and at least 2 Roman (1028).[33] Here we have, for the first time, non-Athenians participating in Athenian reli-

---

31. *IG* II² 1006.29, 1008.18; *Hesp.* 16 (1947): 170–71, #61, line 21.

32. A private association whose known members were both men from Alexandria and Antioch was, in 112–110, devoted to the Theoi Megaloi (*SEG* 21.535–36). On this *oikos* and on the Theoi Megaloi in Athens, see Robert, 1970, 7–14. For the lack of an intrinsic connection between Mithridates and the cult of the Theoi Megaloi, see Sanders and Catling 1990, 331–32.

33. Tracy 1988a, 252. On the foreign ephebes see Follet 1988; Reinmuth 1929.

gious cults in an organized, systematic, and long-term manner. The Roman and other foreign youth would not only compete in games of some spectacular festivals, as they had done for many years, but would share in the rituals of some of Athens' oldest religious cults, a privilege hitherto limited to Athenian citizens. The religion and domestic politics of Athens were now becoming internationalized, and for Athenians the model for such multinational participation in state cults was no doubt Delos. There, as we have seen, because of peculiar historical circumstances virtually all the cults were international in membership, and in Athens the inclusion of foreigners among the ephebes was a significant initial move in the same direction.

Thus far we have observed in the ephebic religious activities elements that appear to be (1) continuations of traditional practices, (2) restorations or slight changes of traditional practices, and (3) wholly new practices and deities. This sets the pattern as we now look at the remaining evidence for the period 166–86 B.C., treating first the traditional practices; second, new elements modeled on the old; and, finally, significant innovations.

Throughout the period the prytanists continued their customary sacrifices to Apollo Prostaterios, Artemis Boulaia, Artemis Phosphoros, and the other traditional gods "for the health and safety of the Boule, the Demos, the children and women, and the friends and allies."[34] These sacrifices, held before meetings of the Ekklesia, had apparently changed little since first attested in 273/2 (above, chapter 4, pp. 113–14). Artemis Boulaia had joined Apollo by 254/3 (*Agora* XV, #89) and remained with him to the last of the prytany documents of our period, *Agora* XV, #254 of 104/3. Artemis Phosphoros first appeared in the record in 182/1 (#183; see above, chapter 6, pp. 194–95) and in this period appears intermittently.[35] Singular among the prytany decrees of the period is *Agora* XV, #240 of 140/39. It records, in addition to the usual sacrifices to Apollo Prostaterios, Artemis Boulaia, and Artemis Phosphoros, sacrifices to Demeter and Kore, to Theseus and Apollo, and the erection of the *eiresionē*. The sacrifice to Demeter and Kore occurred at the Stenia, a festival that is mentioned occasionally in earlier

34. *Agora* XV, #219 and 220 of 164/3; #222 of 161/0; #225 of 155/4; #238 of 145/4; #240 of 140/39; #243 of 135/4; #246 of 131/0; #249 of 125/4; #252 of 122/1; #253 of 118/7; and #254 of 104/3.

35. *Agora* XV, #246 of 131/0; #249 of 125/4; #253 of 118/7. Restored in #219 and 220 of 164/3, #240 of 140/39; #251 of 124/3, and #254 of 104/3.

prytany decrees (chapter 4, pp. 113–15). The sacrifice to Theseus was part of the current, renewed interest in his cult. The sacrifice to Apollo and the *eiresiōnē* are evidence of a much larger revival of Apollo's cult, which I shall describe shortly.

The cult of Athena Polias also flourished during this time; perhaps, to judge by the distribution of epigraphical texts and the families of the honorees, it returned to the prominence it had last enjoyed in the age of Lycourgos. The cult of this goddess was served primarily by women, and it was a time when women could be publicly honored for such service. As a result we know something of the priestesses, *errēphoroi*, and *ergastīnai* of Athena Polias. We have already met Philtera (*PA* 14786), daughter of Pausimachos, the priestess in the last third of the second century who was proud of her Eteobutad family and her ancestors, the statesman Lycourgos and the liberator of Athens Diogenes (*IG* II² 3474; see chapter 6, pp. 171–72). A successor to her as priestess of Athena was Chrysis (*PA* 15583), daughter of Nicetes who received two statues (*IG* II² 3484, 3485), one of them dedicated by her three cousins (3484), and, for service as priestess of Athena on a Pythaïs to Delphi in 106/5, a full array of civic honors from the Delphians (1136). Another priestess, Philippe, daughter of Medeios ([Plut.] *X Orat.* 843B), was the sister of the archon Medeios of 101/0.[36]

Each year two Athenian girls, once called *arrēphoroi* but now *errēphoroi*, participated in Athena's Arrephoria and wove the *peplos* presented to her in the Panathenaia; for this service they had been honored in dedications made by family members since at least 220/19.[37] But now young women could receive also another public honor. Panarista, the *errēphoros* honored in *IG* II² 3488, had served as an *ergastīna* ("workeress") in 103/2 (*IG* II² 1034 d II 9). *IG* II² 1034 best describes the duties of the *ergastīnai*:

Whereas the fathers of the maidens who, for Athena, worked the wool for the *peplos* approached the Boule and revealed that the (*ergastīnai*) have followed all the decrees voted by the Demos about these things and have done what is just and, according to the things assigned, have made the procession in a manner most beautiful and seemly, and have themselves from their own funds made a silver *phialē* worth 100 drachmas, a *phialē* which they wish to dedicate to Athena as a memorial of their piety toward the

---

36. On these and other known priestesses of Athena Polias, see Lewis 1955, 7–12.

37. On the *errēphoroi*, the Arrephoria, and the dedications, see above, chapter 6, p. 199.

goddess, and [the fathers urge the Boule and Demos to allow the dedication of the *phialē;*][38]

[With good fortune it was decided by the Boule that the presiding officers at the next meeting of the Ekklesia treat these matters and report the opinion of the Boule to the Demos, that it seems right to the Boule that they be allowed to dedicate the *phialē* which the maidens have made for Athena and to praise the maidens and crown each of them with a crown of olive because of their piety toward the gods and their generosity toward the Boule and Demos. . . .]

Appended to the decree is a list of the *ergastīnai* to be so honored, arranged by tribe (cf. *IG* II² 1942). The surviving portion, listing eleven girls of the Akamantis tribe, suggests that, in all, ca. 120 girls served this year.[39] And these girls were from the families most prominent politically, socially, and economically. In his prosopographical study of these *ergastīnai*, Pierre Brulé (1987, 100–105) has shown that 80 percent of the recognizable girls on these lists came from known families. Acestion (*PA* 468), daughter of Xenocles, was a member of the Kerykes, and her great-grandfather, grandfather, father, husband, brother, and son each served as *dādouchos* of the Eleusinian Mysteries (Paus. 1.37.1); Megiste (*PA* 9707) was a daughter of the Zenon who served as *epimelētēs* of Delos; Demo's (*PA* 3728) father Miltiades we shall soon see as the wealthy *agōnothetēs* of both the Theseia and the Panathenaia; and Ctesicleia (*PA* 8856) belongs to the Eumolpidai. Several of these girls served also, in other years, as *kanēphoroi* on Delos or at Delphi. Xenostrate (*PA* 11264), daughter of Agias, had been an *errēphoros* (*IG* II² 3473), and three of the girls—Miccion (*PA* 10192), Parion (*PA* 11635), and Peitho (*PA* 11763)—served at least twice as *ergastīnai*.

The *ergastīnai* are first attested in 103/2. They may well have been doing their weaving since the classical period, as most scholars assume, but it is not impossible that they were a late-second-century innovation. The institution would serve two proclivities of the time. First, it would expand the opportunities for wealthy and prominent families to find honor for their daughters in what now seems to be the most prestigious state cult, and we have seen how strong that impulse was in this period. The *arrēphoroi* were, by tradition, limited to two, but the institution of the *ergastīnai* may have been created at this time to allow

38. The last portion of *IG* II² 1034 is lost, but the meaning can be restored, as here, from *IG* II² 1036.16–22.

39. On the enrollment and on the join of *IG* II² 1034 and 1943, see Tracy 1990a, 217–19.

greater participation and recognition. Second, the 100–150 *ergastīnai* form a group comparable in size to the contemporary ephebe corps of young men, and, perhaps, as Brulé argues (1987, 99–105), as *ergastīnai* the girls too received some formal training, in this instance in the "womanly" art of weaving. Whatever their history, the *ergastīnai* make a brief appearance on the record at the very end of the second century B.C.

Throughout these years the Panathenaia was celebrated regularly,[40] but, at least in the 140s, there were problems. *IG* II² 968 records honors given by the state to Miltiades, son of Zoilos (*PA* 10215), who, in addition to other offices, served as *agōnothetēs* of the Theseia in 153/2 and of the Panathenaia in or shortly after 144/3.[41] In the latter role he solved a financial crisis, giving an interest-free loan and contributing "not a little" of his own funds. He also repaired "the things needing work" on the Acropolis, in the Odeion, and, perhaps, in the Anakeion. He gave "equipment made of tow," no doubt ropes for the Panathenaic "ship-cart," and what else was lacking for the transport of the *peplos*. He performed generously "all the things for the procession and the sacrifices owed to the gods," and he put on the contests in a manner worthy of his office and of the Demos that had elected him. He chose his own daughter as *kanēphoros*, as was now common. In sum, he put on the Panathenaia illustriously and well, and, apparently, paid for it himself (41–55). Under Miltiades the Panathenaia was in good hands, but when he assumed office he must have found both the finances and the physical properties of the festival in disarray and needed to use his own considerable wealth to rectify the situation.

The Eleusinian cults, like those of the Acropolis, were prosperous in this period. The Eleusinia, the agonistic festival, was being held regularly and was sufficiently popular to continue being a forum for the publication of honors decreed by the state.[42] In 166/5 the demarch of

40. The Panathenaia is attested as planned or celebrated in 166/5 and 162/1 (*Hesp.* 60 [1991]: 189 *bis*, cols. 2, 3), 161/0 (*IG* II² 956.34), 160/59 (*ID* 1497 *bis* 12–14, 20–22), 157/6 (*IG* II² 957.19, 2316, on which see Tracy and Habicht 1991, 218 = Habicht 1994, 123), 153/2 (*IG* II² 958.30), 144/3 (968.41–55), 127/6 (*SEG* 15.104.36), 122/1 (*IG* II² 1006.42), 118/7 (1008.36), 116/5 (1009.18), 108/7 (1036.23), 106/5 (1011.26), 101/0 (1028.49, 100), and 98/7 (1029.32; *SEG* 32.218.211).

41. As *agōnothetēs* of the Theseia, Miltiades spent more than 3,390 drachmas of his own funds (*IG* II² 958.14–16).

42. The Eleusinia was being expected in 161/0 (*IG* II² 956.34), 160/59 (*ID* 1497 *bis* 13, 21), 157/6 (*IG* II² 957.19), 153/2 (958.30–31), 127/6 (*SEG* 15.104.36–37), 122/1 (*IG* II² 1006.42–43), 118/7 (1008.36), 116/5 (1009.18), 106/5 (1011.26), 101/0 (1028.16), 100/99 (1028.49, 100), and 98/7 (1029.32).

Eleusis, Pamphilos, son of Archon (*PA* 11542), sacrificed to Demeter, Kore, and the other traditional gods at the Haloa and the Chloia;[43] with the hierophant and priestess made the sacrifice and put on the procession of the Kalamaia;[44] produced an Eleusinian Dionysia with a sacrifice, procession, and contests in the theater; paid for all of these things from his own funds; and reported to the Boule that the sacrifices which he made "for the health and safety of the Boule, Demos, children and women, friends and allies" turned out well (*IG* II² 949). The Mysteries retained their international prominence. The Amphictiones of Delphi in 117/6 listed them as one of Athens' great contributions to the Greek world (*IG* II² 1134.17–19), and in *De Oratore* (3.20.75) Cicero has the distinguished orator L. Licinius Crassus fuming that, ca. 110 B.C., he arrived in Athens two days late for the Mysteries and could not convince the Athenians to "repeat" (*referrent*) them for him.

Somewhat larger trends of Athenian religious history may also be revealed in the microcosm of the dedications being made to Demeter at Eleusis in this and earlier periods. First, after a virtual void of dedications to her in the third century, in both the city and at Eleusis,[45] a significant number survive from the second and first centuries, though not nearly so many as from the fourth century. This pattern probably reflects the isolation of Eleusis from the city before 229 and the reunification of Attica thereafter. Second, considerably more than half of the fourth-century dedications to Demeter come from the city, most from the Agora,[46] whereas most of Demeter's dedications of the second century and later have been found in Eleusis.[47] In the latter period Deme-

---

43. The Haloa was last attested ca. 211 B.C. (*IG* II² 1304.46–47). For earlier attestations see [Dem.] 59.116; *IG* II² 1672.124 and 144 of 329/8; *IG* II² 1299.9–14, 29, and 77 of ca. 236/5. On the Haloa, see above, chapter 5, p. 159.

Demeter Chloe ("Verdant") had a cult in the Marathonian tetrapolis (*IG* II² 1358.49; cf. 1356.16) and a sanctuary on the western slope of the Acropolis where she received an offering in Thargelion (Ar. *Lys.* 835; Paus. 1.22.3; Philochoros, *FGrHist* 328 F 61 and commentary). The Eleusinian Chloia, attested only here, presumably celebrated this aspect of the goddess. See Deubner 1932, 67–68.

44. The Kalamaia, a harvest festival, was celebrated also in Piraeus in the mid–fourth century (*IG* II² 1177.9). See Deubner 1932, 67–68.

45. Tracy (1995, 43–44, 171–74) now dates *IG* II² 2971, a dedication to Demeter and Kore by troops stationed at Eleusis, Panakton, and Phyle, to mid–third century B.C.

46. Fourth-century dedications to Demeter from Athens and environs: *IG* II² 3849, 4025, 4562, 4588, 4597, 4640, 4642, 4662, 4663; *SEG* 16.160, 171, 174, 17.83–86, 19.188. From Eleusis: *IG* II² 2840, 2841, 4552, 4608, 4639, 4664; *SEG* 24.224.

47. Second- and early-first-century dedications to Demeter from Athens and environs: *IG* II² 2868; *SEG* 16.164, 33.197. From Eleusis: *IG* II² 3487, 3495, 3874, 4701, 4708, 4709, and the following dedications in honor of "initiates from the hearth": *IG* II² 3475 + 3476,

ter's public cult was apparently increasingly limited to Eleusis, and the Eleusinion adjoining the Agora may have lost importance as a cult center. Third, few of the fourth-century dedications to Demeter honor officials of the cult, whereas the majority of those later—although dedicated to Demeter and Kore—are, like the dedications to Apollo on Delos (see above, chapter 7, pp. 219–21), essentially honoring officials for their service.[48]

Most common among the Eleusinian "officials" honored in the late second and first centuries B.C. are the "initiates from the hearth." Dedications in their honor first appear in this period,[49] but Kevin Clinton's study of them (1974, 98–114) shows that these child-initiates had existed from at least the mid–fifth century. The children ($\pi\alpha\hat{\iota}\delta\epsilon\varsigma$) offered prayers and sacrifices on behalf of the initiates. In the classical period the child was selected by the archon basileus by lot from candidates volunteered by their fathers. In the second and first centuries, when we first know the names of the children, it is clear, in Clinton's words (113), that "the vast majority are . . . from families which were among the most active and distinguished in the civic and religious life of Athens. . . . Many were children or descendants of Eumolpidae or Kerykes." Only boys are indicated in the sources for the classical period, but among those recorded in the Hellenistic period all but one (*IG* II² 3478) are girls. One girl, in addition to serving in this role, was also a *kanēphoros* on a Pythaïs and at the Panathenaia (*IG* II² 3477). The role of "initiate from the hearth" provided another opportunity, as did the *errēphoroi, ergastīnai,* and assorted *kanēphoroi,* for prominent and wealthy Athenians to bring honor to their daughters and their families. The service was commemorated usually by family members, but on occasion even by the state (*IG* II² 3477, 3498).

Amid all these indications of the prosperity of the Eleusinian cults

---

3477, 3478, 3480, 3498, 3499; *SEG* 33.197. On these "initiates from the hearth" and their dedications, see Clinton 1974, 98–114, and the discussion later in this chapter.

48. Fourth-century dedications to Demeter honoring officials: *IG* II² 2840, 2841, an *epimelētēs* of the Mysteries; *SEG* 16.160, a priestess. Mid–third century dedication: *IG* II² 2971, a general honored by troops. Second- and first- century dedications: *IG* II² 3487, an *exēgētēs;* 3495, a priestess; *SEG* 19.124, the hierophant. Cf. *IG* II² 4701. The practice of honoring cult officials became even more common at Eleusis in the Roman period. See, e.g., *IG* II² 3490, 3507–9, 3512, 3513, 3517–19. Honors for girls who held multiple offices, including an Eleusinian one, might be dedicated to Demeter but could be erected in Athens (*SEG* 33.197). Cf. *IG* II² 3477.

49. See note 47 above.

after 166 B.C. there is one discordant note, not unlike Miltiades' need to overhaul the Panathenaia ca. 144/3. Around 150 B.C. Aristocles of Perithoidai (*PA* 1881), hierophant since 183/2, was honored by the Eumolpidai for having regularized matters concerning the registration fee and for having made and had the state provide financing for sacrifices, many of which had lapsed for several years (*SEG* 19.124).[50] Here, as in Miltiades' efforts, we see a Lycourgan impulse to provide *kosmos* ("order" and "adornment") to both the ritual and financial affairs of the cult.[51]

Throughout the period the City Dionysia, with its procession, sacrifice, and dramatic competitions, was regularly celebrated.[52] But we should note that in a partial record of victors in the dramatic competitions, *IG* II[2] 2319–2323, it is expressly stated that in some years the competition for comedies was *not* held.[53] Tragedies remained the premier event, and honors for citizens continued to be announced "at the new contest of tragedies."[54] We also have attested for this period, after a lapse of at least 150 years, Dionysia with dramatic contests in Piraeus, Eleusis, and Salamis.[55] The increased level of private support for public cults is found also here, with a large number of Athenians contributing from

50. On *SEG* 19.124, see Clinton 1974, 24–27. On Aristocles' career as a hierophant, see also Tracy 1990a, 155–56.

51. On further regulations of the Mysteries in this period, see *SEG* 21.494.

52. The City Dionysia are attested for 169/8, 168/7, 164/3, 163/2, 162/1, 161/0, 157/6, 156/5, and 155/4 in *IG* II[2] 2319–2323.205–6, 220–24, 230–32. They were planned or celebrated also in 160/59 (*ID* 1497 *bis* 12, 20–21), 157/6 (*IG* II[2] 957.19), 153/2 (958.29–30), 128/7 and 127/6 (*SEG* 15.104.15–16, 36), 123/2 and 122/1 (*IG* II[2] 1006.13, 42), 119/8 and 118/7 (1008.14–15, 35–36), 116/5 (1009.17), 107/6 and 106/5 (1011.11, 26), 102/1 and 101/0 (1028.17–19, 48, 99–100), and 98/7 and 97/6 (1029.11–12, 31–32).

53. Comedies were not presented in 164/3–162/1 and 157/6–156/5 (*IG* II[2] 2319–2323.220–22, 230–31). The earliest datable omission of comedies is 188/7 (144), but the practice can be traced back to at least ca. 215 (99). On *IG* II[2] 2319–23 and the occasional omission of the comedies, see Pickard-Cambridge 1988, 73, 83, 107–11.

54. E.g., *IG* II[2] 1008.69. For the terminology, see above, chapter 4, pp. 116–17.

55. Piraeus: *SEG* 15.104.25–26 for 128/7. Cf. *IG* II[2] 1008.13–14, 1011.12, 1028.16–17, 1029.11. The last previous and datable occurrence of the Piraeic Dionysia was in 307/6 (*IG* II[2] 456.32–33), but *IG* II[2] 1214.19–25 is probably from the mid–third century. On the Dionysia in the Piraeus and for the numerous fourth-century attestations, see Garland 1987, 124–26; Pickard-Cambridge 1988, 45–47.

Eleusis: *IG* II[2] 949.31–34 of 165/4. All previous attestations of this festival are from the fifth and fourth centuries: *IG* II[2] 1186, 1187, 1192–94, 3100. See Pickard-Cambridge 1988, 47–48.

Salamis: *IG* II[2] 1227.31–32 of 131/0. Cf. *IG* II[2] 1008.82, 1011.58. The Dionysia on Salamis is last attested in the late fourth century ([Arist.] *Ath. Pol.* 54.8). On this festival, see Taylor 1993, 169–73.

100 to 5 drachmas each to the repair of the theater in Piraeus in the mid–second century (*IG* II² 2334). The residents of Hephaistia on Lemnos, Athenian cleruchs, were now also holding Dionysia with contests in tragedy (*IG* II² 1223.8). The founding and refounding of these "literary" festivals is a clear indication of the prosperity and tranquillity of the times and of the Athenian impulse, in such times, to reestablish the traditions of their ancestors.

We have seen (above, chapter 4, pp. 117–22) the formation, in the 280s, of the Athenian guild of *technītai* ("craftsmen") of Dionysos. At that time these guild members put on productions of tragedy, comedy, and musical events at a number of festivals throughout the Greek world. The Amphictionic Council of Delphi guaranteed to these Athenian *technītai* safe passage and freedom from taxes and military service. Soon after this, although other guilds thrived, from the Athenian *technītai* we have only one honorary decree (*IG* II² 1320) until ca. 130, when the Amphictiones, in response to a delegation of Athenian chorus trainers and a poet, renewed the guarantees given to the Athenian *technītai* in 278/7, "unless something is contrary to (what) the Romans (wish)" (*IG* II² 1132.40–94).[56]

IG II² 1132.40–94 shows the guild already (re)established by 130, and this is confirmed by the honors that the guild decreed for the philhellene Ariarathes V, king of Cappadocia from 163–130, and his wife Nysa (*IG* II² 1330). The *technītai* honored them with statues; a sacrifice on their behalf; dedication of the fourteenth day of Metageitnion, his birthday, to the king and the fifteenth to his queen and children; the naming of these days each month after them; and an annual festival with musical and dramatic competitions. Ariarathes had promoted the growth of the guild and, like the Amphictiones, assured its members safety and freedom from arrest and taxes. The honors given to Ariarathes and his queen are typical of those being given elsewhere in the Greek world at the time, but not of those at Athens. The *technītai* of Dionysos, individually probably much traveled and experienced in the ways of the contemporary Greek world, seem more in touch with current religious developments than the Athenians back home.

An embassy of Athenian *technītai* to the Amphictionic Council of Delphi in 117/6 resulted in the following decree of the Amphictiones, one of the more remarkable documents of this period:

---

56. On the various guilds in these times and on the relevant epigraphical texts, see Pickard-Cambridge 1988, 279–21. Cf. *IG* II² 1331, 1332, 3211.

Whereas it happened that a guild (σύνοδον) of *technītai* first arose and was assembled among the Athenians, whose Demos, as the founder (ἀρχη-γός) of all good things among men, led men from the bestial life into domesticity (ἡμερότητα) and was responsible for the interaction of men with one another by introducing the tradition of the (Eleusinian) Mysteries and by announcing to all, through these, that social interaction (χρῆσις) and trust are the greatest good among men, and, in addition, was (the founder) of the laws concerning men given by the gods and of education (παιδείας); and similarly (the Demos of the Athenians) privately received the gift of the tradition of harvest (καρποῦ) and gave to the Greeks the common use of it, and first of all peoples brought together a guild of *technītai* and first made musical and scenic contests of competitors—and it happens that the very many private poets of the city attest to this and the city itself shows clearly the truth, recalling that it is the metropolis of all dramas, having invented and developed tragedy and comedy— . . .

. . . .

So that the Amphictiones may appear to be very concerned with Dionysos Melpomenos and similarly with the other gods who hold the city of the Athenians, and with the *koinon* of the *technītai*, it has been resolved by the Amphictiones that the priests put in office by the *technītai* in Athens may wear gold for the gods in all the cities in their traditional ways and may also wear garlands, and no city, official, or private citizen is to prevent them (from doing so). (*IG* II² 1134.16–28, 41–46)

This almost theatrical encomium of Athens is a reflection of a major religious movement of the period—the establishment of close ties between Athens and Delphi—which we shall take up shortly. Here, however, it is significant in that it reflects the international recognition being given to two elements of Athenian religion just considered, the Eleusinian and Dionysiac cults. Athenian propaganda for the Panhellenic value of these cults, attempted sporadically in the fifth century, appears regularly in the fourth century and now, with the virtual renaissance of Athens internationally after 166, has come to fruition. The terms in which the Amphictiones praised the Eleusinian cult are virtually those set, much more elegantly, by Isocrates in 380 for an international audience (4.28–29, 38–39). It is not surprising that in praising the Athenian *technītai*, the Amphictiones should glorify Athens' contributions to the dramatic, musical, and literary arts. The relevance of the Eleusinian cults to the document becomes more apparent, however, when we learn, from *IG* II² 1338, that before the sack of Sulla the *technītai* of Dionysos as a group participated in the Mysteries—making sacrifices and libations, singing paeans, founding an altar, and then, after the sack, helping to rebuild the sanctuary. The encomium of *IG* II² 1134 would suggest that already by 117/6, the *technītai* had begun playing a significant role in the Eleusinian cult and were internationally recognized for doing so.

Apart from his patronage of the City Dionysia and the *technītai*, Dionysos seems to have been receiving little attention in Athens. Three altars (*IG* II² 2949, 4990, 4993),[57] two private dedications (3479, 4693), and one dedication by the Boule (2801) have been dated to the period.[58] What are notably *not* attested in Athens in this or earlier periods are Dionysiac mysteries of the type described by Walter Burkert (1993) for Egypt, Pergamum, and Cos.[59] Such mysteries were performed by private or publicly appointed *telestai* ("initiators") and were often linked to or co-opted by the ruling dynasties. In Egypt and on Cos the *technītai* seem to have had a role in these Dionysiac mysteries. In Athens, the natural inclination of Dionysiac *technītai* toward Dionysiac mysteries may have been diverted by the existence of the already established and politically and religiously powerful Eleusinian Mysteries in which, as we have seen, by now the Athenian *technītai* of Dionysos had taken a part.

The dedications to Asclepios strongly suggest that of all Athenian cults, his was, both in this period and throughout the Hellenistic period, the one most patronized by individuals as individuals, and this is not surprising given his role as a healing deity. Because the dating of the private, inscribed dedications is usually based on letter forms, prosopographical information, or both, it is seldom exact; but if we use the dates given in *IG* II², roughly sixty-seven private, inscribed, marble dedications to Asclepios survive from the fourth century, sixteen from the third, and seven from the second.[60] To these must be added the hun-

---

57. On *IG* II² 2949, see Freeden 1985.

58. The sanctuary whose property was inventoried in 161/0 may also have belonged to Dionysos (*SEG* 34.95), but see Tracy 1990b.

59. Also, none of the hitherto discovered gold lamellae of these mystery cults has come from Attica (Graf 1993, 257–58).

60. By "private dedications" I mean those made neither by the state nor by officials of the cult. The numbers of dedications per century were established by adding to the texts dated to one century one-half of those dated uncertainly to it or to a following or preceding century. E.g., half of the texts dated third/fourth were given to the fourth century B.C., half to the third century B.C.

Dedications for fourth century B.C., *IG* II² 4351–63, 4365–66, 4368–81, 4388–91, 4395–404, 4406–8, 4410–23, 4425, 4427, and *SEG* 21.775, 23.124, 30.163; for fourth/third, *IG* II² 4428–30, 4468; for third, *IG* II² 4437–41, 4443–50; for third/second, *IG* II² 4454–55; for second, *IG* II² 4457–60 and *SEG* 16.177; for second/first, *IG* II² 4461–62. To the inscribed dedications of the fourth century B.C. should be added the nearly 170 uninscribed votive reliefs found in the Asclepieion. For a list, see Hausmann 1948, 164–85.

dreds of private dedications recorded on the inventories of the sanctuary of the south slope of the Acropolis, ranging in date from ca. 350 to the late second century.[61] The marble dedications varied little over the centuries, with most containing the dedicant's name, the god's name (occasionally joined by Hygieia), and the name of the year's priest. Individuals might make them as a result of a vow (e.g., *IG* II² 4366, 4372), on behalf of children (*IG* II² 4351, 4400, 4403, 4449, 4458) or on behalf of a spouse (*IG* II² 4372). Women as well as men made dedications (e.g. *IG* II² 4415, 4422, 4448). Rarely do we have a text like *SEG* 23.124 of the fourth century, which makes palpable the reason it was inscribed:

HEGEMACHOS, SON OF CRATAIMENES, OF LAMPTRAI.

To Asclepios.
Eurymedon, son of Hegemachos, saved, after having seen and
    suffered many terrible things, dedicated this in the priesthood of
    Theophilos
to Asclepios and Hygieia.

Because, in the healing process, the god might appear directly to the human in a dream, we find the god as early as the fourth century "ordering" an individual to erect an altar (*IG* II² 4358) or other dedication (*IG* II² 4410; cf. 4355, 4969). Asclepios interacted more directly with his worshippers than did most Athenian private and state deities, and in this was more similar to and anticipates the "oriental deities" on Delos, who likewise "ordered" the erection of altars and dedications (above, chapter 7, pp. 223, 229).

The priests of Asclepios, since the mid–fourth century, had been elected, in the cycle of tribal rotation, for one-year terms.[62] The priest of Asclepios was awarded a crown in 165/4 for his services (*SEG* 18.22.1–21):

In the archonship of Pelops, in the twelfth prytany, that of the tribe Ptolemais, on the sixteenth day of Skirophorion, the sixteenth day of the prytany. The Ekklesia (was held) in the theater. It was decided by the Boule and Ekklesia. Aischeas, son of Theopeithes, of Kephisia proposed:

Whereas Protagoras, son of Nicetes, of Pergasai,[63] priest of the Asclepios in the city, came to the Boule and reported that in the sacrifices which

---

61. On these inventories, see Aleshire 1989; Straten 1981, 105–22. On the demographics of the dedicators and on the process of dedication, especially in the third century B.C., see Aleshire 1992.

62. For a chronological list of known priests, see Aleshire 1989, 370–73.

63. For the family tree of Protagoras (*PA* 12284), see Aleshire 1991, 175–78.

he made the omens were good and saving (σωτήρια) for all Athenians and for those dwelling in the cities of the Athenians;[64] and he has overseen the good order (εὐκοσμίας) of the sanctuary and has sacrificed all the sacrifices in accord with the decrees; and he has behaved in a manner orderly and befitting his priesthood;

With good fortune, it has been resolved by the Boule that the presiding officers selected by lot consider these matters at the coming Ekklesia and report the opinion of the Boule to the Demos, that the Boule thinks it right to praise the priest of the Asclepios in the city and to crown him with a garland of olive because of the piety and generosity which he continually has employed toward the gods, and to inscribe this decree on a stone stele and to stand it in the sanctuary of Asclepios.

Throughout the Hellenistic period the priests of Asclepios, as did the priests of other cults, regularly sacrificed "for the Boule, Demos, children and women," often with "health and safety" specified.[65] In a somewhat fuller but fragmentary decree honoring the priest of 138/7 (*SEG* 18.26), we learn that, among other activities, he had "sacrificed well and piously the inaugural sacrifices (εἰσιτητήρια) for Asclepios, Hygieia, and the other gods to whom it was traditional (to sacrifice)"; sacrificed an ox at the Asclepieia, Epidauria, and Heroa;[66] put on the all-night festivals (παννυχίδας) of these; had his daughter serve as *arrēphoros* at the Epidauria; and appointed his son *kleidouchos*. The priest's daughter, though having the title *arrēphoros*, was no doubt a *kanēphoros*,[67] known to participate in the Epidauria already from the fourth or early third century (*IG* II² 3457). But his son is the first *kleidouchos* attested for the cult of Asclepios (cf. *IG* II² 1944, 4456), and the office may have been established in this period on the model of the similar office in cults on Delos. That the priest should appoint his own children to these roles is a sign of the times.

Among his other good services Protagoras had overseen the "good order" (εὐκοσμία) of Asclepios' temple (lines 10–11), and this may have

64. "The cities of the Athenians" are, in this context, Athens and Piraeus. See Gauthier 1982, 275–78.

65. Cf. Schwenk, #54 of 328/7; *SEG* 18.19, 21, 26, 27. In the 240s Antigonos Gonatas was to benefit from the sacrifices of a priest of Asclepios, but his name was later erased from the text (*SEG* 18.19.15–16).

66. Of the two major festivals for Asclepios in Athens, the Asclepieia was last attested for 331/0 (*IG* II² 1496.142) and the Epidauria by a late-fourth- or early-third-century dedication for a *kanēphoros* (*IG* II² 3457). The Heroa is otherwise unknown. On these festivals, see Clinton 1994; Hubbe 1959, 191 n. 57. On the text of *SEG* 18.26, see Aleshire 1989, 91–92.

67. For the terminology, see above, chapter 6, p. 199.

included the handling, display, and repair of the dedications that at times no doubt overwhelmed the site.[68] Throughout the Hellenistic period the priests inventoried and had repaired dedications; on occasion they had those of precious metals melted down and remade into new ones.[69] This activity continued also in the late second century, and the very fragmentary *SEG* 18.25 honors a priest for handling such matters and establishes a commission to assist him.[70]

The cult of Asclepios on the south slope of the Acropolis was founded, apparently, by a private group of citizens and was then, about mid–fourth century, taken over by the state. After this, private associations, in Athens and elsewhere in Attica, were devoted to this deity, but they seem all to have disappeared by the early second century (chapters 1, pp. 36–37, and 5, p. 145). After ca. 200 B.C. Asclepios' cult appears to have been practiced only by individuals or, through its priest, by the state, not by *koina*. This may serve as another indication that private religious associations, so commonly assumed to have been a feature of Hellenistic religion, may actually have been on the decline in Athens after their (very humble) floruit in the third century.

We close this discussion of Asclepios' late Hellenistic cult in Athens with a hymn to Apollo and Asclepios, inscribed and erected in the sanctuary of Asclepios on the south slope of the Acropolis (*IG* II² 4473 + *SEG* 23.126):[71]

MACEDONIOS OF AMPHIPOLIS WROTE THIS AFTER THE GOD ORDERED IT.

Sing of the well-quivered, silver-bowed Delian son of Zeus
    with an eager heart and a fair sounding tongue. Ie Paian
Put in your hand the beautiful olive branch of a suppliant
    and the glorious bough, young men of Athens. Ie Paian
And may a faultless hymn sing of the son of Leto
    [——————— Ie Paian]
Who once begot the helper against diseases and human misery,
    Asclepios, an eager young man. Ie Paian
On the peaks of Pelion a centaur taught him the craft
    and wisdom that ward off pains for mortals.

---

68. For a description of the display and storage of the dedications inside the temple in the third century, see Aleshire 1991, 41–46 and pl. 11. For εὐκοσμία as primarily the maintenance of discipline in the sanctuary, see Hubbe 1959, 184.

69. On this see Aleshire 1989.

70. On *SEG* 18.25 see Aleshire 1989, 354–69.

71. *IG* II² 4473 = Edelstein and Edelstein 1945, T593.

He is the child of Coronis, gentle to men, a most revered deity.
From him were begotten the young men Podaleirios and Machaon,
    two healers of the spear's (wounds) for Greeks, [Ie Paian]
and Iaso, Arceso, Aigle, and Panaceia, the daughters
    of Epione, together with the very distinguished Hygieia. Ie Paian
Hail, great benefit to mortals, most famous deity, [Ie Paian]
Asclepios, and grant that we, singing of your wisdom, always flourish
    In life with most pleasant Hygieia. Ie Paian
May you always come and save the Attic city of Cecrops. Ie Paian
Be gentle, blessed one (μάκαρ), and keep away hated diseases. Ie Paian

This hymn, with its epic language and allusions, provides a fit conclusion to our review of Asclepios. The high regard and even affection for the gentle and wise healer and provider of health are self-evident. Asclepios' children—Iaso ("Healing"), Arceso ("Helper"), Aigle ("Radiance"), Panaceia ("All-healing"), and Hygieia ("Health")—are all patently personifications, the largest such group we have seen thus far. But they are not new to the cult. A relief depicting Asclepios, Arceso, Iaso, Panaceia, and Asclepios' wife Epione ("Gentleness") survives from the fourth century (*IG* II² 4388).[72] Hygieia had been associated with Asclepios in Athens since earliest times. Even the two Homeric heroes mentioned in the hymn, Podaleirios and Machaon, received a fourth-century dedication (*IG* II² 4353). However "literary" and poetic, and despite being composed by a non-Athenian, Macedonios' hymn appears to capture cultic realities and perhaps sentiments of worshippers in the cult of Asclepios in the Athens of its time.

The major cults we have examined thus far—of Demeter at Eleusis, of Dionysos of the City Dionysia, and of Asclepios—were clearly prospering but had been affected little, in details at most, by the Athenian experience on Delos. The case is otherwise for Apollo. In more recent years, since at least 273, Apollo's role in state cult seems to have been primarily as Prostaterios, to whom, along with his sister, the prytanists regularly sacrificed "for the health and safety of the Boule, the Demos, the children and women, and the friends and allies." In the fourth century Apollo had had numerous cults under various epithets, especially in the rural demes. On the Erchian deme calendar alone, for example, he bore six different epithets, evidence of six different cults: Apo-

---

72. For more fourth-century Athenian reliefs depicting Asclepios and his children, see Hausmann 1948, 172–73, 178–79. On Asclepios' family in myth and cult, see Edelstein and Edelstein 1945, 2:85–91.

tropaios, Delphinios, Lykeios, Nymphegetes, Paion, and Pythios.[73] By the close of the fourth century and certainly by the middle of the third this variety of Apolline cults and epithets disappears from the epigraphical record. The causes may be several: the general lack of inscriptions from the countryside; disruptions to rural cults from various invasions and occupations by foreigners, especially the devastation caused by Philip V in 200 (above, chapter 6); and Athens' general isolation from both Delphi and Delos, the wellsprings of Apolline cult. Also, Apollo in Athens, apart from his role in household cult as Agyieus ("Of the Street"), was more a "corporate" than a personal deity. Even in the fourth century there were few private dedications to him.[74] Apart from state cult, Apollo was worshipped, often as Patroös, by phratries and demes,[75] and as these political/social structures suffered under the Macedonians in the countryside, so did their deity.

Recent events, however, spurred Athenian interest in Apollo. After the Romans evicted the Aetolians from Delphi in 189, the Athenians played a major role in 186–185 in reestablishing, through the Romans, the authority of the Amphictiones (themselves among them) over Delphi.[76] And, no less important, the Athenians acquired Delos. Athenians were now serving, year by year, as delegates to the Amphictionic Council at Delphi and as the prestigious priest of Apollo on Delos; all this may have contributed to the decision, in 138/7, to renew the tradition of sending a *theōria*, the Pythaïs, from Athens to Delphi. The previous last attested and perháps last celebrated Pythaïs was in 326/5, when Lycourgos and nine others, including many of those active in Lycourgos' other religious programs,[77] served as *hieropoioi* arranging the

73. Daux 1963.

74. If we exclude dedications from the ephebic circles where Apollo is associated with Hermes and Heracles (e.g., *IG* II² 3002 of the first century B.C.) and those for literary or athletic victories (e.g., *IG* II² 3141 of the third century B.C. and 3148 of ca. 170), the most likely private dedications to Apollo are, from the fourth century B.C., *IG* II² 4556 (Paian), *SEG* 17.82 (with Pan and the Nymphs), *IG* II² 4979 (Nikaios); from the third century B.C., *IG* II² 4674. No private dedications are securely dated to the second or first century B.C. Several of the undated dedications (*IG* II² 4850–54) and altars (5009–10) are quite probably from the fourth century. Of the four dated dedications above, three are from the countryside, and the provenance of the fourth is unknown. Cf. *IG* II² 4631, 4557, 4984.

75. By phratries: Therricleidai (*IG* II² 4973) and Achniadai (4974). By demes: Eleusis (1363.7–8), Erchia (above, pp. 268–269), Halai Aixonides (*SEG* 38.124), Ikarion (*IG* II² 4976), Lamptrai (2967), the Marathonian Tetrapolis (1358.25–26), Plotheia (1172.8), Thorikos (*SEG* 33.147.20, 24, 41, 43). By a *genos*: the Salaminioi (*SEG* 21.527.89) and Elasidai (*IG* II² 2602). On Apollo and phratries, see Lambert 1993, 211–18, 282; de Schutter 1987.

76. Habicht 1987 = 1994, 202–15.

77. *SIG*³ 296. On this Pythaïs and the *hieropoioi* involved, see above, chapter 1, p. 34.

expedition. The Pythaïs, renewed in 138/7 and repeated in 128/7, 106/5, and 98/7, had from three to five hundred participants, including the nine archons, the herald of the Areiopagos Council, the hoplite general, the priest of Apollo, a *mantis*, two *exēgētai*, the corps of ephebes and of cavalrymen, the *archetheōroi* of the various groups of *theōroi*, female *kanēphoroi* and *pyrophoroi* ("fire bearers"), representatives of noble families and of the Marathonian Tetrapolis,[78] other Pythaïstai "selected by lot" (κληρωτοί), and assorted others.[79] The purpose of the Pythaïs was to deliver first-fruits (ἀπαρχαί) to Apollo "for the health and safety of all the citizens, children, women, friends, and allies" (*FD* III.2.48.8–10), and the ceremonies included a choral presentation and equestrian and literary contests.[80]

In 103/2 the Athenians began keeping a record of the Athenian officials who contributed for the forthcoming Pythaïs of 98/7 (*SEG* 32.218). Donations ranged, each year, from 200 to 50 drachmas per person; and in addition to the state officials, the thirty donors of 103/2 included the *epimelētēs* of Delos and eight of the Athenians holding priesthoods on the island. The plan was, apparently, to raise 18,000 drachmas for the first-fruits of the 98/7 Pythaïs. Stephen Tracy's (1982a) detailed analysis of this complicated text and of the many officials involved establishes it as the record for the Delphic Pythaïs and reveals that the regularity of contributions of the first year was not maintained throughout; in particular, the priests from Delos were dilatory or failing in their contributions in the later years. This, he suggests, may have been the result of rivalry between the Delian and Delphic cults (105, 150). Deficiencies in the later years were made up by multiple contributions of the ultrarich Medeios and Sarapion.

The explicit purpose of the Pythaïs of 98/7 and of the earlier ones was to present *aparchai* to Apollo "for health and safety." In more gen-

---

78. By the mid–third century B.C. the Marathonian Tetrapolis had reestablished its close ties with Delphi, sending delegates and perhaps even its own Pythaïs there. The Delphic texts honoring the Tetrapolitans (*FD* III.2.18–22) date from ca. mid–third to mid–second century B.C. Daux (1936, 532–40, 549–51) argues that the state Pythaïs, first recelebrated in 138/7, replaced that of the Marathonian Tetrapolis and hence a special role was reserved for the Tetrapolitans. On the Marathonian Pythaïs, see Philochoros, *FGrHist* 328 F 75 and Jacoby's commentary.

79. In *IG* II² 1136 the Delphians honored the priestess of Athena who participated in the Pythaïs of 106/5.

80. On the numbers, titles, and roles of the participants and on the changes in these in the four Pythaïdes from 138/7–98/7, see Tracy 1975b; Daux 1936, 548–61. The Pythaïs of 106/5 was the largest, and a clear diminution is seen in 98/7.

eral terms it was, according to Tracy (1982a, 150–52), "to renew old traditions and, by so doing, to reassert the importance of Athens in Greek affairs." The latter, promoted especially by the important role of the *technītai* of Dionysos in the *theōria*, looked primarily to "Athens' cultural leadership in Greece, especially in the field of drama where she could indeed lay special claim to pre-eminence."

The role the *technītai* assume in the Pythaïs, like their role in the Mysteries, is indicative of their vastly increased importance in state religion, a development unique to this period. They probably did not inaugurate the new bond between Athens and Delphi, but they capitalized on and developed it. They were absent, as a group, from the Pythaïs in 138/7, but sixty-one of them, as a group, attended that of 127/6, thirty-nine of them performing as a chorus. In the Pythaïs of 98/7 eighty-eight participated.[81] We have seen (above, p. 263) the encomium of Athens with which the Amphictiones responded to a delegation of the *technītai* in 117/6. After the Pythaïs of 98/7 the Amphictiones gave them even higher praise:

Whereas the *technītai* around Dionysos, those in Athens and their *epimelētēs* Alexandros, son of Ariston, a comic poet, are pious toward the divine (τὸ θεῖον), honor their own Demos, and wish to increase things pertaining to the gods because they were the first inventors of all education (πάσας παιδείας) and the founders of dramatic contests; and have been concerned with all things that lead to a good reputation, for which they (now) have ἀσυλία and the other honors that lead to safety and a good reputation from the Amphictiones and the other Greeks and the Roman hegemons. And now, since the Athenians according to their ancestral practices and decrees have sent the holy, traditional Pythaïs after an eight-year period, in accordance with the oracle of the god, for the health and safety of all the citizens, children, women, friends, and allies; and since they performed the ancestral sacrifices in a grand way for the god; and they marshaled and adorned (ἐπεκόσμησαν) the procession well and worthily of the god, their own fatherland, their guild, and of their own good reputation and virtue in all things; and they made sacrifices, *aparchai*, and overseeings much more numerous than those before, and they sang the ancestral paean grandly . . . (*FD* III.2.48.2–12)

By 98/7, in the eyes of the Delphians at least, the Athenian *technītai* of Dionysos, members of a private association, almost overshadow the role of the state of Athens in the Pythaïs, a prominence that developed only

81. Daux 1936, 564–67.

since their first participation in 127/6. We must be wary of the hyperbolic praise characteristic of such documents in the period, but the *technītai* do seem now to have a major role in all elements of the festival. And, as we have seen, they did not limit themselves to Dionysos or Apollo Pythios. They had also taken on major roles in the Mysteries. Clearly the *technītai* of Dionysos have become, rather suddenly, a major force in Athenian state religion. We shall soon see the results of their activity in both politics and religion when these devotees of Dionysos throw their support behind the "new" Dionysos, Mithridates VI Eupator of Pontos.

A decree (*SEG* 21.469C) passed in 129/8, the year before the second Pythaïs, shows that the new Athenian interest in Apollo affected domestic cults as well:

It was resolved by the Boule and Demos.
Xeno[. . . . .], son of Sopatrides, of Sounion proposed:

> Whereas it is traditional (πάτριον) and a custom for the Demos of the Athenians and handed down by their ancestors to make of greatest importance piety toward the gods, and because of this they have acquired a good reputation and fame for the most glorious deeds on land and sea in many infantry and naval expeditions, always beginning their piety (ό-σιότητος) toward the gods with Soter; and since Apollo Pythios is Patroös for the Athenians and an *exegētēs* of the good things, and the son of Leto and Zeus similarly is the common savior of all the Greeks; and the god through his oracles has ordered them to pray to the god surnamed Patroös and to make the ancestral sacrifices to Apollo on behalf of the Demos of the Athenians at the appropriate occasions of the year, sacrificing as it is traditional for the Demos (to do); and, because of these things, Timarchos of Sphettai, treasurer of the Boule, approached the Boule and renewed the oracles and the honors that had first been assigned to the god through the laws;

In order that the Boule and Demos may appear not only preserving the traditional practices (τὰ πάτρια) but also increasing the sacrifices and honors well and piously, in order that they also may acquire the worthwhile favors from the gods, with good fortune, it has been resolved by the Boule that the allotted *proedroi* for the next Ekklesia bring up these matters for consideration and report to the Demos the opinion of the Boule, that it is resolved by the Boule to do the other things for Apollo in accord with the oracles [. . .], and that the basileus and archon of each year and the generals sacrifice for him in the ways prescribed by the decrees, and that they perform the sacrifices and processions in the festival of the Thargelia in Kepoi each year, leading out the sacrificial victims as beautifully as possible

[. . .]. And at the Thargelia, after they have spoken the prayers, let the priest of Apollo Pythios, the *exēgētai*, the other priests, the nine archons, the *hierophantēs*, the *dādouchos*,[82] those coming with them, the *agōnothetai* of the contest performed near the Pythion, and whoever are *chorēgoi*, and the *hieropoioi* make the procession [. . .]. And similarly release the household slaves from their tasks and all the public slaves from all their service. And let the basileus, the priest, the herald of the Areiopagos Council, and the *thesmothetai* sacrifice in these ways. Let the priest of Apollo Pythios take care of the appropriate sacrifice at Kepoi at the Pythion, presenting a perfect sow to Apollo Alexikakos ("Warder Off of Evil"), and a cow to Patroös, and a cow to Apollo Pythios, taking (for himself) the same parts as before. And let the treasurer of the military fund from the revenues of the year sacrifice a cow on behalf of the Demos of the Athenians, their children and wives, and the Romans, and let him give the sacrificial victim to the *hieropoioi*. And let the treasurers of the grain fund and the treasurer of the Boule also sacrifice. And let the prytanists who happen to be serving all sacrifice the six-month offering, and let the treasurer of the military fund give money for the sacrifice and the procession [. . .].

Just one year before the second Pythaïs, this decree mandates the restoration, based on old oracles and decrees, of several sacrifices for Apollo and in particular of a major local festival, the Thargelia. In classical times this festival included a sacrifice, procession, and literary contest. A forty-year series of choregic victory dedications (*IG* II² 3064–69; *SEG* 27.12–19) comes to an end in 344/3 (*IG* II² 3068), and the contest of the festival is last attested for 325/4 (*IG* II² 1629.196–99). It may be that when the *chorēgiai* were abolished by Demetrios of Phaleron at the end of the fourth century (chapter 2, pp. 54–56), the choral performances of the Thargelia were lost. If so, *SEG* 21.469 is restoring the Thargelia, as the Athenians had already done for the Pythaïdes, to the stature it last had in the age of Lycourgos. More interesting, however, is the attitude underlying the restoration: pride in Athenian piety and the favors of the gods and the military successes that resulted from that, and the recognition of Apollo as their ancestor (Patroös) and as the "common savior of all the Greeks."[83] Although nostalgia no doubt played a role (great military victories belonged to the very distant past), the widespread participation of Athenian officials here, the involvement of many segments of the Athenian population in the Pythaïdes, and the

---

82. On the *exēgētai* and the role of other Eleusinian officials here, see Clinton 1974, 89–93.

83. See Chaniotis 1995, 153–54.

significant outlays of money by both individuals and the state all indicate a serious and popular movement to reestablish Athenian ties with
this most prominent Olympian god.

The Romans were surely included among the "friends and allies" who,
like the children and women, were to benefit from the sacrifices made
"for health and safety" by the prytanists, the ephebes, and other Athenian officials to various deities.[84] But, as we examine innovations in the
period, we may ask if the Romans played a new, more significant role
in the state religion. It is generally assumed they did.[85] Ferguson (1911,
366–67) claims that as *euergetai* ("benefactors"), Roman senators and
magistrates "were henceforth entitled to divine honours on coming to
Athens."[86] Similarly it has been thought that there was, by 149/8, a new
state festival, the Romaia. The ephebes did regularly provide an escort
for visiting Roman *euergetai*,[87] and they certainly sacrificed each year
"to the gods and the *euergetai*,"[88] but it is not certain that these latter
euergetai necessarily were Romans. One, at least, was the long-dead
Macedonian liberator of Athens, Diogenes (*IG* II² 1011.14–15). Simply
stated, if the *euergetai* who received sacrifices from the ephebes were
the same "Roman *euergetai*" the ephebes escorted in *IG* II² 1006.21, then
individual Romans were receiving sacrifices for their services to the
Demos (cf. *IG* II² 1009.36–37); but this identification is not assured. In
any case, if Cicero's account is to be taken seriously, L. Licinius Crassus certainly did not think he was treated as a "deity" by the Athenians
on his visit ca. 110 B.C. (above, p. 259).[89]

The status of the festival Romaia is also uncertain. It is attested only
by a list of *hieropoioi* of 149/8 (*IG* II² 1938), and it is hard to believe that

84. In the prytanists' sacrifices to Apollo Prostaterios and Artemis Boulaia, e.g., *Agora*
XV, #238.14, 243.12; and in sacrifices by Eleusinian officials, *SEG* 16.92.15; *IG* II² 949.16–17.
Cf. *IG* II² 990.7, 1000.12–13, 1011.68–69. A sacrifice "to" the Demos of the Romans has
been restored in *Agora* XV, #180.11 of 184/3. It would be unique among the prytany decrees and among the other pre-Sullan sources.

85. Mellor (1975, 102) has in Athens by or shortly after the battle of Pydna in 168 "cults,
priests, and statues" of the goddess Roma, but for this there is no evidence. The evidence
for Roma in Athens, collected in Mellor, is in fact all post-Sullan. For the Romaia of *IG*
II² 1938, see below.

86. Cf. Green 1990, 526.

87. *IG* II² 1006.21 (εὐεργέταις ʿΡωμαίοις). Elsewhere the recipients of the escort are
termed simply "Romans," without the designation *euergetai* (*IG* II² 1006.75, 1008.13,
1011.18).

88. *IG* II² 1006.15–16, 68–69; 1008.26, 59, 1009.36–37; 1011.14–15, 39–40.

89. Relevant here are Nock's comments (1972, 725–26) on Romans as *euergetai*.

a major festival honoring the Romans in this period was celebrated or attested only once. It is more probable that the festival for which these men served was the well-known Romaia on Delos, a festival which the Athenians administered and in which they commonly participated.[90] In sum, there probably was not a Romaia in Athens in this period, and the evidence is not conclusive that Romans, either individually or collectively, were receiving divine honors in Athens from Athenians.

Of the originally foreign cults we have encountered thus far in our survey of Hellenistic Athens, only that of the Mother of the Gods in Piraeus clearly survives into this period. After its shadowy beginnings in the fourth century, it had become entirely a citizen cult by 213/2 and remained that throughout the third, second, and first centuries (above, chapter 5, pp. 142–43). In the first century the surviving dedications are by Athenians: one by a husband and wife as a *charistērion* (*IG* II² 4710), another by Euphris of Probalinthos (*PA* 6100) (*IG* II² 4703), who, with other ephebes of 106/5, had also made a dedication to Hermes (*IG* II² 2984). Both of Euphris' dedications were found in Piraeus.[91] Although this cult was foreign in origin, it had by now been practiced in Athens for over two hundred years and was probably no longer viewed as alien. If *IG* II² 1334 is in fact from Piraeus, it would indicate that the cult remained private, in the hands of *orgeōnes* who chose their priestess by lot each year.

We have seen the popularity of the Sarapis and Isis cult on Delos and the extensive participation in it by Athenians there (chapter 7, pp.

---

90. Above, chapter 7, pp. 221–22. *IG* II² 1938 records two *hieropoioi* for the Romaia and over sixty for the Ptolemaia. The large majority of these *hieropoioi* were Athenians, but there were also foreigners from Alexandria, Thessaly, Rhodes, Rome, and Sardis, including some leading Stoic philosophers, notably Panaitios (Ferguson 1911, 339). The Ptolemaia with its athletic contests, unlike the Romaia, is frequently attested for Athens in this period (e.g., *IG* II² 956.34–35 of 161/0, 1028.100–101 of 101/0). It seems to have come to an end with the invasion of Sulla in 86: it does not appear on the ephebic inscriptions thereafter (*IG* II² 1039–43). On the Ptolemaia in this period, see Habicht 1992a, 83–85 = 1994, 155–56.

Hieropoioi are listed on *IG* II² 1937 of 156/5 and *SEG* 32.216 of ca. 150 for a festival termed the "Athenaia." According to the later lexicographical tradition, Athenaia was an early name for the Panathenaia and an alternative name for the Chalkeia (see Jacoby on *FGrHist* 325 F 18). It was also the name of the festival the Athenians appended to the Delian Apollonia (above, chapter 6, p. 219). Habicht (1982a, 177 = 1994, 58–59) associates these *hieropoioi* with the Chalkeia, but I think it more likely that they served the Delian Athenaia. For a roughly comparable situation, see Tracy 1990a, 199, on *IG* II² 2459.

91. The identity of Nicias of *IG* II² 2950/1 cannot be ascertained.

229–31). The first attestation of the cult of Isis in Athens had been the rights granted to Egyptians to purchase land for a sanctuary before 332/1. Centuries later Pausanias, as he moved from the Prytaneion to the lower city, saw a sanctuary of Sarapis, a god whom, he claims, the Athenians introduced "from Ptolemy" (1.18.4).[92] If Pausanias is correct, this was presumably Ptolemy III Euergetes, whose benefactions to Athens and influence were predominant ca. 224.[93] To be associated with this Sarapieion is, perhaps, a *koinon* of foreign Sarapiastai functioning in 216/5 (above, chapter 6, pp. 180–81). But it is not until 133/2, undoubtedly as a result of their experiences on Delos, that we have unmistakable evidence of Athenians themselves participating in the Egyptian cult in Athens; and in Athens, as on Delos, the Athenians preferred Isis over Sarapis.[94] The priest of that year, Niconymos of Oinoe, made a dedication to Isis and Anoubis and included mention of his *zakoros*, Metrodoros of Calchedon (*SEG* 24.225). Similarly Sosos of Aithalidai, whose father had been a *hieropoios* of the Delian Romaia in 127/6 (*ID* 2596.5) and who was himself to be a *thesmothetēs* in 85/4 (*IG* II² 1715.8), served as priest in Athens (*IG* II² 4702); his *zakoros* was also a foreigner, Zopyros of Miletos, whose own son was an ephebe in 102/1 (*IG* II² 1028.145).[95] The Egyptian gods were now well established in Athens, and, as on Delos, prominent Athenians served their cult.

And, finally, there are several indications that the Athenian Isis cult was virtually identical to the Delian. The dedication from Sosos' priesthood (*IG* II² 4702) was made, by an Athenian, to Isis Dikaiosyne, and to her, with the same epithet, Gaios of Acharnai (*PA* 2937) as a former

---

92. For discussion of the possible site and of inscriptions related to it, see Wycherley 1963, 161–62.

93. Above, chapter 6, pp. 178–81. See Habicht 1992a, 74–76 = 1994, 145–46; Dow 1937a; Ferguson 1911, 171.

94. Dow (1937a, 198–201, 227–32) argues, from letter forms, that *IG* II² 4692—a dedication made to Isis, Sarapis, and, probably, Anoubis in the priesthood of an otherwise unknown Athenian—must date ca. 210–170, and he concludes that a state cult was founded ca. 226/5–222/1, to be associated with the Ptolemaic Sarapieion mentioned by Pausanias (1.18.4). The text of *IG* II² 4692 is, however, so similar to those dated nearly a century later (e.g., *IG* II² 4702; *SEG* 24.225) that Dow's early date and reconstruction of the history of Athenian participation in the cult remain open to question. Habicht (1992a, 76 = 1994, 147–48) follows Dow in dating the state cult to ca. 200 B.C., but see also Habicht 1980, 4 = 1994, 50.

95. A Zopyros, interestingly, was also the *tamias* of the private Sarapiastai of 216/5 (*IG* II² 1292). On *IG* II² 4072, see Dow 1937a, 212–13.

priest of Sarapis on Delos made a dedication there just after 115/4 (*ID* 2079).[96] But the best indicator is *SEG* 42.157:[97]

> To Isis Sarapis
> Anoubis Harpocrates.
> Megallis, daughter of Magas of Marathon,
> for her daughter Demarion and her sons[98]
> as ordered (κατὰ πρόσταγμα),
> in the priesthood of Menandros,
> son of Artemon, of Alopeke,
> when Asopocles of Phlya,
> was *kleidouchos*,
> and Sosicrates of Laodicea
> was *zakoros*,
> and Dionysios of Antioch
> was interpreting dreams.

This inscription, found in Athens and dated ca. 116/5–94 B.C., reveals a cult structure so similar to that on Delos that it was long thought the inscription must have originated on Delos. Pierre Roussel (1916a, 268 n. 2) and Sterling Dow (1937a, 208–12) proved, however, that this cult of Sarapis was Athenian and not Delian, although it duplicates the Delian cult, as Dow states, "in the facts that the deities are the same, that they are listed in the same order, allowing for the prominence given Isis; that the officials are the same, that they are listed in the same order; and that the *zakoros* and interpreter of dreams are foreigners" (212). Clearly the Athenian cult was modeled on the Delian.

Among the remaining foreign cults attested for Athens in this period, two others also had Delian ties. A *koinon* of the Theoi Megaloi honored its own cult officials in 112/1 and 111/0 (*SEG* 21.535–36). Its identifiable officials were from Alexandria and Antioch, and it is unlikely that the procession and regatta held by the state for the Theoi Megaloi were associated with this private cult.[99] *IG* II² 1337 of 97/6 records a decree of *orgeōnes* of the "Syrian Aphrodite" in Piraeus. The term *orgeōnes* for the membership would indicate that all or some were citizens, and the one known member, Satyros of Aixone (*PA* 12588), was an Athenian.

96. Of the five dedications to Egyptian deities in Athens from the period, three were made by Athenians (*IG* II² 4702, *SEG* 21.796, 24.225), one by Aphrodisios of Tyana (*IG* II² 4697), and one by a dedicator (*IG* II² 4692) who cannot be identified.

97. Most recently edited by Tracy 1975a, 72–73, #13. See also Dow 1937a, 208–12.

98. They may be the sons or grandsons of Megallis. See Dow 1937a, 211.

99. On this *oikos* see Robert 1970, 7–14.

The priestess was Nicasis of Corinth.[100] The goddess, originally Atargatis in Syria and on Delos, then Aphrodite Hagne under Athenian influence on Delos, needs in Athens itself still to be identified by her ethnic, "Syrian." That she and the Theoi Megaloi now appear, however briefly, in Athens is due to the prominence and Athenian interest in these cults on Delos.[101]

To another, probably distinct Aphrodite was dedicated a *koinon* of *orgeōnes* who in 138/7 honored their *epimelētēs*, Sarapion of Heracleia.[102] Only Sarapion is named in the decree, no Athenians or others, but the involvement of Athenian citizens is made probable by the inclusion, uniquely on decrees of private cults, of a clause indicating that the sacrifices were on behalf not only of the members of the *koinon* and their families but also of "the Demos of the Athenians."[103]

There also appear some *synodoi* ("assemblies"), apparently a now-fashionable term for *koina*.[104] A *synodos* of Heracles in 159/8 had an Athenian priest and at least four other Athenian members (*SEG* 36.228). The other ten members were all foreigners, two certainly from Antioch. An Athenian made a dedication to Zeus Naios, usually associated with Dodona, and his *synodos* (*IG* II² 4707). And in 112/1 Diognetos of Oion (*PA* 3866) was the treasurer of a *synodos* made up of ship captains and merchants, devoted to Zeus Xenios. This *synodos* received permission from the state to honor their benefactor, Diodoros of Halai (*PA* 3935), who was *epimelētēs* of Piraeus harbor (*IG* II² 1012). In all probability most members were foreigners for whom Zeus Xenios ("Protector of Foreign Guests/Friends") would be appropriate. To these we may add

100. The goddess naturally had a priestess; the establishment of a priest for her by the Athenians on Delos was a bureaucratic not cultic appointment (above, chapter 7, pp. 225, 232–35).

101. On the Theoi Megaloi on Delos, see above, chapter 7, pp. 225–26; on Atargatis, pp. 232–35. There are also a few foreign cults with no apparent Delian connection, all attested by single inscriptions: a dedication to Artemis Nana in the Piraeus (*IG* II² 4696) and "to the gods" by a Tyrian (*IG* II² 4698). A Sidonian was honored by fellow Sidonians of his *koinon* for building a portico for their temple of Ba'al in Piraeus (*IG* II² 2946). This last text, in both Greek and Phoenician, has been dated variously to after 265 (Ameling 1990) and to 96/5 (Tracy 1990a, 247–48).

102. *AM* 66 (1941): 228, #4. For the relief accompanying this decree and representing Sarapion, his wife, Aphrodite, and a cult statue holding a spear, see Lawton 1995, #61. The find spot of this inscription, near the church of Hagios Sostos on Leoforos Syngrou, would appear also to disassociate it from the cult of Aphrodite Hagne in Piraeus.

103. Kyparissis and Peek 1941, 231.

104. σύνοδος perhaps initially meant the "sum total of dues paid," and developed from the fact that members of a *koinon* φέρειν τὴν σύνοδον (*IG* II² 1326.6, 1012.14–15).

the Sabaziastai of 103/2 (*IG* II² 1335). Their priest was Zenon of Antioch; their treasurer, secretary, and *epimelētēs* was Dorotheos of Oa (*PA* 4617). Of the fifty-three members listed, thirty-seven are Athenians; one, in addition to the priest, is from Antioch, two from Laodicea, three from Miletos, and other single individuals from various areas including Macedon, Apameia, and Heracleia. One, Agathocles (line 58), was apparently a slave. In 330 B.C. Demosthenes had derided Aeschines for participating in the exotic rituals of this Thraco-Phrygian god (18.259–60), a god whose cult was already established in Piraeus (*IG* II² 2932). The Sabaziastai of 103/2 were apparently using the same (long-abandoned?) sanctuary as the devotees of Sabazios had in 342/1.

In this period membership in cults of foreign deities remained private and small, but here too we may see affects of the Delian experience. Now for the first time we have unmistakable evidence of Athenians in Athens participating side by side with foreigners of various nationalities, often those nationalities that were well represented on Delos. Private cults in Athens, like most cults on Delos, were becoming international. But even in these late times the foreign cults were few—fewer even than they had been in the third century—small, and, apparently, marginal. Their importance in religion of the time pales by comparison to the great efforts and participation in the traditional state cults we have surveyed.

We now come to the end of this period, the years just preceding the sack of the city by the Roman general Sulla on March 1, 86 B.C. On the political side the catastrophe was caused in large part by Athens' turn to Mithridates VI Eupator, king of Pontus, whose many military successes suggested he might successfully oppose the Romans under whose support, in Athens, Medeios of Piraeus (*PA* 10098) and Sarapion of Melite (*PA* 12564) were flourishing.[105] Medeios held the archonship in 101/0 and then for three successive years beginning in 91/0, clearly setting himself up as a tyrant with at least Roman acquiescence. In religion Medeios' dominance in these last years is apparent in the multiple offices he held: in 99/8 alone he served as *agōnothetēs* of both the Panathenaia and the Delian Delia; for these and other offices, he contributed 1,150 drachmas for the Pythaïs of 98/7. In one year Sarapion served as *agōnothetēs* of the Eleusinia, Panathenaia, Delia, and one other

---

105. On the careers of Medeios and Sarapion, see Tracy 1982a, and above, chapter 7, pp. 239–41.

festival. He also, as hoplite general, headed the Pythaïs of 98/7. In a sense this financial support of major state festivals by a very few wealthy individuals is the culmination of a long tradition. Even in the early classical period members of the richest families were assigned, on a cyclical basis, to provide a chorus or another expensive item for a drama or athletic contest. Lycourgos, as we have seen, questioned the value of such liturgies (chapter 1, pp. 15, 34), and Demetrios of Phaleron eliminated them (chapter 2, pp. 54–58). Demetrios' replacement of *chorēgoi* by *agōnothetai* was decisive for the funding and, perhaps, the atmosphere of the major festivals. The financial support and thus the splendor of a year's festivals would henceforth be dependent on one individual. Throughout our period the *agōnothetai* remained Athenian citizens, and so the festivals remained administered and financed by citizens. But here, at the end, the assumption of so many religious responsibilities, just as of so many political offices, by a small group of individuals reveals how small and closed the group in authority had become. Despite this, however, as Athenians entered into these troubled years, the full program of state festivals and cult was apparently still being maintained. The last securely dated list of ephebic activities, *IG* II² 1029 of 98/7 B.C., shows a program of religious activities scarcely different from that of 215/4, examined in chapter 6, or that of 123/2 B.C. with which this chapter began.

In 89/8 the beleaguered Athenian state sent an emissary to Mithridates to represent its interests. The emissary was a Peripatetic philosopher, Athenion, described by a very hostile critic as half slave-born and a self-declared citizen. For the account of these events we must depend on that same critic, a Stoic philosopher of the time, Poseidonios of Apamea, who was pro-Roman, anti-Mithridates, and pro-Sulla.[106] Here, with an emphasis on religious matters and a de-emphasis of the calumny, I summarize his account, preserved in Athenaios' *Deipnosophistai* 5.211E–215B (*FGrHist* 87 F 36).

After Athenion's stay with Mithridates (89/8), during which he was received and treated as a friend and confidant, he returned to Athens. The populace of Athens rushed out to welcome him: "for this spectacle men, women, children ran together. . . . And also the *technītai* of

106. On Poseidonios' account in Athenaios, on the biases of both, and on the possible confusion of Athenion with Aristion and of the actions correctly or incorrectly attributed to one or the other, see Bugh 1992. In my account I simply follow Athenaios' narrative, the many problems of which Bugh explicates. On the relationships of Athens, Rome, and Mithridates and on Athenian internal politics at this time, see Badian 1976.

Dionysos met him and invited the messenger of the new Dionysos to their common hearth and to the prayers and libations around it." Athenion was put up in the ornate house of a rich man and then appeared, trailing after him a shiny cloak and wearing a gold ring with the image of Mithridates. "In the sanctuary of the *technītai* of Dionysos sacrifices were performed to celebrate the presence of Athenion and, with a herald's proclamation, libations were offered." At a public meeting in the Agora the next day, Athenion told the Athenians "things that had never been expected, things that never had been dreamed of": that King Mithridates controlled Bithynia, Cappadocia, and all Asia Minor up to Pamphylia and Cilicia. Every city, he said, was welcoming Mithridates "with honors beyond those of a man" (ταῖς ὑπὲρ ἄνθρωπον τιμαῖς) and was calling the king a god (θεόν). Oracles from everywhere were predicting his rule over the inhabited earth (τὸ κράτος τῆς οἰκουμένης). "Let us not," Athenion continued, "overlook the fact that the sanctuaries have been closed, that the gymnasia are dry and dirty, that the theater has no gatherings, that the law courts are silent, that the Pnyx, consecrated by the oracles of the gods, is robbed of its Demos. And, Athenian men, let us not overlook that the sacred cry of Iacchos has been silenced, the sacred *anaktoron* of the two goddesses has been closed, and the haunts of the philosophers are silent."

We see here, not so much in the events as in the attitudes revealed, much that should now be familiar. The losses felt most deeply are, first, that the sanctuaries have been closed; that the gymnasia, the training grounds of the ephebes, are abandoned; that the theater, always Athens' claim to international pride, is silenced; that the law courts and Pnyx, two critical elements of democracy, have ceased to function. The Eleusinian Mysteries too have been suspended, and, finally—what was perhaps particularly annoying to the Peripatetic philosopher Athenion —the philosophical schools were closed. But, I stress, standing among the losses of theater, philosophy, and democracy are those of religion and cult.

We see also here the now-familiar attitude toward a benefactor, toward a foreigner who could eliminate political oppression and restore democracy and who could provide "things that never had been expected, things that had never been dreamed of." For such a man, Demetrios Poliorcetes, the Athenians willingly voted divine honors in 307/6 B.C. (see chapter 3). He too was a Dionysos. Now, over two hundred years later, it appears that not the citizens through state cult but the *technītai* of Dionysos—the actors, poets, and professionals of Dionysos—take the lead in honoring the new Dionysos. It is in their sanctuary and at their altar that the messenger of the new Dionysos is honored. We have also noted above that the *technitai* were now playing a new, larger role in the Eleusinian Mysteries, and this, as well as their historical importance, may have earned special mention of the Mysteries in Athenion's speech.

After this rousing speech Athenion was chosen hoplite general and given virtually dictatorial powers, which, according to Poseidonios, he wielded maliciously against citizen and foreigner, friend and foe alike. In addition to other atrocities he also "reached out for Apollo's money from Delos." He sent there Apellicon, another Peripatetic and a naturalized citizen of Athens from Teos, a man who had bought the library of Aristotle and had stolen from the archives the entire collection of Athenian state decrees! Apellicon set out with an army for Delos, "more in the manner of a religious celebration than of a military expedition." On Delos a Roman general led an attack on the negligent, drunk, and sleeping Athenian forces, killing six hundred "like cattle" and taking captive around four hundred. Apellicon and a few others escaped, but neither he nor Athenion was to be heard of again. Shortly afterward Mithridates' forces took control of Delos and massacred 20,000 residents there, mostly Italians, an act in keeping with Mithridates' systematic massacre of 80,000 Italians on one day in the cities of Asia Minor.[107] Pausanias, two hundred years later, recounts the sack of Delos in his story of a mysterious statue of Apollo that washed up on the shores of Cape Malea in the Peloponnesos:

> The cult statue of Apollo, which is now here, once was set up on Delos. Delos was then a market for Greeks and seemed because of the god to provide security for those working there. Menophanes, a general of Mithridates, either himself scorned the god or did what was ordered by Mithridates—for when a man goes after profits, religious matters ($\tau\grave{a}$ $\theta\epsilon\hat{\imath}a$) are second to financial gains. Since Delos was unwalled and the residents did not possess weapons, Menophanes sailed in with triremes and murdered both the foreigners resident there and the Delians themselves. After he had carried off much money belonging to the merchants and all the dedications, after he had enslaved the women and children, he leveled Delos. And while the island was being sacked and pillaged, one of the barbarians in insolence ($\acute{\upsilon}\pi\grave{o}$ $\mathring{\upsilon}\beta\rho\epsilon\omega\varsigma$) hurled this statue into the sea. The current took it up and carried it to this part of the land of the Boiatai, and for this reason they call this place Epidelion.

107. Appian *Mith.* 22–23, 28, 58, 62.

Neither Menophanes nor Mithridates himself escaped the wrath from the god. Straightway those of the merchants who had escaped set up with their ships an ambush and sank Menophanes after he had set sail leaving Delos. The god later forced Mithridates to commit suicide after his rule had been destroyed and he was being chased from all sides by the Romans. . . . Such things happened to these men who had behaved impiously. (Paus. 3.23.3–6)

With the deaths or disappearances of Apellicon and Athenion after the Delian fiasco, Poseidonios' account comes to an end. For the rest we depend on Plutarch, who describes Sulla's role in these events, and on Appian, who in his *Mithridatic Wars* gives the broader picture of Roman involvement with the king of Pontos. We now take up the siege and destruction of Athens and Piraeus by Sulla. We begin with what appears to be a significant new element in mainland Greek religious history: the seizure of sacred treasures by generals simply to obtain cash. It had, of course, happened or been threatened on occasion throughout Greek history. In early times it was a mark of barbarism and alienation from Greek culture. In Athens it had been done only by the desperate tyrant Lachares, and, in one account at least, he was fittingly punished for it (chapter 3, pp. 90–92). Philip V certainly destroyed a number of sanctuaries in Athens and throughout Greece, but probably more for vengeance than profit. But Plutarch and Appian make it all too clear that the robbing of sanctuaries was, in the first century B.C., becoming routine. If Poseidonios were a less hostile witness we could easily accept his claim that Athenion sent Apellicon to seize the treasures of Delos. It is, however, conceivable and perhaps more likely that Apellicon was sent to protect the many Athenians there against the large Roman and Italian population. There is no doubt, however, of Sulla's purposes as he was engaged in the siege of Athens:

Since Sulla needed much money for the war, he was disturbing those places of Greece that were sacrosanct, sending for the most beautiful and expensive dedications, in part from Epidauros, in part from Olympia. He wrote also to the Amphictiones at Delphi, saying that it was better for the god's treasures to be brought to him. For, he said, he would guard them more securely or, if he used them, he would pay back no less. And he sent one of his friends, the Phocian Caphis, and ordered him to receive each item by weight. When Caphis came to Delphi, he was hesitant to touch the sacred items and in the presence of the Amphictiones wept much over the necessity of it. And when some said that they heard a lyre sounding in the inner chamber of the temple, Caphis, either because he believed it or because he wished to throw the fear of god into Sulla, wrote to Sulla about it. Sulla jokingly wrote in response that he was surprised that Caphis did not understand that the singing was not of an angry god but of a happy god, and, since the god was cheerfully giving, he ordered Caphis to take the treasures confidently.

Most Greeks did not realize that the other treasures were being sent away (from Delphi), but when because of the weight the pack animals could not take up the silver *pithos*, the last remaining one of the royal (dedications of Croesus), the Amphictiones were forced to cut it into pieces. As they did so, they remembered Titus Flamininus, Manius Acilius, and Aemilius Paulus. One of them drove Antiochos out of Greece, the others defeated in war the kings of the Macedonians. But all three of them not only kept their hands off the Greek sanctuaries but even gave them gifts, honor, and great respect. But those were some of the prudent men who had learned to serve their leaders in silence, who commanded according to the law, who themselves kingly in spirit and thrifty in their spending used public expenditures moderately and as assigned, men who believed that fawning over their soldiers was more shameful than fearing the enemy. But the generals (in Sulla's time) got their leading positions by violence, not by virtue. And because they needed weapons more against one another than against the enemy, they were forced to play the demagogue in their generalships. In buying their soldiers' services with the money they were spending on their soldiers' pleasures, these generals did not realize that they were putting their whole country up for sale, that they were enslaving themselves to the worst men for the purpose of ruling their betters. (Plut. *Sulla* 12.3–9)[108]

We should not discount the prejudices of Plutarch himself, once a priest at Delphi, but he is no doubt correct in the fact of the robbing of the major sanctuaries and in the motives, personal wealth and pay of soldiers, that lay behind it. All of this could give little hope to the Athenians who were still defending their city against Sulla and his army.

Aristion, an Epicurean philosopher who was apparently little better than Athenion, was now, with the support of Mithridates and with money from the sacred treasury of Delos (Appian *Mith*. 28), ruling Athens and commanding the defense against the siege.

Sulla had a terrible and inexorable passion to capture Athens, either because in some kind of jealousy he was shadowboxing against the city's ancient glory or because he was angry at the jokes and obscenities with which the tyrant Aristion, dancing and ridiculing, used to provoke him and (his

108. Cf. Appian *Mith*. 54. On the situation in Delphi after Sulla's thefts and on the end of the Soteria, see Nachtergael 1977, 376–78.

wife) Metella from the walls. Aristion had a soul made up of licentiousness and savagery, and had taken up the worst of the diseases and passions of Mithridates. In these last times he imposed the fatal blow on a city that had escaped countless wars and many tyrannies and civil wars. Wheat was selling for 1,000 drachmas a bushel in the city, and men were eating the feverfew that grew around the Acropolis and were boiling their shoes and leather flasks for food. But Aristion himself was constantly having midday drinking parties and revels, was dancing in armor and telling jokes on the enemy. He paid no attention when the sacred lamp of (Athena in the Erechtheum) went out for lack of oil,[109] and when the priestess asked for a quart of wheat he sent pepper. When members of the Boule and priests begged him to pity the city and settle with Sulla, Aristion scattered them with a volley of arrows.

Late and reluctantly Aristion sent out two or three of his drinking companions to negotiate for peace. They asked for nothing that could bring safety but spoke solemnly about Theseus, Eumolpos, and the Persian Wars. Sulla replied, "Go away, gentlemen, and take with you these speeches. I was sent by the Romans to Athens not to learn history but to put down rebels." (Plut. *Sulla* 13.1–4)

The fall of Athens and Sulla's sack followed shortly thereafter:

Sulla broke down and leveled the section of wall between the Piraeic and Sacred Gates, and he entered the city about midnight. He was terrifying because of the many trumpets and bugles, the cries and shouts of the army that was let loose to pillage and murder and was rushing through the narrow streets with drawn swords. No count could be made of those who were killed, but the number is still now measured by the area covered by the flowing blood. For, apart from those killed in the rest of the city, blood and gore in the Agora covered all the Cerameicos inside the Dipylon, and many say it washed through the gate and over the area outside. So many died in this way, but no fewer committed suicide in pity and longing for their country which they thought would be destroyed. This made the best men despair and even fear survival because they expected no humaneness or moderation in Sulla.

The exiles Medeios and Calliphon begged Sulla and groveled before him, and Sulla's fellow senators on campaign with him asked him to spare the city. And Sulla himself, now sated with vengeance, spoke an encomium of the ancient Athenians and said that, as a favor, he granted the few to the many, the living to the dead. In his *Memoirs* Sulla says that he captured Athens on March 1, which is the first day of (the Athenian month) Anthesterion. In Anthesterion, by chance, the Athenians celebrate several

---

109. Cf. Plut. *Numa* 9.

memorials of the destruction and devastation of the great flood because about that time of the year the flood occurred.

After the city was taken the tyrant Aristion fled to the Acropolis and was besieged there by Curio to whom the task was assigned. Aristion held out for some time but finally, oppressed by thirst, he gave himself up. And straight away the divine (τὸ θεῖον) gave a sign. For at the same hour of the same day that Curio was bringing Aristion down (from the Acropolis), clouds formed in a clear sky and filled the Acropolis with water. Soon thereafter Sulla took also the Piraeus and burned most of it. (Plut. *Sulla* 14.3–7)[110]

According to Appian (*Mith.* 38–39, 41) Sulla burned Piraeus but allowed his soldiers to pillage but not burn the city. He gathered from the Acropolis alone ca. 40 pounds of gold and 600 pounds of silver, much of it, no doubt, in the form of religious dedications. Virtually all Athenian sanctuaries must have been stripped of valuables. Later rebuilding programs suggest that the buildings of the sanctuaries in the city probably survived but many of those in Piraeus and the countryside were ruined. As part of the post-Sullan rebuilding the Athenians had to forbid the private sale or purchase of sanctuaries, a provision which reveals the chaos in religious administrative structure that the sack had caused. They also had to restate the "ancient tradition" that no one was to give birth or die in a sanctuary, and this suggests that some after the sack had taken up residence in the ruined and abandoned sanctuaries.[111]

Interestingly, Sulla soon returned to Piraeus and had himself initiated into the Eleusinian Mysteries (Plut. *Sulla* 26.1), the only element of Athenian religion that seems to have appealed to the Romans of the time (cf. Cic. *Leg.* 2.36). Centuries later, however, Pausanias (1.20.7) offered what was perhaps the later Athenians' view of their goddess' final revenge on Sulla. Mithridates had paid for his impieties toward Apollo of Delos, and so too was Sulla to suffer for an impiety he committed in Athens.

Some time later Sulla was afflicted with the (fatal) disease (of mites in the bowels)[112] with which I hear also the Syrian Pherecydes was taken. Sulla's

110. Cf. Appian *Mith.* 38–39.

111. The very fragmentary *SEG* 26.121 records a post-Sullan rebuilding program and originally listed ca. 80 sanctuaries being repaired or cleansed in Piraeus, on Salamis, elsewhere in the countryside, and in Athens. On this text and the sites, see Culley 1975, 1977. For the date see also Freeden 1983, 145–80; Shear 1981, 365–67.

112. For a graphic description of this disease, see Plut. *Sulla* 36. On the pathology and historicity of the disease, commonly fatal to impious tyrants, see Africa 1982; Keaveney and Madden 1982.

deeds toward the majority of Athenians were more savage than were be-fitting a Roman man. But I do not think that they were the cause of his misfortune later. The disease was rather an expression of the wrath of (Zeus) Hikesios ("Protector of Suppliants"), because Sulla dragged off and killed Aristion after he took refuge in the sanctuary of Athena.

Conclusion

My purpose has been to show the status of Athenian public and private religious institutions and, where possible, beliefs at the beginning of the Hellenistic period and the developments they underwent in the years down to the siege and pillaging of Athens by the Roman general Sulla and his soldiers in 86 B.C. In this concluding chapter we review major events and the general lines of development, both of which may occasionally have gotten obscured in the detailed accounts of earlier chapters. We proceed again chronologically but pause at appropriate moments to note the later development or significance of ideas or practices introduced during the period under discussion. These discussions and then remarks at the end of the chapter will, I trust, help fit the religion of Hellenistic Athens into the larger picture of both religion and society in the Greek Hellenistic world.

The defeat of Athens in the battle of Chaeroneia by the Macedonian forces commanded by Philip II in 338 B.C. had eliminated her independence in international political affairs, had endangered her democratic government, and had even threatened her existence. Immediately thereafter, under the leadership of the statesman Lycourgos, the Athenians undertook a national revival that involved rebuilding the walls and navy, establishing an educational program for their young men, invigorating the economy, and, no less important, refurbishing the finances, sanctuaries, and festivals of their traditional deities. On the religious side of this national revival the Athenians were clearly looking back to the age of Pericles, restoring dedications and buildings to the beauty and grandeur they had last had before the disastrous Peloponnesian War. The effort was broadly based, with financial and personal support from a large number of prominent Athenians and with the approval of the Athenian Demos. Lycourgos himself was clearly influential, on the cultic side as priest of Poseidon-Erechtheus and as an unofficial expert on religious matters, and on the financial side both as a private fund-raiser and as administrator of the state treasury. He also was a powerful spokesman for traditional religious values, as his speech against Leocrates demonstrates.

We must take care here not to think of these activities, by Lycourgos or the Athenians in general, as "nostalgic" or "pietistic." Success as an individual or as a state was always, in the Greek tradition, in part the result of "honoring the ancestral gods in the ancestral ways," and forward-looking and visionary statesmen in late-fourth-century Athens, if they wished to attain again the prosperity of fifth-century Athens, would naturally undertake to reestablish the religious sanctuaries, dedications, and rituals that had brought fifth-century Athenians their successes. The Greek instinct, in times of stress and failure, was (usually) not to give up on the ancestral gods or to seek new gods, but to return to the rituals and customs of earlier, better times. And thus the age of Lycourgos looked back, in religion particularly, to the age of Pericles, and herein we see continuity between high classical religion and that practiced in Athens at the outset of the Hellenistic period. And, I argue, the religion of the Lycourgan period itself became the model to which the Athenians in following centuries then returned after various dislocations caused by national and international events.

For Lycourgan Athens we have no contemporary statement about a conscious desire or systematic program for a national revival or for religion's part in it. But a survey of what was then being done would naturally lead us to conclude that such a desire existed. The historian Polybius, writing in the third quarter of the second century, offers a useful account of the same general outlook as he records what his fellow Achaians did in the 220s after a series of brutal wars in the Peloponnesos (5.106.1–3): "The Achaians, as soon as they had put aside the war, . . . and the other cities throughout the Peloponnesos were trying to reacquire the same (lives they had before the wars): they were tending the land, and they were renewing their ancestral (πατρίας) sacrifices and festivals and the other traditions that they each individually had concerning the gods. For it was as if a forgetfulness (λήθην) about such things had occurred for most of them because of the unbroken sequence of wars that had gone before." In the worst of wartimes the land and the religious cults might be "forgotten" and neglected, but the Greek instinct was, as soon as circumstances allowed, to renew the land and to renew the ancestral religious traditions.

So too the Athenians responded after Chaeroneia—a relatively minor disaster for them, in comparison to that of the Achaeans—when the war was short and neither their land nor sanctuaries were damaged. All the more they turned to religious matters after the ravages of Lachares and the disastrous siege of Demetrios Poliorcetes in 294, after their freedom from Demetrios in 287/6, and then again after the Chremonidean War in the 260s. Finally, after the escape from Macedonian domination in 229, under Eurycleides' leadership they devoted attention to the land as well as to their religious institutions. But in an increasingly impoverished Athens, major, wholesale physical damage like that brought to the rural sanctuaries by Philip V in 201 could not be repaired. And likewise the damage—physical, economic, and psychological—wrought by Sulla in 86 was so extensive and Athens was so poor that thereafter permanent changes of much greater magnitude resulted. Now, for the first time, the restorations were qualitatively different—but that brings us to the end of the Hellenistic age in Athens and is a topic for another book.

In the Lycourgan period Athens was still relatively prosperous and had the funds and energy to devote to a religious revival. At the center of the this movement, as at the center of fifth-century state religion, was the cult of Athena Polias. Very early in Lycourgos' administration work was completed on the Panathenaic Stadium for Athena's major festival, the quadrennial Panathenaia. Various measures were taken to establish secure and lasting funding for the annual Lesser Panathenaia. Gold and silver processional vessels and gold jewelry for one hundred *kanēphoroi* were made for the procession of the Panathenaia. Most important symbolically for the association with the Periclean period was the restoration of the seven gold Nikai that had been melted down in the difficult times at the end of the Peloponnesian War. Authority over the cult of Athena Polias was held by Lycourgos' family, with himself and later his sons serving as priests of Poseidon-Erechtheus and a female from another branch of the Eteobutadai holding the goddess' priesthood. Lycourgos had special concerns with this cult, but happily his personal interest coincided with his statesman's role of promoting the state as a whole. In enhancing his and his family's cult he was also enhancing the major state cult of Athens.

Also fundamental to reasserting the essential place of religion in the Athenian social structure were the new buildings and remodeling of the sanctuaries of Apollo Patroös, one (along with Athena) divine ancestor of the Athenians; perhaps of Zeus Phratrios and Athena Phratria, the patrons of the phratries, which were key units in determining identity as Athenians; and of the eponymous heroes, the patrons of the political structure of the ten tribes. Further Lycourgan efforts were directed to the traditional but distinctively Athenian cults of the Dionysos of the theater and of Demeter and Kore at Eleusis. The theater enjoyed a major renovation, and significant new construction of a bridge and buildings was undertaken for Eleusis. Lycourgos, whose interest in tragedy is manifest in the *Leocrates*, himself was responsible for the law, exceptionally important for the survival of Athena drama, establishing canonical texts of Aeschylus, Sophocles, and Euripides. At Eleusis he not only tended to financial details but also introduced a law of ritual, forbidding women from riding on wagons in the great procession. And both Dionysos and Demeter also prospered from Lycourgos' more general financial innovations promoting the *kosmos* and securing the future for all cults.

A major addition to state cult was the acquisition of the healing sanctuary of Amphiaraos at Oropos and the creation of a new quadrennial Amphiaraia. This was new but hardly innovative in religious terms. Athens had long laid claim to the sanctuary, and the new festival was, from all appearances, very much along traditional lines. The acquisition of the Amphiaraion may have increased Athenian interest in healing cults in general, but this interest had probably been growing since the introduction of Asclepios to Athens in 420/19. Amphiaraos could provide, through dreams, some oracular information but apparently only that concerned with his own cult matters. There is no indication that the Athenians used his cult, as, for example, that of Apollo at Delphi or of Zeus at Dodona, as an oracle for state affairs. The Athenians lost Oropos after the Lamian War in 322, may have regained it from Demetrios Poliorcetes in 304/3, but then had lost it again by 287/6. Their claim to it and the Amphiaraion remained in the national consciousness, however, and in the late second century the ephebes annually made a day trip to the Amphiaraion, sacrificed there, and were reminded of the Athenian claims of ownership.

The one true cultic innovation in the Lycourgan age was the approval, by the state, of the purchase of land in Piraeus by the Citian devotees of Aphrodite Ourania for a cult site of their Cyprian goddess. This cult, limited to Citian nationals, was probably introduced as a favor and convenience to them, as the cult of Isis had been introduced for Egyptians some years before. We shall see that the introduction of foreign cults for foreign devotees in Piraeus occurred not irregularly in the following centuries but left virtually no evidence of an effect on Athenian state or private religion. The Citian cult of Aphrodite Ourania does, however, serve as our first if very small indicator of what will be a major factor in religious change later in the Hellenistic period: namely, the increasingly common phenomenon of Greeks and foreigners living abroad. We shall see that after the acquisition of Delos in 167/6 the effect on Athenian religion and Athenians was far greater when Athenians lived abroad as foreigners than when foreigners lived in Athens.

The Lycourgan innovation that was eventually to have a major impact on Athenian state religion was, in fact, not cultic or religious. It was the introduction or major remodeling of the *ephēbeia*, the program of two years of military training and acculturation for Athenian young men aged eighteen to twenty. Probably initially and throughout the Lycourgan period the *ephēbeia* was intended primarily as military and civic training, but it would become, within two centuries, a vehicle for the performance of a broad range of state sacrifices, rituals, and festivals. Just after Demetrios of Phaleron the *ephēbeia* was reduced in the number of participants and the length of term served, now just one year, and for a century the records are scant. After 229 the ephebic corps remained relatively small, only twenty to fifty young men each year, but the ephebes by that time have assumed a major role in the many state religious processions, contests, and sacrifices. We cannot date precisely the beginnings of this new religious activity of the ephebes, but the *terminus ante quem* is 215/4 (*SEG* 29.116). The most likely time for this major innovation is just after the liberation of Athens from the Macedonians in 229, in part because of the ephebes' association with Diogenes the "liberator" of Athens but also, and more tellingly, because several of the ephebes' activities now and in the next century had a strongly nationalistic, pro-democratic cast. These included the Aianteia and the procession for Demokratia on Salamis, the display in arms at the Epitaphia, the participation of the priest of Demos and the Charites, and later, among others, the display at the Theseia, the offering to the Marathonian dead, and the day trip to Oropos. The *ephēbeia* would grow, involving more than a hundred Athenian young men by 128/7, and the Athenians were, after 229, clearly indoctrinating the ephebes in a complex system of national and religious traditions.[1] The ephebes were also providing similar ritual and service functions in a wide range of public festivals, including the City Dionysia and the Eleusinian Mysteries. Whenever a procession, a contest, an escort, or a sacrifice requiring manpower was required, the ephebes were called upon.

There soon followed this "youth movement" for boys a "youth movement" for girls. In the classical and earlier Hellenistic period women were occasionally, girls hardly ever, honored publicly for their service as priestesses or other religious offices. But beginning as early as 220/19, we find increasingly large numbers of girls—numbers equaling those of ephebes—participating in major cults as *errēphoroi, ergastīnai*, and *kanēphoroi* and being publicly honored with statues and other dedications for their service. There is also a trend for Athenian priests to appoint their daughters and sons *kanēphoroi* and *kleidouchoi*. There had always been some participation of children in official cult at Athens,[2] but the numbers now, the greater range of activities, and the public honoring of the child participants are distinguishing features of religion in late Hellenistic Athens and reflect the more general interest in children in the Hellenistic literature and art.[3] This movement, intended perhaps as acculturation to Athenian national and religious traditions and no doubt as a venue for acquiring social prestige, grew throughout the period, culminating in the last years of the second century B.C. Then young men and women were participating regularly, some almost weekly it seems, in a wide array of national and international festivals. The mechanism for their involvement in religious affairs was put into place, however, by the institution or the remodeling of the *ephēbeia* in the Lycourgan age.

What is most evident, and what was clearly intended, in the age of Lycourgos is continuity with the past, with the religious traditions of the classical period. If we are careful not to telescope the evidence, significant changes that point to the future are few.[4] First and foremost is

---

1. On this aspect of the *ephēbeia* in Athens and elsewhere, see Nilsson 1967–74, 2:61–67.

2. Golden 1990, esp. 41–50, 65–72, 76–79.

3. Pollitt 1986, 128–130; Herter 1927.

4. Those who have studied the age of Lycourgos have tended, quite naturally, to focus their attention on it for its own sake, or, occasionally, on its relationship to the past, to the classical period. Few have considered its importance in the area of religion as a seminal time for the future. Sally Humphreys has addressed the issue most directly (1985, 1986), but even then in passing remarks. She sees, as elements of Hellenistic religion in the age of Lycourgos, the following: (1) the young are participating more extensively in cult; (2)

the establishment of the *ephēbeia*. Second is the now apparently systematic exploitation of the wealthy to support, in this period, the building and remodeling of religious buildings. Now we find some officials contributing substantial sums for such purposes to the cults they administered. In later periods the priests themselves were expected to do the same, apparently for the routine sacrifices and affairs of the cult they headed. And last, an important difference not so much in the administrative structure of religion as in psychology, is the first attestation of a phrase that soon becomes formulaic for expressing the purpose of a broad range of state religious activities: "For the health and safety of the Boule and Demos of the Athenians and their children, wives, and other possessions."

In "for health and safety" we may be seeing a first sign of a changed religious outlook, one that is now becoming defensive, perhaps even pessimistic in contrast to the higher expectations and optimism of the fifth century. Recent political and military events could certainly have

---

priests are supplementing funds for sacrifices in their cults; (3) interest in cult is moving from the cult center (the Acropolis) to the edges (Eleusis and Oropos); and (4) the introduction of foreign cults shows a "growing taste for the exotic in religious ritual, a feeling that only what was wild, strange, and altogether different from ordinary life was truly religious" (1986, 108). I would disagree with or limit each of these propositions. First, the young were not participating significantly more in cult than they had in the classical period, *but*, as we have just seen, the mechanism for this change, the *ephēbeia*, was put into place. There is, however, no evidence that the ephebes in the Lycourgan period were making a major contribution to Athenian religious life. Such a claim is possible only by retrojecting late-second- and first-century B.C. ephebic activity into the Lycourgan period, and the evidence does not warrant this. Second, some individuals were making financial contributions—as priests, officials, or as private citizens—to religious cults and in particular to the construction of religious buildings, probably at the urging of Lycourgos himself, and there is very little evidence of this (except for *chorēgiai*) from earlier periods. But the practice had apparently not, as it would later, become institutionalized in the sense of priests and other religious officials being routinely expected to use their own funds. Third, there is *no* evidence that religious interest in the Lycourgan period was moving from the Acropolis to the geographical "edges." Eleusis was prosperous and popular throughout the classical period, and the Athenians had always laid claim to Oropos. That they reacquired it in 335 and developed the cult there is an accident of history. Lycourgos himself was the priest of Poseidon-Erechtheus on the Acropolis and was by family and personally devoted to the cult of Athena Polias; much of his sacred building and restructuring of cult featured her cult. If anything it was a period of reassertion of the centrality of Acropolis cults. Lycourgos' interest in Piraeus can be explained militarily and economically, and there is no indication that development there was at the expense of Acropolis or Agora cults. And, finally, the introduction of cults of Isis and Aphrodite Ourania for a few foreigners in Piraeus would have had virtually no effect on state or private religion. The impact of foreign cults in Athens lay far, far in the future.

motivated this change, and future ones would certainly further its development. Most revealing among the latter were the introduction, in 307/6, of the cult of Antigonos I and Demetrios Poliorcetes as *Sōtērēs* and then the dismantling of this cult twenty years later. In 307/6 and for a few years afterward these Macedonian generals were providing "health and safety" to Athens in immediate ways much welcomed and appreciated by the Athenians; hence they were the Soteres, their festival was the Soteria, and concerns for "health and safety" were no doubt directed largely to them. Immediately after getting rid of Demetrios in 287/6 the Athenians, if my analysis is correct, transferred the festival to a new Zeus Soter and Athena Soteira, imported from Piraeus perhaps; henceforth throughout the Hellenistic period Athenian sacrifices and prayers "for health and safety" are directed to the gods, not to men. In addition to Zeus Soter and Athena Soteira, prayers for this purpose are widely attested for Dionysos, Asclepios, Amphiaraos, Apollo Prostaterios and Artemis Boulaia and Artemis Phosphoros as group, Demeter and Kore, Aglauros and Ares and Helios and the Horai as a group, Athena Polias, and Eirene. And very often is added, to the gods specified by name, "the other gods" or "the other ancestral gods," thus bringing all the state's gods into play. It is noteworthy that all these gods are expected to protect both "health" and "safety." Zeus Soter is asked for "health" as well as "safety;" Asclepios and Amphiaraos for "safety" as well as "health." The phrase "health and safety" encapsulates what the Athenians of the Hellenistic period were wanting from the gods for their government, for their wives and children, for their friends and allies, and for themselves.

We should like to be able define more precisely what Hellenistic Athenians meant by "health" and by "safety," but we are given little help from the texts.[5] "Health" would seem rather transparent, but it was not, I expect, the curing of diseases and the mending of broken bones. For that the healing gods Asclepios and Amphiaraos would suffice; Zeus Soter would not have a role. I suspect that the Athenians here meant more the "things necessary for a healthy life"; in these often very lean times, punctuated even with occasions of general starvation, such things

5. On the nature of "safety" and "saving gods" in this period, see Z. Stewart 1977, 551–57. On the terms "Soter" and "Euergetes" as applied to both gods and men, see Nock 1972, 720–35, esp. 720–27. On the relatively high proportion of new festivals founded for such "saving gods" in Greek cities in the Hellenistic period, see Chaniotis 1995, 153. For an excellent summary of the physical, political, economic, and other dangers that Greeks of the mainland were subject to in the Hellenistic period, see Nilsson 1967–74, 2:42–51.

would include food and other such essentials. "Safety" is often taken to mean "political safety," usually in the context of the preservation or restoration of the democratic institutions.[6] So it might naturally be understood in "the safety of the Boule" and perhaps even in "the safety of the Demos." Constituting the Demos, however, were also individual citizens, and by "the safety of their children and wives" was no doubt meant personal physical safety—safety from military attacks and the dangers of war that so immediately threatened and were, for the most part, now well beyond the control of Athenians. In the classical period the Athenians largely controlled their own food supplies and determined largely themselves when, where, and with whom they would make war.[7] After Chaeroneia and increasingly as time progressed, the Athenians were dependent on others for their food supply and were at the whim of powerful foreign generals and kings who might or might not invade, besiege, or even destroy Athens and massacre its residents. In these circumstances the Athenians understandably turned ever more to the gods "for health and safety," a phrase that apparently encompassed a large range of personal as well as political concerns. Emily Kearns (1990, 325) sees the areas of Greek life requiring "safety" or "deliverance" as breaking down into two groups: for the individual, death, disgrace, illness, injury, and poverty; for the city, defeat (in war), plague, famine, civil disturbance, and natural disasters. One can see how the phrase "health and safety" might come to be used to encompass all, or nearly all, of these.

Preoccupation with Macedonian expansionism had dominated Athenian politics since the 350s, and for the century after Philip's victory at Chaeroneia in 338 Athenian religion too was dramatically affected, directly or indirectly, by Macedonian influences. One might even perversely claim that Philip's victory motivated Athens' religious revival under Lycourgos. But after Athens' unsuccessful revolt against Macedon in the Lamian War and the occupation and garrisoning of Attica in 322, Macedonian influences on Athenian social, political, and religious life became much more immediate and would continue to be so for nearly

6. For the phrase "safety of the city" or "of the Demos" reflecting services rendered to Athenians during and after their revolt from Demetrios Poliorcetes in 287/6, see Shear 1978, 71 n. 201. For σωτηρία τῆς πόλεως as a technical term involving debates and decrees concerning the physical protection and general welfare of the state, see Rhodes 1972, 231–35.

7. Green, in contrasting the Hellenistic and classical periods, speaks of the "special kind of confidence that only self-determination can produce" (1990, 53).

a hundred years, until 229 B.C. The effects on Athenian religious life were varied: economic, psychological, artistic, physical, and institutional.[8]

The Macedonian garrison occupied the Mounichion Hill overlooking Piraeus on Boedromion 20, 322 B.C., the very day that initiates made their procession from Athens to Eleusis for the Mysteries. In his account of this traumatic event Plutarch (*Phoc.* 28.1–3) has the Athenians question the gods. In their despair they thought that the gods were no longer protecting even their own rituals. Nor, for that matter, were they protecting their own sanctuaries. The Macedonians chose, as their major fortress, the very hill immediately above the sanctuary of Artemis Mounichia, the goddess who had, a century and a half previously, helped the Athenians defeat the Persians. For Artemis the break with her Athenian devotees would have been physical as well as psychological. Because of the fort the Athenians probably could not reach the sanctuary and they certainly would not have sent their wives and daughters to the area. It is hardly surprising that the cult of Artemis Mounichia and her sister cult at Brauron disappear from the record for nearly two hundred years.

The presence and, in 229, the departure of Macedonian garrisons may well help to explain other elements of Athenian religious history. The cult of Theseus, the legendary synoecist of Attica, received a major boost with the recovery of his bones by Cimon in 476/5. But the cult of Theseus and the several festivals associated with him—the Synoikia, Oschophoria, Deipnophoria, and so on—disappear from the record during the period of Macedonian occupation, only to reappear when, after 166, Athens regained all of Attica and many of her former overseas possessions. The causes again may be both psychological and physical. When foreigners held much of Attica, Athenians had little cause to celebrate the hero who had unified it. And, physically, it would have been difficult and perhaps impossible to hold the processions to Phaleron required for several of these festivals.

During Macedonian occupation Piraeus was, at various times, under tighter or looser Macedonian control, but it appears throughout to have been quite isolated from the city.[9] Piraeus was, no doubt, impoverished, and this may have led to the loss of some major festivals. But

8. A. Stewart (1979, 27) speaks of the period 261–229 as an "almost total cultural hiatus." For more general accounts of the period in economic and social terms, see Day 1942, 4–14, 23–26; Rostovtzeff 1941, 215–18; Ferguson 1911, 182–85.

9. On Piraeus under Macedonian domination, see Taylor 1993, 214–26; Garland 1987, 45–53.

in its isolation Piraeus seems to have operated, in religious affairs, more as an independent country than a deme, as it did in earlier times. Piraeic deities, in particular Zeus Soter and Athena Soteira, appear more independent and national in character, less affiliated with Athenian state cults than similar deities in other demes. The isolation from Athens thus affected religion in Piraeus, but more significant for Athenian religious history is the impact on the city of Athens. In part the Macedonian occupation of Piraeus probably meant that now Athens, in contrast to the classical period, was largely cut off from trade with the rest of the Greek world, especially from the movement of foreign cults that were usually transported and established by foreign merchants and sailors. And even what foreign cults might find their way to Piraeus were then cut off from access to Athens itself. Foreign cults in Greek cities often got their foothold in harbor towns, as did those of the Egyptian Isis and the Cyprian Aphrodite Ourania in Piraeus in the fourth century. From the harbor towns those foreign cults which appealed to citizens might move inland to the larger population centers. In Athens this natural development was thwarted for the nearly hundred-year separation of Piraeus and Athens, and the closing off of Piraeus by the Macedonians helps explain the relative lack of foreign cults in both Piraeus and Athens itself in the early Hellenistic period.

In the aftermath of the Lamian War the Macedonian general Cassander controlled Athens, and as his "overseer" of Athens he installed an Athenian, Demetrios of Phaleron, in 317/6. Among the various measures introduced by the "tyrant" Demetrios during his ten-year reign, two were to have a lasting effect on Athenian religion. His limitation on the size and nature of funerary monuments brought to an end the rich tradition of sculpted funerary reliefs that had flourished since the 420s. These now were replaced by columns, plaques, and other such simple monuments, and the elaborate reliefs, with a few possible exceptions, were not to appear again until the mid–second century B.C.[10] Demetrios also eliminated the *chorēgia*, the classical but recently criticized system by which individual wealthy citizens each year were appointed to pay for individual dithyrambic choruses and for the productions of individual tragic and comic poets at the City Dionysia and other such festivals. He replaced the forty-five *chorēgoi* with a single, annually elected individual, the *agōnothetēs*. The Demos itself now became the *chorēgos*, but the *agōnothetēs* administered the contests of the major

---

10. Schmidt 1991, 43–44.

festivals and, probably from the very beginning, contributed significant funds of his own for the embellishment of the festivals. In one sense the innovation was democratic: the Demos, by the election of the *agōnothetēs* and by financial support, took control of its own festivals. But the establishment of one individual over the contests of major festivals simultaneously narrowed citizen participation in the production of the festivals.[11] The replacement of the *chorēgoi* by the *agōnothetēs* under Demetrios may be a sign that these festivals were beginning to be put on "*for*" the Demos by the government and by a single wealthy individual rather than "*by*" the Demos for the Demos. The actors were now professionals; many of the playwrights were foreign; and, one suspects, unlike in much earlier times when more or less ordinary fellow citizens were chorus members, actors, poets, and *chorēgoi*, the audiences now felt themselves increasingly to be spectators at events staged in their behalf.[12] The *agōnothetai* even in the third century contributed large sums of money to ensure the success of the festivals of their years, but the culmination of this new trend came only at the end of our period when, in 99/8, the ultrarich Medeios apparently himself financed a good share of Athens' whole religious program. But the narrowing of the citizen base for the financial support of the festivals that made these later developments possible and perhaps even inevitable is owed to Demetrios of Phaleron.

Demetrios the tyrant was also a philosopher, a leading Peripatetic of his time, and his career offers a rare opportunity to see the intersection of politics, religion, and philosophy in the period. Demetrios' innovations in religious institutions may well owe their origins, if not their details, to contemporary discussions in philosophical circles. Like Demetrios the philosophers of the time, including Aristotle and Theophrastos, were patronized by Macedonians and were themselves pro-Macedonian in their politics. Unlike Demetrios they were almost all foreigners who had no right by birth and who showed no inclination as foreign residents to participate in or to contribute to Athenian state cult. They were well-known and respected, often publicly honored members of the social community, and they no doubt attended literary, musical,

---

11. As Green puts it, the elimination of such liturgies was "one more nail in the coffin of individual civic pride, of personal involvement in the affairs of the *polis*" (1990, 46).

12. Cf. Green (1990, 527) on the "increasing trend toward professionalism: one more symptom of that move away from all-round amateur involvement that had been the hallmark of the *polis* in its classical heyday; one more similarity with our own age, a world of spectator sports, or organized shows, of passive, non-participating audiences."

and athletic contests at the major festivals, but they would not as members of the religious community sacrifice or be included among the beneficiaries ("the Demos of the Athenians, their children and wives") of sacrifices and other rituals performed by Athenians. Moreover, living abroad they would be isolated from the religious rituals of their various homelands. These foreign philosophers formed at the Academy, in the Lyceum, and elsewhere quite separate, independent societies with, in each case, a cult of the Muses as their patrons. But these philosophical societies were hardly religious in the conventional sense, and there is no evidence that they had any formal or informal associations with Athenian public cult. These philosophers prospered under Macedonian rule in Athens, but in the moments of Athenian rebellion or independence they could become victims.

Charges of impiety were raised against Aristotle at the time of the Lamian War and against Theophastos a few years later, in Aristotle's case for giving greater than human honors to his friend and patron, Hermeias the tyrant of Atarneus. There was no doubt an anti-Macedonian political element to the bringing of these charges, as there was a political element in the attacks on Socrates at the beginning of the century. And in both cases religious accusations were a convenient weapon. But in both cases the specific charges must have arisen from popular concerns of the time, and for Aristotle the charge was that he was treating a human ruler as one usually treated a god. And with Aristotle's devotion to Hermeias and likewise with the devotion of Plato's successors to the Academy's founder, the philosophers may have opened the door conceptually, in Athens, to ruler cult.

Scholars have often assumed ruler cult to be a fundamental and distinguishing characteristic of Hellenistic Greek religion, an important and widespread mechanism for constructing the new political, social, and religious realities.[13] In Athens, in fact, ruler cult had a very brief history, essentially that of Demetrios Poliorcetes from 307/6 to 287 B.C.; and then, after a brief flirtation with Antigonos Gonatas, it ended. Only at the very end, two hundred years later, do we find the misguided partisans of Mithridates speaking of their champion as a god, as a New Dionysos. Athens' two tries at ruler cult, the aborted one for Alexander in 324 and that for Demetrios Poliorcetes in 307/6, were both di-

---

13. For the development of Hellenistic ruler cult and its relationship to contemporary beliefs about gods and heroes, see Price 1984, 23–40; Z. Stewart 1977, 562–77; Nilsson 1967–74, 2:132–85.

rected toward Macedonians and were both formal enactments of the Ekklesia. The debate about Alexander's divinity in 324/3 generated sarcastic comments from Demosthenes and Lycourgos, but, for largely political reasons, the Ekklesia voted to make Alexander a god. The cult, if it was in fact ever established, certainly came to an end shortly with Alexander's death and the Lamian War. The complaints of the orator Hyperides about the now-defunct Alexander cult in his funeral speech over the Athenian dead of the Lamian War are, interestingly, the last recorded criticisms from the Greek world about the inappropriateness of ruler cult on general or theoretical grounds.[14]

The circumstances and the motives for the cult of Demetrios Poliorcetes and his father Antigonos Monophthalmos were significantly different from those of Alexander. Antigonos promised and Demetrios delivered to Athens in 307/6 and later in 304/3 political freedom, a restoration of democracy, physical safety, and food, all elements of Athenian life thought to be owed in good part to the gods.[15] Antigonos and Demetrios did, basically, provide divine services to the Athenians, and the Athenians in an outpouring of gratitude and relief honored them as *Sōtēres* and established for them the apparatus of divine cult: an altar, sacrifices, festival, hymn, and golden statues.

I have discussed in *Honor Thy Gods* (1991) and, more briefly, here in chapter 3 how, in the Greek tradition, "honor" is a notion fundamental to understanding much of divine cult. "Honor" was what was due to gods for great services, and that "honor" toward the gods was rendered through the "gifts" of sacrifice, hymns, dedications, and other such things. And it is important that the "honor" rendered to gods was not, generically, unlike that rendered to men for their service, but, in the classical period, the services provided by men to their fellow men were of a different and lower order than those provided by the gods and so were the "gifts" expressing that honor. For the Athenians the deeds or "services" of Antigonos and Demetrios now surpassed the usual, human level, and so the "gifts" expressing "honor" were elevated to the divine level. Alexander, we might recall, when he asked an Indian Gymnosophist the impossible question "How might a human

14. F. Walbank 1987, 380.

15. On this important point, see Tarn and Griffith 1952, 52–54, who, however, view ruler cult exclusively as political: "It had nothing to do with religious feeling." Significantly, they comment: "The Olympians conferred no personal salvation, no hope of immortality, little spirituality." If that is our definition of "religious feeling," classical Greek religion lacked it also.

being become a god," was told, "If he should do something which it is impossible for a human being to do" (Plut. *Alex.* 64.4). Alexander found that answer acceptable.

The change in the types of "gifts" now given to these exceptional men was certainly significant, but it was facilitated and is understandable in the Greek tradition, I would argue, because the feelings of "honor" owed to gods and men were not fundamentally different.[16] Aristotle offers us the best ancient and nearly contemporary commentary on this:

> Honor is a indicator of a reputation for benefaction, and justly and especially those who have provided a benefaction are honored. But in addition also one able to provide a benefaction (but not yet having done so) is honored. The benefaction may concern either safety and the other things responsible for existence, or wealth, or any of the other good things of which the acquisition is not easy, either in general or at a given place or time. Many men receive honor for what seem to be small things, but for that the places and situations are the reason. The constituent parts of honor are sacrifices, memorials in verse or prose, gifts of honor, sanctuaries, front-row seating at public events, tombs, statues, board at state expense, the things given by non-Greeks such as *proskynēsis* and yielding place, and gifts that are, in each people, held in honor. (Arist. *Rhet.* 1361a28–b2)

In the *Rhetoric*, completed in the 330s,[17] Aristotle shows that the linkages I see fundamental to the nature of Greek ruler cult were established even before any such cult of Macedonian kings had been broached in the Greek world: "honor" directly results from good services properly recognized; the areas of "good service" involve safety, things necessary for life (presumably food, water, and good health), and financial prosperity; and gifts express this "honor." Note too that Aristotle simply lists, with no fundamental distinction, the "constituent parts of honor" belonging to gods (sacrifices, written memorials, and sanctuaries) and those belonging to men (front-row seating, tombs, statues, etc.). Finally, relevant in the context of ruler cult is Aristotle's comment that "Many men receive honor for what seem to be small things, but for that the places and situations are the reason." In 307 and in 304 B.C., it was in fact the specific situations that led the Athenians to give divine "honors" to Demetrios Poliorcetes for what must certainly *not* have seemed small matters to them.

16. Cf. Z. Stewart 1977, 565.
17. On the date of Aristotle's *Rhetoric*, see Kennedy 1991, 6.

If this is all correct, one should be wary of the many scholarly discussions of ruler cult that distinguish sharply between "genuine religious belief" (usually left undefined) and the awarding of "godlike honors."[18] The awarding of divine honors, I would claim, is central, not peripheral, to "genuine religious belief" in the Greek tradition. However much we may disparage it, Greeks and even Athenians for a time were honoring these rulers as "gods"—not because they thought them immortal, but because they were receiving from them what, in the circumstances, only gods could give.

Initially support for the new gods was broadly based and widely advocated. Demetrios himself in cult was assimilated to Dionysos, Zeus (Kataibates), Apollo Pythios, and Demeter. But in 304/3 when the *Sōtēr* moved to Athens for a year, when he brought his debaucheries to the Parthenon and indulged himself playing Dionysos, his welcome began to fade. Opposition emerged from a few prominent religious and political figures, but, more important, Demetrios himself turned from benefactor of democratic Athens to its oppressor with the brutal siege of 295/4. His band of supporters in Athens continued to shower him with ever-more extravagant divine honors, but the Athenian populace quite probably was by now, for political and religious reasons, alienated from him. The divine honors given enthusiastically to Demetrios in 307/6 had become, largely through the behavior of Demetrios and his supporters, a travesty, and most Athenians were no doubt happy to see their Macedonian Dionysos depart in 287/6.

Among the honors Antigonos and Demetrios received in 307/6 was to be named eponyms of two new tribes, Antigonis and Demetrias, and thus to join the ranks of legendary eponymous heroes such as Erechtheus and Ajax. These tribal cults survived the "de-Demetricizing" of Athenian religion after 287/6, and in fact only this "heroic" honor persisted in later Athenian "ruler cult." Ptolemy III Euergetes, apparently because of assurances of protection to Athens, was made eponym of a new tribe, Ptolemais, in 224; and in 200, after Antigonis and Demetrias had been eliminated, a new ally, Attalos the king of Pergamon, was given his tribe, Attalis, at the outset of the Second Macedonian War. These tribal honors can, however, scarcely be understood as ruler cult in the usual sense, because the religious elements are limited to one segment, about one-twelfth of the population. There is no evidence that the hero received statewide sacrifices, altars, or prayers in the role of

18. For a recent example of drawing such a distinction, see Green 1990, 402–3.

Sōtēr or benefactor (*euergetēs*).[19] Perhaps as a result of their experience with the divine Demetrios the Athenians henceforth limited the role of their benefactors, whether Macedonian, Egyptian, or Pergamene, to being—along with themselves, their children, and their wives—the beneficiaries and not the recipients of sacrifices and prayers. These benefactors were brought into the religious community, not set above it. The experience of true ruler cult in Athens was bitter, but short.

At the ouster of Demetrios Poliorcetes in 287/6 the Athenians began to de-Demetricize their cults and repair the damage. This process was long, was interrupted by the Chremonidean War, and could not be said to have been completed until the 240s. However, it was necessary, setting the stage for the resurgence of traditional, Lycourgan state religion when Athens finally gained her independence in 229. The Athenians first removed the Demetrieia from the City Dionysia, renewed the celebration of the Mysteries and the Eleusinia at Eleusis, and held again, after an interruption of four or eight years, the Great Panathenaia. These were all accomplished by 282 at the latest. The Soteria, the major festival of Demetrios and his father, was remodeled into a festival of Zeus Soter and Athena Soteira. Just at this time we see traces of a short-lived attempt to establish Zeus Eleutherios/Soter as the primary protector of Athens' political freedom, a diminution of the role of the Acropolis cult of Athena Polias in this regard. For a time Athena, now as Ergane, was to look more to Athens' economic and business interests, and Athenians directed more attention to Agora cults for protection of the state as a whole. This, if the slight evidence is not misleading, would be a major effect of Demetrios' desecration of Athena's cult on the Acropolis. The three cults of Athens co-opted by Demetrios thus underwent major changes upon his departure, as Dionysos and the Eleusinian deities returned to their Lycourgan status, and Athena was temporarily transformed. And, finally, again soon after the king's ouster the Athenians began officially to participate again in international religious festivals, the Ptolemaia of Ptolemy II and the Soteria established by the Amphictionic Council to celebrate the Greek victory over the Galatians at Delphi in 279.

Of particular interest is that now, after the two decades of the divine

19. Athens' relationships with one such tribal eponym can best be understood from Habicht's survey (1990a = 1994, 184–201) of her benefactions from and honors to Attalos I and the members of his family who succeeded him as king of Pergamon. Attalos and his successors are "kings" not "gods," and they are awarded human, not "godlike," honors.

Demetrios, sacrifices "for health and safety" again are made to the traditional deities: to Asclepios, Dionysos, Demeter and Kore, and to the newly popular Apollo Prostaterios, Zeus Soter, and Athena Soteira. During his domination of Athens Demetrios Poliorcetes was the *Sōtēr* of Athens, and as such would naturally receive the appropriate offerings. But immediately upon his departure the Athenians took up again the practice, begun in the age of Lycourgos, of making such offerings to the gods; they would do so throughout the rest of the Hellenistic period.

Athens' growing prosperity and eagerness to recover Piraeus led her, in the early 260s, to form a Greek alliance and revolt against Demetrios' son, Antigonos Gonatas. After two sieges, the war ended disastrously, and in 262/1 Antigonos through appointees and garrisons took tight control of Athens and Attica. The evidence is sparse, but it appears that the major Athenian cults did not recover from this catastrophe until the late 250s or the 240s. The Great Panathenaia first reappears in 254, just after Antigonos had somewhat relaxed his hold on Athens. Around 255/4 the City Dionysia is again attested after a lapse of fifteen years. In this same period there was inventorying of dedications to Asclepios (Aleshire, #V), the first such inventory in thirty years, and of dedications on the Acropolis (Pollux 10.126). By the 240s the status of Athenian cults seems to have been stabilized from both the desecrations of Demetrios and the effects of the Chremonidean War. Eleusis was functioning normally, the major festivals of the Panathenaia and City Dionysia were being held, and Asclepios and the Acropolis deities were accumulating dedications. Sacrifices were being made to a number of traditional deities for "the health and safety of the Demos, their children and wives," and added to these beneficiaries, not as a god but as a man, was Antigonos Gonatas. And, finally, in 246/5, for the first time since the 270s, the Athenians again participated in the Delphic Soteria. Athena Polias and Aglauros, both Acropolis-oriented deities, are prominent in the evidence for the 240s; together with the renewal of other cults described above, they suggest that finally, after forty years, the Athenians had successfully restored their religious system to its pre-Demetrian, Lycourgan status.

In 229 the Athenians bought their freedom from the Macedonian garrisons and control. The changes we have surveyed in Athenian religious affairs since 323 were surely by-products of the Macedonian dominance, not the result of any systematic Macedonian policy. The temporary loss of Artemis Mounichia, the effects on foreign cults of the isolation of

Piraeus, and even Demetrios' bizarre behavior that tarnished Athena Polias and soured the Athenians on ruler cult resulted only secondarily from the Macedonians' other purposes and concerns. The original deification of Demetrios Poliorcetes and his father was, I think, a spontaneous outpouring of emotion and gratitude by Athenians at large, but the extension and extravagance of later honors were orchestrated by that group of now-powerful Athenians who owed their authority to Demetrios. The Macedonians are always there in the background, but the real changes in Athenian religion in the period are the product of Athenian internal politics and social life. The case is otherwise for the Macedonians' devastating final, parting shot. In 201 Philip V in a fit of rage systematically and barbarically had Attica's rural shrines, temples, altars, and tombs destroyed—irreparably destroyed. This was apparently the fatal blow to very many rural and deme cults that had been a vibrant element of Athenian religious life in the classical period but had been struggling since at least the end of the fourth century. Henceforth Athenian public religion, or at least our evidence for it, is largely restricted to the urban centers of Athens and Piraeus and to Eleusis and the forts. The later increased participation we shall see in the urban cults may be a result in part of the greater urbanization and prosperity of Athenian life, but in part also of the impoverishment or loss of rural cults and their priesthoods, sacrifices, occasional festivals, and treasuries. Those rural cults that reappear after Philip's destruction were primarily those reflecting Athenian nationalism: monuments, tombs, and sanctuaries associated with the great victories at Marathon in 490 and Salamis in 480. But to judge from the epigraphical and archaeological evidence, hundreds and perhaps thousands of other rural cults ceased to exist.

Also owed quite directly to Macedonian kings and generals was the internationalizing of Athenian tragedy and comedy. This led in turn to the formation of the Athenian (and other) *technītai* of Dionysos, the guild of professional poets, actors, and musicians. Alexander shared his grandfather's and father's taste for Athenian drama and brought to perform and converse at his banquets numerous Athenian poets and actors. As Alexander and his successors then undertook to stage magnificent festivals on the Greek model, they needed ready and organized troupes to perform, and the Athenian *technītai* and other guilds were formed to satisfy this need. The result was often a separation of the Dionysiac contests from festivals of Dionysos, with tragedy and comedy now produced at festivals of other deities or even in secular settings. In Athens itself there was an increased professionalism and internationalism in the poets, performers, and contests of the dramatic festivals. In a sense Athenian tragedy and comedy had become less "Athenian" and more "Greek."

Underlying the whole Macedonian period is the Athenian impulse, after each dislocation caused by external or internal forces, to restore τὰ πάτρια, the "ancestral practices." After 287/6 the Athenians began a forty-year effort, itself interrupted by a war and further losses, to reclaim the damage that they, the divine Demetrios, and his successor Antigonos Gonatas had done to traditional religion. The model of "the ancestral traditions" was, for this generation of Athenians, the age of Lycourgos, and those traditions had been kept alive throughout this period in part by the Atthidographers. From Chaeroneia to the Chremonidean War, Phanodemos, Philochoros, and their fellow Athenian writers were putting on record even the most archaic and esoteric Athenian religious traditions, and as prominent Athenians the Atthidographers must have been a force for revival after Demetrios as Phanodemos had been after Chaeroneia. This religious revival after 287/6, interrupted by the Chremonidean War, was not complete until the late 250s or the 240s, but that was well in time for the resurgence of an independent Athens after 229. Just as Athens attempted to return, in times of freedom, to the Lycourgan democracy and democratic institutions after oppressions of foreign or foreign-supported tyrannies and oligarchies, so in religion she returned to the Lycourgan model. The return, of course, could not be complete. Precedents had been set, such as the tribal cults for Demetrios and Antigonos, and not everything was rooted out; but the changes that survived the restorations, in comparison to the continuity, were few, small, and relatively inconsequential. The history of Athenian religion in this period is not flat and is not linear. It is a sequence of waves, of dislocations followed by restorations, and the classical traditions as formulated and interpreted by the Lycourgan age formed the model for the restorations.[20]

Upon their liberation in 229 the Athenians created, near the Stoa of Zeus in the Agora, a new cult: that of Demos and the Charites. This new cult, I have argued, was intended to express Athenian gratitude to the

20. For a study of the changing styles of Athenian sculpture during the Hellenistic period, of the negative effect on Athenian sculpture and sculptors of the Macedonian occupation, and of the revival after 229 and especially after 167/6, all in many ways offering intriguing analogies to religious changes in these times, see A. Stewart 1979.

foreigners who had assisted them *and* to promote what impoverished and war-torn Athens at this time particularly craved: democracy, peace, and agricultural prosperity. It was a new cult in a new location, but it was closely affiliated with some of the most ancient and revered cults of Athens.

It was Diogenes, the Macedonian commandant and (now) Athenian citizen, whom the Athenians convinced, with 150 talents, to remove the garrisons in 229. Then or shortly thereafter they rewarded him, as a benefactor (*euergetēs*), with divine honors, a palaestra in his name (Diogeneion), and a festival (Diogeneia). Diogenes, like Demetrios Poliorcetes in 307/6, had restored freedom and democracy to Athens, a feat beyond the power of Athenians themselves. The cult, palaestra, and festival of Diogenes were all intimately and primarily associated with the ephebes, and we find just in these years after the liberation of Athens a resurgence of interest in the *ephēbeia*, the *ephēbeia* that had essentially been created in not dissimilar circumstances in the national revival after Chaeroneia.

The epigraphical evidence, virtually the only evidence we have for religious activity in this period, would indicate that Athenians and their families were still participating widely in state but not in private cults.[21] For the time from independence (229/8) to the takeover of Delos in 167/6, only three "private" citizen cults—that is, cults not financed by the state and not directed to the welfare of the state as a whole or a traditional subunit of it—are attested: a *koinon* of Asclepiastai on the south slope of the Acropolis; the Piraeic cult of the Mother of the Gods, which, following its uncertain origins, had become entirely citizen and was now flourishing; and the fifteen *orgeōnes* of the Piraeic *koinon* of Dionysiastai founded and headed by the members of one family.[22] The latter two cults in particular had as members some prominent Athenians and give us our best evidence of private cults standing apart from state, local, and domestic cults. It would appear that apart from the one Piraeic cult of the Mother of the Gods, most such cults in this and earlier times were very small and short-lived. With the exception, again, of the Mother of the Gods, the private Athenian *koina* surveyed in chapter 5, mostly of the late fourth century and early third century, have all

21. Tarn and Griffith (1952, 93–95) note that most private clubs, religious or secular, of the Hellenistic period were for foreign, not citizen, residents of a state.

22. On these cults, see chapters 5, pp. 145–46, and 6, pp. 203–06. On the Amphiarastai of this period, see above, chapter 5, p. 150.

disappeared from the record by this time. There may well have been other private cults that left no epigraphical record, but if such cults were numerous one would expect to find, at the least, inscribed altars or boundary stones.

The case is much the same for cults practiced by foreigners. Bendis, Ammon, Sabazios, Isis, the Citian Aphrodite Ourania, Tynabos, Zeus Labraundos, and the *thiasos* of Artemis have all disappeared. Sarapis is the only new foreign deity to emerge in this period, with a substantial following of foreign Sarapiastai allowed and perhaps encouraged to honor this deity because of the growing Athenian pro-Ptolemaic and pro-Egyptian sentiments after 229. Some foreign cults too may have escaped the epigraphical record, but there is no evidence to indicate that either private or foreign cults were a major factor in religion in Athens at this time. This is all the more noteworthy since such cults are usually considered characteristic of Hellenistic religion.[23] The real exposure of Athenians to foreign deities and the real participation of Athenians in their cults was to come only when the Athenians took over and managed religious affairs on Delos.

Individualism, whether in domestic political attitudes, philosophy, art, or religion, is commonly considered a distinguishing feature of the Hellenistic period, in Athens as elsewhere.[24] In religion, it is almost universally claimed, individuals found state cults and deities unsatisfying and abandoned or ignored them, turning instead to foreign deities who offered more direct, personal, and meaningful relationships and to private cult associations that offered a more immediate sense of community.[25] For Athens there is, as we have seen, little evidence, certainly no more (despite fuller records) than in the classical period, either for the introduction of foreign deities or for participation in private cult associations. Increased individualism in Athenian religion of the Hellenistic period is instead much more subtle, to be found *within* state cult and not apart from it. The evidence is insufficient to chronicle the full development, but in very general and simplistic terms, I see it as follows. In classical Athens state cult—whether it be the festivals of the Pana-

23. For a general survey of the spread of foreign cults in the Hellenistic period, properly broken down by deity, date, and region, see Nilsson 1967–74, 2:119–31.

24. For the rise of individualism in general in the Hellenistic period, see Green 1990, 337, 567, 587–91, 602, 609; in Athenian sculpture, A. Stewart 1979, *passim*, but esp. 115–26, 141; in philosophy and its Athenian environment, Long 1974, 2–4, 163.

25. Tarn and Griffith 1952, 338.

thenaia or the City Dionysia, sacrifices of the demesmen of Erchia, or the secret rites of the Arrephoria—was thought to be performed by, paid for, and done for the sake of the Demos at large. Individuals, of course, performed the sacrifices, carried the baskets in the processions, sometimes (if ordered to do so) paid the costs of choral performances, and so forth, but they did so largely as anonymous members (πολῖται) of the Demos. Despite exceptional cases and despite exceptional types of roles (*chorēgoi*, for example), one performed one's religious duties and services in state cult primarily as a member of the state community, with, compared to later periods, relatively little attention paid to or sought for oneself.[26] By the late Hellenistic period, however, we find that individuals were being, and no doubt wanting to be, widely honored by name, with statues, and on inscriptions for their service as priests, priestesses, *kanēphoroi, ergastīnai,* and *arrēphoroi;* for their dedications; and especially for their financial contributions for religious purposes. Fathers and mothers honored their daughters, children honored their parents, the Ekklesia honored priests, and long lists of financial contributors to the Pythaïdes and other religious festivals were inscribed on stones displayed publicly. Put in another way, there were now far more new statues representing identifiable men, women, and children in a sanctuary than there were new statues and dedications representing the deity. This is, of course, just part of the broader trend of Hellenistic Greeks to honor one another with crowns, statues, decrees, and titles for an increasing variety of reasons (no doubt itself another sign of individualism).[27] But in the context of religion, these types of honors do tend to set the individual apart from the corporate body of citizens worshipping together and through one another in the classical period. More precisely, I think, in Athens it tends to isolate for attention individual families from the corporate body; nearly as many Hellenistic religious honorific decrees stem from or emphasize the family of the honoree as honor the one individual him- or herself. We have seen how many stat-

---

26. Demosthenes (23.198) noticed a similar difference between his time and the early fifth century when discussing "honors" given by the state: "There is no one of that time who would say that the sea battle at Salamis belonged to Themistocles. No, he would say it belonged to the Athenians. Nor that the Battle of Marathon belonged to Miltiades; rather it belonged to the city. But now many say that Timotheos took Corcyra, that Iphicrates cut down the Spartan force, that Chabrias won the sea battle at Naxos."

27. On this trend in Athens and especially through portrait sculpture, see A. Stewart 1979, *passim*, esp. 115–26. On the nature and spread of such honors throughout the Hellenistic world, see Habicht 1995.

ues and other dedications there are now honoring children, often erected by their parents, and in chapter 6 we saw how many fathers and other family members appointed relatives to religious posts under their jurisdiction. Individuals now wanted and expected public recognition for themselves and their families for their religious services. Counterexamples certainly exist of self-promotion in religious affairs in the classical period and of group identity in the Hellenistic periods, but I would argue that the evidence in aggregate indicates significant new and growing interest in such individual and family honors in the Hellenistic period. Individualism in the religion of Hellenistic Athens was played out *through*, not apart from, state cult; and, perhaps at the expense of social unity, it involved the recognition of individual families as much or more than that of single people.[28]

In 167/6 the Romans gave Athens Delos in return for her help in the Third Macedonian War. The Delians were banished from their own island, and suddenly the Athenians were faced with managing the complex and internationally prominent cult structure of the prior inhabitants. Among the existing cults were those of Apollo and Artemis, the particularly Delian cults of Hestia, Zeus Cynthios, and Anios, and also the relatively new cults of Asclepios, the Megaloi Theoi, the Cabeiroi, and Sarapis. As we have seen in chapter 7, the Athenians had recourse to their usual administrative practices and divided the Delian cults into ten units, some having more than one god, and annually selected ten priests from among themselves, one to tend each of the ten cultic units. The Athenians tended to "Atticize" some of these cults, most notably by adding an Athenaia to the Apollonia and by adding or emphasizing an Athena Cynthia alongside Zeus Cynthios. More important, however, some of the annual Athenian priests became personally quite interested in the deities they served, erecting dedications and even contributing major buildings. Athenian priests and laymen showed attention particularly to the cults of Zeus Cynthios and Athena Cynthia, the combined cults of the Theoi Megaloi, Dioscouroi, and the Cabeiroi in the Samothrakeion, and the cult of the Egyptian Isis and Sarapis. By 150 B.C. the Athenians had also allowed the establishment of a cult of the

---

28. "Individualism" in religion for a foreigner living in Athens would have been quite different from that for a citizen, of course. There is very little evidence for the former, but Graf (1995) offers valuable comments on the well-documented case of the religious activities of Artemidoros of Perge when he lived in Thera.

Syrian deities Atargatis and Hadad, and this cult found quick favor among the Athenians themselves. By 112 the deities have been given Greek names, Aphrodite Hagne and Zeus Hadatos, and have an annual Athenian priest. These Athenian priests and Athenian laymen also contributed numerous dedications and major buildings to the sanctuary. In 110/09 even the Athenian Demos, at the request of Aphrodite Hagne, dedicated a building to her on Delos.

The cults of Sarapis and Atargatis seem particularly to have captured the attention of the Athenians, and both are notable in being largely foreign to Athenian traditions. Both had oriental-type cult structures; there were Athenian priests, along with *kleidouchoi* and *kanēphoroi* (often relatives of the priest), but foreigners and even slaves served in other capacities. The deities of both cults also could order, through dreams probably, their devotees, their priests, and even the Athenian state to make dedications. On Delos these two cults had also a strongly international following, and in these and some other cults there Athenians had their first experience of worship, side by side, with Syrians, Romans, and citizens of many other states, and with freedmen and slaves. And in several of these cults the Athenians would have found themselves a small minority of the devotees.

The Athenians, I expect, were relatively isolated from much of the Greek and Eastern world during the nearly hundred years of Macedonian dominance and occupation, from the loss of the Lamian War in 322 to their final freedom in 229. There were, of course, philosophers from many Greek states teaching and studying in Athens during this period, but there is little evidence that they influenced Athenian society at large. The closure of Piraeus to the free movement of trade and people was an important determinant, especially in religious matters. It almost certainly inhibited the cosmopolitanism of Athens, in both religious and social terms, in the early Hellenistic period. Delos was, in 167/6, more cosmopolitan in social and political terms, but traditional religion remained very strong for the Delians themselves. The peculiar historical situation of Delos in 167/6, the expulsion of the Delians, the Athenian takeover of the cults, and the swarms of foreign merchants, traders, and sailors favored quick changes in the religious situation there. Eastern cults were promoted at the expense of traditional and local Delian cults, and new foreign cults were welcomed. And the Athenians themselves, living abroad and less restricted by their own domestic religious traditions, appear to have participated energetically in many of these new cults.

When living on Delos the Athenians as priests, other cult officials, or simply as individuals practiced cults like those of Sarapis and Atargatis. But interestingly, these same Athenians—many of whose families we can follow—back in Athens still themselves (or members of their families) continued to follow the old Athenian traditions, serving Athena Polias, Asclepios, and other state deities. There is little evidence that Athenians who had experienced life on Delos then immediately transported back to Athens wholesale the more exotic cults they had practiced when abroad. The importation to Athens of the cult of the Theoi Megaloi was apparently not successful, and only a few private dedications survive for an Athenian Aphrodite Hagne. The real effect on Athenians of the Delian experience was cosmopolitanism, which was in turn to have its real effect on Athenian religion in the rebuilding and perhaps even reconception of many Athenian cults and practices after the devastation of the city by Sulla and his troops in 86 B.C. For our period the clearest indication, in Athens itself, of this new cosmopolitanism is the admittance, from 123/2 on, of foreigners into the Athenian *ephēbeia*. In 123/2 only 14 of the 127 ephebes were foreign, but by 102/1 40 of the 141. Since by now the ephebes as a corps were heavily involved in the activities of the oldest and most traditional state cults, the shift means that now foreigners, for the first time in Athenian history, were participating in a regular, pro-grammatic, and long-term manner in native Athenian cults. Foreigners were not as yet officials of cult, but through the *ephēbeia* Athenian reli-gion itself was beginning to be internationalized. We see also signs of Delian-inspired cosmopolitanism now in the appearance of some Athe-nians and foreigners worshipping together in Athens in cults of Isis, of Aphrodite Hagne, and of other foreign deities. This incipient cos-mopolitanism in Athenian cult would become an important factor in the reconstruction of Athenian religion after Sulla.

On Delos the Athenian religious service at the end of the second cen-tury was characterized by multiple offices and even multiple priesthoods (though not in one year), by the high social status of these officehold-ers, by the often very large and expensive dedications and defrayals of cultic expense by the priests, and by the involvement in the cult of sev-eral members of the families of the officeholders. Most significantly, de-spite our rather extensive evidence there is no indication of exclusive devotion to one cult or one deity. Even those who served Isis and Sara-pis or Aphrodite Hagne might, the next year, serve another quite differ-ent cult, and their children might well be involved in other cults on Delos or in very traditional cults back in Athens.

These features of Athenian religious activity on Delos can be paralleled in Athens itself and surely reflect the times, politically as well as religiously. The major development in these years in Athens, from ca. 100 to 90 B.C., is that, rather suddenly, fewer individual families participate in the state cult and these fewer families assume much larger financial burdens for religious activities. Eventually Medeios of Piraeus (*PA* 10098) and Sarapion of Melite (*PA* 12564), who were also political leaders in a now narrow oligarchy, held multiple religious offices each year and between them provided much of the money required for the major festivals. The close association of financial and cultic support with a few political leaders meant, of course, that the success and future of state cult was now dangerously tied to the political fortunes of these few leaders; this too was a new situation in the religious history of Athens, new at least since the tyranny of Peisistratos in the sixth century. The chaos in religious life just after the forced departure of the anti-Mithridatic Medeios, Sarapion, and their like is reported by Poseidonios of Apamea: sanctuaries were closed, the theater had no gatherings, and the Eleusinian Mysteries were not being celebrated. Quite remarkably it seems to have been the *technītai* of Dionysos, that guild of internationally experienced actors, musicians, and poets, who for a short time moved into the void. This guild was formed in the 280s and by the beginning of the first century B.C. was playing a major role in Athens' religious dealings with Delphi and even in the Eleusinian Mysteries. It was they who welcomed Mithridates' agent at their sanctuary with libations and prayers. Mithridates, another "Dionysos," was being promoted by the *technītai* of Dionysos, and he was promising to the Athenians much of what Demetrios Poliorcetes had promised them two hundred years earlier: freedom from political oppression and restoration of the democracy. Had events taken a different turn, no doubt the Athenians would have honored Mithridates, as did other cities, with the same type of divine honors they had given Demetrios. But now, in the beginning of the first century, it was a much more violent world and the Romans were on the scene. Mithridates' massacre of the Italians in 88 and Sulla's campaign against him led quickly to the punishment of all pro-Mithridatic states, including Athens. Sulla's siege of the city and the pillaging of it by his troops in 86 B.C. were devastating to Athenian life, politics, and religion, and it would take the Athens more than two generations to recover. In the rebuilding, Athenian state cult and religion would become quite different. Had Sulla not let his men slaughter the citizens and pillage the city, and had he not systematically destroyed or damaged some of the major political and religious monuments, Athens might have been able to recover from the political and religious anomalies and chaos of the previous decade, as the city had so many times before. But the devastation caused by Sulla in 86 truly brought the end, I believe, to centuries of continuity in much of Athenian religion.

Change is always easier and more interesting to describe than continuity, but I would like to stress, one final time, that the distinguishing feature of Athenian religion in the Hellenistic period is continuity, a conscious continuity of the Lycourgan period with the classical period and an implicit continuity of Hellenistic times with the Lycourgan age.[29] We have charted several disruptions to the traditional practices and beliefs of the Athenians, disruptions caused usually by foreign potentates and their supporters in Athens. But each time the Athenians freed themselves from the power of these foreigners, they reestablished, not perfectly but to a good degree, their traditional political and religious practices.

In the current state of scholarship it is difficult to compare religion in Hellenistic Athens to that in other cities of either mainland Greece or Asia Minor. Much good work has been done on individual cults and cult practices in various cities, but only rarely have scholars attempted a comprehensive study of the religion of a single city in the Hellenistic or any other period. And thus, with the few exceptions discussed below, cities to which to compare Athens in the Hellenistic period are lacking. Most general studies of religion in Hellenistic times have instead been based largely on literary and philosophical writings culled from throughout the Greek world. These studies tend to overlook the distinctions of place and time that I discussed in the introduction, thereby neglecting significant differences between, for example, second century B.C. Alexandria and Athens and between sources from the third century B.C. and the second century A.D. Many of these studies are also based on the assumption that there was a Panhellenic *koinē* of religion in the Hellenistic period and that the writings of Hellenistic and Graeco-Roman poets, philosophers, novelists, and other literary figures

29. For studies that emphasize the importance of the continuity from Hellenistic to classical religion, see Z. Stewart 1977 (Athens in particular, 517–19); Nilsson 1967–74, vol. 2 *passim*, but esp. 1–10. Note also the recent comments of Graf 1995.

reflect this *koinē*. Both assumptions may be mistaken,[30] and we can now offer Athens as a touchstone for evaluating what these studies commonly attribute to "Hellenistic religion."

This is not the place to review all that has been attributed to "Hellenistic religion," but let us examine some recent views of two scholars, one from the area of religious study and one from social and political history, for comparison to the evidence from Athens.[31] I chose both because they offer lucid, lively, informed, and relatively traditional views of religion in Hellenistic Greece. H. S. Versnel in an excellent essay on Dionysos and Euripides' *Bacchae*, in which he argues that Euripides' Dionysos is "Hellenistic avant la lettre," offers what he terms nine "well-known features of the religious mentality of the Hellenistic and Roman periods."[32] I give or paraphrase each:

1. Cosmopolitan pretensions and claims to universal worship by individual deities and cults.

2. Miracles and epiphanies serving as evidence of a god's greatness and as an incentive to worship.

3. Expressions of beatitude (*makarismoi*) as the effect of the immediate divine presence, here and now, with the interdependence of bliss and devotion and of the liberating qualities of the god.

4. The dogmatic elevation of one god above all others and the concomitant *affective* exclusion of other gods.

5. The interpretation of worship as personal submission or devotion to the god, even to the effect of being "possessed" or "enslaved" by the deity.

6. The refusal to believe in and, consequently, to honor a particular god.

7. The futility of resisting a god, and the divine triumph over atheists and sinners.

---

30. On the latter point and on the tendency to compare Athens of the classical period not to Athens of a later period, but to what may be found of Hellenistic religion elsewhere, see Z. Stewart 1977, 505–6.

31. For other, very recent specialized studies on religion in Hellenistic Greece, see, on the structure and nature of festivals and particularly on the attested Athenian festivals, Chaniotis 1995; on honors for the dead, especially in civic cult, Herrman 1995.

32. Versnel 1990, 189–205.

8. The severe punishment of those who "fight the god" (*theomachoi*).

9. Public confession of guilt toward the god, either as a token of reverence or as an instrument of propaganda or both.

Peter Green in his bold and thought-provoking survey of Hellenistic political, artistic, intellectual, and social history, *Alexander to Actium* (1990), attempts to place the religion of the time into a much larger intellectual and political context. He draws a very definite line between state and private religion. In the former there is "the steady erosion of the old Olympian pantheon (still accorded traditional public honors, but progressively more peripheral)" (396). Zeus, Athena, and Poseidon "retain their official civic status: their worship and calendar were too deeply embedded in the structure of *polis* life; they were part of the obsolescent fabric to which Greek city dwellers obstinately clung" (396). But "This did not mean that the gods themselves, in the business of everyday life, were always taken seriously. Ethical and scientific advances had robbed them of many of their original functions as anthropomorphized natural forces, and middle-class city dwellers had long looked askance at their indifference to civic morality" (397). Concerning ruler cult, he found it "Small wonder that, as the years went by, the traditional civic gods were not so much rejected—public ritual has always been the most stubbornly conservative of phenomena—as shunted off into a vague, blissful, remote, Elysian heaven, and left with no direct impact on, or interest in, human existence. Real men had, in the end, outperformed their own anthropomorphic deities" (57). Nevertheless, "We sometimes forget the stubborn, glacial resistance, at a lower level, to what must seem, in retrospect, a general collapse of faith. . . . Were not the Olympian deities still officially worshipped? Did not every *polis* retain its traditional divine patron? All true; and yet the image had grown dead and hollow, eaten away at the heart by the boreworms of political impotence, creeping secularism, social fragmentation, loss of cohesive identity" (399, 587).

In the sphere of private religion Green finds, in summary, "that curious underworld of exotic cults and associations, often foreign in origin; of curse tablets, spiked wax dolls, and formulas guaranteed to induce passion or dispose of enemies; of a proliferating variety of demons, friendly or malevolent; of mystery cults, syncretic distillations of Pythagoreanism and Orphism, oracles, miraculous cures, and, above all, astrology" (586). Times had changed:

Olympianism had been strongly bound up with family and *polis*, but now the individual was adrift in an indifferent world and free to choose his own gods. Not surprisingly, he tended to pick those that could best replace the emotional and cultural support structure that he had lost. . . . We also find a proliferation of private religious clubs, whose members call themselves Apolloniasts or Sarapiasts, Hermaists or Iobacchi. Again, one senses a desperate reaching-out after identity and community: those who can no longer be meaningfully involved with their society can at least strive for oneness with God. The ties of the *polis* had broken down, and these clubs enabled persons isolated in the new urban solitude of megalopolis to reach out, through formal worship and shared banquets, not only to a communal deity, but also to one another. (586, 590–91)

Of the period 221–168 B.C., Green notes, "Religious traditionalism, the fear of divine retribution, still had a strong grip on the majority of Athenians, and fostered, in an increasingly godless age, remarkable susceptibility to any exotic cult with emotional drawing power" (399).

These brief quotations to indicate Green's and Versnel's positions do little justice to the detailed arguments, evidence, and scholarly traditions on which they are based. They do serve, however, as good markers of current (and often past) views of Hellenistic religion in general, and they can be measured against what we have found for Athens.

For most of what Versnel and Green describe there is no evidence in Hellenistic, pre-Roman Athens: of claims by deities to universal worship (except perhaps for the late developing and, at this time, very small cult of Isis); of *markarismoi*-oriented devotion; of the elevation of one god to the exclusion of the others; of personal submission or servility to the worshipped god; of worship through public confession of guilt; of a proliferating variety of demons, good or bad; of individuals turning from state cult to private cult; of Pythagorean- or Orphic-based cults; or of astrology as a practice and not a part of a philosophical system. Yet other of Versnel's and Green's "Hellenistic" elements had been evident in the classical period in Athens, and indeed some were more evident in the classical period than later: miracles and epiphanies causing foundation of or new interest in cult (more commonly attested for classical Athens);[33] the refusal to believe in a deity, followed by the de-

---

33. Pfister 1924 collected the examples of epiphanies from throughout the Greek and Roman world, making important distinctions of terminology and distinctions between those epiphanies described in epic and other literature, between those in dreams and in person, and between cultic and noncultic contexts. We have noted the dreams associated with Asclepios and some oriental deities on Delos (chapter 7, pp. 223, 229, and 8. p. 265.)

ity's anger and ultimate triumph over the rebel (a theme of classical tragedy, unattested in Hellenistic Athens); the magic of curse tablets and "spiked wax dolls" (to judge from archaeological finds, common in Athens of the fourth century but almost nonexistent in the third and second centuries);[34] oracles;[35] and miraculous (i.e., Asclepios') cures.[36]

---

but, apart from them, no epiphanies are recorded for Hellenistic Athens. For classical Athens, the cult of Pan was founded because of the god's appearance to Pheidippides in 490 B.C. (Hdt. 6.105; Paus. 1.28.4, 8.54.6; Suda s.v. "Ἱππίας") and that of the hero Echetlaios for his appearance at the Battle of Marathon (Paus. 1.32.5). On these and on other matters related to the introduction of new gods in the classical period, see Garland 1992. On the general lack of ephiphanies, especially of gods as contrasted to heroes, in classical Athenian religion, see Mikalson 1991, 21, 65. In this regard one should note also Nilsson's (1967–74, 2:183–84) discussion of the title ἐπιφανής in Hellenistic ruler cult.

34. Without an archaeological context these curse tablets are difficult to date. Therefore Wünsch (1897) in his early collection of Attic tablets offered dates for only 21 of 220 whole or fragmentary tablets: ten (#26, 38, 47–50, 78, 89, 100, 107) he put into the fifth and fourth centuries B.C.; two (#72–73) before the end of the third century B.C.; one (#57) in early third century B.C.; and six (#31, 35, 36, 60–62) into the Roman period. Jordan (1985) records Attic curse tablets for which there is clear archaeological evidence for dating, #1–14 from the Cerameicos and #20–38 from the Agora. *All* the Cerameicos tablets are from fifth or fourth century B.C. From the Agora one (#20) is fourth century B.C., one (#21) is first century A.D., and all the rest are from the third century A.D. Of all the fifty-four Athenian tablets in Jordan's list, only two (#15, 49) may date to the third century B.C. (or fourth), none to second or first century B.C. From the finds to date, in Athens the Hellenistic period was *not* a time of the efflorescence of such tablets. Quite the contrary: the use of curse tablets then was negligible compared to both earlier and later periods. Similarly, in Athens datable lead "voodoo dolls" associated with curses date to the fifth and fourth century B.C., one possibly to third century B.C., none later (for a list, see Faraone 1991, 200–201). The distribution of Athenian curse tablets may not be unusual. A survey of the ca. 150 non-Athenian curse tablets in Jordan's inventory shows more than twice as many attributed to sixth, fifth, and fourth century B.C. as to the Hellenistic period. On the nature and use of such tablets and dolls throughout the Greek and Roman world, see Gager 1992.

35. Of the seventy-five Delphic oracles deemed "historical" by Fontenrose (1978, 244–67), twenty-three were directed to Athenians or the Athenian state. Seven (H1–3, 8–11) are from the fifth century B.C.; nine (H12, 18, 21, 24, 27–30, 33) are from the fourth century B.C., all before the death of Alexander; only two (H51, 57) are Hellenistic; and five (H58, 59, 64, 66, 75) are from the Roman period. On the somewhat limited role of the Delphic and other oracles in the Hellenistic period, see Nilsson 1967–74, 2:103–13, 229–31.

36. "Miracle cures" are, of course, at least as old as the cult of Asclepios, and that brings us to the mid–or late sixth century B.C. in Epidauros and to 420/19 in Athens. The four inscriptions (*IG* IV² 1.121–124) from Epidauros that offer our first written descriptions of such cures have drawn great attention and are a staple of discussions of religion in the Hellenistic period. The inscriptions date from the second half of the fourth century B.C. but probably collect and remodel earlier material. Many—perhaps all—of the tales may thus be classical. In a sense these inscriptions are just the verbal narrative of events implied in the earlier votive plaques, reliefs, and dedications of body parts found in Asclepios'

Some of the religious elements that Versnel and Green put into the Hellenistic period are, I think, characteristic of some cults and some levels of religion in Athens in the Roman period: that is, after, in some cases centuries after, the battle of Actium in 31 B.C. In more general terms, even a cursory look at the date, nature, and milieu of the sources commonly used by scholars writing on "Hellenistic religion" will indicate that much that is usually termed "Hellenistic" in Greek religion is in fact Graeco-Roman, from Roman imperial times.[37] Although seeds may have been sown in the Hellenistic period, these new plants did not really appear and certainly did not flourish until Roman times; to do so, they quite probably needed the political and social environment of the Roman imperial world, not that of the Greek Hellenistic world. We may be making serious errors in our understanding of the history of Greek religion and of the history of religion in the Mediterranean world by retrojecting these Graeco-Roman developments into the Hellenistic Greek world, thus creating the impression that they appeared centuries before we have evidence for them. We would certainly be wrong to impose them on Hellenistic Athens.

If we turn from the more general studies of "Hellenistic religion" to those of the cults and deities of specific cities, we find much that corroborates what we have found for Athens. This, again, is not the place nor am I the person to survey all that has been discovered for all Greek cities of the Hellenistic period, but we have one excellent source in Fritz Graf's *Nordionische Kulte* (1985). Graf exhaustively collects, dates, and surveys what is known of the cults and deities of the Ionian city-states of Chios, Erythrai, Clazomenai, and Phocaia for the archaic, classical, Hellenistic, and Roman periods. The formal developments of the two best-documented cities, Chios and Erythrai, parallel, in the Hellenistic period, what was happening in Athens. Each had its own elaborate cult structure, the product of its own heritage and of influences from its neighbors, but in the new developments in the Hellenistic period and in the continuity with the classical period these city-states are similar

---

sanctuaries since their beginnings. As such they stand much closer to the classical traditions than to the ruminations of the second-century A.D. orator and hypochondriac Aelius Aristides to which they are often compared. On the Epidaurian "cure" inscriptions, see now LiDonnici 1989.

37. On the critical need to distinguish between Hellenistic and Graeco-Roman sources in the study of Hellenistic religion, see Z. Stewart 1977, 504 n. 1; Nilsson 1967–74, vol. 2.

to one another and to Athens. For Chios (see 140–46 for summary) the various classical state cults of Athena, Zeus, Apollo, and Dionysos continued to be practiced in the Hellenistic period. The ephebes training in the gymnasia made dedications to Hermes and Heracles and performed in agonistic festivals in their honor. In the third century, interestingly, young women performed contests for Leto, an activity for which the girl might be publicly honored with a dedication not unlike those honoring girls in contemporary Athens. Asclepios appears early in the Hellenistic period, as in Athens worshipped sometimes by a private cult association. Aristocratic *genē* on Chios, as in Athens, maintained long-standing "private" cults in their regions of predominance on the island.[38] The Egyptian gods, as at Delos, were introduced in the second or first century B.C. by private individuals. Otherwise, private cults—especially those of the more exotic oriental deities, some of which are found in the Roman period—are noticeably lacking in the Hellenistic period. No cult of Hellenistic rulers is attested, and the cult of the goddess Roma is introduced here relatively early—sometime after the peace of Apamea in 188, the Roman intervention so important for this part of the world and this island.[39]

For Erythrai the epigraphical evidence is far better in both quantity and quality (see 367–75 for summary). Fifty-four priesthoods (including five of Athena and seven of Apollo) are listed on one inscription (*IE* 201) of ca. 300–260, and all served cults with apparent archaic or classical origins.[40] The one clear exception is that of Alexander the Great, who gave the city its independence and hence was and was honored as a genuine benefactor. His cult was quite probably founded during his lifetime and, unlike in Athens, lasted into Roman times. On a very fragmentary Erythraian sacred calendar of ca. 188–150 B.C. (*IE* 207) we have further evidence of ruler cult, with monthly offerings: one for Antiochos I and, as on Chios and no doubt for the same reasons, one for Roma. Elsewhere we learn that Seleucos I received a cult and festival associated, like that of Demetrios Poliorcetes in Athens, with the

---

38. For the continuing importance of Athenian aristocratic *genē* in religious cults in the Hellenistic period, see MacKendrick 1969.

39. On the importance of Apamea see Graf 1985, 17.

40. Possible exceptions are Agathe Tyche and Eirene. The leasing of the priesthoods recorded in this text is not known for Hellenistic Athens or other mainland cities. It was limited to the Greek cities of Asia Minor and the adjoining islands. On such sale or leasing of priesthoods, see Graf 1985, 149–53; Z. Stewart 1977, 516–17; Nilsson, 1967–74, 2:77–82.

Dionysia.[41] Clearly Erythrai, unlike Athens and Chios, had throughout the Hellenistic period a strong and continuous cult of the Macedonian kings. The Erythraians also had one of the earliest (early third century B.C.) attested cults of Demos, but this Demos was, unlike in Athens, often associated with deities such as the Dioscouroi and Zeus Soter. On the second century B.C. calendar appear also the abstract deities Homonoia ("Concord"), Arete ("Virtue"), and Nike ("Victory"), all quite possibly Hellenistic in origin. Asclepios came to Erythrai ca. 370 B.C.; the Egyptian cult of Sarapis, Isis, and Anubis, at the end of the second century B.C. Private cult in Erythrai, as Graf says, remained "konservativ," limited to the traditional gods of Greek belief. Only in the third century A.D. do we find attested exotic cults like that of the Persian Anait.

These two cities are not, of course, documented nearly as well as Athens, but the pattern appears much the same. They all display maintenance of traditional and classical cults throughout the Hellenistic period; some ruler cult, the extent and success of it probably depending on local circumstances; late (i.e., second century B.C.) introduction of the Egyptian gods; no evidence for other, even more exotic oriental gods; no evidence for the rise and little evidence even for the presence of private cult standing apart from the traditional units of the city, tribe, family, and so on; and some indication of increased recognition and perhaps activity of women and children in religious cult.

The sources for the religion of Hellenistic Chios and Erythrai are largely those available, but in far greater quantity, for Hellenistic Athens: inscriptions and occasional (usually passing) remarks in historians and geographical writers. What these sources for Chios, Erythrai, and Athens record is what W. K. C. Guthrie called "the routine of religion which was accepted by most of the citizens . . . as a matter of course" (1950, 258); what Peter Green, much less charitably, speaks of as "the obsolescent fabric to which Greek city dwellers obstinately clung" and "the stubborn mindless glacis of public faith" (1990, 396, 596); and what I would term the "popular religion" of the time—that is, the religion actually practiced by the vast majority of the citizens, dwelling in cities or not, in the Hellenistic period. Since we have been led by those writing on Hellenistic social, philosophical, and intellectual history to expect so much religious change, so many new deities, and such fundamentally different relationships between human and gods

41. For the contributions of the Seleucids to Erythrai, see Graf 1985, 158.

and between individual and state religion, it is important for those concerned with religious history and its postclassical and pre-Christian periods to recognize how very strongly the classical traditions maintained themselves, in Athens certainly and I expect in many other Greek states as well, to the very end of the Hellenistic period.

Cross-References
for Epigraphical Texts

Supplementum Epigraphicum Graecum (SEG)

14.64 = *Hesp.* 23 (1954): 287–96, #182
15.104 = *Hesp.* 24 (1955): 220–39
15.111 = *BCH* 80 (1956): 57–63
15.112 = *BCH* 80 (1956): 64–69
16.58 = *Hesp.* 7 (1938): 297, #22
16.63 = *Hesp.* 26 (1957): 54–55, #11
16.92 = *Hesp.* 16 (1947): 163, #61
16.160 = *Hesp.* 26 (1957): 79–80, #25
16.164 = *Hesp.* 26 (1957): 88–89, #32
16.171 = *Hesp.* 26 (1957): 80, #26
16.174 = *Hesp.* 26 (1957): 80–81, #27
17.36 = *Hesp.* 26 (1957): 209–10, #57
17.83 = *Hesp.* 26 (1957): 200–203, #50
17.84 = *Hesp.* 26 (1957): 203–6, #51
17.85 = *Hesp.* 26 (1957): 206, #52
17.86 = *Hesp.* 26 (1957): 216, #66
18.19 (*IG* II² 775 + 803) = Hubbe 1959, #3
18.20 (*IG* II² 820) = Hubbe 1959, #5
18.21 (*IG* II² 996) = Hubbe 1959, #6
18.22 (*IG* II² 950) = Hubbe 1959, #7
18.25 (*IG* II² 1019) = Hubbe 1959, #9
18.26 (*IG* II² 974) = Hubbe 1959, #10
18.27 (*IG* II² 975 + 1061) = Hubbe 1959, #11

18.33 (*IG* II² 1293) = Hubbe 1959, #4

18.87 = *Hesp.* 28 (1959): 278–79, #7

19.125 = *Hesp.* 29 (1960): 21, #27

19.188 = *Hesp.* 29 (1960): 37, #45

21.435 = *AM* 76 (1961): 127–41, #1

21.458 = *Hesp.* 32 (1963): 20–21, #20

21.522 = *Hesp.* 32 (1963): 14–15, #13

21.527 = Ferguson 1938, 3–5

21.532 = *Hesp.* 30 (1961): 227–28, #26

21.533 = *Hesp.* 30 (1961): 228, #27

21.534 = Sokolowski 1962, 210–12

21.535 = *Hesp.* 30 (1961): 229, #28

21.536 = *Hesp.* 30 (1961): 229–30, #29

21.541 = *BCH* 87 (1963): 603–34

21.562 (*IG* II² 1642) = Woodward 1962, 13

21.775 = *Hesp.* 30 (1961): 267–68, #92

21.779 = *Hesp.* 32 (1963): 45, 438, #61

21.785 (*IG* II² 4641) = Oikonomides 1964, 58–59, #15

21.796 = *Hesp.* 32 (1963), 47, #68

22.116 = Threpsiades and Vanderpool 1964

22.128 = *PAAH* 1958, 35–36

23.124 = *AD* 18B (1963): 20

24.156 = *AD* 23A (1968): 1–6

24.224 = *AD* 21A (1966): 140–41, #1

24.225 = *AD* 20B (1965): 97, #2

25.89 = *Hesp.* 7 (1938): 100–109, #18

25.90 = *Hesp.* 4 (1935): 562–65, #40

25.96 (*IG* II² 772) = Sokolowski 1969, 74–75, #40

25.141 see *SEG* 30.69

25.186 = *Hesp.* 37 (1968): 284–85, #21

25.220 = *Hesp.* 37 (1968): 286–87, #24

26.72 = *Hesp.* 43 (1974): 158–88

26.98 = *Hesp.* 45 (1976): 296–303

26.121 (*IG* II² 1035) = Culley 1975, 1977

26.139 = *Hesp.* 46 (1977): 259–67

27.12 = *AD* 25A ([1970] 1971): 143–49, # 1

27.13 = ibid., #2

27.14 = ibid, #3

27.15 = ibid., #4

27.16 = ibid., #5

27.17 = ibid, #6
27.18 = ibid., #7
27.19 = ibid., #8
28.60 = Shear 1978, 2–4
29.116 = *Hesp.* 48 (1979): 174–78
30.69 (*SEG* 25.141) = Woodhead 1981
31.112 = Petrakos 1981, 72, #28
31.162 = Petrakos 1981, 68–69, #21
31.177 (*IG* II² 4436) = Petrakos 1981, 60–62, #10
31.731 (*ID* 2256+) = *BCH* 50 (1981): 171–73
32.86 = *Hesp.* suppl. 19 (1982): 173–82
32.117 (*IG* II² 778+) = *Hesp.* 7 (1938): 119–21, #23
32.169 (*IG* II² 1705+) = *Hesp.* 8 (1939): 45–47, #13
32.201 = Petrakos 1983, 126, #2
32.216 = *AM* 97 (1982): 171–84
32.218 (*IG* II² 2336) = Tracy 1982b
32.238 (*IG* II² 2791) = Palagia 1982, 111
33.115 = *Hesp.* 52 (1983): 48–63
33.147 = Daux 1983
33.197 = *Hesp.* 52 (1983): 155–61, ##1, 2
33.201 = Petrakos 1983, 126, #2
35.74 = Palagia and Clinton 1985
35.887 = Will 1985, 101
36.164 = *Horos* 4 (1986): 11–18
36.740 (*ID* 2249+) = *Horos* 4 (1986): 79–83
40.657 (*ID* 1562) = *ABSA* 85 (1990): 327–32
41.75 = Petrakos 1992, 31–34, #15
41.86 = Petrakos 1992, 34–37, #16
41.90 = Petrakos 1993, 21–24, #1
41.162 = Petrakos 1992, 18–19, #2
41.164 = Petrakos 1992, 19–20, #4
41.165 = Petrakos 1992, 19, #3
42.157 = Tracy 1975, 72–73, #13

Aleshire Inventory

Inv. III (1989) = *IG* II² 1533
Inv. IV (1989) = *IG* II² 1534A
Inv. V (1989) = *IG* II² 1534B + 1535
Inv. VI (1989) = *SEG* 28.116

Inv. VII (1989) = *IG* II² 1539
Inv. VIII (1989) = *IG* II² 1536
Inv. IX (1989) = *IG* II² 1019

Reinmuth

#6 = *AM* 76 (1961): 143, #2
#9 = *Hesp.* 9 (1940): 59–66, #8
#13 = Pouilloux 1954, III, #2 *bis*
#15 = *AE* 1918, 73–100, ##95–97

Schwenk

#6 = *Hesp.* 21 (1952): 355–59, #5
#13 = *IG* II² 1255
#17A = *Hesp.* 28 (1959): 239–47
#17B = *IG* II² 334
#21 = *IG* II² 333
#27 = *IG* II² 337
#28 = *IG* II² 338
#40 = *IG* VII 4252
#41 = *IG* VII 4253
#48 = *IG* II² 351 + 624
#50 = *IG* VII 4254
#52 = *IG* II² 1256
#54 = *IG* II² 354
#56 = *AE* 1917, 40–48, #92
#77 = *IG* II² 1257
#79 = *IG* II² 365

Bibliography

Abramson, H. 1975. "The Olympieion in Athens and Its Connections with Rome." *CSCA* 7: 1–25.

Africa, T. 1982. "Worms and the Death of Kings: A Cautionary Note on Disease and History." *Classical Antiquity* 1: 1–17.

Aleshire, S. B. 1989. *The Athenian Asklepieion*. Amsterdam.

—— 1991. *Asklepios at Athens*. Amsterdam.

—— 1992. "The Economics of Dedication at the Athenian Asklepieion." In *Economics of Cult in the Ancient Greek World*, edited by T. Linders and B. Alroth, 85–99. Boreas 21. Uppsala.

—— 1994. "The Demos and the Priests: The Selection of Sacred Officials at Athens from Cleisthenes to Augustus." In *Ritual, Finance, Politics*, edited by R. Osborne and S. Hornblower, 325–37. Oxford.

Ameling, W. 1989. "Das neue attische Dekret für Oropos: Ein Datierungsvorschlag." *ZPE* 77: 95–96.

—— 1990. "Koinon *TΩN ΣΙΔΩΝΙΩΝ*." *ZPE* 81: 189–99.

Arnim, J. von. 1903–24. *Stoicorum Veterum Fragmenta*. 4 vols. Stuttgart.

Atkinson, K. M. T. 1973. "Demosthenes, Alexander, and Asebeia." *Athenaeum* 51: 310–35.

Austin, C. 1974. "Catalogus Comicorum Graecorum." *ZPE* 14: 201–25.

Badian, E. 1976. "Rome, Athens, and Mithridates." *AJAH* 1: 105–28.

—— 1981. "The Deification of Alexander the Great." In *Ancient Macedonian Studies in Honor of Charles F. Edson*, edited by H. J. Dell and E. N. Borza, 27–71. Thessaloniki.

Badian, E., and T. R. Martin. 1985. "Athenians, Other Allies, and the Hellenes in the Athenian Honorary Decree for Adeimantos of Lampsakos." *ZPE* 61: 167–72.

Balsdon, J. P. V. D. 1950. "The 'Divinity' of Alexander." *Historia* 1: 363–88.

Baslez, M. F. 1977. *Recherches sur les conditions de pénétration et de diffusion des religions orientales à Délos*. Paris.

———. 1984. *L'étranger dans la Grèce antique*. Paris.

Bayer, E. 1942. *Demetrios Phalereus der Athener*. Stuttgart.

Benjamin, A. S. 1963. "The Altars of Hadrian in Athens and Hadrian's Panhellenic Program." *Hesp.* 32: 57–86.

Bickerman, E. J. 1963. "Sur un passage d' Hypéride." *Athenaeum* 41: 70–85.

Billows, R. A. 1990. *Antigonos the One-Eyed and the Creation of the Hellenistic State*. Berkeley.

Bosworth, A. B. 1994. "A New Macedonian Prince." *CQ* 44: 57–65.

Bourriot, F. 1976. *Recherches sur la nature du genos*. Lille.

Boyancé, P. 1937. *Le cult des Muses chez les philosophes grecs*. Paris.

Brulé, P. 1987. *La fille d'Athènes*. Paris.

Bruneau, P. 1970. *Recherches sur les cultes de Délos à l'époque hellénistique et à l'époque impériale*. Paris.

———. 1987. "Deliaca (VI)." *BCH* 111: 313–42.

Bruneau, P., and J. Ducat. 1983. *Guide de Délos*. Paris.

Bugh, G. R. 1990. "The Theseia in Late Hellenistic Athens." *ZPE* 83: 20–37.

———. 1992. "Athenion and Aristion of Athens." *Phoenix* 46: 108–23.

Burkert, W. 1966. "Kekropidensage und Arrhephoria." *Hermes* 94: 1–25.

———. 1970. "Buzyge und Palladion." *Zeitschrift für Religion und Geistesgeschichte* 22: 356–68.

———. 1983. *Homo Necans*, translated by P. Bing. Berkeley.

———. 1993. "Bacchic *Teletai* in the Hellenistic Age." In *Masks of Dionysus*, edited by T. H. Carpenter and C. A. Faraone, 259–75. Ithaca, N.Y.

Camp, J. M. 1992. *The Athenian Agora: Excavations in the Heart of Classical Athens*. London.

Chaniotis, A. 1995. "Sich selbst feiern? Städtische Feste des Hellenismus im Spannungsfeld von Religion und Politik." In *Stadtbild und Bürgerbild im Hellenismus*, edited by M. Wörrle and P. Zanker, 147–72. Vestigia 47. Munich.

Clay, D. 1982. "Epicurus in the Archives of Athens." In *Studies in Attic Epigraphy, History, and Topography*, 17–26. *Hesp.* supplement 19. Princeton.

———. 1986. "The Cults of Epicurus." *Cronache Ercolanesi* 16: 11–28.

Clinton, K. [1971] 1972. "Inscriptions from Eleusis." *AE* 81–136.

———. 1974. *The Sacred Officials of the Eleusinian Mysteries*. Transactions of the American Philosophical Society 63.4. Philadelphia.

———. 1988. "Sacrifice at the Eleusinian Mysteries." In *Early Greek Cult Practice*, edited by R. Hägg, N. Marinatos, and G. C. Nordquist, 69–79. Stockholm.

———. 1992. *Myth and Cult: The Iconography of the Eleusinian Mysteries*. Stockholm.

———. 1994. "The Epidauria and the Arrival of Asclepius in Athens." In *Ancient Greek Cult Practice from the Epigraphical Evidence*, edited by R. Hägg, 17–34. Stockholm.

Cole, S. G. 1984. *Theoi Megaloi: The Cult of the Great Gods at Samothrace*. Leiden.

Conomis, N. C. 1970. *Lycurgi Oratio in Leocratem*. Leipzig.

Culley, G. R. 1975. "The Restoration of Sanctuaries in Attica: *IG* II² 1035." *Hesp.* 44: 207–23.

———. 1977. "The Restoration of Sanctuaries in Attica, II." *Hesp.* 46: 282–98.

Cuvigny, M. 1981. *Plutarque: oeuvres morales.* Vol. 12. Paris.

Daux, G. 1936. *Delphes au IIe et au Ier siècle.* Paris.

———. 1963. "La grande démarchie: un nouveau calendrier sacrificiel d'Attique (Erchia)." *BCH* 87: 603–34.

———. 1983. "Le calendrier de Thorikos au Musée J. Paul Getty." *AC* 52: 150–74.

———. 1984. "Sacrifices à Thorikos." *J. Paul Getty Museum Journal* 12: 145–52.

Davies, J. K. 1967. "Demosthenes on Liturgies: A Note." *JHS* 87: 33–40.

———. 1971. *Athenian Propertied Families.* Oxford.

———. 1984. "Cultural, Social and Economic Features of the Hellenistic World." In *Cambridge Ancient History,* edited by F. W. Walbank, A. E. Astin, M. W. Frederiksen, and R. M. Ogilvie, 7.1:257–320. 2nd ed. Cambridge.

Day, J. 1942. *An Economic History of Athens under Roman Domination.* New York.

de Schutter, X. 1987. "Le cult d'Apollon Patrôos à Athènes." *AC* 56: 103–29.

Derenne, E. 1930. *Les procès d'impiété.* Paris.

Deubner, L. 1932. *Attische Feste.* Berlin.

Develin, R. 1989. *Athenian Officials, 684–321 b.c.* Cambridge.

Di Vita, A. 1952–54. "Atena Ergane in una terracotta dalla Sicilia ed il culto della dea in Atene." *ASAA* 30–32: 141–54.

Dinsmoor, W. B. 1931. *The Archons of Athens in the Hellenistic Age.* Cambridge, Mass.

———. 1950. *The Architecture of Ancient Greece.* 3rd rev. ed. London.

Dontas, G. S. 1983. "The True Aglaurion." *Hesp.* 52: 48–63.

Dorandi, T. 1989. "Epigraphica Philosophica." *Prometheus* 15: 37–38.

Dörpfeld, W. 1884. "Ein antikes Bauwerk im Piräus." *AM* 9: 279–87.

Dow, S. 1937a. "The Egyptian Cults in Athens." *HTR* 30: 183–232.

———. 1937b. *Prytaneis. Hesp.* supplement 1. Athens.

———. 1960. "The Athenian *Epheboi;* Other Staffs, and the Staff of the *Diogeneion." TAPA* 91: 381–409.

———. 1963. "The Athenian Honors for Aristonikos of Karystos, 'Alexander's Σφαιριστής.'" *HSCP* 67: 77–92.

———. 1965. "The Greater Demarkhia of Erkhia." *BCH* 89: 180–213.

———. 1985. "The Cult of the Hero Doctor." *BAPA* 22: 33–47.

Dow, S., and R. F. Healey. 1965. *A Sacred Calendar of Eleusis.* Harvard Theological Studies 21. Cambridge, Mass.

Dreyer, B. 1996. "Der Beginn der Freiheitsphase Athens 287 v. Chr. und das Datum der Panathenäen und Ptolemaia im Kalliasdekret." *ZPE* 111: 45–67.

Dunand, F. 1973. *Le culte d'Isis dans le bassin oriental de la Méditerranée.* Leiden.

Düring, I. 1957. *Aristotle in the Ancient Biographical Tradition.* Göteborg.

———. 1966. *Aristoteles.* Heidelberg.

Durrbach, F. 1932. *Lycurgue.* Paris.

Edelstein, L., and E. Edelstein. 1945. *Asclepius.* 2 vols. Baltimore.

Edmunds, L. 1971. "The Religiosity of Alexander." *GRBS* 12: 363–91.

Edwards, C. M. 1984. "Aphrodite on a Ladder." *Hesp.* 53: 59–72.

———. 1985. "Greek Votive Reliefs to Pan and the Nymphs." Ph.D. diss., New York University.

Ehrenberg, V. 1946. *Aspects of the Ancient World: Essays and Reviews*. New York.

———. 1962. *The People of Aristophanes*. 3rd ed. New York.

Engelmann, H., and R. Merkelbach. 1972–73. *Die Inschriften von Erythrai und Klazomenai* I–II. Bonn.

Errington, R. M. 1990. *A History of Macedonia*. Berkeley.

Faraguna, M. 1992. *Athene nell'età di Alessandro*. In *Atti della Accademia Nazionale dei Lincei*, ser. 9, 2.2:163–447. Rome.

Faraone, C. A. 1991. "Binding and Burying the Forces of Evil: The Defensive Use of 'Voodoo Dolls' in Ancient Greece." *Classical Antiquity* 10: 165–220.

Ferguson, W. S. 1907. "Researches in Athenian and Delian Documents, I." *Klio* 7: 213–40.

———. 1911. *Hellenistic Athens*. London.

———. 1929. "Lachares and Demetrius Poliorcetes." *CP* 24: 1–31.

———. 1932. *Athenian Tribal Cycles in the Hellenistic Age*. Cambridge, Mass.

———. 1938. "The Salaminioi of Heptaphylai and Sounion." *Hesperia* 7: 1–74.

———. 1944. "The Attic Orgeones." *HTR* 37: 61–140.

———. 1949. "Orgeonika." In *Commemorative Studies in Honor of Theodore Leslie Shear*, 130–63. *Hesp.* supplement 8. Baltimore.

Follet, S. 1988. "Éphèbes étrangers a Athènes: Romains, Milésiens, Chypriotes etc." *Centre d'Etudes Chypriotes* 9: 19–32.

Fontenrose, J. 1978. *The Delphic Oracle*. Berkeley.

Foster, G. V. 1984. "The Bones from the Altar West of the Painted Stoa." *Hesp.* 53: 73–82.

Frantz, A. 1979. "A Public Building of Late Antiquity in Athens (*IG* II² 5205)." *Hesp.* 48: 194–203.

Fredricksmeyer, E. A. 1979. "Divine Honors for Philip II." *TAPA* 109: 39–61.

———. 1981. "On the Background of Ruler Cult." In *Ancient Macedonian Studies in Honor of Charles F. Edson*, edited by H. J. Dell and E. N. Borza, 145–56. Thessaloniki.

Freeden, J. von. 1983. *ΟΙΚΙΑ ΚΥΡΡΗΣΤΟΥ: Studien zum sogennanten Turm der Winde in Athen*. Rome.

———. 1985. "*ΠΙΣΤΟΚΡΑΤΗΣ ΚΑΙ ΑΠΟΛΛΟΔΩΡΟΣ ΣΑΤΥΡΟΥ ΑΥΡΙΔΑΙ* (IG II² 2949)." *ZPE* 61: 215–18.

Gager, J. G. 1992. *Curse Tablets and Binding Spells from the Ancient World*. Oxford.

Garlan, Y. 1978. "Décret de Rhamnonte voté par des *ΥΠΑΙΘΡΟΙ*." *BCH* 102: 103–8.

Garland, R. 1982. "A First Catalogue of Attic Peribolos Tombs." *ABSA* 77: 125–76.

———. 1985. *The Greek Way of Death*. Ithaca, N.Y.

———. 1987. *The Piraeus*. Ithaca, N.Y.

———. 1989. "The Well-Ordered Corpse: An Investigation into the Motives behind Greek Funerary Legislation." *BICS* 36: 1–15.

———. 1992. *Introducing New Gods*. Ithaca, N.Y.

Gauthier, P. 1979. "La réunification d'Athènes en 281 et les deux archontes Nicias." *REG* 92: 348–99.

———. 1982. "Les villes athéniennes et un décret pour un commerçant (*IG* II² 903)." *REG* 95: 275–90.

———. 1985a. "Les chlamydes et l'entretien des éphèbes athéniens: remarques sur le décret de 204/3." *Chiron* 15: 149–63.

———. 1985b. *Les cités grecques et leurs bienfaiteurs*. Athens.

Gehrke, H. J. 1978. "Das Verhältnis von Politik und Philosophie im Wirken des Demetrios von Phaleron." *Chiron* 8: 149–93.

———. 1990. *Geschichte des Hellenismus*. Munich.

Ghiron-Bistagne, P. 1976. *Recherches sur les acteurs dans la Grèce antique*. Paris.

Golden, M. 1990. *Childhood in Classical Athens*. Baltimore.

Goldstein, J. A. 1968. *The Letters of Demosthenes*. New York.

Gomme, A. W. 1937. *Essays in Greek History and Literature*. Oxford.

Gow, A. S. F., and D. L. Page, eds. 1965. *The Greek Anthology*. 2 vols. Cambridge.

Graf, F. 1985. *Nordionische Kulte*. Rome.

———. 1993. "Dionysian and Orphic Eschatology: New Texts and Old Questions." In *Masks of Dionysos*, edited by T. H. Carpenter and C. A. Faraone, 239–58. Ithaca, N.Y.

———. 1995. "Bemerkungen zur bürgerlichen Religiosität im Zeitalter des Hellenismus." In *Stadtbild und Bürgerbild im Hellenismus*, edited by M. Wörrle and P. Zanker, 103–14. Vestigia 47. Munich.

Grant, F. C. 1953. *Hellenistic Religions*. New York.

Green, P. 1990. *Alexander to Actium: The Historical Evolution of the Hellenistic Age*. Berkeley.

Gruen, E. S. 1984. *The Hellenistic World and the Coming of Rome*. Berkeley.

Guthrie, W. K. C. 1950. *The Greeks and Their Gods*. London.

Habicht, C. 1956. *Gottmenschentum und griechische Städte*. Munich.

———. 1961. "Neue Inschriften aus dem Kerameikos." *AM* 76: 127–48.

———. 1970. *Gottmenschentum und griechische Städte*. 2nd ed. Zetemata 14. Munich.

———. 1979. *Untersuchungen zur politischen Geschichte Athens im 3. Jahrhundert v. Chr.* Vestigia 30. Munich.

———. 1980. "Bemerkungen zum P. Haun. 6." *ZPE* 39: 1–5.

———. 1982a. "Eine Liste von Hieropoioi aus dem Jahre des Archons Andreas." *AM* 97: 171–84.

———. 1982b. *Studien zur Geschichte Athens in hellenistischer Zeit*. Hypomnemata 73. Göttingen.

———. 1985. *Pausanias' Guide to Ancient Greece*. Berkeley.

———. 1987. "The Role of Athens in the Reorganization of the Delphic Amphictiony after 189 B.C." *Hesp.* 56: 59–71.

———. 1988a. "Die beiden Xenocles von Sphettos." *Hesp.* 57: 323–27.

———. 1988b. *Hellenistic Athens and Her Philosophers*. David Magie Lectures. Princeton.

——. 1989. "Pytheas von Alopeke, Aufseher über die Brunnen Attikas." *ZPE* 77: 83–87.

——. 1990a. "Athens and the Attalids in the Second Century B.C." *Hesp.* 59: 561–77.

——. 1990b. "Zum Text eines athenischen Volksbeschlusses von 304/3 v. Chr. (*SEG* XXX, 69)." *Hesp.* 59: 463–66.

——. 1991. "Zu den Epimeleten von Delos 167–88." *Hermes* 119: 194–216.

——. 1992a. "Athens and the Ptolemies." *Classical Antiquity* 11: 68–90.

——. 1992b. "Der Kyniker Teles und die Reform der athenischen Ephebie." *ZPE* 93: 47–49.

——. 1993. "Attische Fluchtafeln aus der Zeit Alexanders des Grossen." *Illinois Classical Studies* 18: 113–18.

——. 1994. *Athen in hellenistischer Zeit*. Munich.

——. 1995. "Ist ein 'Honoratiorenregime' das Kennzeichen der Stadt im späteren Hellenismus?" In *Stadtbild und Bürgerbild im Hellenismus*, edited by M. Wörrle and P. Zanker, 87–92. Vestigia 47. Munich.

Hadzsits, G. P. 1908. "Significance of Worship and Prayer among the Epicureans." *TAPA* 39: 73–88.

Hamilton, R. 1992. *Choes and Anthesteria*. Ann Arbor, Mich.

Harding, P. 1994. *Androtion and the Atthis*. Oxford.

Harris, D. 1992. "Bronze Statues on the Athenian Acropolis: The Evidence of a Lycurgan Inventory." *AJA* 96: 637–52.

Harrison, A. R. W. 1968–71. *The Law of Athens*. 2 vols. Oxford.

Harrison, E. B. 1990. "Aphrodite Hegemone in the Athenian Agora." In *Akten des XIII. Internationalen Kongresses für Klassische Archäologie*, 346 and pl. 50.1. Berlin.

Hartigan, K. 1979. *The Poets and the Cities*. Meisenheim am Glan.

Hausmann, U. 1948. *Kunst und Heiltum: Untersuchungen zu den griechischen Asklepiosreliefs*. Potsdam.

Hedrick, C. W. 1988. "The Temple and Cult of Apollo Patroos in Athens." *AJA* 92: 185–210.

Henrichs, A. 1983. "The 'Sobriety' of Oedipus: Sophocles *OC* 100 Misunderstood." *HSCP* 87: 87–100.

Henry, A. 1992. "Lyandros of Anaphlystos and the Decree for Phaidros of Sphettos." *Chiron* 22: 25–33.

Herrman, P. 1995. "Γέρας Θανόντων: Totenruhm und Totenehrung im städtischen Leben der hellenistischen Zeit." In *Stadtbild und Bürgerbild im Hellenismus*, edited by M. Wörrle and P. Zanker, 189–97. Vestigia 47. Munich.

Herter, H. 1927. "Das Kind im Zeitalter des Hellenismus." *Bonner Jahrbücher* 132: 250–58.

——. 1939. "Theseus der Athener." *RhM* 88: 244–326.

Houser, C. 1982. "Alexander's Influence on Greek Sculpture." *Studies in the History of Art* 10: 228–38.

Hubbe, R. O. 1959. "Decrees from the Precinct of Asklepios at Athens." *Hesp.* 28: 169–201.

Humphreys, S. 1985. "Lycurgus of Butadae: an Athenian Aristocrat." In *The*

Craft of the Ancient Historian, edited by J. W. Eadie and J. Ober, 199–252. Lanham, Md.

———. 1986. "Dynamics of the Greek Breakthrough: The Dialogue between Philosophy and Religion." In *The Origins and Diversity of Axial Age Civilizations*, edited by S. N. Eistenstadt, 92–110. Albany.

Jacoby, F. 1949. *Atthis: The Local Chronicles of Ancient Athens*. Oxford.

Jacquemin, A. 1981. "Notes sur quelques offrandes du gymnase de Délos." *BCH* 105: 155–69.

Judeich, W. 1931. *Topographie von Athen*. 2nd ed. Munich.

Kearns, E. 1989. *The Heroes of Attica*. BICS supplement 57. London.

———. 1990. "Saving the City." In *The Greek City*, edited by O. Murray and S. Price, 323–44. Oxford.

Keaveney, A., and J. A. Madden. 1982. "Phthiriasis and Its Victims." *Symbolae Osloenses* 57: 87–99.

Kennedy, G. A. 1991. *Aristotle: "On Rhetoric."* Oxford.

Kertész, I. 1978. "Bemerkungen zum Kult des Demetrios Poliorketes." *Oikumene* 2: 163–75.

Knoepfler, D. 1993. "Adolf Wilhelm et la penteteris des Amphiaraia d'Oropos." In *Aristote et Athenes*, edited by M. Pierart, 279–302. Paris.

Kock, T. 1880–88. *Comicorum Atticorum Fragmenta*. 3 vols. Leipzig.

Koester, H. 1982. *Introduction to the New Testament*. Vol. I. Philadephia.

Kolb, F. 1981. *Agora und Theater, Volks- und Festversammlung*. Berlin.

Kreeb, M. 1985. "Zur Basis der Kleopatra auf Delos." *Horos* 3: 41–61.

Kron, U. 1976. *Die zehn attischen Phylenheroen*. Berlin.

Kyparissis, N., and W. Peek. 1941. "Attische Urkunden." *AM* 66: 228–39.

Lalonde, G. V., M. K. Langdon, and M. B. Walbank. 1991. *Inscriptions: Horoi, Poletai Records, Leases of Public Lands*. The Athenian Agora 19. Princeton.

Lambert, S. D. 1993. *The Phratries of Attica*. Ann Arbor, Mich.

Lane, E. 1971–78. *Corpus Monumentorum Religionis Dei Menis*. 4 vols. Leiden.

Langdon, M. K. 1976. *A Sanctuary of Zeus on Mount Hymettos*. *Hesp.* supplement 16. Princeton.

———. 1987. "An Attic Decree Concerning Oropos." *Hesp.* 56: 47–58.

Lardinois, A. 1992. "Greek Myths for Athenian Rituals: Religion and Politics in Aeschylus' *Eumenides* and Sophocles' *Oedipus Coloneus*." *GRBS* 33: 313–27.

Lauter, H. 1989. "Das Teichos von Sunion." In *Marburger Winckelmann-Programm 1988*, 11–33. Marburg.

Lawton, C. L. 1995. *Attic Document Reliefs*. Oxford.

Lawton, C., and D. Harris. 1990. "Aias and Eurysakes on a Fourth-Century Honorary Decree from Salamis." *ZPE* 80: 109–15.

Le Bohec, S. 1993. *Antigone Dôsôn*. Nancy.

Leiwo, M. 1989. "Philostratus of Ascalon, His Bank, His Connections, and Naples in c. 130–90 B.C." *Athenaeum* 67: 575–84.

Lewis, D. M. 1954. "Notes on Attic Inscriptions." *ABSA* 49: 17–50.

———. 1955. "Notes on Attic Inscriptions (II)." *ABSA* 50: 1–36.

———. 1959a. "Attic Manumissions." *Hesp.* 28: 208–38.

———. 1959b. "Law on the Lesser Panathenaia." *Hesp.* 28: 239–47.

——. 1968. "Dedications of Phialai at Athens." *Hesp.* 37: 368–80.

——. 1973. "Attic Ephebic Inscriptions." *CR* 23: 254–56.

——. 1983. "A Loyal Husband?" *ZPE* 52: 48.

——. 1985a. "The Archonship of Lysiades." *ZPE* 58: 271–74.

——. 1985b. "Temple Inventories in Ancient Greece." In *Pots and Pans*, edited by M. Vickers, 71–81. Oxford Studies in Islamic Art 3. Oxford.

——. 1988. "The Last Inventories of the Treasurers of Athena." In *Comptes et inventaires dans la cité grecque*, edited by D. Knoepfler and N. Quellet, 297–308. Neuchâtel.

LiDonnici, L. R. 1989. "Tale and Dream: The Text and Compositional History of the Corpus of Epidaurian Miracle Cures." Ph.D. diss., University of Pennsylvania.

Linders, T. 1987. "Gods, Gifts, Society." In *Gifts to the Gods*, edited by T. Linders and G. C. Nordquist, 115–22. Boreas 15. Uppsala.

Long, A. A. 1974. *Hellenistic Philosophy: Stoics, Epicureans, Sceptics*. London.

Lund, H. S. 1992. *Lysimachus*. London.

Lynch, J. P. 1972. *Aristotle's School*. Berkeley.

Maass, M. 1972. *Die Prohedrie des Dionysostheaters in Athen*. Munich.

MacDowell, D. M. 1962. *Andokides: On the Mysteries*. Oxford.

——. 1990. *Demosthenes: Against Meidias*. Oxford.

MacKendrick, P. 1969. *The Athenian Aristocracy, 399 to 31 b.c.* Cambridge, Mass.

Marasco, G. 1984. *Democare di Leuconoe*. Florence.

Marcovich, M. 1988. *Studies in Graeco-Roman Religions and Gnosticism*. Leiden.

McInerney, J. 1994. "Politicizing the Past: The Atthis of Kleidemos." *Classical Antiquity* 13: 17–37.

Meiggs, R., and D. M. Lewis. 1969. *A Selection of Greek Historical Inscriptions*. Oxford.

Mellor, R. 1975. *ΘΕΑ ΡΩΜΗ: The Worship of the Goddess Roma in the Greek World*. Göttingen.

Meritt, B. D. 1963. "Apollo Pythios or Patroios." *AJP* 84: 419–20.

Meritt, B. D., and J. S. Trail. 1974. *Inscriptions: The Athenian Councillors*. The Athenian Agora 15. Princeton.

Merkelbach, R. 1972. "Aglauros (Die Religion der Epheben)." *ZPE* 9: 277–83.

Merker, I. L. 1986. "Habron the Son of Lykourgos of Boutadai." *Ancient World* 14: 41–50.

Mette, H. J. 1977. *Urkunden dramatischer Aufführungen in Griechenland*. Berlin.

Meyer, H. 1988. "Zur Chronologie des Poseidoniastenhauses in Delos." *AM* 103: 203–20.

Mikalson, J. D. 1975a. *The Sacred and Civil Calendar of the Athenian Year*. Princeton.

——. 1975b. "ἡμέρα ἀποφράς." *AJP* 96: 19–27.

——. 1977. "Religion in the Attic Demes." *AJP* 98: 424–35.

——. 1982. "The Heorte of Heortology." *GRBS* 23: 213–21.

——. 1983. *Athenian Popular Religion*. Chapel Hill, N.C.

———. 1984. "Religion and the Plague in Athens, 431–423 B.C." In *Studies Presented to Sterling Dow*, edited by K. J. Rigsby, 217–25. *GRBS* Monograph 10. Durham, N.C.

———. 1989. "Unanswered Prayers in Greek Tragedy." *JHS* 109: 81–98.

———. 1991. *Honor Thy Gods: Popular Religion in Greek Tragedy*. Chapel Hill, N.C.

Miller, S. G. 1995a. "Architecture as Evidence for the Identity of the Early Polis." In *Sources for the Ancient Greek City-State*, edited by M. H. Hansen, 201–43. Copenhagen.

———. 1995b. "Old Metroon and Old Bouleuterion in the Classical Agora of Athens." *Historia Einzelschriften* 95: 133–56.

Miller, S. G., and S. N. Koumanoudes. 1971. "*IG* II² 1477 and 3046 Rediscovered." *Hesp.* 40: 448–58.

Mitchel, F. W. 1962. "Demades of Paeania and *IG* II² 1493, 1494, 1495." *TAPA* 93: 213–29.

———. 1970. *Lykourgan Athens: 338–322*. Lecture in Memory of Louise Taft Semple. Cincinnati.

Mueller, K. 1898. *Fragmenta Historicorum Graecorum*. Vol. 2. Paris.

Mylonas, G. E. 1961. *Eleusis and the Eleusinian Mysteries*. Princeton.

Nachtergael, G. 1977. *Les Galates en Grèce et les Sôtéria de Delphes*. Brussels.

Nagy, B. 1978. "The Athenian Athlothetai." *GRBS* 19: 307–13.

———. 1984. "The *Peplotheke*: What Was It?" In *Studies Presented to Sterling Dow*, edited by K. J. Rigsby, 227–32. *GRBS* Monograph 10. Durham.

———. 1991. "The Procession to Phaleron." *Historia* 40: 288–306.

Nilsson, M. P. 1967–74. *Geschichte der Griechischen Religion*. 2 vols. 3rd ed. Munich.

Nock, A. D. 1928. "Notes on Ruler-Cult, I–IV." *JHS* 48: 21–43.

———. 1972. *Essays on Religion and the Ancient World*, edited by Z. Stewart. Cambridge, Mass.

Norman, N. J. 1983. "'The Panathenaic Ship.'" *Archaeological News* 12: 41–46.

Novotny, F. 1977. *The Posthumous Life of Plato*. The Hague.

Obbink, D. D. 1984. "*POxy.* 215 and Epicurean Religious Θεωρία." In *Atti del XVII Congresso Internazionale di Papirologia*, 2:607–19. Naples.

———. 1989. "The Atheism of Epicurus." *GRBS* 30: 187–223.

Oeconomides-Caramessini, M. 1976. "The 1973 Piraeus Hoard of Athenian Bronze Coins." *AAA* 9: 220–23.

Oikonomides, A. N. 1964. *The Two Agoras in Ancient Athens*. Chicago.

———. 1982. "The Cult of Diogenes 'Euergetes' in Ancient Athens." *ZPE* 45: 118–20.

———. 1986. "The Epigraphical Tradition of the Decree of Stratokles Honoring 'Post Mortem' the Orator Lykourgos." *Ancient World* 14: 51–54.

Oliver, J. H. 1960. *Demokratia, the Gods, and the Free World*. Baltimore.

Osborne, M. J. 1981. "Some Attic Inscriptions." *ZPE* 42: 171–78.

———. 1981–83. *Naturalization in Athens*. 4 vols. Brussels.

———. 1989. "The Chronology of Athens in the Mid Third Century B.C." *ZPE* 78: 209–42.

Osborne, M. J., and S. G. Byrne. 1994. *A Lexicon of Greek Personal Names.*
Vol. 2. Oxford.

Osborne, R. 1985. *Demos: The Discovery of Classical Attika.* Cambridge.

———. 1990. "The *Demos* and Its Divisions in Classical Athens." In *The Greek City*, edited by O. Murray and S. Price, 265–93. Oxford.

Palagia, O. 1982. "A Colossal Statue of a Personification from the Agora of Athens." *Hesp.* 51:99–113.

———. 1989–90. "A New Relief of the Graces and the *Charites* of Socrates." *Sacris Erudiri* 31: 347–56.

———. 1994. "No Demokratia." In *The Archaeology of Athens and Attica under the Democracy*, edited by W. D. E. Coulson, O. Palagia, T. L. Shear Jr., H. A. Shapiro, and F. J. Frost, 113–22. Oxford.

Palagia, O., and K. Clinton. 1985. "A Decree from the Athenian Asklepieion." *Hesp.* 54: 137–39.

Palagia, O., and D. M. Lewis. 1989. "The Ephebes of Erechtheis, 333/2 B.C. and Their Dedication." *ABSA* 84: 333–44.

Palaiokrassa, L. 1989. "Neue Befunde aus dem Heiligtum der Artemis Munichia." *AM* 104: 1–40.

———. 1991. Τὸ Ἱερὸ τῆς Ἀρτέμιδος Μουνιχίας. Βιβλιοθήκη τῆς ἐν Ἀθήναις Ἀρχαιολογικῆς Ἑταιρείας 115. Athens.

Parke, H. W. 1977. *Festivals of the Athenians.* Ithaca, N.Y.

Parker, R. 1983. *Miasma: Pollution and Purification in Early Greek Religion.* Oxford.

———. 1987. "Festivals of the Attic Demes." In *Gifts to the Gods*, edited by T. Linders and G. C. Nordquist, 137–47. Boreas 15. Uppsala.

Pélékidis, C. 1962. *Histoire de l' éphébie attique.* Paris.

Peppas-Delmousou, D. 1984. "Le théâtre attique dans le monde hellénistique." In *Actes du VIIIème congrès internationale d' épigraphie grecque et latin*, 62–68. Athens.

Peters, F. E. 1970. *The Harvest of Hellenism.* New York.

Petrakos, B. C. 1968. Ὁ Ὠρωπὸς καὶ τὸ Ἱερὸν τοῦ Ἀμφιαράου. Βιβλιοθήκη τῆς ἐν Ἀθήναις Ἀρχαιολογικῆς Ἑταιρείας 63. Athens.

———. [1979] 1981. "Νέες ἔρευνες στὸν Ραμνούντα." *AE* 1–81.

———. [1981] 1983. "Ἀνασκαφὴ Ραμνοῦντος." *PAAH* 118–40.

———. 1986. "Προβλήματα τῆς βάσης του αγάλματος τῆς Νεμέσεως." In *Klassische griechische Plastik*, edited by H. Kyrieleis, 89–107. Archaische und klassische griechische Plastik 2. Mainz.

———. [1989] 1992. "Ἀνασκαφὴ Ραμνοῦντος." *PAAH* 1–37.

———. [1990] 1993. "Ἀνασκαφὴ Ραμνοῦντος." *PAAH* 1–39.

Pfister, F. 1924. "Epiphanie." *RE* suppl. 4:277–323.

———. 1951. *Die Reisebilder des Herakleides.* Vienna.

Pickard-Cambridge, A. W. 1946. *The Theatre of Dionysus in Athens.* Oxford.

———. 1962. *Dithyramb, Tragedy and Comedy*, revised by T. B. L Webster. 2nd ed. Oxford.

———. 1988. *The Dramatic Festivals of Athens*, revised by J. Gould and D. M. Lewis. 2nd ed., with supplement and corrections. Oxford.

Pirenne-Delforge, V. 1994. *L'Aphrodite grecque. Kernos* supplément 4. Liège.

Pleket, H. W. 1981. "Religious History as the History of Mentality." In *Faith, Hope, and Worship*, edited by H. S. Versnel, 152–92. Leiden.

Plezia, M. 1977. *Aristotelis Privatorum Scriptorum Fragmenta*. Leipzig.

Pollitt, J. J. 1986. *Art in the Hellenistic Age*. Cambridge.

Pouilloux, J. 1954. *La forteresse de Rhamnonte*. Paris.

——. 1956. "Trois décrets de Rhamnonte." *BCH* 80: 57–75.

——. 1969. "Un nouvel archonte d' Athènes au III siècle dans un décret d' Éleusis?" *ZPE* 4: 1–6.

Price, S. R. F. 1984. *Rituals and Power*. Cambridge.

Raubitschek, A. E. 1943. "Greek Inscriptions." *Hesp.* 12: 12–88.

——. 1962. "Demokratia." *Hesp.* 31: 238–43.

Reinmuth, O. W. 1929. *The Foreigners in the Athenian Ephebia*. Lincoln.

——. 1971. *The Ephebic Inscriptions of the Fourth Century b.c.* Leiden.

Rhodes, P. J. 1972. *The Athenian Boule*. Oxford.

——. 1993. *A Commentary on the Aristotelian Athenaion Politeia*. 2nd ed. Oxford.

Richter, G. M. A. 1962. *Greek Portraits IV*. Brussels.

Rider, B. C. 1916. *The Greek House*. Cambridge.

Ridgway, B. S. 1992. "Images of Athena on the Akropolis." In *Goddess and Polis*, edited by J. Neils, 119–42. Princeton.

Rist, J. M. 1972. *Epicurus: An Introduction*. Cambridge.

Ritchie, C. E., Jr. 1989. "The Lyceum, The Garden of Theophrastos, and the Garden of the Muses." In Φίλια ἔπη εἰς Γεώργιον Ε. Μύλωναν, 3:250–60. Athens.

Robert, L. 1960. "Sur une loi d'Athènes relative aux petites Panathénées." In *Hellenica*, 11–12:189–203. Paris.

——. [1969] 1970. "Inscriptions d' Athènes et de la Grèce centrale." *AE* 1–58.

——. [1977] 1979. "Une fête de la paix à Athènes au IVe siècle." *AE* 211–16.

Robertson, N. 1983. "The Riddle of the Arrephoria at Athens." *HSCP* 87: 241–88.

——. 1984. "The Ritual Background of the Erysichthon Story." *AJP* 105: 369–408.

——. 1985. "The Origin of the Panathenaea." *RhM* 128: 231–95.

——. 1986. "A Point of Precedence at Plataia." *Hesp.* 55: 88–102.

Rocchi, M. 1980. "Contributi allo culto delle Charites (II)." *Studii clasice* 19: 19–28.

Rosivach, V. J. 1987. "The Cult of Zeus Eleutherios at Athens." *La Parola del Passato* 42: 262–85.

——. 1991. "IG 2² 334 and the Panathenaic Hekatomb." *La Parola del Passato* 46: 430–42.

Rostovtzeff, M. 1941. *The Social and Economic History of the Hellenistic World*. Oxford.

Rotroff, S. I. 1978. "An Anonymous Hero in the Athenian Agora." *Hesp.* 47: 196–209.

Roussel, P. 1908. "Les Athéniens mentionnés dans les inscriptions de Délos." *BCH* 32: 303–444.

——. 1916a. *Les cultes égyptiens à Délos*. Paris.

————. 1916b. *Délos colonie Athénienne*. Paris.

Roux, G. 1979. *L'amphictionie, Delphes et le temple d'Apollon au IVe siècle*. Lyons.

Sanders, G. D. R., and R. W. V. Catling. 1990. "From Delos to Melos: A New Fragment of *I. Delos 1562*." *ABSA* 85: 327–32.

Schmidt, S. 1991. *Hellenistische Grabreliefs: Typologische und chronologische Beobachtungen*. Cologne.

Schmitt, H. H. 1969. *Die Staatsverträge des Altertums*. Vol. 3. Munich.

Schwenk, C. J. 1985. *Athens in the Age of Alexander*. Chicago.

Shear, T. L., Jr. 1970. "The Monument of the Eponymous Heroes in the Athenian Agora." *Hesp.* 39: 145–222.

————. 1973. "The Athenian Agora: Excavations of 1971." *Hesp* 42: 121–79.

————. 1978. *Kallias of Sphettos and the Revolt of Athens in 286 b.c.* *Hesp.* supplement 17. Princeton.

————. 1981. "Athens: From City-State to Provincial Town." *Hesp.* 50: 356–77.

————. 1984. "The Athenian Agora: Excavations of 1980–1982." *Hesp.* 53: 1–57.

————. 1995. "Bouleuterion, Metroon, and the Archives at Athens." *Historia Einzelschriften* 95: 157–90.

Siewert, P. 1977. "The Ephebic Oath in Fifth-Century Athens." *JHS* 97: 102–11.

Simms, R. R. 1988. "The Cult of the Thracian Goddess Bendis in Athens and Attica." *Ancient World* 18: 59–76.

————. 1989. "Isis in Classical Athens." *CJ* 84: 216–21.

Simon, E. 1983. *Festivals of Attica*. Madison, Wis.

Sokolowski, F. 1962. *Lois sacrées des cités grecques (Supplément)*. Paris.

————. 1964. "Aphrodite as Guardian of Greek Magistrates." *HTR* 57: 1–8.

————. 1969. *Lois sacrées des cités grecques*. Paris.

Stambaugh, J. E. 1972. *Sarapis under the Early Ptolemies*. Leiden.

Stanley, K. 1961. "Notes on an Athenian Prytany Decree." *AJP* 82: 425–27.

Stewart, A. 1979. *Attika: Studies in Athenian Sculpture of the Hellenistic Age*. London.

Stewart, Z. 1977. "La Religione." In *Storia e civiltà dei Greci*, edited by R. Bianchi Bandinelli, 8:503–616. Milan.

Stichel, R. H. W. 1990. "Zur hellenistischen Nekropole im Kerameikos von Athen: Demetrios von Phaleron." In *Akten des XIII. Internationalen Kongresses für Klassische Archäologie*, 546–47. Berlin.

————. 1992. "Columella—Mensa—Labellum: Zur Form der attischen Grabmäler in Luxusgesetz des Demetrios von Phaleron." *AA* 107: 433–40.

Straten, F. T. van. 1976. "Daikrates' Dream." *Bulletin Antieke Beschaving* 51: 1–38.

————. 1981. "Gifts for the Gods." In *Faith, Hope, and Worship*, edited by H. S. Versnel, 65–151. Leiden.

Stroud, R. S. 1974. "An Athenian Law on Silver Coinage." *Hesp.* 43: 158–88.

Tarn, W. W. 1913. *Antigonos Gonatas*. Oxford.

Tarn, W. W., and G. T. Griffith. 1952. *Hellenistic Civilisation*. 3rd ed. London.

Taylor, M. C. 1993. "The Geographical Dimensions of the Polis: The History of Salamis from the Sixth to the Third Century B.C." Ph.D. diss., Stanford University.

Thompson, D. B. 1944. "The Golden Nikai Reconsidered." *Hesp.* 13: 173–209.

Thompson, H. A. 1981. "Athens Faces Adversity." *Hesp.* 50: 343–55.

Thompson, H. A., and R. E. Wycherley. 1972. *The Agora of Athens.* The Athenian Agora 14. Princeton.

Threpsiades, J., and E. Vanderpool. 1964. "Themistokles' Sanctuary of Artemis Aristoboule." *AD* 19: 26–36.

Tod, M. N. 1948. *A Selection of Greek Historical Inscriptions.* Oxford.

Tölle-Kastenbein, R. 1994. *Das Olympieion in Athen.* Vienna.

Tracy, S. V. 1975a. *The Lettering of an Athenian Mason. Hesp.* supplement 15. Princeton.

———. 1975b. "Notes on the Pythaïs Inscriptions." *BCH* 99: 186–218.

———. 1979. "Greek Inscriptions from the Athenian Agora." *Hesp.* 48: 174–79.

———. 1982a. "Agora I 7181 + *IG* II² 944b." In *Studies in Attic Epigraphy, History, and Topography*, 157–61. *Hesp.* supplement 19. Princeton.

———. 1982b. *I.G. II2 2336: Contributors of First Fruits for the Pythaïs.* Beiträge zur klassischen Philologie 139. Meisenheim am Glan.

———. 1984. "Greek Inscriptions from the Athenian Agora." *Hesp.* 53: 369–77.

———. 1988a. "Ephebic Inscriptions from Athens: Addenda and Corrigenda." *Hesp.* 57: 249–52.

———. 1988b. "Two Attic Letter Cutters of the Third Century: 286/5–235/4 B.C." *Hesp.* 57: 303–22.

———. 1990a. *Attic Letter-Cutters of 229 to 86 b.c.* Berkeley.

———. [1984] 1990b. "The Date of the Athenian Archon Achaios." *AJAH* 9: 43–47.

———. 1991. "The Panathenaic Festival and Games: An Epigraphic Inquiry." *Nikephoros* 4: 133–53.

———. 1994. "*IG* II² 1195 and Agathe Tyche in Attica." *Hesp.* 63: 241–44.

———. 1995. *Athenian Democracy in Transition: Attic Letter-Cutters of 340 to 290 B.C.* Berkeley.

Tracy, S. V., and C. Habicht. 1991. "New and Old Panathenaic Victor Lists." *Hesp.* 60: 187–236.

Traill, J. S. 1975. *The Political Organization of Attica. Hesp.* supplement 14. Princeton.

Travlos, J. 1971. *Pictorial Dictionary of Ancient Athens.* London.

Tritle, L. A. 1988. *Phocion the Good.* London.

Tsakos, K. 1990–91. "Θησαυρός Ἀφροδίτης Οὐρανίας· ἡ ἐπιγραφή." *Horos* 8–9: 17–28.

Usener, H. 1887. *Epicurea.* Leipzig.

Vermaseren, M. J. 1982. *Corpus Cultus Cybelae Attidisque.* Vol. 2. Leiden.

Versnel, H. S. 1990. *Ter Unus.* Leiden.

Vidman, L. 1969. *Sylloge Inscriptionum Religionis Isiacae et Sarapiacae.* Berlin.

———. 1970. *Isis und Sarapis bei den Griechen und Römern.* Berlin.

Vikela, E. 1994. *Die Weihreliefs aus dem athener Pankrates-Heiligtum am Ilissos.*

Mitteilungen des Deutschen Archäologischen Instituts, Athenische Abteilung 16. Berlin.

Walbank, F. W. 1933. *Aratos of Sicyon*. Cambridge.

———. 1940. *Philip V of Macedon*. Cambridge.

———. 1957–79. *A Historical Commentary on Polybius*. 3 vols. Oxford.

———. 1981. *The Hellenistic World*. Brighton.

———. 1987. "Könige als Götter: Überlegungen zum Herrscherkult von Alexander bis Augustus." *Chiron* 17: 365–82.

Walbank, M. B. 1982. "Regulations for an Athenian Festival." In *Studies in Attic Epigraphy, History, and Topography*, 173–82. *Hesp.* supplement 19. Princeton.

———. 1990. "Notes on Attic Decrees." *ABSA* 85: 435–47.

Weber, G. 1995. "Herrscher, Hof und Dichter." *Historia* 44: 283–316.

Wehrli, F. 1949. *Demetrios von Phaleron*. Die Schule des Aristoteles 4. Basle.

Welter, G. 1923. "Das Olympieion in Athen II." *AM* 48: 182–89.

West, M. L. 1972. *Iambi et Elegi Graeci*. Vol. 2. Oxford.

———. 1982. *Greek Metre*. Oxford.

Westermann, A. 1845. *Biographoi: Vitarum Scriptores Graeci Minores*. Braunschweig.

Whitehead, D. 1977. *The Ideology of the Athenian Metic*. Cambridge.

———. 1983. "Competitive Outlay and Community Profit: φιλοτιμία in Democratic Athens." *Classica et Medievalia* 34: 55–74.

———. 1986. *The Demes of Attica*. Princeton.

Wilamowitz, U. 1881. *Antigonos von Karystos*. Berlin.

Will, E. 1985. *Le sanctuaire de la déesse Syrienne*. Exploration archéologique de Délos 35. Paris.

Williams, J. M. 1987. "The Peripatetic School and Demetrius of Phalerum's Reforms in Athens." *Ancient World* 15: 87–98.

———. 1989. "Demades' Last Years, 323/2–319/8 B.C.: A 'Revisionist' Interpretation." *Ancient World* 19: 19–30.

Winiarczyk, M. 1989. "Bibliographie zum antiken Atheismus." *Elenchos* 10: 103–92.

Woodbury, L. 1965. "The Date and Atheism of Diagoras of Melos." *Phoenix* 19: 178–11.

Woodhead, A. G. 1981. "Athens and Demetrios Poliorcetes at the End of the Fourth Century B.C." In *Ancient Macedonian Studies in Honor of Charles F. Edson*, edited by H. J. Dell and E. N. Borza, 357–67. Thessaloniki.

Woodward, A. M. 1962. "Athens and the Oracle of Ammon." *ABSA* 57: 5–13.

Wormell, D. E. W. 1935. "The Literary Tradition Concerning Hermias of Atarneus." *YCS* 5: 57–92.

Worthington, I. 1992. *A Historical Commentary on Dinarchus*. Ann Arbor, Mich.

Wünsch, R. 1897. *Defixionum Tabellae*. IG III.3. Berlin.

Wycherley, R. E. 1957. *Literary and Epigraphical Testimonia*. The Athenian Agora 3. Princeton.

———. 1962. "Peripatos: the Athenian Philosophical Scene—II." *GR* 9: 2–21.

———. 1963. "Pausanias at Athens, II." *GRBS* 4: 157–75.

———. 1964. "The Olympieion at Athens." *GRBS* 5: 161–79.

———. 1978. *The Stones of Athens*. Princeton.

Ziebarth, E. 1934. "Neue Verfluchungstafeln aus Attica, Boiotien und Euboia." In *Sitzungsberichte der preussischen Akademie der Wissenschaften, Phil.- Hist. Klasse*, 1022–50. Berlin.

General Index

For Athenians either the deme, or when the deme is not known, the *PA* number is given. In the case of homonymous individuals, the Athenians are given first, by deme, then the foreigners.

kanéphoroi, 21, 28, 32, 102, 198–99, 220,
    227, 230–31, 233–34, 238–40, 257–58,
    260, 266, 270, 290, 293, 310, 312
κατὰ πρόσταγμα, 223, 229–30, 235, 265,
    267, 277, 312
kleidouchos, 220, 223, 230, 233, 238–40,
    266, 277, 293, 312

Lachares, *PA* 9005, 90–92, 106, 110, 116,
    283, 290
Lamia, 88
Lamian War, 37, 46, 48, 71, 78, 102, 111,
    249, 291, 296, 298, 300–1, 312
Laodamia of Piraeus, 239
Leaina, 88
Lenaia, 36, 54–55, 59, 118–19, 122, 211–12;
    on Delos, 211, 227, 240
Leochares of Pallene, 39
Leocrates, *PA* 9083, 11–19, 25, 31–32, 39,
    289
Leocritos, *PA* 9096, 104
Leon of Aixone, 202
Leonides: of Melite, 238; of Phyle, 163
Leos, 42
Leto, 115, 267, 272; on Chios, 321; on
    Delos, 209–11, 219, 240
Licinius Crassus, Lucius, 259, 274
Ludi Megalenses, 119
Ludi Romani, 119
Lyceum, as gymnasion, 21–22, 168, 190–
    91; as philosophical school, 48–49, 54,
    60–61, 64, 66–68, 122, 129, 244, 299,
    300
Lyciscos of Cephallenia, 118
Lycomedes of Diomeia, 20
Lycon of Scarpheia, 118, 120
Lycourgos of Boutadai, 3–8, 11–45, 47–51,
    55–59, 67–69, 72–77, 79, 92, 98, 103, 105–
    111, 130–31, 135, 164–67, 170–72, 180,
    196, 198, 200, 206–7, 240–41, 253, 256,
    261, 269–70, 273, 280, 288–94, 296, 301,
    304–5, 307, 315
Lysias of Syracuse, 59
Lysimachos of Macedon, 76, 82, 99–101,
    118–19, 197
Lysippos, 168
Lyson, 112

Macedonian Wars: First, 170, 181, 242;
    Second, 170, 176, 187, 189, 242, 303;
    Third, 170, 194, 242, 311

Macedonios of Amphipolis, 267–68
Machaon, 268
Medeios of Piraeus, 239–41, 256, 270,
    279–80, 285, 299, 314
Megallis of Marathon, 277
Megiste of Marathon, 257
Megistos Ares Ouranios, on Delos, 235
Meixigenes of Cholleidai, 42
Melanthios: *PA* 9770, 130–32; of Rhodes,
    68
Menander of Kephisia, 62–63, 69–71, 107
Menandros: of Alopeke, 277; of Eitea,
    157–58
Menesaichmos, *PA* 9983, 25, 41
Menis of Heracleia, 103
Menophanes, 282–83
Menyllos, 58
Mercury, 227
Metella, wife of Sulla, 285
Metrodoros: of Calchedon, 276; of
    Lampsacos, 127
Miccion of Lakiadai, 257
Micion: of Kephisia, 164, 170, 173–74,
    176–77, 194; of Semachidai, 217
Miltiades: of Lakiadai, 310; of Marathon,
    257–58, 261
Mithridates V Euergetes, 220
Mithridates VI Eupator, 226, 231, 242–43,
    254, 272, 279–86, 300, 314
Mother of the Gods, 139, 142–44, 148,
    151–55, 203–4, 206, 244, 247–48, 275,
    308; on Delos, 230
Mounichos, 42, 52–53
Musaios, 64
Muses, 64–68, 120, 300
Mynniskos of Chalcis, 118
Mysteries at Agrai, 89, 107, 133, 160, 162,
    182–83
Mystion of Paiania, 230

Nausiphilos of Kephale, 141–42
Nemean Games, 34, 41, 156–57, 160
Nemesia, 192, 195
Nemesis, 156, 158, 192; on Delos, 230, 237
Neoptolemos: of Melite, 27, 34–36; of
    Scyros, 118–21
Nicanor, 58–59, 188–90
Nicasis of Corinth, 278
Niceratos of Kydathenaion, 33–34
Nichomachos of Paiania, 158
Nicocles of Hagnous, 42

Index of Epigraphical Texts Cited

See also the Appendix for original or earlier places of publication of some epigraphical texts in this index.

Designer: Ina Clausen
Compositor: Integrated Composition Systems
Text: 10/13 Galliard
Display: Galliard
Printer: Thomson-Shore, Inc.
Binder: Thomson-Shore, Inc.